DISCOURSE AND DEFIANCE UNDER NAZI OCCUPATION

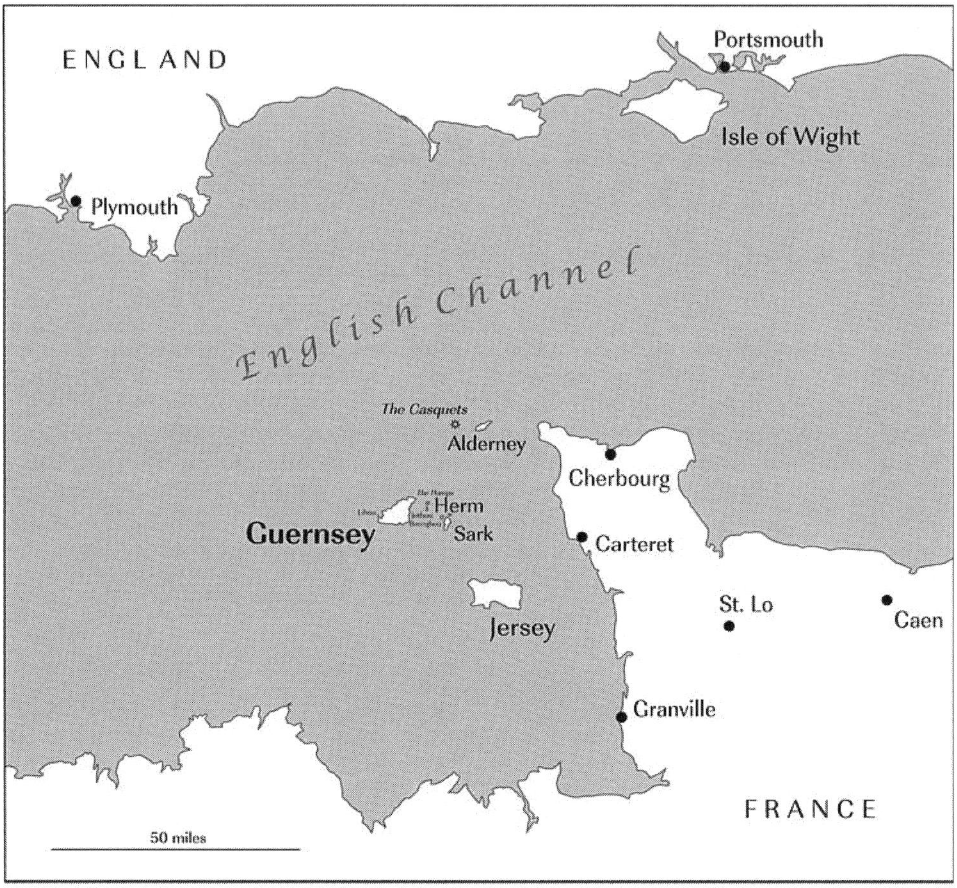
ENGLAND
Portsmouth
Isle of Wight
Plymouth
English Channel
The Casquets
Alderney
Cherbourg
Herm
Guernsey
Sark
Carteret
Jersey
St. Lo
Caen
Granville
FRANCE
50 miles

E. White

DISCOURSE AND DEFIANCE UNDER NAZI OCCUPATION

Guernsey, Channel Islands, 1940–1945

Cheryl R. Jorgensen-Earp

Michigan State University Press
East Lansing

∞ The paper used in this publication meets the minimum requirements of ANSI/NISO Z39.48-1992 (R 1997) (Permanence of Paper).

Michigan State University Press
East Lansing, Michigan 48823-5245

Printed and bound in the United States of America.

19 18 17 16 15 14 13 1 2 3 4 5 6 7 8 9 10

LIBRARY OF CONGRESS CATALOGING-IN-PUBLICATION DATA
Jorgensen-Earp, Cheryl R., 1952–
Discourse and defiance under Nazi occupation : Guernsey, Channel Islands, 1940–1945 / Cheryl R. Jorgensen-Earp.
pages cm
Includes bibliographical references and index.
ISBN 978-1-61186-082-5 (cloth : alk. paper)—ISBN 978-1-60917-369-2 (ebook) 1. World War, 1939–1945—Channel Islands—Guernsey. 2. Channel Islands—History—German occupation, 1940–1945. 3. Guernsey (Channel Islands)—History—20th century. 4. Government, Resistance to—Channel Islands—Guernsey—History—20th century. 5. Guernsey (Channel Islands)—Social conditions—20th century. 6. Guernsey (Channel Islands)—Politics and government—20th century. I. Title.
D760.8.G8J67 2013
940.53'42342—dc23
2012044850

Book design by Scribe Inc. (www.scribenet.com)
Cover design by TG Design

Front cover image is of Major Knackfuss with an unknown Guernsey man, © Imperial War Museum (HU 2932), used with permission. Diarists pictured on front cover are (left to right) Rev. Robert Douglas Ord, Gertrude Mabel Corbin, Arthur Mauger, Elizabeth Doig, Alf Williams, and Dorothy Higgs.

green press INITIATIVE Michigan State University Press is a member of the Green Press Initiative and is committed to developing and encouraging ecologically responsible publishing practices. For more information about the Green Press Initiative and the use of recycled paper in book publishing, please visit www.greenpressinitiative.org.

Visit Michigan State University Press at www.msupress.org

Dedicated to the Memory of
Alfred C. "Alf" Williams
1921–2006
Guernseyman and Resister

Contents

Acknowledgments

BECAUSE THE RESEARCH AND WRITING THAT WENT INTO THIS STUDY HAS SPANNED many years, I have many people and institutions to thank. I would like to start with Richard Heaume, founder and director of the German Occupation Museum in Forest, Guernsey. Richard has been invariably kind and helpful whenever I have descended upon him (often with very short notice). I will always be grateful that he introduced me to Alf Williams in 2003 and invited me on some of the fascinating "rambles" with the Channel Islands Occupation Society. The photographs taken at the German Occupation Museum are presented here with his permission. Recently, Richard was appointed MBE (Member of the Order of the British Empire), a well-deserved honor for a man who has spent his life preserving the history of the Occupation period.

I am very grateful to the Island archivist, Dr. Darryl Ogier, for his expert advice and to Nathan Coyde, Vikki Ellis, Rachel Guilbert, Sarah Lowe, Lawrence West, and the entire team at the Island Archives in Guernsey for their thoughtful guidance through the research, permissions process, and image production for this book. The photographs of the diarists, taken from the identity cards housed at the Island Archives, were produced by the Archives and appear here with permission. In addition to the identity photos and forms for the adult population of Guernsey, the Archives also houses the diaries of Kenneth Lewis, Herbert Williams, Arthur Mauger, and Gertie Corbin among its varied and rich resources. I also want to thank Ms. Amanda Bennett and the staff at the Priaulx Library for their help and for access to a variety of sources including the diaries of the Reverend Robert Douglas Ord, Ambrose Robin, and Elizabeth Doig. I spent many happy hours at both the old and the beautiful new Island Archives, as well as at the Priaulx Library seated at a desk before a particular sunny window. Curators, archivists, and librarians make research possible, and Guernsey is graced with some of the finest.

The cartoon of the girls with the V-sign is by Edmund Blampied, the well-known artist who spent the Occupation in his home island of Jersey. It is reproduced here with the kind permission of the Edmund Blampied estate, and I particularly appreciate Alan Blampied's help with its inclusion. My thanks also go to Louise Downie of Jersey Heritage and Andrew Hall for their assistance, as well as to Ingrid Gallie for information that she provided. I would like to thank Nigel Lewis for permission to quote from the diary of his father, Kenneth Lewis; Peter Sauvarin and Janice Williams for permission to quote from the diary of their father, Herbert Williams; Peter Bachmann (the very young "Peter-John" in his mother's account) for permission to quote from Kitty Bachmann's published diary; and Nigel Higgs and family for permission to quote from Dorothy Higgs's published diary. I would like to thank Mrs. Bronwyn Henderson, Mrs. Hilary Richardson, and Mrs. Jane Pearson of the Ladies College, Guernsey, for their help in granting permission to quote from Winifred Harvey's published diary. One of the surprises of this research was finding the microfilm of William

Arthur Warry's diary in the Albert and Shirley Small Special Collections Library at the University of Virginia. The original copy of the diary is held by the Guernsey Museums and Galleries, and my thanks go to Lisa Burton, Matt Harvey, and the Guernsey Museums and Galleries for granting permission to quote from it. I am particularly indebted to Daphne Gemmill for providing some fascinating information about W. A. Warry and for granting permission to quote from her grandfather's diary. Finally, I would like to thank Michael Elstob, the great nephew of the Reverend R. Douglas Ord, for permission to quote from Rev. Ord's wonderful and detailed diary.

With so many experts to draw on in Guernsey, I have relied on much helpful advice, such as that provided by Jeremy Marquand of the *Guernsey Press and Star* and Herbert Winterflood. A very special form of expertise was provided by Bill Le Page, Marion Legg, and Maud Smyth, and I thank them so much for filling out questionnaires that allowed me to tap their memories of the Occupation years. Lynchburg College has been very generous with travel grants that have allowed me to complete this research despite the distance involved. I owe a great debt of gratitude to Dr. Martin J. Medhurst, Martha Bates, Annette Tanner, Kristine Blakeslee, Elise Jajuga, Travis Kimbel, Ellen White, and all of those at Michigan State University Press who have shepherded the original manuscript toward publication.

On a personal note, I would like to send my special appreciation to Kevin and Marcia Le Page for their encouragement and support. I would also like to thank Steve and Denise Le Page (and the rest of the Le Page family) for their hospitality and some delightful evenings in Guernsey. I send my special love to my late father and to my mother, so recently parted from me. They were also members of the extraordinary World War II generation, although their experiences during the time were far different from those of the Guernsey Islanders. And my love goes always to my husband, Dar, and son, Ethan, who accompanied me on many research trips and explored all the twists and turns of modern Guernsey. Those days shine brightly in my happiest memories.

Introduction

The attack came, quite literally, from the clear blue sky. On June 28, 1940, as German bombs poured down on the Guernsey Harbor, those at some distance were torn between seeking shelter and the need to watch with horrified fascination. The Reverend Robert Douglas Ord, having finished tea with guests in his garden beneath a "perfect blue sky," stood with the others at the French window overlooking the garden "that we might take together whatever might be our fate." His spaniel Judy, of a less philosophical and more practical bent, huddled in fear under the stairs.[1]

Many in Guernsey just escaped being closer to the action, having been drawn into town to hear the Procureur, Mr. Ambrose Sherwill, speak about the Island's situation now that France (only 40 km distant) had fallen to the Germans. Eighteen-year-old Ken Lewis had gone with his mate Ralph to Smith Street, near the harbor in St. Peter Port, in order to listen to the speech. Returning to Ralph's home in the Steam Mill Lanes after Sherwill's address, they were standing on the lawn with Ralph's father when the German planes came over. Enthralled by minute details of military equipment, an interest he would maintain over the subsequent years, Ken quickly identified the planes as three Dornier 215s flying abreast. While they watched, the center plane suddenly dropped back from formation, exuding small puffs of smoke as they heard the sound of machine-gun fire. Simultaneously, there was the accelerating scream of a bomb, and Ralph's father threw himself to the ground while they heard the "crump" of bombs hitting the harbor Weighbridge. Any spell of being mere observers was broken. The trio ran first to the garage, finding it covered in broken glass. Seeking next a refuge behind a large chair in the house, they finally ended up under the table with Ralph's mother and a neighbor woman "singing hymns and praying" as the house shook and the raid continued.[2]

Grower Jack Sauvary had worked hard to pack up thirty-nine baskets of tomatoes for shipment that morning. Tired from the effort, Jack "had a little snooze" and went to St. Peter Port for a haircut, just in case he "slipped off" in one of the boats evacuating Islanders to England. Following the crowd up the High Street to hear Sherwill's address, he stood for a while shooting the breeze with a friend about the pros and cons of remaining in Guernsey. As the crowd surged down the Quay Steps after the speech, Jack managed to outpace them enough to catch the bus to his home in the parish of St. Sampson. He had barely walked through his house to the back door when the attack began, and he ran to put on his Air Raid Precautions "tin hat" and take shelter in the corner of his small office under the bathroom.[3]

Jack was lucky in avoiding the more immediate trauma suffered by Mrs. Elizabeth Doig and Winifred Harvey. In her terse diary entry, Elizabeth Doig reported being caught in the Grange, an area just up the hill from the harbor, and taking shelter with twenty others in a house, a thoroughly unforgettable and "nerve racking experience."[4] Most dramatic of all was the experience of Winifred Harvey. Like so many, she wavered between evacuating to

England and riding out whatever might come in Guernsey. Coming into town on Friday morning, she picked up two embarkation tickets for Tuesday, the Friday tickets having all been handed out. Yet, still she wasn't sure what to do. Listening to Sherwill's speech provided new information; when asked if the planes seen overhead were German, Winnie recorded Sherwill's response in her diary: "'Yes,' he said, 'some of them were, but what of it?'" Sherwill next warned those whose entire income came from England that they might be cut off for a time without resources and thus be a "burden on the island." That was the deciding argument for Winnie. With a new resolve to leave Tuesday, she tiredly sought a way to get home. The crowds were too great to reach the bus stop up the hill, so she turned back through Smith Street to walk home. In what could serve as a metaphor for things to come, Winnie came upon "a stray wee tortoiseshell kitten, defying some big dogs." She watched as an old lady walking with her husband picked the kitten up, and the couple followed Winnie up the street. At the sound of three planes overhead, they all looked up, saw puffs of smoke like those described by Ken Lewis, heard a whistle and a loud explosion. "Get under those trees and lie down!" Winnie shouted to the old couple as they raced across the road.[5]

In her diary, Winnie described how the German planes bombed the harbor, machine-gunning people: "The first bombs fell plumb in the middle of the long line of tomato lorries waiting for the boat, creating havoc. They circled round and came back again and again." People on the pier tried to take shelter underneath the lower landing, but they were not the only ones being gunned down. An ambulance on the other side of St. James' Church, ferrying the wounded to the hospital, was machine-gunned, killing Joseph Way, the driver.[6] During a lull, the old couple with the kitten and Winnie's friends Colonel and Mrs. Carey, who had joined them on the ground under the trees, made off for their homes. Winnie lay there alone, looking over the newspaper in a strange state of calm. She finally rose and ran most of the way to the First Aid post where she was a volunteer, "looking for cover in every street."[7]

The saddest, most personal account of this unprovoked attack on civilians came from the diary of Arthur J. Mauger, a grower from Kings Mills, Castel. In ledger books scripted in his beautiful flowing hand, he had long recorded an account of daily life. On June 28, he started with his usual report of the weather; the day was "Fine." He described how he "messed about the place" doing odd jobs with the men. In the afternoon, all the men, including his step-grandson Frank, left to go to the White Rock (referring to the pier off of the South Quay of the harbor) to see to the arrival of cattle abandoned by those evacuating the Island of Alderney. Thus, the men were in precisely the wrong place, standing on the pier when the air raid occurred.

Arthur recorded in his entry for the 28th: "Frank was one of the seriously wounded. Frank Le Page and his two sons are missing and probably killed, also P. Le Noury, all neighbours . . . Frank was chatting to his workman and others, but was the only one in that lot to be hit." His next entry on Saturday, the 29th, confirmed his worst fears: "A very sad day for nearly all of us neighbours. Good old Frank my step grandson died last night about 3 a.m. through the terrible wounds he had in the last evening 'airraid' he was 32 and 2 months 18 days. Frank Le Page [from] Millmount and his two sons were killed outright last evening. Also P. Le Noury, in fact there was 25 killed and 33 injured, the wives are in an awful state . . . Frank Le Page was 49, the sons 19 and 14 respectively."[8] The final count would actually be thirty-four dead and dozens more wounded, the surreal horror of an attack on innocent farmers loading their crops captured in the memoirs of Guernsey journalist Frank Falla: "The blood of the wounded and the dying mingled with the juice of the tomatoes."[9]

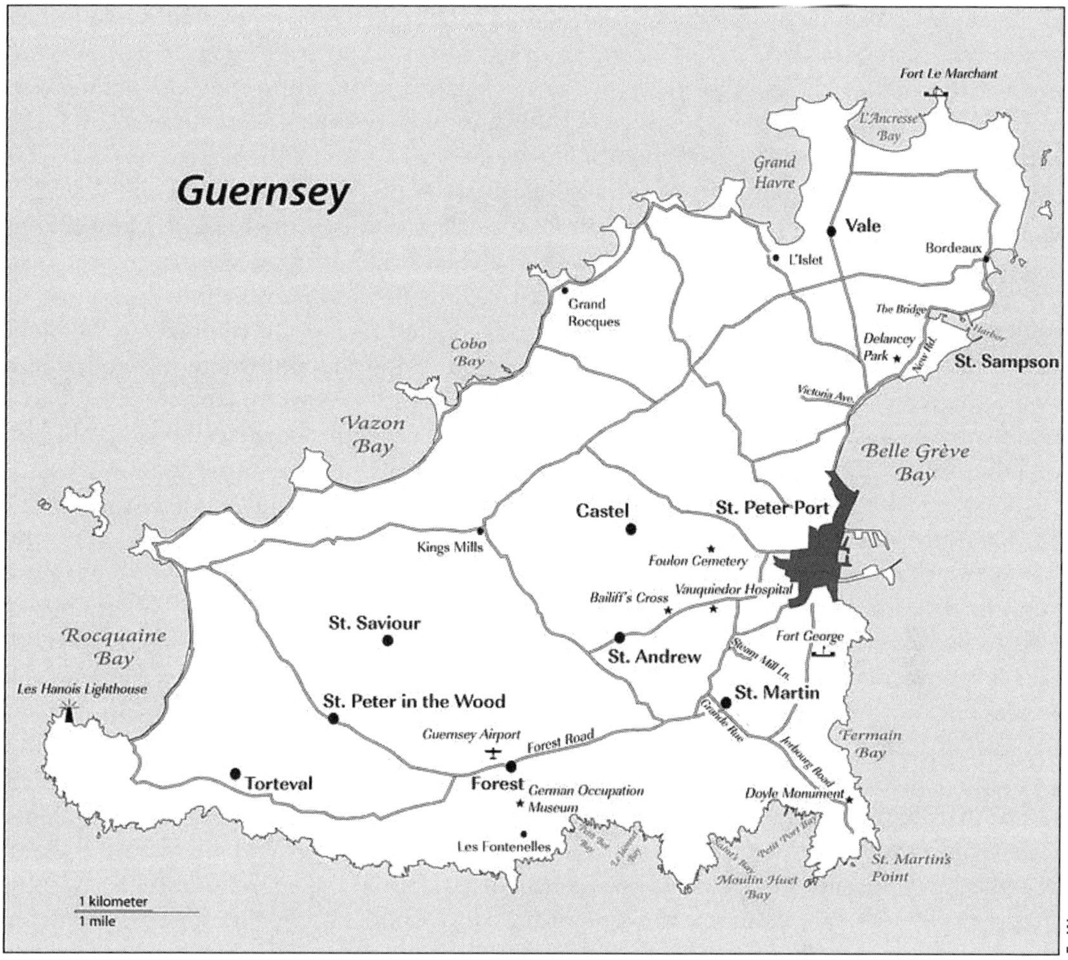

E. WHITE

This, what builder and grower Jack Sauvary called in his own diary "the eventful outrage,"[10] was the first contact the people of Guernsey were to have with the Germans who would occupy them for the next five years. Military occupation during and following wars is a recurrent situation, and one whose rhetorical aspects have yet to be fully explored. In recent decades, our understanding of resistance under occupation has expanded greatly, developed in part through studies by Roderick Kedward and others of the German occupation of France.[11] Slowly, there has developed a new appreciation of formerly "unrecognized resistance,"[12] and this has helped redefine resistance as a whole. We could take as a broad definition of resistance the one offered by Christopher Lloyd: "the struggle for personal and political liberty against an oppressive, external force."[13] Yet, we know that the struggle against domination is often internally as well as externally directed, particularly when we look at oppressive power inequities outside of a military situation. Resistance strategies develop in the struggle of workers against domination within an oppressive corporation, or as a response to slavery or economic servitude within an oppressive society. Even under military occupation, particularly in instances of widespread or official collaboration, resistance becomes internal as well as external. Kedward makes the point that, in the case of Vichy, "what started as a national defeat by an *external* enemy had quickly become a civil conflict between *internal* enemies."[14]

If we can expand Lloyd's definition of resistance to encompass opposition to internal as well as external oppression, then his use of the term "struggle" opens the concept of resistance to a myriad number of covert as well as overt acts. In the case of military occupation, the very fact that an occupied people are held under force of arms provides an expectation that the counters to that power will be overt and hold the potential for violent overthrow. This view is not unreasonable in many situations of military occupation, and there are multiple studies of resistance activities, both organized and unorganized, that have met military power with sabotage and counterforce. However, the fact that such resistance does exist in certain cases has led to the mistaken notion that resistance is synonymous with violence, or at the least with quantifiable overt actions. Even in situations that lend themselves to violent opposition, discrete acts of resistance tend to be isolated eruptions, whose very visibility shelters the size and complexity of a submerged supporting structure of psychological defiance.[15] And that underlying foundation of community mindset is constantly shaped and structured by the ebb and flow of events, information, and opportunities.

Modern Americans and Britons have learned from our own experience in Iraq what others have learned before us. Violence or sabotage may be the apparent problems for occupying forces, but these acts are facilitated by psychological resistance. "Hearts and minds" truly are at its root, and dramatic or violent actions are simply the most visible forms of an opposition to power. "Resistance," Andrea Muhi Brighenti claims, "may be helped by invisibility, which furnishes a place to hide from domination." Thus, Brighenti finds in resistance a need to seek "the realms of the informal, the implicit and even the trivial." Particularly in military contexts, the resister is unlikely to prevail in a struggle head to head on the battlefield of the powerful, and thus must seek new, and often hidden, locations where resistance may flourish. While invisibility may prevent detection, it also hinders acknowledgment that resistance has even taken place.[16] Therefore, some forms of resistance, often those that are psychological and expressed symbolically, have largely gone unrecognized. As Hazel Knowles Smith states, "Even harder to quantify and evaluate is the case for resistance of opinion,"[17] but this is the very case that I intend to make in this study.

Capturing the nature of occupation resistance has been difficult for scholars, and this problem has resulted in some slippery terminology. The desire has been to find a descriptor that would separate the bulk of Island resistance from the type of organized resistance movement that developed on the Continent and that tends to constitute resistance in most people's minds. Specific acts during the Guernsey Occupation have been referred to as "passive patriotism,"[18] "silent resistance,"[19] "spiritual resistance,"[20] and even (when describing the actions of Salvation Army resister Marie Ozanne) "Christian resistance."[21] All of these terms are perfectly accurate in the specific instances to which they were applied, but none can fully capture the vast sweep of resistance, some of which was passive and personal and some active and organized, some silent and some anything but silent. Perhaps the best way to encompass all of the resistant activities in Guernsey is to consider them forms of rhetorical resistance, for all in some way involve the manipulation of discursive or nondiscursive symbols, and all are designed (however subtly) to "induce to attitude or action,"[22] which is the purview of rhetoric.

The concept that there is a resistance that relies on symbolic forms arising from the common people[23] and serving as "rhetorical antidotes"[24] to power is not entirely new, and its treatment has already served as the basis for many new understandings of subjugated people. Our view of the resistance wielded by African-Americans during slavery and under Jim Crow has been widely expanded by an attention to the subtle discursive and nondiscursive means of

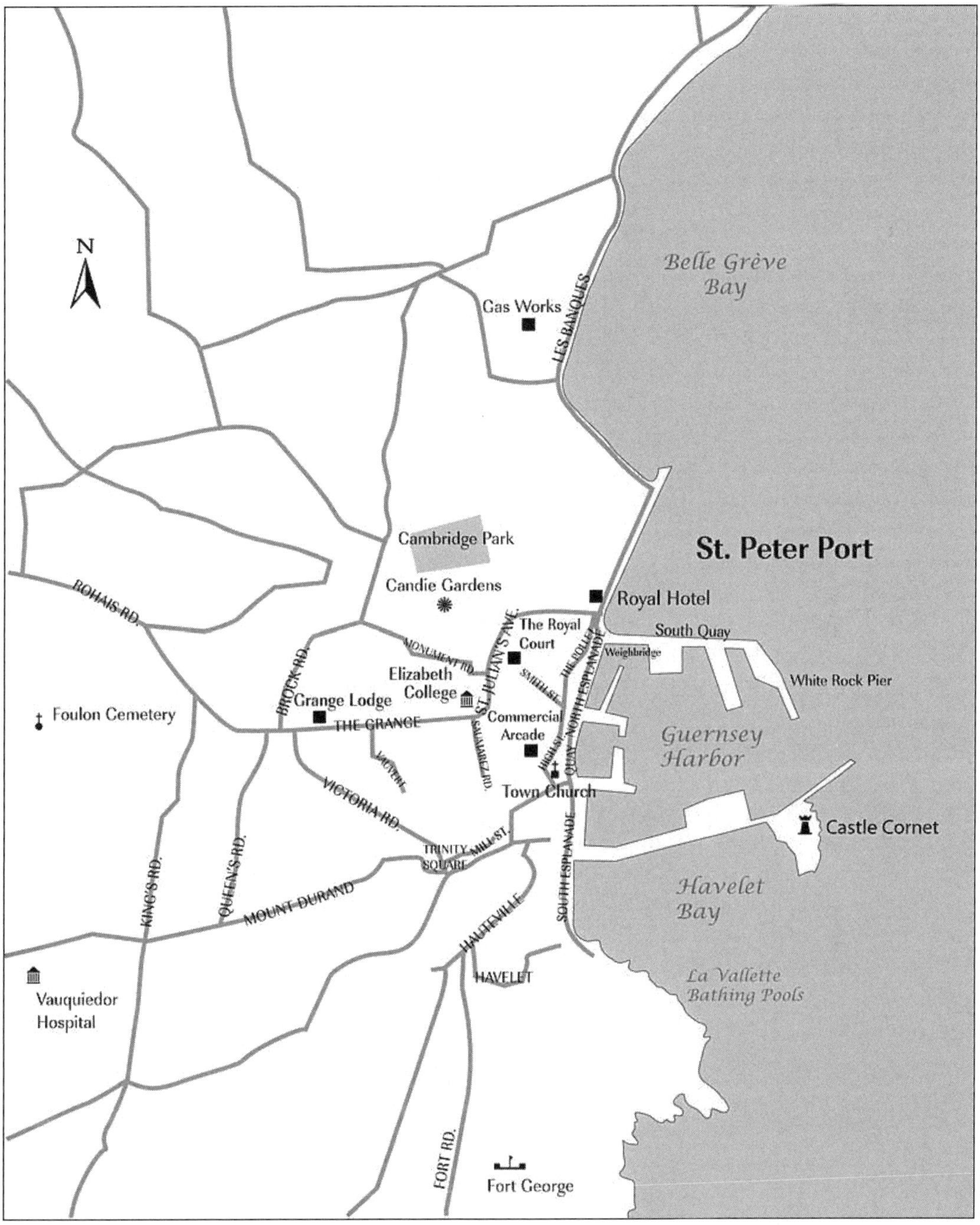

E. WHITE

opposing power. The past few decades have provided detailed studies of these tactics, where spirituals, work slowdowns, folk tales, and feigned illness or ignorance were some of the many subtle methods of countering oppression.[25] The same re-visioning has taken place in women's history, as what was previously taken to be female passivity and acceptance of a subjugated position in society has been transformed by close attention to private and public rhetorical means of challenging male domination.[26] Despite these successes and the many calls to approach "vernacular discourse" as a worthy object of critical study and thus to expand our understanding of resistance,[27] we are often slow to acknowledge the extent of the impact of rhetorical resistance.

Scholars have been particularly hesitant to make claims for the power of rhetorical resistance as a counter to the force of arms, leaving it primarily as a preparatory stage for movements of "real" resistance or actual revolution. I believe that this tendency has to do with the realities of the specific opposition movements examined thus far, where symbolic means of resistance often emerged early on and then were overshadowed by more overt acts of subversion. For example, the concept of symbolic means of resistance as a forerunner of an organized movement may be seen in Nathaniel Hong's study of the German occupation of Denmark, and his detailing of some of the methods used from 1940 to 1942 (graffiti, leaflets, posters, songs, chain letters, movie demonstrations) until the emergence of "an active resistance movement." Hong's description of these tactics is fascinating, and he posits that "The simplicity, even crudeness, of these strategies made them well suited to the first stage of resistance."[28] More recently, Kerry Kathleen Riley's excellent study of the grassroots social movement in the German Democratic Republic prior to the fall of the Berlin Wall situates this form of symbolic opposition as one part of "a story of rhetorical resistance, reclamation, rebellion, and revolution." In the case of the GDR, what began as private resistant exchanges, often in the form of jokes, would evolve into the "quasi-public sphere" of group work and prayer services in the Evangelical Lutheran Church, and then blossom into the slogans, banners, and marches of the "demonstration culture," finally to be fulfilled in the revolution, the "winning of the street."[29]

In these studies that highlight a symbolic resistance as the forerunner or companion of a more overt resistance movement, we are able to appreciate the value of subtle oppositional tactics, or "everyday subversions," in Riley's phrase. But what can we make of its efficacy when rhetorical resistance is not an appetizer or side dish but the main course, when it is practically the sole means of opposition to domination under force of arms? In this study, I would like to approach rhetorical resistance under conditions of military occupation as a complete and very real form of resistance in itself, with its own identifiable structure and its own value as a long-term method of opposition to power. In doing so, I begin with a series of questions about the shape of a more subtle form of resistance, one rooted in discursive and nondiscursive symbols.

In conditions of military occupation where the overt actions of a full resistance movement are unlikely to be cultivated, is there a distinct pattern to a covert resistance that can be identified? While granting that all military occupations are unique, are there conditions that encourage the development of a resistance that is primarily discursive and symbolic? Can we further detail the components of this rhetorical resistance, cultivated around the manipulation of discourse and the control of information? Finally, does the pattern of rhetorical resistance extend to other situations where there is an extreme power differential and where a community finds itself in a condition of powerlessness? I believe that the answer to all of these questions is yes. It is a search for the outline of a rhetorical resistance that led me to the five years of the Guernsey Occupation, which will serve as the focus of this book.[30]

There are multiple reasons for the choice of the Guernsey Occupation as the means to identify the pattern of rhetorical resistance, not the least of which is the recent controversy that has sprung up over the nature of resistance versus collaboration in the Channel Islands during World War II. Although historians have examined the Occupation, until recently there were fewer studies than such an intriguing episode would warrant. Most of the early studies were published by Channel Island presses and are not readily available outside the Channel

Islands, with the exception of Charles Cruikshank's scholarly 1975 study, *The German Occupation of the Channel Islands.*[31] Until 2007, the one book widely circulated on the Occupation had been Madeleine Bunting's *The Model Occupation.*[32] Bunting has an undergraduate degree in history, having taken part also in a prestigious postgraduate fellowship, but her career has been as a polemical journalist, writing opinion columns for the London-based *Guardian.* This background actually held promise for attaining interviews that would add depth to what has tended to be dry recitations of Nazi emplacements, or tales of starving Islanders making jelly from carrageen moss. Thus, I looked forward to reading her book when it was published in 1995, but came away deeply disappointed. The interesting interviews, the nuggets of previously unknown information, the focus on lesser-known stories of the Occupation (such as the experience of liberated Russian slave laborers, or Dolly Joanknecht, a young Guernsey girl who fell in love with and subsequently married a German soldier) are all there.[33] Yet, imposed throughout are Bunting's conclusions, ones that do not seem to match her own evidence.

Just an example or two will point up this problem and give insight into the impact her study has had on Occupation scholarship. It will also reveal the difficulties in understanding resistance when only the overt and forceful are identified as resistant acts. In her chapter on Channel Island resistance, Bunting acknowledges that, of the entire Empire, the islands had given one of the highest percentages based on population of young men and women to the war effort. The population that remained, often too old or too young for active war duty, had different tasks: "to endure and survive, not to indulge in ineffective and costly gestures of resistance." Indeed, she lays out the excellent Island reasons why a traditional resistance would have been foolish. Bunting then follows up with her conclusion that this argument makes Islanders "uneasy." She intuits their discomfort because they are "quick to point to resistance activities, however petty, that they may have been involved in." What she repeatedly in the book calls their "defensiveness" over the issue comes, she claims, from their unexpressed belief that "their stock of brave exploits is meagre."

Yet, in the very next paragraph the reader learns the "further twist" about Island resistance: "Most islanders are reluctant to mention that there were instances of significant resistance." The emotion she assigns to the Islanders this time is "embarrassment" because they could not approximate the courage of their greatest resisters. The reader cannot help but be puzzled. Are the Islanders defensive because there was *no* effective resistance, proven by the quickness with which they gave Bunting personal examples of attempts to resist? Or are they embarrassed because there *was* substantial resistance to which their own personal attempts could not measure up? Either way, Bunting's style of analysis takes all evidence—positive, negative, or neutral—and reads it as proof of Islander failure.[34]

Bunting's description of defensive Islanders whitewashing a dark secret would come as a surprise to those who have visited Guernsey, the island that is the specific focus of this study. Bunting dismisses any counters to her own reading as part of a "sanitised collective memory."[35] Apparently Channel Islanders are not only self-delusional but also dangerous. Bunting claims, "The islanders succeeded in frightening off the last historian to publish a book on the Occupation; he admitted that he had never set foot on the islands for fear of the controversy he may have found."[36] Invariably, I have encountered in Guernsey Islanders an open perspective, and a clear-eyed view that the Occupation is history, a five-year period that needs to be examined in all its facets. They are frank, and Guernsey wry, about the minority rogues gallery willing to throw ethics aside in their bid personally to survive, or financially to thrive, in the Occupation atmosphere. More, they are fascinated by what they see as the vast majority of Guernseymen and women who resourcefully walked the ethical tightrope of the Occupation, emerging with their lives, self-respect, and British patriotism intact. In Islander eagerness to share their best Occupation stories with her, Bunting senses only deceit and shame. Rather, it is in just such apparently mundane accounts that new understandings of the Occupation and the nature of rhetorical resistance lie waiting.

Recent accounts of the Occupation are sometimes mired in the conceptual frame that this was the only part of Britain occupied by the Nazis. In fact, the opening sentence of Bunting's book is "What if Hitler had invaded Britain?"[37] An undertone of "See, you weren't so perfect" versus "Well, do you think you could have done half so good?" colors discourse between some mainland British writers and Islanders, and fuels a tabloid-exposé mentality bent on uncovering the "real" story. For example, in her final chapter, Bunting devolves into manufactured outrage, predicated on the blanket charge that Islanders failed as British subjects. Following passing references to Churchill's "fight them on the beaches" speech, and claims from Leonard Woolf that some of the Bloomsbury group had purchased poison to commit suicide if Hitler invaded, Bunting continues: "But Channel Islanders did not fight on the beaches, in the fields, or in the streets. They did not commit suicide, and they did not kill any Germans . . . the islanders had not lived up to Britain's wartime ideals. Indeed, they had dismally failed them."[38] Imagine the surprise of Islanders when they read these lines. Only by flinging themselves willy-nilly off a local cliff en masse, or an equally suicidal attack—armed with broom handles and saucepans—on German forces could they meet Bunting's (or her projection of wartime Britain's) high standards for British patriotism. Through such dramatic and extreme conclusions, Bunting changed the dynamic of open inquiry and reasonable argument in Occupation studies. She also confines resistance to those explicit acts that provide counterforce to the German occupiers, treating other forms of defiance as unimportant or vaguely collaborative.

As Louise Willmot writes, in reference to the controversy engendered by Bunting, "None of this encourages an objective assessment of island resistance."[39] Willmot believes that such resistance is underestimated because it was largely "unorganized" rather than falling neatly into "a resistance 'movement' akin to those which existed on the continent." Negative judgments based on such a comparison, in Willmot's words, "fail to do justice either to the conditions the islanders faced, or to the resistance they did offer," and she urges researchers to "move beyond what has become a sterile debate."[40] Although Willmot had in mind academic studies, in an interesting turn of events, the charming fictional account *The Guernsey Literary and Potato Peel Pie Society*, published in 2007, may have done the most thus far to capture the unique flavor of that particular time and place and introduce it to a wider audience.[41]

Although academics and journalists are now slowly approaching the Islanders' history with new appreciation,[42] there is an underlying structure to the Guernsey Occupation that has never been examined in depth. As a rhetorician, I will view this time through the frame provided by my own field, and an interest in persuasive discourse and the ebb and flow of communication. This study seeks an understanding not just of *what* happened during the Occupation, but *why* resistance took the very specific form that it did. When information is restricted through the fiat of occupiers' control and through the physical remoteness of an island location, information itself becomes a nexus of power and resistance. As new orders came down from the German occupying forces forbidding access to outside information by confiscating wireless sets and censoring the press, the Islanders immediately undertook countermoves, sometimes at great personal risk. The verbal and symbolic defiance of the Islanders, such a notable aspect of the Occupation, was neither simple "smarting off" nor a harmless means to blow off steam, as sometimes portrayed. There appeared to be a tacit understanding between occupier and occupied that this struggle for control of information and limits on acceptable expression were important aspects of domination. These discursive and symbolic elements would construct an Occupation resistance of subtlety, depth, and complexity.

A desire to step outside past debates about the Occupation and to uncover a broader sense of rhetorical resistance that could be applied to other situations led me to the Guernsey Archives, the Priaulx Library, and the Imperial War Museum. In order to study discourse contemporaneous with the Occupation and thus avoid the unconscious structuring of memory that comes in the wake of historical controversy, I decided to focus on private diaries kept in Guernsey from June 1940 to May 1945.[43] By examining diaries written during the Occupation of Guernsey, I am seeking the larger story of discourse and rhetorical resistance during those five years. Within these diaries lies the largely unexamined "hidden transcript" of the Guernsey Occupation. James C. Scott, in his book *Domination and the Arts of Resistance: Hidden Transcripts*, poses the question "How do we study power relations when the powerless are often obliged to adopt a strategic pose in the presence of the powerful and when the powerful may have an interest in overdramatizing their reputation and mastery?"[44] Scott argues that the dominated develop a "hidden transcript," one that offers an appraisal of power that may only be safely uttered in private, "behind the back of the dominant."[45] In fact, both the dominated *and* the dominant in a power situation develop hidden transcripts, and an understanding of these discourses is vital to an accurate reading of the public transcript, and to the recognition of resistance when it appears.[46]

Although aspects of the hidden transcript of the powerless may leak into public view, they appear in disguise and in a coded form designed to shelter the weak from peril.[47] Scott argues that the more dangerous the situation for the powerless, the richer will be their attending hidden transcript.[48] When those who experienced the Occupation revel in stories of small defiances, coded insults, and the deft turning of tables on their occupiers, it is not "defensiveness," but the recognition and appreciation of this hidden transcript. As Scott puts it, to read a hidden transcript of the powerless,

> we enter the world of rumor, gossip, disguises, linguistic tricks, metaphors, euphemisms, folktales, ritual gestures, anonymity. For good reason, nothing is entirely straightforward here; the realities of power for subordinate groups mean that much of their political action requires interpretation precisely because it is intended to be cryptic and opaque.[49]

The Guernsey diarists of this study are my guides in discovering this world of coded discourse and disguised subversion.

Generally this hidden transcript is lost to history, or the ability to decode it is challenged by its incomplete and sheltered nature. We are left with the documents and performances of a public transcript that is little more than "the *self*-portrait of dominant elites as they would have themselves seen."[50] Part of the problem in the more controversial studies of the Occupation has been a naive reading of a public transcript (the "open interaction"[51] between the occupier and occupied) that was largely a fiction of power. It behooves the dominant to portray resistance as easily controlled "pinpricks," to amplify their mastery and control of the dominated. When historians privilege the public transcript, bolstered by only certain aspects of the hidden transcript of the powerful, they complete the work that the dominant hoped to achieve through a structuring of image and history.

Secret war diaries kept in Guernsey provide new insights into resistance as practiced under Occupation. Generally, personal diaries meet Jennifer Sinor's criteria for "ordinary writing," writing that is "typically unseen and ignored" and generally considered "discardable."[52] What lifts these diaries out of the ordinary is the narrative they have to tell about extraordinary events.[53] The reader has been introduced to some of the diarists who will guide us through their experiences during the years of Occupation. The premier diary, over a thousand typed pages in length, was kept by a Methodist minister, the Reverend R. Douglas Ord.[54] Ord was based at Brock Road Church from 1938 to 1948 and, as his diary entries reveal, was an intellectual of piercing insight. Having spent substantial time as a prisoner of war during World War I, Ord was the only minister in the Island who spoke German. He flatly refused to serve as an official interpreter for the Germans, but his facility with the language would be a skill he brought to bear in a variety of interventions on behalf of the Guernsey population. As this study will show, he became a point of contact for certain anti-Party Germans, and his ability to manipulate information for productive ends is one of the more interesting stories of the Guernsey Occupation.

Juxtaposed against the intellectual sophistication of Rev. Ord is the fresh perspective of Ken Lewis. Just eighteen at the start of the Occupation, Ken is wide-eyed and frank about all that he encounters, and records his experiences in three substantial volumes without any hint of self-editing. Thus, we are treated to a boy's fascination with the soldiers newly in his midst, his calf-love (even his prayers and dreams) for a young woman who evacuated before the Occupation, and his heartfelt concerns that the great adventure of the war was passing him by. Ken's unselfconscious ethics and concern for others come through clearly, and because he goes to work for the States of Guernsey as a clerk for Louis Guillemette, Sherwill's secretary, he provides a window into the thinking at the highest level of Guernsey government.

Ambrose Collas Robin, a fifty-three-year-old man at the start of the Occupation and blind in his right eye, in some ways overlaps Rev. Ord and Ken Lewis. Like both of them, he was part of the Methodist "set" of an island where one can still go and stand on the rock, or visit the Assembly Rooms, where John Wesley preached. Like Ken Lewis, Ambrose Robin also worked for the States, being deeply involved with gathering statistics concerning the health of the community, and ultimately being put in charge of the Oddfellows Friendly Societies.[55]

Quite a different perspective is provided by Herbert Williams in his entertaining, frank, and substantial diary. Bert comes late to starting a diary, beginning his entries in January 1942. At the beginning of his journal, he records his memories of being a special constable, serving at the airport during the raid and the subsequent Occupation. A reader gets the sense right away that Bert is an everyman, bouncing around from situation to situation. His is a dark, sarcastic view of others who might be out for an advantage, and he has little use for authority—enjoying the process of indicating whenever the emperor has no clothes. Although his is a wealth of negative commentary, occasionally appending a series of dramatic question marks to his entries to show his skepticism of others, he ultimately comes across as soft-hearted and likable. To Bert's great disgust, German authorities dismissed him as a constable, declaring him to be too short. Even though he finally settled in as an electrician for the Lyric Theatre, his great love was his avocation as a bandleader. Thus, Bert Williams gives us much in the way of conventional-wisdom commentary, a revealing view of Occupation tensions and joys within his circle of family and friends, and a backstage view of the Occupation.[56]

Like Bert Williams, William Arthur Warry had a unique perspective to offer as a diarist. Bill Warry ran a shop in the Guernsey Arcade in St. Peter Port and lived with his wife in rooms over the shop. Therefore, he was in a position to see the impact of Occupation on the shops and markets in the middle of Guernsey's largest town. Bill appears to have started his diary mainly as a scrapbook, wherein he affixed articles cut out from the German-controlled local paper. He began by writing brief commentary around these articles, but soon the commentary took over, and the scrapbook became a diary with the pictures and articles taking second place to Bill's observations of life in the center of town.[57]

Located north of St. Peter Port in the neighboring St. Sampson's Parish, Jack Sauvary was sixty-four when the Occupation commenced. His diary reflects the variety of views one would expect from a longtime builder, grower, douzenier (parish representative), and churchwarden. More than broadness of experience, Jack's writings have the wistful tone of a man deeply missing his wife, who died in 1939. With so much of his family evacuated, there is a lonely feel to his entries despite his many deep relationships with friends and remaining family. In his diary, the reader encounters the attachment to nature and the rhythm of life in an island of breathtaking beauty and physical isolation. At age seventy-nine, Arthur Mauger also provides the perspective of an old Guernsey grower living on the far side of the Island from the harbor of St. Peter Port. He is a bit of a romantic for a farmer, marking weddings by drawing a heart in the margins, and over/underlining deaths with a Victorian black banding.

Although many of the secret diaries from the Occupation years were kept by men, women also took the risk to record their views on daily life. One of the finest of all the diaries was kept by Winifred Harvey, a woman born in Guernsey in 1888 (making her fifty-two at the advent of the Occupation). A product of the Ladies College in Guernsey, a school run according to the plan for women's education advocated by the reformers Miss Buss and Miss Beale,[58] Winnie Harvey was intensely active in public service. She was the classic "old girl" of the college, serving on its board of governors and raising money on its behalf. But Winnie's great love was Guiding—the Girl Guides, or in her case, the Island Guides, being the original of the Girl Scout movement in the United States.

The diaries of Dorothy Higgs and K. M. (Kitty) Bachmann are in a different format from those of Winifred Harvey or the male diarists. Dorothy Higgs wrote a series of letters to her sister Phyllis in England, and, because there was no way to send them, tucked them aside as a diary for her sister to read in anticipation that the Island would one day be free of German control. Kitty Bachmann did much the same thing, with her journal arranged as if it were a series of letters to her mother, who had evacuated to England. Both Dorothy and Kitty were women in their prime during the Occupation, and the sense of direct address provided by the letter format of their diaries make them particularly compelling reading. Dorothy was of a problem-solving mentality, and her account is laced with her new avocation raising animals and devising makeshift recipes using substitute ingredients, culinary inventions so popular that she shared them in a column for the Guernsey paper.[59] Kitty was a young mother, longing for her firstborn, Diana, evacuated to England, and reveling in her new son, Peter-John, born during the Occupation.[60]

Elizabeth Doig, a widow who stayed in Guernsey for the sake of her brother, represents older women, who composed a substantial part of the Occupation population. Of enough economic standing that she had a maid at the beginning of the Occupation, Elizabeth had her four-story home confiscated by the Germans during the first year. From then on, she bounced around in her living conditions, recording the stresses of continual moves, isolation, and various health concerns. Finally, I will also make brief references to the diary of Gertie Corbin, a middle-aged woman I began to think of as the Angel of Death for her emphasis on tragic deaths and injuries. Her pithy asides give a sense of the dry humor that became a primary psychological buffer against despair during this time.[61]

Because, during the Occupation, certain key events stood out like signposts across the unfolding five years, the diarists are often commenting upon the same public occurrences. Since diaries are a private expression of inner contemplation, each event is filtered through the perception of the diarist and is affected by such factors as age, gender, social/economic factors, and closeness to the event. Metaphorically, I think of the diarists' entries on common public events as resembling photographs taken by a number of individuals on the same tour through a foreign country. Most will choose to photograph major landmarks, and there will be similarities among the photographs. Yet, the angle of the shot, the people chosen for inclusion, any number of other factors of the photographer's taste and personality will be unique. Examining all of the photos taken of the same landmark together will give the viewer a new overall perspective of the place. Yet, each photographer will also take pictures that are not replicated anywhere else: photographs of friends and family, little moments that tell the real story of the journey for that individual. Perhaps it is these wholly individual pictures (like some wholly personal diary entries) that have the most important truth to tell.

To extend this metaphor just a bit farther, most of us are not avid photographers on a daily basis; it takes something unusual—a major trip, a new child, a Christmas holiday—to trigger our desire to record what is happening. Most of the writers whose diaries I will examine here had never kept a regular diary before. Arthur Mauger seems to be an exception in a group mostly new to keeping a diary. His diary was the apparent habit of many years of keeping a farm record, with his account of the Occupation starting in the middle of ledger book 21. Although he had kept a brief diary for many years, his entries during the Occupation took on greater length, detail, and apparent importance to him. I will discuss later the importance of the sense-making process as it applies to much of the discourse of the Occupation, including these diary entries.

More specifically, in describing the impetus to record in diaries, Alex Aronson speaks of the "inner need to save the momentary impact of experience from oblivion."[62] Such an act takes on its greatest meaning during wartime, for the "illusion of stability and permanence" provided by recording daily events is most valued when the diarist is in "greater need of a shelter from the viciousness and malice of the world."[63] Still, most pictures taken on a vacation tour are only shared among close friends and family. Most people believe, and rightly so, that others will be easily bored with the minutiae of our own experiences. The same could be said of these private diaries; they were not intended for public consumption, but as a later aid to the memory of the writer (or for the entertainment of family and friends).

The immediacy and intermingling of the mundane with the important, as well as the simple beauty of the diary process, is captured well by Kitty Bachmann. On Sunday, May 10, 1942, she wrote:

> A day of much-needed steady rain, Peter [her husband] is reading by the fire, which he glimpses behind the ever-lasting washing, while the Cherub [their infant son] sleeps in his room, allowing me to relax and add a few lines to this spasmodic journal . . . As I write, two Germans are leading their horses to the stalls in the garden garage, Lily is aimlessly chewing the cud in the field, and the

> rain pursues its steady course down the window-panes. Not an exhilarating prospect as we await news of the Spring Offensive. Perhaps Winston will be more optimistic tonight.[64]

As actual letters became impossible, Kitty's "one-way conversation"[65] via her diary/letters became the only illusion of contact she had with a daughter growing up without her. Thus, Kitty berates herself for "every day that I allow to pass without adding something to this diary. Somehow, this task I have set myself, has forged a precious link with you all."[66]

Many of the other diarists also acknowledge a potential reader, some in almost as specific a manner as Kitty Bachmann or Dorothy Higgs. When disappointed that messages could not come through from his children, Jack Sauvary ended one entry, "Good night, Darlings. I hope you are all safe."[67] At other times, he questioned or spoke to family directly, but simultaneously acknowledged that their answer would come at some distant time: "Do you all agree? I think you will." And occasionally he seemed to question the purpose of his writing by pondering, "I don't know if this news will interest you to read, but it will give you some idea how we fared during the Occupation."[68]

The ideal reader in Elizabeth Doig's mind only became apparent in a 1944 entry, upon her hearing from Scotland about the deaths of close friends: "I had so looked forward to seeing them again & giving them my experiences on this Island during these years of occupation & I always imagined the Prov. [Provost] & Hugh Menzies reading this diary of mine with great interest."[69] Yet, most of the diarists kept their journal for themselves, as a spur to memory in later years. Later in the Occupation, Kitty Bachmann expressed a darker reason for being glad that she kept an account. In the horrifying swirl of bombings that followed D-Day, she feared that the Island "could be reduced to a heap of rubble." In the event that she and her husband would not be alive to welcome the evacuees home, "I again pray that you will discover this book in its secret place, so that love's labour will not have been lost."[70]

This writing also seems to have been therapeutic, for the diary functions as the "invisible shoulder" for the writer.[71] Dorothy Higgs stated quite frankly that she mostly wrote when depressed, and long intervals between entries marked a better frame of mind rather than a lack of interesting events.[72] This was not consistent with Dorothy, because the sudden starvation death of her gardener triggered such emotions that she had "not had the heart to write lately."[73] The therapeutic aspect of writing out events is particularly apparent with Winnie Harvey. Her first diary entry was written in August of 1940, although it details the week of June 16 to June 25 of that year. Her diary begins:

> It is extremely difficult to write now in August, about this week, the worst I have lived through. I have been putting it off and off but chiefly because I dreaded to write of the 19th, the death of my Rolfie; but if I write it now perhaps I shall get it over and feel better.[74]

Her desire to come to grips with the death of her little dog, discussed in chapter 1, was the trigger for her recording of the entire Occupation experience. Whatever Winnie anticipated about the healing power of writing, she would return to Rolfie's death repeatedly over the years, like a tongue touching a sore tooth.

As is typical of our human condition, the diarists were blind to the future and knew only what their current position allowed them to see. The judgments of history are often based in hindsight: on our perfect knowledge that Germany would lose the war, that the Occupation would end in five years, that something incredibly dark was happening in those German concentration camps. Reading these accounts reminds us that for the diarists, the future was a closed book. Despite their hopes and belief in the Allied forces, they could not know whether their position in thrall to Germany would be permanent. They were also blind to their own fates, and one of the diarists would not survive for the long-anticipated liberation and reunion with family. Others wrote longingly of family and friends they would see again, only to find later that these loved ones had been dead for many months. They were wary (and condemning) of any "bad players" among their neighbors; they were supportive of their local Guernsey officials, but impatient with their mistakes. In these diaries, they complain and they worry and they dream, as all people do. They provide an excellent, uncensored window on the Occupation, and one that does not fall prey to anachronistic thinking. And, without any intention of doing so, they reveal the structure of rhetorical resistance as it develops under conditions of domination.

Now, when I say that these diaries are uncensored, I must separate the published accounts from those that are only available in archives as unpublished manuscripts. Both Rev. Ord's and Ken Lewis's diaries remain unpublished, although they are the most fascinating and detailed accounts of the period. Unpublished also are the diaries of Arthur Mauger, Bert Williams, Gertie Corbin, Ambrose Robin, William Arthur Warry, and Elizabeth Doig. The other four diaries have been published: Dorothy Higgs's as *Life in Guernsey under the Nazis, 1940–45* in 1947, Kitty Bachmann's as *The Prey of an Eagle* in 1972, Jack Sauvary's as *Diary of the German Occupation of Guernsey, 1940—1945* in 1990, and Winifred Harvey's as *The Battle of Newlands* in 1995. The problem with a published diary is the possibility that editors, often family, will "clean up" the diary and remove the very immediacy and frankness that make the diary useful to begin with. Because these four diaries were published prior to Bunting's book (or in Harvey's case, during the same year) and thus prior to any extensive revisions of history, they are unlikely to be cleansed of controversial material. I find the published diaries to be consistent with the tone and information in the unpublished accounts, and I have not hesitated to utilize them. However, the reader may assign different weight to the published diaries at his or her discretion.

It is also important to note that these diaries, for all their frank directness, were censored to some degree by the authors as they wrote. There was a certain level of danger involved in keeping these secret accounts of the Occupation. On March 14, 1943, Rev. Ord recorded in his diary and underlined for its ironic importance: "*Someone in Jersey has been imprisoned for keeping a diary!*"[75] More often, the writers were concerned that the information recorded could get themselves or their neighbors into trouble. Thus, some are politic in what they record and give hints of interesting stories untold. Kitty Bachmann put it this way: "There are many things which could be recorded if caution were not the constant watchword. The subjects exempted from these pages reduce the rest to trivialities."[76] It was her opinion that "the pen is more dangerous than the sword,"[77] although this belief did not seem to hamper her recording the more comical foibles of herself and others.

What appear to be withheld in these instances are accounts of activities incompatible with the goals of the occupiers. It is only the resistant that needed protecting from German officials, and there seemed to be little hesitation in outing collaborators, sexual dalliers, or black-marketeers. Some, like Dorothy Higgs, use easily deciphered code for their own illegal activities, such as listening to the BBC over wireless sets. Thus, there are references to how they needed to "sort the beans" in the attic at a given time.[78] Despite concerns that they, or their neighbors, might be condemned by their own writing, some diarists (Rev. Ord and Ken

Lewis, notably) are shockingly frank and detailed. It is disturbing to imagine the repercussions had these two diaries fallen into German hands.

An objective study of this period has its difficulties because World War II is a period of high drama. Those heroic figures that risked all for those in peril, those unique souls who have been designated "righteous among the nations," deserve to have their stories told and retold. So, too, do the resistance fighters throughout Europe, and the common Allied soldiers who faced uncommon dangers in prosecuting the war. It should in no way lessen our admiration of the extraordinary to acknowledge the quieter efforts of the ordinary. Not everyone has the presentiment to anticipate coming dangers for self or others, not everyone is composed of the steel needed for incredible deeds, and not everyone is in a position where such deeds are even possible. This is a study of average people trapped in a situation that would challenge their resourcefulness, sometimes on a daily basis, for five long years.

Much of the scholarship on the Occupation attempts in some way to evaluate the patriotism of the civilians caught up in the situation. Given the apparent tensions with mainland Britain over the Occupation, it is important to state that I do not seek to compare the residents of Guernsey to other people in other situations during the war. In fact, I am only examining the experience of this one Channel Island, as I believe that even the experience of the larger Island of Jersey had its own particular ethos. By examining accounts written at the very time that the people of Guernsey were living this experience, I hope to avoid both the vagaries of memory and the emphasis on controversy that seems to follow modern historical analysis of civilians during the war. It is only through a close reading of one particular instance of Occupation that a detailed understanding of rhetorical resistance is likely to emerge, and Guernsey's experience of Occupation will provide us with that text.

A common metaphor in the communication discipline speaks of the control of information as being like a dam: information will still flow, but by carving its way in new courses around the obstacle. Thus, to understand the type of resistance that emerged in Guernsey, the situation under which the Islanders lived must also be understood. Chapter 1 introduces the panoptical nature of an Occupation that took place in this small island in the English Channel. Counter-surveillance and the "reading" of the occupier developed quickly, and a discussion of these elements provides a frame for the key events that occurred during the five years of Occupation. Chapter 2 introduces the two foundational elements that are prerequisite to the development of rhetorical resistance. The story of the Guernsey Occupation involves interpersonal communication: with family and friends who remained in Guernsey, with evacuated family and neighbors, and with the occupying forces in their midst. Through communication and the everyday handling of the deprivations of Occupation, Islanders developed, first, the sense of support necessary to community action. The second vital element is a sense of trust and commonality, a belief in shared community values, and support for a counter-ideology to that of the dominant.

These foundational aspects of support and trust build to a study in chapters 3, 4, and 5 of the three-pronged approach to resistance undertaken by the Guernsey Islanders during the war years. In detailing a rhetorical resistance, this study examines the secondary discourse that undercut official methods of communication. Specifically, I examine the functioning of rumor and gossip, by which discourse moved in its own path around the Island, and which served as a means of manipulation and control (chapter 3); the implications of common narratives—of propaganda and counterpropaganda, of jokes and stories and other unofficial discourse (chapter 4); and the structure of acts of symbolic resistance, many of them clustered around coded discourse and the illegal wireless sets retained by Islanders at great personal risk (chapter 5). The conclusion examines the final year of Occupation, the Liberation of Guernsey, and certain instances of public memory as structured immediately after the Occupation and over time. It brings together the many elements discussed in this study to pose an outline for rhetorical resistance applicable to other instances of prolonged military occupation and to other situations of domination.

This study will show that the Germans viewed the occupation of the Channel Islands in different terms than they did the occupation of Europe. Despite the brutal and in some ways inexplicable air raid, the Germans initially viewed the Islanders as potential allies, with many of the troops convinced that they would be greeted as liberators when they "freed" the Islands from England. Even though they were quickly relieved of that misconception, German officials were correct in anticipating that the Island situation was not analogous to that in Europe. Guernsey was an island far closer to then-occupied France than to free England. It was actually considered so strategically unimportant by the British that an invasion and retaking of the Island did not occur even after D-Day.

As I will discuss later, the Germans knew they were unlikely to face the equivalent of European young men who grabbed guns, attacked with subversive skill, and disappeared into the mountains. As Norman Le Brocq, a Jersey resister, said in a postwar interview, "You couldn't take to the mountains in Jersey with arms in hand. First we've got no mountains and second we had no arms."[79] What was true of the larger Island of Jersey was certainly the case in Guernsey, with its 24.3 square miles and minimal places to hide. In fact, this study will attempt to replace comparisons to the French Resistance with more accurate analogies that better match the isolated situation of the Channel Islands. Once freed from cinematic notions that violence is the only means to confront evil, we can then appreciate the rationale behind a nonviolent resistance based on the manipulation of information. It would be primarily individuals fighting this battle for psychological control during the Occupation, and the struggle took place in an atmosphere where superior knowledge served as the counter to power, and communication became the means of command.

The German occupiers clearly had as part of their agenda the desire to control the mental universe of the occupied. To counter this control, the Islanders became adroit inventors of new psychological resources to help them navigate the shifting ground they found all around them. In some instances, they designed labyrinthine community networks of information as protection for their fellow citizens and impediments to the occupation forces. This study will show that the Germans were well aware of the special nature of this resistance and took countermeasures along the same lines. Thus, the five-year Occupation of Guernsey becomes a story of new channels circumventing the control of information, and of a subjugated people devising methods of sufferance and endurance to buy the time needed to survive with their spirits intact. Rather than the received view of a simple passivity in average Islanders that bordered on collaboration, this study of the German Occupation of Guernsey reveals a quiet defiance and a rhetorical insurgence of depth and nuance. For the occupied population of Guernsey, it would be a subtle resistance.

CHAPTER ONE

The Panoptical Occupation

Everyone seems to be in a dreadful hurry. If you wander today through the narrow, winding streets of St. Peter Port, you may hear rapid footsteps behind you as young and not so young Islanders walk briskly past. I once felt the light, sharp rap of a woman's cane on my leg (eighty, if she was a day) to urge me out of the way as I lollygagged through the Pollet, the extension of High Street that curves gently down toward the harbor. It almost seems that these busy people will run out of room and continue walking purposefully right off the Island and into the English Channel. But there has always been an energy here that runs counter to expectations of sleepy island life.

Guernsey is not simply a place for wealthy British tax exiles and tourists drawn by the harbors, beaches, and pleasant little shops. It is a thriving investment and banking center, and the digital revolution has thrown its invisible net of modernity over the ancient buildings and narrow, cobbled streets. It is a place that wears its long history comfortably while closing its hand firmly around the future. The sleek sailboats and little fishing vessels of today sail the same waters where the Romans had their harbor and later privateers and smugglers worked a darker trade. The ferries from England and France daily pass the brooding Castle Cornet, which in its various forms has guarded the harbor since the thirteenth century. And, a visitor walking the narrow streets and precipitous stairs that rise in layers from the harbor may stop to examine the plaque commemorating the burning of three women for heresy in 1556. Reading that Perotine Massey gave birth to her son in the inferno, only to have him rescued alive and thrown back into the flames at the order of the Bailiff, provides a chill even in the midsummer Guernsey sunshine. Or, the visitor may continue on to visit Hauteville House, the home of Victor Hugo during his fifteen-year exile, where he penned *Les Miserables* while he designed its exquisite garden and eccentric gothic-funhouse decor.

Leaving St. Peter Port, or one of the other little towns dotting the edge of the Island, might lead to a walk through a dark, fragrant forest or along the many high cliff paths with their endless views to sea and vertigo-inspiring plunges to the rocks and salt spray below. Yet, the interior of Guernsey holds a storybook feel, not flat and barren as islands sometimes seem, but rich with undulating green and fields surrounded by the hedgerows, stone walls, and the shady lanes of a British countryside. Waiting for one of the large green and yellow buses that somehow squeeze their way through the narrow roads, you might look over to a twelfth- or thirteenth-century church and its graveyard, or to a house with a "witch's seat." These stones that jut out of the chimneys of ancient houses provided a resting spot for passing witches, preventing them from flying down the chimneys and cursing the residents. In a field close by there likely will be Guernsey cows comfortably grazing, each attached by a long rope to her individual stake like a dog in a suburban backyard. Yet walk down another lane back toward the sea and there it stands, cold and stark against the sky: a German watchtower.

The Island of Guernsey is a palimpsest, written on so repeatedly by history that the physical markers of previous eras seep through to give intriguing glimpses of the past. Even so, there is something jarring about the juxtaposition of Nazi Germany with its ancient towns and narrow streets. The fact that so much left from the Occupation can be found in concrete bunkers, underground tunnels, and the detritus of war makes this time period substantially different in its physical remains as well as its ethos. Although the imprint of violence and war is not unique to the Occupation period, there is a clear aura of control and containment. In Islander emphasis on the ring of jackboots in the Pollet or the sound of German martial music echoing off the buildings of the High Street is some sense of violation, but also a fascination with the simple incongruity of it all.

It may have been that very air of unreality that made evacuating Guernsey in 1940 such a difficult individual decision, despite the imminent threat of invasion. That is where this story of communication and information restriction begins, before the first German occupier set polished boot on Island soil. In this chapter, I will give an overview of some of the major periods of the Occupation as defined by events and the changing circumstances that defined the Guernsey people's relationship with their occupiers. This is not a history book per se, but the primary markers of events will provide a Baedeker as we later traverse the Occupation years in a nonchronological fashion. This was not one Occupation with a consistent set of rules and players, but a multi-tiered experience requiring continual adjustment and rethinking.

This chapter will first discuss the evacuation period and the initial period of Occupation, lasting roughly until the early months of 1941. This would be a time of tentativeness and sizing up on both sides, requiring a painful alteration of the Islanders' self-view as a sovereign people. During this time, Guernsey residents became adept, as have other subjugated peoples, at the survival skill of "reading" those in power over them. As the German command put in place a domination based on surveillance and the restriction of communication, the populace countered with surveillance of their own, where their gaze was turned upward toward those in power. Their ability to observe and control the observation of others set the framework of resistance to power that would only expand during the following five years. In the next part of this chapter, I will examine the second major iteration of the Occupation from February 1941 to June 1944, when much of the mask of occupier compassion or restraint fell away and the stakes became considerably higher. These changes forced a "rereading" of their masters, and an increased need for oppositional techniques. During the final year of Occupation, stretching from D-day in June 1944 to Liberation Day on May 9, 1945, the Germans were so isolated as to become co-prisoners with the Guernsey citizenry. Although the Occupation technically continued, that year had such a unique flavor that I will discuss it separately in the final chapter.

As the Islanders moved from the confusion of evacuation through the lenient early days of German rule and into the tightened restrictions and ongoing threat of the primary years of Occupation, they quietly developed a repertoire of resistance appropriate to the changing conditions. The initial step for those who would develop resistance consisted of understanding the face of the occupier while constructing a dual identity of their own: an inscrutable public face of passivity that sheltered a private face of opposition.

"WATCHMAN, WHAT OF THE NIGHT?"

This text from Isaiah 22:11–12 would provide the theme of Rev. Ord's sermon for June 16, 1940, capturing well the sense of an uncertain people turning for guidance to those in a better position to know.[1] It is at this point from the 16th to the raid on the 28th that confusion, silence, and contradictory information led average Islanders to make irrevocable decisions and caused Dorothy Higgs to write, "We seem to have lived half a lifetime in the last fortnight."[2] As early as the 18th, Winifred Harvey mentioned hearing that all the major Islands (Guernsey, Jersey, Alderney, and Sark) were to be demilitarized, and that the governor and all troops were evacuating Guernsey that day.[3] There was still confusion between Whitehall in London and the Guernsey government as to the proper steps to take, with the Germans sweeping inexorably through France and toward the Channel Islands. The War Office believed demilitarization would be the deciding factor in removing any need for German attack. Despite the urging of the Home Office to make this decision public, particularly to the Germans, the War Office demurred, believing that such information would constitute an open invitation for the Germans to invade.[4] This confounding decision to shelter the knowledge of demilitarization from the Germans (the very audience for whom the action was performed) contributed in no small part to the German air raid of the 28th.

Confusion was also intense as to whether there should be mass evacuations, with the director of Sea Transport believing that the Home Office considered it unnecessary, and others in the same Sea Transport department telling the Guernsey Bailiff that transport off the Island would be provided for all.[5] To complicate matters, a new governmental arrangement had been formed in Guernsey to deal with the Germans should events play out in that direction. Including the Procureur (Sherwill), Mr. R. O. Falla, Jurat Leale, and other prominent men, it was, in effect, a cabinet. Their task would ostensibly be to coordinate the work of the various States committees, and thus they had been given the name the Controlling Committee (on Jersey, the Supreme Council).[6] This new arrangement did not sit too well with Winifred Harvey, who observed, "They have dictator's powers over everything though the Bailiff is the nominal head."[7] The change in the men at the top could only add to the contradictory messages coming out of London, and the Guernsey press magnified the confusion. Kitty Bachmann described notices published in the local press, apparently originating with States officials, that would only be replaced with conflicting new notices in the following issue. Kitty summed it up well by describing their minds, had they been visible, as "some extravagant Heath-Robinson concoction," the eccentric cartoon machines whose American equivalent was Rube Goldberg.[8]

The Islanders ricocheted off official notices, rumor, and their own inferences and expectations, leading them to make decisions, unmake them, and make the same decisions over again. Kitty's husband, Peter, saw firsthand the confusion wrought by the initial "official" announcement in the *Press* stating that anyone desiring to evacuate must register at their local douzaine room by eight o'clock that evening. Because so many people did not see a copy of the paper until six o'clock, that gave little time to comply with what seemed to be an ultimatum. Peter went to their local Vale Douzaine Room to register and was stunned by the "surging crowds" he found surrounding the building. Realizing that the committee was overwhelmed by sheer numbers, Peter climbed through a window to help with the registration task. A number of the people there were proxy-registering for invalids, elderly, or other family and neighbors unable to attend in person. Babies were present in their perambulators and in their parents' arms.

Expectant mothers were registering, and Peter noted one unmarried mother in particular, weeping because she was deserted and alone. But in all the confusion, he did not see the shoving, yelling, or hysterical need to push to the front that is the hallmark of panic. From what the Bachmanns observed, there did not seem to be widespread panic, at least not among relatives and friends as they prepared to leave. Kitty attributed this to the Guernsey "traditional mulishness," a trait that, combined with strength of character, had long lent the Islanders the nickname of "Guernsey Donkeys."[9] Yet, Kitty was the first to admit that she was not among the "dense crowds swarming the jetties" as ships left for England, and that she was probably "not competent to judge" the overall level of Island fear.[10]

This would not be the last time that the diarist's specific location in Guernsey determined what he or she experienced. If Kitty was unaware of panic in the Island, she was definitely in the minority. Arthur Mauger, writing from his farm in Castel, headed the entry for June 22nd, "people panicky."[11] This assessment was borne out by Winifred Harvey, who heard from a neighbor that all children must be evacuated and everyone needed to register at the Constables' Office by 7:00 that evening. Without a newspaper to confirm or deny this news, and believing that registration and evacuation were now compulsory, Winnie braved the crowds. She described the scene: "The crush was awful, people squeezing and pushing from three sides . . . Coming out by the same door you went in. It was frightful, people fainting and being pulled out of the crowd." At one point, having stood in the press of bodies for well over two hours, a movement of the crowd frightened Winnie and she let out a sudden "Oh!" A man near to her believed that she was about to faint and convinced the police to push her in through the door, with Winnie dragging an old lady in with her. Winnie managed to register and was told to come back in the morning for further instructions.[12]

It was at this point that Winifred Harvey, and many others, made a fatal decision that would haunt them for the rest of the Occupation and beyond. Her friend Vera Carey was close to her in the crowd and asked if Winnie had put her little dog, Rolf, to sleep yet. "You are not allowed to take him. Do have it done. Lainé [the veterinarian] did my Donald this afternoon." Deeply upset, Winnie asked the man conducting the registration if Rolf could go with her to England since she had obtained a permit for him. He replied, "No, Miss Harvey, I do beg of you to have him put to sleep. Mine was done this afternoon." Now convinced that she would be compelled to leave the Island, and that Rolf could not be left to die from neglect, Winnie sought out both the veterinarian and the animal shelter, both of whom were too busy at the sad task of mass euthanasia to help her. Winnie best describes what happened next:

> So, we all got in my car, Mrs. Perry held Rolfie who kissed my cheek and we drove to Mr. Foote. I put my little Rolfie on the wall and just walked away and Foote shot him and he fell without a cry, not knowing anything. I went back and stroked his lovely head, my little companion and friend. He is buried there.[13]

Across the Island, others made this same sad decision. Rev. Ord, in reporting these days of panic, described the many valuable dogs and cats that were killed, "to the distress not only of their owners but of the vets themselves." Worse than the decision itself, Ord reported, was the fact that "Amateurs killed their own pets, sometimes, it is to be feared, with unnecessary cruelty." Ord had been told of a bird fancier forced to wring the necks of his prize birds himself before he "cleared off" to England.[14] Others opted to let their pet birds fly free to fend for themselves, and Winnie described her garden as "full of budgerigars and canaries." Those who ultimately stayed in Guernsey would spend days trying to collect these birds and rescue the dogs and cats abandoned in locked houses by evacuees.[15]

Winnie, for one, would never completely recover from this terrible act, performed with the most loving of intentions, and she spent the remainder of the Occupation revisiting the decision. Even when lying in the street, under the bombardment of the air raid on the harbor on the 28th of June, she was thinking, "'Thank God Rolf is out of this!' Mrs. Kinnersley's lovely young red setter went mad and had to be shot. Rolfie was so upset by noise that it might have been the same with him."[16] Yet, no amount of rationalization could ease Winnie's obvious grief and regret. She wrote in August, "I think sometimes that I did right by Rolf and some times it was a frightful mistake. But I have missed him every day frightfully."[17] Rolfie's death became her touchstone, symbolic of all the decisions large and small in the years to come. These early days of disinformation, panic, and forced decision making under the worst conditions would spawn many regrets for the diarists and the remainder of the Guernsey population. When the announcement finally came from the elderly Bailiff, Victor G. Carey, that evacuation was voluntary, considerable damage had already been done. As Rev. Ord wrote in his diary, "Had this announcement been made a day earlier, much misunderstanding and wretchedness had been avoided."[18]

Not only were pets euthanized or abandoned, poultry slaughtered, and cows left in fields to wander loose and unmilked, but property of all kinds took on a lesser significance to its owners. As Ord put it, "Car owners gave away their cars to friends—some for twenty shillings. Others did the like with property: 'There's my house and furniture; do what you like with it. I'm off!'"[19] One of the more amusing stories of the sudden relinquishing of property was provided by Bert Williams, who was working at Fort George in the electrical department of the Royal Engineers staff. All seemed normal when he finished up work at 6 P.M. on June 19, but on his arrival at 7 A.M. the following morning, Bert found the fort deserted and turned upside down. Bert and a few others wandered around the fort to the "smashed up" canteen, where a barrel of beer had been left with its tap open and beer spilling all over the floor. Never one to miss an opportunity, Bert said, "The lads soon stopped the beer from running to waste by drinking it up. I came across the piano & so all hands settled down to a sing song with beer." This same morning, George Collivert, the owner of the Albert Arms, came to the decision to "give his pub away" and began to hand out beer, liquor, and tobacco gratis to all who appeared. Bert snagged the final bottle of Pony Ale, by which time Collivert's "once spotless bar was afloat with beer and all the lads of the village were definately [*sic*] under the weather."[20]

The rationale for such giveaways appeared to be unwillingness by evacuees to allow their property to fall into Nazi hands.[21] In some parts of the Island, the Germans confiscated the homes of those who evacuated almost immediately as housing for the troops.[22] Quick confiscation of evacuee property for German housing appears to have been less common in other areas. Thus, as late as December 1941, Jack Sauvary wrote of his friend Stafford, who had taken on the task of "looking after evacuees' homes," along with "women [who] ventilate and clean them each week."[23]

The decision to evacuate to England or to stay behind and suffer a German invasion was not merely predicated on panic, but on a variety of personal factors. It is important to recognize that many Islanders anticipated not a relatively peaceful Occupation, but becoming the new frontline of the war. They expected an all-out battle between England and Germany on their soil, with the very real possibility of Guernsey being flattened by Allied air raids. Quite naturally, they turned for advice to spiritual advisors, and Rev. Ord reported being "besieged" by both old friends and total strangers seeking counsel: "We are depending on you; what you say goes for us!" Ord did his best with these requests, but privately filtered them through his dry wit, musing, "It is curious how, in times of crisis, people turn to a Minister of religion when they ignore him at other times."[24]

Some of the decisions to evacuate were easier than others. Resident soldiers were demobilized, and men of military age, considered to be from age twenty to age thirty-three, were invited to leave the Island. They would be in especial danger with a German invasion and were of considerable value to Great Britain for war duty.[25] It is unfortunate that Ken Lewis does not write about the decision that led him to stay in Guernsey. At the age of eighteen, he fell between the two stools of being considered too young for overseas duty and being considered of conscription military age. Conscription age would change to eighteen later in the war. At this point, however, adolescents of the time were particularly helpful to their families, and Ken stayed in Guernsey, as did some of his "mates." With no way to become involved in the great cause, they would form a particular point of resistance and bedevilment for the occupying forces.

Many families made the wrenching decision early on to evacuate their children, and nearly entire schools left together, generally with a small group of teachers accompanying. The steamers were often delayed, and Ord described how "the bairns nevertheless marched along the jetty singing and putting on a brave smile."[26] For many children, this must have seemed an exciting adventure, and evacuating by school group was a clever way to give the sense of a school outing. For other more prescient or cautious children, the magnitude of the experience could not be sheltered from them. As Kitty Bachmann tucked in her daughter the night before evacuation, Diana said to her, "I shall try to forget you and Daddy, then I shan't be too sad." Diana already sensed that her parents would not be joining her in England, although that decision had not yet been made. Kitty described her daughter "as she lay the next morning, dishevelled after a restless night, sprawled across the bed, fast asleep, with flushed cheeks, her new identity disc on its silver chain slipped on to a bare shoulder, oblivious to the fact that I was standing there in mental agony, forcing myself to waken her and send her away, literally and irrevocably into the unknown."[27] Any parent can understand the pain and the peculiar bravery of relinquishing a child to an uncertain but seemingly safer fate. Yet, just as in the evacuation of schoolchildren from London during the Blitz, not all families were able to make this decision or to do so in time.

At the other end of the life cycle, the elderly posed particular problems when decisions were made whether to go or stay. More than one set of plans to evacuate as a family would be confounded by older residents' inability to endure the travel or unwillingness to leave the only home they had ever known. Arthur Mauger, at nearly eighty and still active at his family farm, seemed not to have seriously considered leaving. Jack Sauvary apologized to his children often in his diary for failing to go with them, writing, "You know darlings that I am getting old and to start life again is not very encouraging, not at 64."[28] Today, we would not think of sixty-four as all that old, and Jack seemed extremely vital and involved with everything going on around him. Yet, the recent death of his wife must have made him feel that the best part of his life was behind him. Later, as German orders became harsher, he admitted to worrying that he had made the wrong decision, and then revealed the real tug that kept him in Guernsey, "I was afraid that if we all got killed with bombs there may not be even a small stone to mark Mum's grave."[29]

The decision to go with parents, or stay behind with parents, at times divided families. Kitty Bachmann's family was offered berths on a departing ship with less than an hour's notice. When her mother and sister Audrey called to tell Kitty that there was additional room for two more, Kitty and Peter faced a difficult decision. Peter could not, at such short notice, leave his business as a jeweler, and "neither would his old people entertain, for one moment, the idea of travelling." Sitting there at their breakfast table, he gave Kitty complete choice to go immediately or wait until they could sort out the proper course for the two of them to follow together. Despite her family's entreaties on the telephone, Kitty decided to wait with her husband. The speed of events robbed Kitty of the opportunity for proper goodbyes, a particularly sad thing in light of later events.[30]

Not that everyone was so solicitous about elderly parents. Bessie Clayton, a teacher at the Girls' Intermediate School, rang up Winifred Harvey to tell her that she was evacuating with the school. Winnie asked her, "But what about your mother?" To which Bessie breezily responded, "She will probably follow." And thus, Winnie reports, Bessie departed for England and "left her mother quite stranded and alone." This apparent desertion of "poor old Mrs. Clayton" gnawed at Winnie. She "didn't in the least want to take responsibility for her," but her conscience would not let her ignore the woman's plight and she decided to at least make inquiries. As it turned out, the neighbors were leaving and couldn't take her with them, and even her daily cleaning woman had left for the mainland. As the reader of her diary anticipates, Winnie finally writes, "there seemed nothing for it but to fetch her here."[31]

This theme of abandonment versus bravely standing by one's responsibility took on great importance during and after the evacuation period. There was pressure applied to reduce panic and to encourage valuable members of the community to remain in the Island. Placards bearing what Kitty Bachmann called "the bitterest taunts" appeared all over Guernsey: "DON'T BE YELLOW!" "CHEER UP!" "EVACUATION NOT COMPULSORY!" "STAY WHERE YOU ARE!"[32] Many irreplaceable people had left the Island, and there may also have been considerable pressure from Whitehall, uncertain what to do with the sudden influx of so many refugees.[33] R. O. Falla of the Controlling Committee made a special trip to Winifred Harvey to beg her to stay, saying, "Miss Harvey, while you are here you are an asset to the island, if you go you become a refugee." Even a girl in Le Riches store said to her, "I am so glad you are here, Miss Harvey, we do look to those who should lead us to stand by the island."[34]

Such repeated assurances of her importance to other people's well-being seemed to have the effect on Winnie Harvey of slowing down her decision to leave, and she was not alone in using others' needs as the criterion for staying. Rev. Ord described his quiet discussion with his wife Grae (always called G. in his diary) and their decision: "Unless evacuation is universal and compulsory, I cannot leave. In any case not until the sick or the aged had been embarked could clergy and ministers leave their posts. G. refused to accept my suggestion that she should go herself, though she was apprehensive of what the Nazis might do with those of my calling. So we made our final decision and found essential peace."[35]

So, in an atmosphere of disinformation and conflicting pressures to stay or go, the Guernsey Islanders made their decisions, or delayed until the decision was made for them. There would be plenty of time for regrets for some. Jack Sauvary wrote of Mrs. Stubbs, who was "very upset not to have got away. She blames Dick [her husband] for studying his firm too much."[36] Doubtless, this delay would be a topic of conversation in the Stubbs home for the next five years. One who paid a terrible price for poor decisions made in high places was a British officer, Douglas McLeod. On June 29, the day following the harbor air raid, Kitty Bachmann was in town for supplies. McLeod rushed up to her in great agitation, frantically explaining, "I have just arrived—on leave. I had no idea that Guernsey was being evacuated!"

As he spoke, the two of them looked up, horrified to see German planes overhead. "On no account must I be caught here," McLeod continued. "I simply must get away, even if I have to steal a fishing boat."

Even as he spoke, Kitty knew that his escape would be impossible. The last boat had left during the height of the air raid the day before, pulling away to avoid the bombs so precipitously that people on board merely to say goodbye to family were carried away with them, and some husbands and wives waiting to join their spouses on board were left behind on the jetty. Kitty later learned that McLeod was imprisoned by the Germans in Castle Cornet in the early days of the Occupation, later to be transferred to a prisoner-of-war camp in Germany for the duration. "On whom, one may ask," Kitty pondered in August 1940, "lies the responsibility for sending men on leave to a place in imminent danger of invasion?"[37]

Regardless of personal decisions to evacuate or stay, many clung to the "comfortable illusion" that the Germans would consider Guernsey too tiny to bother occupying or destroying. The air raid of the 28th put an end not only to the option to evacuate but also to such false hopes. Ken Lewis had heard that a German plane landed on Sunday, the 30th, but took off again, and so the family "went to Chapel that evening quite relieved," only to hear later from his dad that subsequent planes had indeed landed and stayed.[38] By eight o'clock the official broadcast came that everyone must "behave and not talk in groups," and Jack Sauvary grimly reported, "It's now official that we are in camp."[39]

Despite the speculation and the evening broadcast, some would not receive definitive news of the Occupation until Monday morning. Winifred Harvey was told by her Hungarian housemaid, Rosa, who announced "with rosy cheeks, eyes and mouth round with excitement, "The Germans are here!" Rosa Toth was one of the many Hungarian, Rumanian, German, Swiss, or Italian girls serving as domestic help in the Island, largely because British girls eschewed domestic service at the time. Winnie actually had a second Hungarian girl, Maria Szabo, who served as her cook.[40] Rosa, and presumably many others, of these girls were intensely excited at the arrival of young German soldiers, anticipating that they would find allies, and perhaps romance, among their ranks. Part of this anticipation was the desire for a reversal of fortunes where the servants would become the mistresses under the new order. Rosa, for example, wanted Winifred Harvey to evacuate to England, and planned to remain in the Island and take up residence in Winnie's house. Rosa and most of these girls refused to evacuate, fearing being interned in England, with many hoping that the Germans might give them free passage back to their homelands.[41]

In any case, this would be the way Winnie heard the momentous news that morning, and having confirmed the truth by way of the milkman, stoically thought, "Well . . . I had best get dressed."[42] Equally practical was Dorothy Higgs, who awakened Monday morning believing she heard the telephone. But when the operator told her that they were not "expecting any more trunk calls," then Dorothy "knew that was that." She even felt a certain "relief to know the sword had fallen and we no longer had to sit shivering under it."[43] And that seems to have been a widespread feeling: a desire to have the agony of uncertainty and waiting at an end. So, with great trepidation, the Islanders prepared to face whatever would come next.

THE VELVET GLOVE

Despite going to bed on Sunday night "with heavy hearts dreading the consequence of the German invasion,"[44] the Guernsey population awoke on Monday morning to news that somewhat assuaged their deepest fears. Special editions of both Island newspapers, the *Evening Press* and the *Star*, had been published overnight and delivered free to every household. The front page was given over to a listing of the initial "Orders of the Commandant of the German Forces in Occupation of the Island of Guernsey,"[45] the details of which were greeted with cautious optimism. Wirelesses would still be allowed, there was no move (despite many rumors that circulated to the contrary) to close churches and chapels, time would move forward by an hour, and the private use of cars was to cease.[46] Considering the treatment of Europe under occupation and the horrors of the initial air raid, the orders seemed "very lenient in the circumstances."[47] Yet, the second of the eleven orders did not escape notice: "We will respect the population in Guernsey, but, should anyone attempt to cause the least trouble, serious measures will be taken and the town will be bombed."[48] The direct threat of a repeat bombing, combined with an order that begged the question of what "the least trouble" actually meant, caused Dorothy Higgs to tartly observe, "So, I rather think we shall behave exactly as they wish!"[49]

Some of these initial orders led to the unconscious human comedy that would shadow more important events throughout the Occupation. The Germans lessened the opportunity for armed resistance with Order Six, requiring that all weapons "except souvenirs" had to be turned in to the Royal Hotel by noon of that very day, along with all ammunition. Jack Sauvary took the bus into St. Peter Port, only to find hundreds already in front of the Royal carrying all sorts of swords, bayonets, and all variety of guns, including the muzzle-loading type. Seeing the different interpretations put on the term "weapon," Jack handed in his old revolvers, all three tied neatly together. The German officer took them, looked them over, and simply said, "Curios I suppose, oh you can take them back."[50] Winifred Harvey topped Jack in her caution by cutting off the points of the hog-spears hanging decoratively in the hall. These she packed up with some ancient swords and sent in by way of "old Roberts," one of her part-time gardeners. Again, the German officer handed this unusual collection appeared flummoxed, exclaiming, "These are souvenirs, we don't want these," whereupon the faithful Roberts brought them all back home again.[51]

There were many reasons for the restraint of the occupier's hand and a "velvet glove" treatment of the populace during these initial weeks and months. Other occupying forces have started with a belief that the least effort and most effective control lay in a benign policy couched in mutual respect. This would be the initial approach taken, for example, by the Northern forces in the occupied South of the American Civil War, where most officers in charge "eschewed mass arrests and mandatory loyalty oaths in favor of a 'rosewater' policy of leniency and suasion."[52] For the German occupiers of Guernsey, three basic factors made an easing into the Occupation the obvious choice: a misperception of Guernsey history, a strategic sense of the value of the Channel Islands, and the personalities of those initially in command.

First, there was some confusion in the German mind over the pedigree of Channel Islanders and whether they considered themselves British, French, or something wholly independent, a confusion that was only amplified by the Channel Islands' position as Crown dependencies. This status means that the Channel Islands are part of the British Isles but not the United

Kingdom and owe allegiance to the monarch rather than Westminster.[53] Hitler reportedly chose to view the Islanders as French and therefore likely to greet the invading German armies as "liberators," a common fantasy it would seem for occupying forces.[54] The Germans' original notions of flowers thrown at their feet by a liberated people were short-lived, and their propaganda based on that theme was mere fabrication.[55] However, the lingering effects of confusion over the Guernsey constitution and national loyalties did lead to some apparent oddities during the Occupation. For example, singing of the national anthem was banned unless special permission was granted, yet prayers for the royal family, viewed by the Germans as wholly separate from Churchill and Parliament, were permitted during church services.[56] In actuality, this policy was a more accurate reflection of Guernsey's special nature as a British Crown dependency.

There also seem to have been confused notions of the actual strategic value of the Channel Islands. Certainly the propaganda value of occupying a corner of British territory was clear to the German hierarchy. Whether the Channel Islands could serve as a launching point for the invasion of the British mainland is questionable, considering that they are located so close to western France. Any attack by sea or air would have been more logical coming directly across the narrowest portion of the English Channel and launched from the northernmost part of France. It is instructive that some of the troops coming ashore, perhaps having been told that an invasion was imminent, believed that they had reached the Isle of Wight or mainland Britain itself.[57]

It was more important for German self-protection to prevent the British from retaking these Islands, so close to German-occupied France, that would then be available as Britain's own invasion launch point. But the true strategic nature of the Islands and the need for a benign advent to the Occupation may have hinged on the rejected July 19, 1940, peace proposal that Hitler made to Britain. As Knowles Smith claims, this proposal surely had some effect on the early Occupation, for "the invader would naturally wish to demonstrate to the British people that they were not cruel barbarians, but a highly civilised and superior race, well able to rule fairly."[58] Plans for this attempted rapprochement were combined with a reported respect that the Germans felt for the British as cultural equals. Many historians have reported the instructions given by his superior to Count von Schmettow, when he was placed in command over the Channel Islands at the end of September 1940, to "remember that it is English territory you are going to, not defeated France."[59]

Confusion over the nature of the Channel Islands and strategic concerns were both instrumental in setting the tone for the earliest days of Occupation. Yet the interplay between the personalities of Ambrose Sherwill and Major Dr. Albrecht Lanz may be the most salient reason for a display of the velvet glove. As the first commandant of the Guernsey Occupation, Lanz brought a scholarly mindset to his position and appears to have formed a strong regard for his opposite number in the Guernsey government. Sherwill was a decorated war veteran of World War I, wounded nine times in combat. On his first meeting with Lanz, Sherwill brought his medals for gallantry in action and placed them on the table before the commandant. Noting that his days as a soldier were behind him, Sherwill said, "I bitterly regret that I am one no longer but there isn't a rifle in the island. Now I realise that I must obey orders."[60] This gesture, realistic but with an edge of defiance, appealed to Lanz and forged an early respect between the two men.

Apparently Lanz had a sense of how to handle large groups of people, assuring them that their concerns were considered and their input taken seriously. He appointed one of his officers, Dr. Maass, to serve as an official liaison with the Island population. Kitty Bachmann described how Dr. Maass kept "fixed hours each day during which Islanders may call on him for advice, on any of the problems arising from the Occupation."[61] He seems to have been successful in defusing a number of situations, and received strong positive reviews for the brief time that he held this position. Although not speaking from personal experience, Winifred Harvey reported that Dr. Maass was "a charming person, I hear."[62]

What is apparent from all accounts is that the replacement of Dr. Maass in August and Dr. Lanz in late September was widely viewed as a bleak omen for the future. Kitty Bachmann announced on August 10 the first shift in German control: "The Chief-of-Staff, Dr. Maas [*sic*], has been replaced. We can hardly expect a change for the better; for, by all accounts, Dr. Maas was always approachable and, at times, even conciliatory."[63] The anxiety felt by Islanders over the removal of Maass and Lanz was not misplaced. Although the true shift in occupier/occupied relationship would not come until early the next spring, only to worsen notably the following year, events of the fall of 1940 served as prelude to still darker times to come. These earliest changes at the top signaled an end to the artificial honeymoon of the first months of Occupation.

THE PANOPTICAL PRISON

Dorothy Higgs could say, with justice, that the residents of Guernsey felt "the iron hand very little" in the early days. She chalked up as "mainly unimportant things" such restrictions as cycling single file and "needing to be careful about phoning." These were all, in Higgs's view, "just policy and not compulsion."[64] I would like to put a different frame on these early orders and the way they may have operated both by chance and by design. These orders basically fell into two groups: censorship of communication and restraint of allowable actions. They were accompanied by a very visible presence of the triumphant German forces, and by what Guernseymen viewed as attempts at "Germanization" of their Island home.

By instituting control by continuing surveillance and the restriction of civilian actions, the German command established an occupation based on "panopticism." This term, coined by Michel Foucault, is a metaphoric play on Jeremy Bentham's eighteenth-century design for a model prison. Bentham's Panopticon was designed with a central tower, having windows facing a ring of cells. Each cell had a large window facing the tower and a small window on the opposite wall, allowing the cell to be flooded by crosslight. Thus, each prisoner was clearly visible, while unable to see the observer in the tower. Walls between the cells prevented contact between prisoners, and so the cells functioned like "so many small theatres, in which each actor is alone, perfectly individualized and constantly visible."[65] Because the prisoners were never sure when they were being watched, they assumed a constant observer, supplying in their own minds a guard who may or may not have been actually present. As Foucault succinctly put it, "Visibility is a trap,"[66] and it was their continuous visibility that allowed control of the prisoners. Shackles and locks were secondary, for the prisoner knew that his every move was being monitored, and only his compliance with regulations could prevent punishment.

Ideally, in the German view, the Island of Guernsey would have to function as a prison without bars, which is the true promise of the Panopticon. There certainly seemed to be enough troops in Guernsey to aid in the necessary surveillance. On July 29, 1940, a census by the States of Guernsey had recorded that there were 23,981 Islanders still in residence.[67] The number of German soldiers in the Island varied, but there were approximately 15,000 soldiers in Guernsey at the peak of the Occupation during the spring of 1942.[68] Yet, even with the massive presence of German troops, something more would be needed to achieve a panoptical effect. The answer lay in the establishment of a sense of constant surveillance that can be seen in the early orders of the German occupiers.

As a preliminary step to surveillance, the Island population would have their movements restricted, with the very first of the initial group of eleven orders forbidding Islanders to leave their homes between 11 P.M. and 6 A.M.[69] By late August, this curfew had been moved back to 10 P.M.[70] and would move forward and back again throughout the Occupation. Due to reconnaissance attempts by the British government in the fall of 1940, access to specific parts of Guernsey was also forbidden or was restricted to certain hours. For example, by December 1940, anyone residing on "the small side roads of the slopes of the South coast of the Island" was forbidden to go outside after dark. Even if in possession of a pass, residents were warned that they were subject to being shot on sight.[71]

As they had in other occupied territories, the German authorities also took steps to list, quantify, and measure residents, like so many new possessions. On Sunday, October 13, Winifred Harvey mildly described as "an unpleasant thing" a demand that those having relations serving in the British Army or reserves provide the name and rank of the British officer, along with their own name and address.[72] This seemed to Winnie mainly to presage a search of homes for hidden spies. More disturbing to Winnie would be the "frightful" November order, the first one listed as "zur Befehl des Führers" (by order of the Fuhrer). The *Bekanntmachung* (order) required the reporting of "every British person, not born on the island or permanently resident here before September 1st, 1939." Unless the report was made by Tuesday, November 5, "the person sheltering them will be shot." "What," Winnie pondered at the time, "does it mean?"[73]

Between these two reports about relations and personal origin came the forms to register for identity cards. Had there been any doubts about German plans to closely monitor the populace, these identity cards put them to rest. By October 1940, the new military commander of the Islands, Oberst Graf von Schmettow, ordered compulsory identity cards for Guernsey and Jersey residents over the age of fourteen. In registering, each applicant had to supply (along with hair and eye color) any distinguishing mark such as scars or a limp.[74] As a douzenier, Jack Sauvary had the job of checking registration cards for accuracy: "I have looked into more ladies' eyes than I ever did in all my life! Had I been colour blind I might have got out of the job!" Even the old and infirm could not escape registration, so constables and douzeniers were to charge one shilling for a home visit to complete the form. "Of course," Jack mentioned in passing, "we have not taken the bob."[75]

Ultimately, these identity cards would be enhanced the following summer with the photograph of the bearer. It took several months to photograph the entire population of the Islands. What is now a remarkable historical record was less impressive to the participants. Generally taken outside in unforgiving light, these usually unsmiling photographs show a population already worn down by a year of Occupation. As Rev. Ord described his and Grae's photos, "We both look somewhat the worse for wear in these pictures."[76] Of course, the larger purpose of these cards escaped no one. They had to be produced whenever and wherever demanded by the Germans: indeed, the ability to leave one's home hinged on the constant possession of the identity card.

Physical restrictions and the cataloging of residents were accompanied in these early days by a tightening on communication. Anything that smacked of communication to the outside world was banned, with wireless transmitters prohibited and earning the possessor a fifteen-year sentence.[77] In October, German soldiers even went door to door and wrung the necks of all the pigeons in the Island, presumably to prevent a more ancient means of message transmission.[78] Communication and physical restrictions were combined in the order that banned all meetings of societies and clubs, not a surprising law given the opportunity for subversion such meetings would provide.[79] Proof of the interplay between restricted communication and panoptical control would come in the passing in late July of what would be commonly known as the "Dangerous Talking Bill." This was an ordinance forbidding speaking "in a way detrimental to the good understanding between the Guernsey people and the German forces."[80]

For Rev. Ord, this was "the first truly sinister ruling we have had and sends a shiver down the spine."[81] Ord's response was the logical one for a minister charged with delivering sermons, and whose speech would be subject to heightened scrutiny. Sure enough, the next day Ord received a typed notification from the chairman of the Channel Island synods urging caution in the wording of sermons and prayers. Reportedly, the term "the forces of evil" had turned up in church services, and the "objectionable significance for the Army of Occupation" was inescapable. Inescapable, too, was the implication that religious services were monitored for content, and even a public petition to God was subject to scrutiny.[82]

On the same day that Ord received this notification, he reported on the case of Mr. Collins, the manager of Mssrs. Le Riches department store, as the "1st victim of the speech laws."[83] For once, Rev. Ord had the order of events wrong, believing that the Germans forced the passing of an ordinance that was then used against Collins for forbidding the use of the German language in his shop. Rumor went around that Mr. Collins had been denounced by a clerk in his own store. The actual events, in at least one published account, involved a Mr. Cheeseborough, who was a clerk at Le Riches. On July 19, he asked Mr. Collins if he should stop his work to translate for another clerk handling a German complaint about a coffee order. Collins told him just to continue his own work, and he would handle it. The complaint against Collins apparently came from the Germans, who wanted preferred treatment, but Mr. Collins had neither forbidden the use of German, nor was he denounced to the Germans by Cheeseborough.[84] It was the States of Guernsey that "rushed through" the speech bill, so that the ailing Mr. Collins could be tried by the court rather than by the Germans.[85] Mr. Collins was subsequently acquitted, and this was the only official case brought under this hastily arranged law.

In Winifred Harvey's eyes, this case was "a definite warning."[86] It is notable that the false rumor of the Collins incident cast a Guernseyman rather than a German soldier as the denouncer. Unlike in a traditional prison setting, the occupying forces could not prevent contact between the Islanders. If, however, the trust between Guernseymen could be broken, then the sense of surveillance could be expanded greatly. "Lateral surveillance," the monitoring by one's peers, expands the number of eyes working at the behest of those in power.[87] As with self-monitoring, an internalized suspicion that neighbors or even family may be part of the "thousands of eyes posted everywhere"[88] can fuel the fear and paranoia conducive to control.[89] Thus, it is the *belief* in constant surveillance that facilitates the power relationship, allowing actual monitoring to be spotty or "discontinuous" in its action while still being "permanent in its effects."[90]

Even in this first half-year, before relations between occupier and occupied hardened, the German command made a warning move apparently designed to heighten the Islanders' monitoring of self and others. In mid-November of 1940, ostensibly because the Guernsey populace "favoured espionage"[91] against the German forces, an order went out requisitioning all civilian wireless sets. If the occupiers wanted to flash their teeth, they could not have found a more effective means than by severing the link the Islanders had with mainland Britain and evacuated loved ones. Only the month before, Guernseymen had crowded around their sets to hear a BBC program on the Channel Islands, including songs and messages in Guernsey patois from evacuated children.[92] However, this punishment for perceived attitudes was short-lived, and just as abruptly at Christmastime the wireless sets were returned.

The sudden reprieve, timed to appear as a Christmas gift from the occupiers, was met with understandable rejoicing. Ambrose Robin, responsible for the live-in care of his elderly Uncle Phil and Aunt Adele, wrote of the "monotony of our lives without reliable news of the outside world."[93] When Phil's set arrived in a delivery van on Christmas Eve, "Phil and I were like two boys with a new toy connecting it up getting it going." But, of course, the wireless was far from a toy and simple source of entertainment, as Robin makes clear:

> After 6 weeks absence we are once again in touch with the land upon which are our cherished possessions, our children. This link opens the door to possibilities that we may yet be fortunate enough to hear news of our fold—all other avenues appear to be bolted and barred.

He closes this small outburst of excitement and anticipation with a prediction that would prove ironic in the years ahead: "In days to come we may look upon this punishment as one of the trivial annoyances of the occupation."[94]

Rev. Ord looked closely at the return order for the wireless sets, "taken in the expectation and under the condition of perfect loyalty on the part of the Island Authorities and population in the future." This order, of course, begged the question of whether the loyalty was to the Island and its continued smooth functioning, or to Germany in the guise of the occupying forces. Yet, for its strategic vagueness, the order made clear that "the whole community would bear the consequences of individual misconduct." By punishing all for the supposed misdeeds of one, and by providing a taste of that punishment, the occupiers heightened the likelihood of lateral surveillance. Ord saw this clearly and noted that this entire wireless incident was little more than a "brandishing of threats to keep us silent mice in the future."[95]

The "new restrictions . . . becoming more rigorous as time goes on," in Kitty Bachmann's words[96]—or as Bert Williams later described it, a "procession of orders and orders"[97]—kept everyone slightly off-kilter, always unsure of their own actions and whether they would call down the wrath of the occupier on the entire community. This perfect climate to foster self-monitoring was enhanced by the very visible presence of German troops. What the Guernsey populace viewed as the occupiers' efforts to "Germanize" them served largely as reminders that Island life was *not* the same and those in control could be watching at any time. Many of the changes to German practice merely simplified life and coordination for German forces. As examples, the move to German time and the shift to German signage ("Zum Hafen," "Zur Flugplatz")[98] were practical measures, albeit with symbolic value.

More obviously a manipulation of symbolism was the order "forbidding processions and emblems," a restriction instituted in November as an anticipation of Armistice Day.[99] Fishing boats could no longer fly the national flag.[100] In fact all display of flags and wearing of badges were banned—save for the flag of the fascist party in England.[101] If the Islanders were forced to censor their symbolic expression, German processions and symbols seemed to be ever present.

Winnie Harvey and other wardens of the ARP (Air Raid Precautions) were forced to do some heavy soul-searching if they needed to venture out after curfew. The air-raid wardens were placed under German authority, and members patrolling post-curfew were required to paint their helmets white, carry a permit, and (the worst insult) to wear armlets complete with a swastika. "None of us wants to go out," Winnie wrote simply. Yet her sense of duty to possible civilian casualties won out: "I hated the idea of wearing a swastika on my arm but this is not the time to resign from ARP work. I think the way to look at it is to remember we are not now free and the swastika and card are only permits."[102]

Such Nazi iconography as the swastika functioned to brand Guernseymen as tools of the Germans, even when they were functioning as autonomous citizens and performing tasks in aid of civilians. The important aspect from the occupiers' standpoint was to be omnipresent if only in symbolic form, and it was not long before the ever-present identity cards were stamped with swastikas. German troops also took special efforts to make themselves seen and heard. On August 16, those living in St. Peter Port were "treated," in Ord's ironic opinion, to the sight of three companies of troops, preceded by their band, marching past the commandant as he stood at the bottom of St. Julian Avenue.[103] Such displays of martial strength and music, particularly at a time when British processions were banned, drove home the occupier's prerogative to act, and the occupied's position as only to be acted upon.

In these early days of Occupation, we can see proof of the power of surveillance and the triumph of panopticism. The restriction of communication between Islanders and with the outside world was coupled with a reasonable belief that their words and actions were monitored by the controlling forces. The Guernsey civilians were thus placed in the position of panoptical prisoners, as "the object of information, never a subject in communication."[104] Ideally, from the viewpoint of those in power, control by surveillance becomes most efficient when it is a self-perpetuating mechanism. Once the prisoner internalizes the rules and expectations and functions under the fear of possible surveillance at any time, the prisoner serves effectively as his own guard.[105]

Of course, panopticism, or discipline by surveillance, was simply one aspect of German control and augmented the power relations already in place by force of arms. As Mark Andrejevic maintains, the panoptical prison created by constant monitoring "does not create the power relations," although it "amplifies, extends, and automates this power."[106] Under a guise of the pleasant and "correct" relations that the Germans sought as the visible face of their occupation of Guernsey lay the "cruel ingenious cage"[107] of panoptical surveillance. The Islanders had every reason to be literally *self*-conscious when simple and natural actions were now banned and could lead to arrest and imprisonment.

READING THE OTHER

The Guernsey Islanders were not without resources in countering panoptical surveillance and turned instinctively to the same techniques that are used to withstand monitoring today. In the twenty-first century, a time of heightened scrutiny due to fears of terrorism, the expanding surveillance by closed-circuit television and security oversight has been met by "undersight" on the part of those monitored. Steve Mann coined the neologism "sousveillance" to refer to "watchful vigilance from underneath," a move where the ones being watched turn their own gaze upward and monitor those in power.[108] From the very beginning of the Occupation, the Islanders became adept at reading their captors while resisting the Germans' ability to understand the Islanders' actions and motivations. It was natural to observe the troops as they came into the town and spread out over the Island, because close contact became inevitable.

One shared observation of the young troops was their voraciousness. Even early on, the Islanders were well aware of their isolated position and the possible lack of new supplies. Articles were appearing in the local papers by the late summer of 1940 urging residents to economize in essentials and warning of shortages in fuel and food, particularly for the coming fall and winter. As the general populace tried to comply, Ambrose Robin reported with disgust that "German troops are buying the very articles we are short of."[109] Rev. Ord was particularly vivid in describing the first glimpse many Guernseymen had of the German occupiers. As buses brought the troops into St. Peter Port, the soldiers "stared open-mouthed at the well-dressed civilians, the clean freshly-painted houses and the shops with their windows invitingly full of good things." Coming from war-torn areas to a land of seeming plenty, the Germans reacted like starving men:

> Every strong point had been occupied immediately—particularly the cafes and confectionery shops! Germans are everywhere—eating, eating, eating. They prove their prowess as trenchermen, ordering omelettes made with eight eggs. From time to time they go out into the street to be sick and then valiantly resume their place at the festive board unless ousted by others.[110]

Observers felt they were gaining some insight into the extent of deprivation in the German army. As Ord maintained, "It was instructive to see Germans eating butter in half pound packets without bread as they went about the streets."[111]

Ken Lewis would be a particularly fascinated observer of the German troops, and he recorded even minor encounters with young soldiers, most of them only a few years older than himself. In one account, he mentioned seeing "about 40 German soldiers in full equipment at the bottom of Saints Road, some even being in the Rector's Garden." On that same morning he "had occassion [*sic*] to pass up Saints Road," an occasion he apparently designed for himself to catch a closer look. He was rewarded for his initiative by having one soldier, standing with another beside the rector's back gate, "say good morning to me."[112] Each contact with German troops was clearly viewed as an adventure untainted by concerns that seemed to beset his elders. One of his great coups came very early in the Occupation in mid-July when, with his mate Ralph, he heard that a troop carrier had crashed near the airport. "Full of curiosity," this Guernsey version of Tom and Huck set out that evening for a little "close investigation." They discovered "a bomber of the Heinkel 111 type" and returned repeatedly over the following days, actually climbing inside the plane at one point: "It was quite a thrill to sit in the Pilot's seat of a German plane and to work the joy-stick and rudder-bar, on these occasions we brought home many souveniers which will prove interesting in the days to come."[113]

Ken and his friends were not the only ones reading the troops and garnering what information they could from their presence—and sometimes their absence—in the Island. In September 1940, Winifred Harvey presented an entire series of observations and the conclusions drawn from them by the population. First, she wrote, "They say a great many Germans have left, there are only a few hundred as on the first days of the occupation. There are certainly fewer about." This apparently positive sign was followed closely by her observation that "the Sentries on the hotel were doubled," and her reading of a German communiqué in the *Press* "that the Reichsmarschall is personally conducting operations in the north of France." Could this mean the reports were true and an important personage ("Is it Goering himself?") was in Guernsey to discuss giving up the Channel Islands?[114] This type of report—a blend of personal observation, interpretive reading of the German troops, rumor, and factual knowledge—was the common model of civilian information-gathering for much of the Occupation.

As the old saying has it, increasing familiarity did seem to breed a level of contempt and, more important, distrust in this first half-year of Occupation. For one thing, the always acute British tendency to puncture inflated egos kicked in when observing German display. Rev. Ord, in observing the August 16 military band review, found it "hard not to laugh at the 'goose step' which was performed with excessive zeal and solemnity. A fitting symbol of a system we instinctively hate. The Germans . . . resent our nickname for it."[115] For the most part, however, any comical take on the visible German culture ran a distant second to unease about hidden German intentions and actions. Kitty Bachmann had heard "many lurid stories of atrocities in Poland and elsewhere." Although she was not prepared to view these stories as untrue, she did think that, at least as she wrote in August 1940, "they seem fantastic in the light of the Germans' present conduct here." Kitty shared with much of the rest of the world a belief that the tales of Nazi atrocities were so outrageous as to beg belief. The Islanders were also hearing that "they usually begin by ingratiating themselves with their victims, in order to get away to a smooth start gradually giving less and less sugar with the pill."[116]

The Reverend Ord was a step ahead of her in his reservations, believing from the very beginning that "In what is bound to be a long-drawn-out affair men chosen for the initial period are undoubtedly a picked lot."[117] Ord was willing to act on his concerns that the Germans' velvet-glove behavior could not last. The minister of information had suggested that because of his knowledge of German, the reverend might serve as a possible interpreter for the German command. He "refused categorically." Ord's reasoning was that "when their 'courtesy' wears thin and they wish to pick their inevitable quarrel for reasons best known to themselves, the Germans might well allege mistranslation with intent to embarrass their administration."[118]

Yet, if individuals were conducting a *sousveillance* by reading the Germans in their midst, the Islanders prided themselves on thwarting the occupiers' ability to read them in return. Winnie relished the rumor that the Germans considered the Guernsey population "the bad boys." Supposedly, the Germans called the Guernsey attitude "dumb insolence" and resented the way the civilians looked "right through them."[119] Most rewarding of all was the knowledge that "*they* can't understand us at all. They have stolen our boats, our cars, our leaders and now our wirelesses and we are as gay, or more so, as ever. It puzzles them awfully."[120] The strongest challenge to panoptical power is to thwart surveillance while simultaneously observing those in power, reading their intentions and (ideally) countering their plans. This sophisticated game of hide-and-seek developed during the early, easier period of Occupation would serve the Islanders well in the difficult years to come.

THE GRIP TIGHTENS

The transition from 1941 to 1942 put the Reverend Douglas Ord in a contemplative mood. "The Year End!" he wrote. "Twelve months ago today I wrote in this diary: I wonder if the New Year will see the wearing out of the 'courtesy' with which the Germans began their regime here.' We have no doubt of the answer now." In fact, Ord continued, it was barely six months from the start of the Occupation before the Germans had managed to alienate "any unhostile disposition" a Guernseyman might briefly have maintained. In the twelve months past, the occupiers had only built on this hostility by bringing "loss and misery and heartbreak" through orders that had "swollen to a mighty flood."[121] This end of the false and tenuous honeymoon between occupier and occupied is a revealing story of German treachery, well-meaning British blunders, and compensatory attempts by Island authorities to avert disaster.

In the remainder of this chapter, I will detail some of the primary events stretching from the start of 1941 until the D-day Invasion in June 1944. The structuring of rhetorical resistance would depend on an accurate understanding of the dark heart of the occupiers. As their grip tightened around the Island, key moves were made by the Germans to heighten control, including the final confiscation of wireless sets, the billeting of soldiers and confiscation of Islanders' homes, and the sudden deportations of many Islanders to German internment camps. I will also examine the way the Guernsey residents reread the Germans in their midst, confirming their earlier belief that there was dark malevolence beneath the polite mask. They quickly developed a series of animalistic metaphors to capture an authoritarian and cruel nature as they found it in the occupiers, an initial synchronizing of perception among the civilian population that would blossom into a counter-ideology fueling resistance. Finally, I will discuss one of the major lessons of the Occupation: that the quality of the individual outweighed group membership and that there were good men within the German forces. Some of these were true anti-Party Germans who opposed Hitler but were caught up in the military for fear of reprisals against their families and charges of treason. There were also those men whose simple humanity transcended the dark times and their role in the German military. Over time, the Islanders developed a means to respond to (and encourage) good when they saw it in the German forces, without compromising their general wariness and their unalloyed opposition to all the Nazi Occupation represented.

"The velvet glove has gone." Winifred Harvey's grim assessment of the evolving Occupation was recorded in late October 1940.[122] Although she was directly describing the imposition of trial by military law, already in force in occupied France, there was a more general meaning to her words. An unmistakable pall had fallen over the tentative understanding established between German occupier and Guernsey citizenry. But what could have caused such a tipping of this delicate balance not even four months into the Occupation? Granting that the apparent bonhomie of early days was more strategic than real on both sides, its premature end could be partially traced to two young men left waiting on a dark beach.

It was on the sands of Petit Port Bay where Lt. Hubert Nicolle and Lt. James Symes stood on September 7, 1940, for three hours at a stretch, repeatedly signaling a Morse "R" with their flashlight out toward the Channel. Despite three nights' effort, the prearranged signal brought no response from the English craft scheduled to pick up the information-gathering team. Nicolle and Symes reluctantly concluded that they were stranded. This was not the first British reconnaissance mission to Guernsey for the twenty-year-old Nicolle.

On the 8th of July, he had been deposited at Le Jaonnet Bay as a part of Operation "Anger," a British attempt to determine the "strength and disposition of the Germans, their attitude to Islanders, and the Islanders view of Germans." It took a particular courage for Nicolle to don civilian clothes and return to his Guernsey home. If caught, he would be disavowed by England and, being out of uniform, most likely shot as a common spy. This initial mission went smoothly mainly because Nicolle's father lived next door to H. H. Collins, the managing director of Le Riches grocery company. Without having to move from his father's house and risk capture, Nicolle had ample information at hand about troop strength and food supplies of the Island.[123]

With this successful mission under his belt, Nicolle had expected a warm reception from the Island government when he returned on September 4, with fellow Guernseyman James Symes, for further information gathering. Through an intermediary he contacted Ambrose Sherwill and asked if the States official had a message for the Home Office. To Nicolle's surprise, Sherwill made clear his opinion that such raids served no practical purpose and merely caused dangerous complications for the Island population. Nicolle later offered his opinion: "Clearly Sherwill was very resentful of our presence and his attitude was, don't bother us, go and fight your war somewhere else."[124] Whether Nicolle wished to acknowledge it or not, Sherwill had good reason to seek an end to spying raids unlikely to be followed by British action. The very submarine that had retrieved Nicolle from Operation Anger deposited two more Guernseymen, Phillip Martel and Desmond Mulholland, meant to prepare the way for a planned commando landing on the night of July 12–13. Much as Nicolle and Symes would later do, Martel and Mulholland stood for three nights signaling for a raiding party that was prevented from landing by bad weather and that finally went to a smaller Channel Island (either Sark or Herm) before returning to their destroyer. A separate landing party that *did* make it onto the sands at Petit Port that night devolved into a series of missteps that would have been comical had the situation not been so serious.

First, the commando party staggered up the incredibly long series of stairs leading to Jerbourg Road, then divided into three separate groups to seek Germans at the old British barracks, to attack a machine-gun post that Nicolle had reported, and to lay down a roadblock (to stop any Germans fleeing the assault on the barracks). Since they found neither Germans nor the machine-gun post, the need for the roadblock they constructed of stones from a farmer's wall was greatly lessened. They then contented themselves with cutting some telephone lines before heading back down the stairs to the bay at three in the morning. The secrecy of their escape was seriously compromised by Lt. Colonel Slater, who tripped on the steep descent, accidentally discharging his pistol. Nor were they in a strong position once they reached the bay. The launches that had brought them ashore could not pick them up due to the high tide, so they piled their equipment into a small dinghy sent to shore by the navy. This seemed to go well until Private Ross vaulted into the dinghy, upending it and sending all the equipment (including Private Drain, who had been perched on the back) into the water.

Faced with swimming to the launches, it was then learned that four commandos sent on a dangerous mission to a Channel Island were nonswimmers! Effectively now, four commandos were stranded as well as Martell and Mulholland. To complicate matters, the Germans would soon be seeking these British visitors to the Island. Not only were there the roadblock (left in place) and cut telephone wires as clues, but rifles, ammunition, and other military gear were left behind at Petit Port Bay. Worse still, a soldier's haversack was found in the parking area of the Doyle Monument. Since the haversack contained fresh cakes in a paper bag marked with the name of a Plymouth bakery, it did not need genius to know that there had been a British landing.[125]

The nonswimming commandos' time at large was brief, for they were picked up the following afternoon as they wandered toward the airport in search of a means to leave the Island. Their next stop would be a French POW camp at St. Lo.[126] The situation was somewhat different for civilian-clothed Martell and Mulholland, who took shelter with family—Martell with his sister and Mulholland with his mother. Although they also futilely sought some means of leaving the Island, it soon became clear that they were compromising the safety of their families. Thus it was that they turned up at Sherwill's door early on the morning of July 29, seeking advice on the proper way to surrender to the Germans. If Sherwill was initially aghast at having responsibility for two men, certain to be shot if they surrendered in civilian garb, he quickly set a clever plan into motion. First, he sent to the town arsenal store for two militia uniforms for Martel and Mulholland. To buy time, since his office was expecting him and the Germans tended to call without warning, Sherwill phoned in claiming to have a sick headache. This simplest of ruses provided time to attire Martell and Mulholland in uniform, give them a final sustaining meal in freedom, and deliver them to the German headquarters on their way to a POW camp in France.

Yet, this rapid and creative action did not save Mrs. Le Masurier, Martel's stepsister, and Mrs. Michael, Mulholland's mother, from being sent to France under house arrest.[127] As the Germans undoubtedly hoped, word of the penalty faced for aiding a British soldier, even when undertaken by a relative, made it swiftly around the Island.[128]

So, it is little wonder that Ambrose Sherwill was less than thrilled when contacted by Nicolle on his second mission to Guernsey in September. Nor would Sherwill's presentiment of further difficulties be incorrect. After their failure to reembark at the end of the mission, Nicolle and Symes returned to family and friends, hoping to "lie low" until the rescue that they felt would come. Sure enough, an attempted rescue took place on September 30, although one marked by the same problems as the commando raid.

An unnaturally thin young Guernseyman, Captain John Parker landed at Corbiere in military uniform, made his precarious way up the cliff, and fell promptly—and loudly—into a German trench. He was blinded by a flashlight beam in his eyes and heard the unwelcome words "For you the war is over."[129] Word reached Nicolle and Symes of Parker's capture, and they feared that rumor of their own presence might find its way to the German authorities. So, once again, Ambrose Sherwill found himself in the familiar position, as with Martel and Mulholland, of having two young soldiers on his hands. In this instance, having witnessed the arrest and deportation of Martel's and Mulholland's relatives, Sherwill took additional steps to protect family members who had, after all, sheltered spies in civilian dress. German Major Bandelow had made clear to Sherwill his belief that British armed forces were still in the Island, and had threatened to shoot not only the soldiers but also those who sheltered them. Further, he maintained that, should such relatives fail to step forward, hostages could well be taken and shot in their place.[130]

Thus began a dangerous game of poker, with Sherwill holding his knowledge of Nicolle's and Symes's presence very close to the vest. Sherwill first talked Bandelow into an exchange of letters designed for publication in the Island papers, all with the goal of eliciting a public promise that any armed forces, either in hiding from the start of the Occupation or entering the Island since that time, would be treated as prisoners of war. Then, as rewrites were going on prior to publication, Sherwill slipped in the concept that relatives sheltering such soldiers would be exempt from punishment. This exchange was published, followed by a signed order appearing in the *Guernsey Evening Press* that set the deadline for surrender at 6:00 P.M. on Monday, October 21, 1940. The order stated that "Members of the British Armed Forces obeying this Order will be treated as Prisoners of War and no measures will be taken against persons who have assisted them."[131] Although, the order went on to state, any soldier found hiding after this time would be treated as the "agent of an enemy power," as would those aiding them. Sherwill believed he had done all that he could to protect those now in hiding. As would happen so often in the coming years, an Islander had thus played concealed information against power in a rhetorical game with the highest stakes. A promise had been extracted and published for all the Island to see; surely such a contract of honor could not then be broken.

Following the order's publication, Nicolle and Symes duly surrendered,[132] and the treachery of the Germans became apparent. Despite the promise in the order, twenty-four people were seized. Perhaps the holding of the immediate families was not surprising seeing that E. W. Nicolle, Lt. Nicolle's father, was secretary to States Committees.[133] Yet, also held were Jessie Marriette, engaged to Lt. Nicolle, and her parents, and Mary Bird, Lt. Symes's fiancée, and her parents. Even Nicolle's eighty-three-year-old grandmother and Mr. Allen (the groundskeeper of the college where the two men sheltered briefly) were detained. At first, it seemed that the Germans would keep their promises in the order, as most of the prisoners were released after interrogation.[134] Then came word that all those connected with Nicolle and Symes had been rearrested and sent to France for trial.[135]

The staggering news for the Island was the treatment of Ambrose Sherwill. Kept on house arrest for a week, interrogated for eleven hours straight in a room with only a single chair, "so that nothing should distract his mind," finally he was hauled aboard an airplane for France with scarcely a half-hour's notice and held in solitary confinement in Cherche Midi Prison.[136] All the prisoners reportedly endured some rough treatment: kept in solitary cells with little food; given a concrete slab with no cover, mattress, or pillow for a bed; and subjected to continuous questioning.[137] As far as the family members knew, Lts. Nicolle and Symes were condemned to be shot, word of their reprieve and status as POWs actually reaching Guernsey before it reached the prisoners in Cherche Midi.[138] It was all too much for Mr. Symes. In despair over his son and under the stress of harsh treatment, he committed suicide on December 22 by opening an artery in his wrist. Only two days later, the family members learned what Guernsey already knew: that they were to be released.[139] A week more, and the families, Ambrose Sherwill, and all connected with the Nicolle/Symes affair, except for the young men themselves, were returned to Guernsey. Although Sherwill was back in the Island, he was forbidden to hold any kind of public office, and the delicate understanding he had pieced together with the Germans was shattered.

The Island at large recoiled at Sherwill's treatment. First, they knew that they had lost a valuable advocate; as Winnie Harvey put it, "He has fought and worked so hard for us and our welfare . . . it is a dreadful shock."[140] Second, Guernseymen learned a larger lesson about the nature of their German masters and drew a comparison with their heritage: "Thus, the Germans have violated the traditional British trust in the given word."[141] Lacking this basic level of trust, one never to be restored throughout the Occupation, the Islanders faced heightened uncertainty. They would seek to reduce this uncertainty through both direct and indirect methods. At this early point in the first fall, British actions had put the Island in an untenable position. The Germans used this series of raids as the ostensible reason for the first confiscation of wireless sets and the imposition of heightened surveillance.

THE MAILED FIST

With the enforced change in the States of Guernsey administration following Sherwill's removal, the game between German military hierarchy and Guernsey States representatives would intensify over the next three years. A revolving door of military commandants had started early in the Occupation, but settled by October 1941 into a more consistent reign of Colonel Knackfuss as the Feldkommandant, and General Müller as the Military Commandant of the Channel Islands. This stability did not mean an improved relationship between occupier and occupied. Knackfuss was a short man, described by William Bell as both stocky and aggressive. The fact that he sometimes wore a monocle would have only reinforced the image of a strutting Nazi popinjay. Müller, too, maintained a façade that was less pleasant and apparently conciliatory than that of earlier commandants. His perpetually red complexion and explosive temper made him an object of fear for the German soldiers and far from an approachable figure for civilians.[142]

With changes in the German leadership, the Guernsey populace was smothered under an incredible array of *Bekanntmachungs*. These orders were rarely rescinded, and thus life was led under layers of rules that were highly detailed but extremely confusing. Some of the orders had an obvious and clear intent to prevent surveillance or to exert control. For example, many diarists mention the order in June 1942 calling in all cameras and all photographic materials of any kind.[143] Some new regulations that were taken very seriously by the Germans seemed meaningless to the average Guernseyman. Firing four experienced constables, a group that included Ken Lewis's father as well as Bert Williams, simply because the Germans deemed the men too short seemed inexplicable.[144] Other orders had mainly symbolic meaning, and this did *not* escape the populace. "*Now*," Bill Warry wrote in August of 1942, "we have to raise our hats when the German National Anthem is played, or . . . ?"[145]

Whether the orders were clear and practical from a German perspective or vague and largely symbolic, the diarists used much the same language to describe the ratcheting up of control from 1941 until D-day. Winnie Harvey considered Knackfuss "a Nazi of the Nazis" and described his orders as his "turning the screw."[146] Bert Williams also described the new regulations as "the screw gradually being put on."[147] Jack Sauvary echoed this language as new rules took effect: "We don't know what to expect from day to day. Things are tightening up all the time."[148] In this manipulation of everyday life, a term that derives from the Latin "manus" or "hand," the Islanders felt the closing grip of control. Rev. Ord described their evolving sense of their situation: "We feel the grip of the German mailed fist upon us without a doubt. The power of the Military and the secret, crafty machinations of the Gestapo, striking in the dark swiftly and silently are brought home to us in many ways. One here, one there, is hauled off to prison."[149]

In August 1942, Knackfuss detailed that any instances of espionage, sabotage, or high treason would result in the death penalty, and he particularly singled out "attacks against communications" as worthy of the ultimate penalty. Therefore, a person performing a common Island action, such as looking out to sea with binoculars,[150] might be open to the death penalty should the action occur at the same time as the cutting of a local telephone line. Further, Knackfuss declared, "Henceforth I reserve to myself the right to nominate certain members of any Parish who will be liable to the Death Penalty." Although never utilized, this threat of hostage taking and execution considerably upped the ante, making the violation of minor orders a potential threat to the entire community.[151]

Despite the possible consequences, Guernseymen did not react to these threats in a uniform fashion. Some developed a policy of caution and the ability to self-censor, but many others took a scofflaw approach. They handled the ridiculous slew of orders by judiciously choosing to violate a certain number of minor ones that imposed on day-to-day life. They then attempted to skirt any trouble through a combination of bluff and brass, whether dealing with the German soldiers or with the Feldgendarmerie, the German police. Thus, the prisons became overstuffed with those caught violating orders—the true cost of these brief prison sentences, some served in Guernsey and some in France, only becoming apparent in 1943.

BILLETING AND EVICTIONS

Early in the Occupation, the Germans took over houses, particularly large ones that belonged to evacuees from the Island. They claimed that anyone who left the Island prior to the German arrival was an official enemy, and they treated the houses, furniture, and personal items left behind as spoils of war.[152] Thus, they moved furniture from house to house and generally destroyed their accommodations, leaving them filthy and often stripping them of fixtures, wiring, and any other item that they considered valuable. In addition to occupying residences abandoned by evacuees, the Germans used billeting as an early method of housing, particularly for officers and civil servants.

Jack Sauvary had two empty bedrooms in his house that drew the attention of the billeting officers.[153] The New Road was particularly valued at that time, and Jack's first officer moved in on October 8, 1941; his batman appears to have been housed elsewhere. Jack's "No. 1 Officer" made himself much at home, requesting the good mahogany table, which Jack relinquished with orders that a tablecloth be used, and dishes. He then brought in a "No. 2 Officer" to spend the night in the adjoining room, "borrowing" (really requisitioning) Jack's bicycle for the evening.

Having a stranger in the house, one who was called on by his batman before six o'clock in the morning, took some getting used to. This was especially true because the Germans felt no need to inform Jack of their movements. Jack's officer came on Wednesday, and on Sunday morning, October 12, he rose early and left for the day, never to return. Jack left the house unlocked for several days but never saw the officer again, deciding that he must have left the Island with a number of other men on the 14th. By the end of the month, the billeting officers were back with news that Jack needed to house a civil servant and a "lady typist" (who ended up staying elsewhere), also providing them with a room in which to work. When Jack met the civil servant that he would come to call "my German" a few days later, the man "clicked his boots, gave me such a salute, and shook hands," a display of politeness that, under the forced circumstances, Jack seemed to find amusing.[154]

For all of the disruption of having a civil servant sleep upstairs and set up shop in his dining room, Jack knew that he was getting off easy. By the following spring, the card that was required to be affixed to the door (THIS HOUSE OCCUPIED) now had to be replaced with a new form detailing any rooms that were still empty. This allowed anyone passing by to "shop" for billeting accommodations simply by reading the form on the door. Jack feared that he soon could have a full house, but considered it far superior to being turned out entirely, a fate that was swiftly descending on many in Guernsey.[155] The worst aspects to billeting appeared to be the lack of privacy, the destruction of property, and the drunken parties that the Germans held into the wee small hours. Jack's German (Erwin) proved to be a friendly, if demanding housemate; his tendency to upset the house with abrupt comings and goings at all hours was somewhat balanced by his gifts of British tobacco bought in Holland as tokens of apology and politeness.

Sunday, July 5, 1942, proved just what an imposition a young German soldier could be on his reluctant Guernsey "host." Erwin, whom Jack occasionally called "The Boss," turned up with a joint of meat, some salt, and bread. Requesting that the joint be cooked, Erwin invited a few civilians, a soldier, and an officer to a sit-down meal that evening. They also brought a barrel of beer, which they attached to two of Jack's stools and set up in the garden, bringing in chocolate and cigarettes for, they said, five people. By the time Jack was back from church, there were twelve. Fueled by bottles of champagne, they danced to wireless music until dark, and then took the beer into the drawing room. By one o'clock, they decided they were hungry and had Jack slice up the remainder of the bread, which they topped with their tomatoes and all of Jack's. They stayed up all night, as did Jack rather than "leaving them the run of the house." The house and garden were littered with broken glass from champagne bottles and some of Jack's glasses, the carpet was ruined (they claimed that they would get Jack a new one, though he knew "that's as far as it will go"), and the neighbors had as little sleep as Jack.[156]

This type of impromptu "ball" was the lot of many of those billeting Germans against their will, their houseguests viewing their "hosts" as little more than servants. Rev. Ord told of a chat one sunny spring day with his neighbor, forced to billet four officers and batmen, who exclaimed heatedly, "I wish all Germans was in 'ell, Sir! That mayn't be the sort of language to use to a Reverend Gentleman like yourself, BUT IT'S FROM THE HEART ALL THE SAME!" Ord well understood his neighbor's feelings, for his house was being slowly ruined by German drunken binges, where broken bottles and wine-stained furniture littered a formerly beautiful home. As Ord sympathetically put it, "The Archangel Gabriel would himself use unbiblical language were his celestial abode similarly treated."[157]

Worse was to follow. In October 1942, Bert Williams announced that the Germans were "turning people out of their houses wholesale," wanting at that point to house the soldiers in zones rather than billeting them individually.[158] Yet, this fall upheaval was the second wave of mass evictions, the first having taken place the previous year. In November 1941, Dorothy Higgs, for all her bravado about German orders, learned that the house where they lived, Alta Vista, was being taken, along with all the houses on the same hill. The Higgses learned through the owner of Alta Vista that they could share a previously abandoned bungalow with caretakers who had been staying there. They gratefully accepted the offer of three small rooms, only to have the caretakers get a chance at another house, leaving the Higgses the entire "White Cottage" to themselves. And this is where Dorothy Higgs's incredible luck and optimistic attitude really came into play. Although small, the White Cottage had a lovely view, a large garden, and trees near the house; it was, in fact, Dorothy wrote, "so lovely—just what I have always dreamed of having." It also would, as we will see later, place Dorothy in the perfect location to ride out the Occupation using her wits and creativity.[159]

Rev. Ord heard account after account of the shabby treatment of evicted families. Houses were chosen, and mere minutes later soldiers appeared in lorries, loading up the furniture for their own taking while the owners stood helplessly by. Generally, the house owners only had ten minutes to fill a suitcase and leave. And all of this, Ord pointed out, occurred in the miserable weather of fall. Hard enough to be turned out on a beautiful day, but "in this drenching, chilly downpour, it is terrible."[160] Even those dangerously ill "encounter the same callousness" and were thrown out in the cold.[161]

Yet, treatment was not equal for those whose houses were taken. The German officers, always hypersensitive to power and rank, seemed to identify with those they perceived as having prestige and culture. Winifred Harvey knew that it would only be a matter of time before covetous German eyes fell upon her beautiful estate of Newlands. First, by spring of 1941 she heard of many large homes being taken: Saumarez Lodge, Springfield—all were falling like dominoes, and seizure was coming her way.[162] The Germans actually came for the house in late October, on a day when the house was at its loveliest, "a glorious sunny morning, flowers about, everything spick and span." They wanted the house for the general, so Winnie knew that there was no point in resisting. Unlike others who had been evicted, Winnie was offered the opportunity to stay, actually billeting in her own home, where the general would take over the entire ground floor and most of the first as well. Winnie asked instead for a week to move out and was granted this extra time.

In fact, she had the luxury of negotiating with Captain Seelig what she could take and what needed to be left in the house. She requested her piano, for music "is a great comfort in these days." "Certainly," replied the captain. She asked for and received her desk and grandfather clock. The captain offered her the drawing room carpet: "It is a shame for boots . . . take it, Madam." He balked at giving her the curtains, and she thought it best not to press for them, although she took the hall drapes. Then it came down to linens and her one table service that had not been sent away before the Occupation; "Let us share it," said the captain. When Winnie later related this part of the exchange to the Hartley-Jacksons, "they all roared with laughter and said it was as good as a proposal."[163]

Thus, Winnie moved to 2 Grange Terrace, taking the ground and first floors, while her landlord Mr. Jehan took the floor above. Feeble and blind Mrs. Clayton was installed in a nursing home, much to Winnie's initial relief, but only three weeks later, the soft-hearted Winnie brought her to live at Grange Terrace.[164] Undoubtedly, money and standing was part of the game of bluster, bluff, and negotiation; it had nothing to do with kindness and respect, as was clear in the Germans' treatment of Rev. K. C. McCartney in his eviction from the St. Andrew's rectory. Ken Lewis was particularly incensed, noting that because the reverend was blind, "he knew every crick and corner of his own home and moving to a new home would seriously restrict his movements." A formal appeal was made on the behalf of Rev. McCartney, but "with the callousness of the Germans they refused to entertain any such idea and he was forced to move."[165] German inconsistency and contempt for weakness combined to distribute hardship unevenly, and it fell mainly on those least able to cope.

The older and frailer the Islander, the more devastating the forced exile from their homes. Arthur Mauger was given three days (better than most) to pack up everything and evacuate his home. Although he resignedly wrote that "it's hard luck after nearly 60 yrs residence there," the true impact can be gauged by a glance at his diary pages. His beautiful flowing script became tremulous, so shaky that it is difficult to read. It is the worst on the actual moving day, returning to normal over the following days, time that he spent weeding the yard and becoming accustomed to his new surroundings. The emotional impact of this uprooting on an eighty-two-year-old man was undoubtedly profound.[166] Jack Sauvary, too, was swept out of his home of twenty-eight years in the New Road during the round of evictions in the fall of 1942. The entire New Road on his side of the street was seized, and he had only days to pack up and clear out. With his usual humor, Jack recounted that he had packed, repacked, and moved in his dreams every time he took a nap during that trying time. Ultimately, he moved in with Mrs. Rowe, who gave him a comfortable bedroom and a place to keep his rabbits in the backyard. The eternal optimist, Jack talked about Mrs. Rowe as being "a brick in every way" and lauded the help of his friends in the move: "So, no regrets. Amen!"[167]

Some Guernsey residents never managed to adjust to these changes. Elizabeth Doig had two officers and two soldiers installed in the flat above her own and found that the tramping on the floor above went on till the "wee awa' 'ours," as she put it. Shortly after that time, her brother John was evicted from his home and took up residence with his family at the Birnaue Court Hotel. Elizabeth spent many of her nights with them.[168] Thus, she was pleased when the entire family decided to quit the hotel for a house, and she joined them in the move, relinquishing her flat.[169] She moved once again on July 27 to stay with a woman in St. Martin, where she would be closer to town. She wrote that she regretted parting from her "dear brother," but then described her new living conditions with the phrase "atmosphere much better hope to enjoy being there." It is not a deep reading to see in this some possible friction with the rest of the family (perhaps John's wife and daughter), a distinct possibility as she was the widowed relative attaching herself to the rest of the family.

By October 8, Elizabeth moved to a boarding house—saying briefly, "expect to be happier here"—an arrangement that worked out for her for almost a year.[170] Then, in September 1943, she moved to a farm in Castel. The boarding house had managed the food situation well, but it had more rules than the independent Elizabeth could stand ("We were treated more like children in a charity institution").[171] So, by September 19, 1943, she was settled on a farm with full-cream milk available and was once again achieving a healthy weight.[172] This peripatetic lifestyle—bouncing from one spot to another—would be the fate of some in the Island. Elizabeth was an outsider, a Scotswoman, with only limited family in Guernsey. She never really regained her footing or a sense of the same community she had when located in her original home.

STRANGLEHOLD

It could be said that those evicted from their homes at least retained their larger home and community of Guernsey, but that too would be stripped from some of them in 1942–1943. German control reached its height during these two years, with regulations moving swiftly past those based on perceived German need (such as housing) and into displays of power and mass punishment. In June 1942, the entire Island was subject to a final confiscation of wireless sets. Rev. Ord recorded the news in all capital letters: CIVILIAN WIRELESS SETS ARE TO BE CALLED IN.[173] Jack Sauvary was equally taken aback, expostulating, "Oh, what devilish news! We are to lose our wirelesses!"[174] If the universal response of despair seems overwrought, one has to remember the extreme importance of BBC programming to a people isolated from their larger nation during time of war. Most followed the war and news of London ardently, finding encouragement and gaining perspective on the actions of their captors.[175] But the real devastation came to those with evacuated relatives on the British mainland, and for whom a loss of even symbolic contact was "a bitter blow."[176] To now have no reliable news and only German propaganda in the local papers effectively widened the distance between parents and evacuated children, Island wives and their husbands fighting in the war, and the population at large from evacuated friends and family members. It was, wrote Elizabeth Doig, "like a death in the house."[177]

The June loss of wireless would pale before the events of September. On the 15th of September, an order by Knackfuss was published in the *Guernsey Press*, confirming rumors that had circulated for several days. All British subjects whose permanent home was not in the Channel Islands (such as those stranded in 1940) were to be deported to Germany. The same order of deportation applied to all men aged sixteen to seventy not born in the Channel Islands, and their immediate families. All of the dentists, most of the bank personnel, many key players in medicine and technical professions would be deported.[178] Intense panic gripped those soon to be confined in a German internment camp, and turmoil spread throughout the Island. A cluster of English women (many close to seventy) cried openly in Bill Warry's shop, and groups of English-born who had lived in Guernsey since childhood could be found on every corner surrounded by their sympathetic Guernsey friends.[179] Rev. Ord tried his best to stem the flood of misery brought on by this devastating news. Ambrose Robin went to Ebenezer Church on Sunday, September 20, to hear Ord "pour out measures of hope and comfort." Robin was aware that Ord had been a German prisoner in World War I for two and a half years, and "this made you feel that what he said was no idle words."[180]

But if Ord could comfort others, he could not stop the anxiety that gripped his own heart, because he, too, was scheduled for deportation. His diary reflected what he carefully kept from others, greeting the news with "Germany! A prison camp! And for the second time in my life. And to have to bear the thought of G. going through what I knew so well—the journey, the food question, the conditions of camp life, the plundering of our home and goods, and ending of my work so dear to me."[181] The situation for ministers was particularly complex, for the German authorities decided that only thirteen could stay. On September 17, a special meeting was held, presided over by John Leale, the head of the Controlling Committee, to sort out what spiritual leadership would be left to the Island. They really had little say in the matter, for ten were already exempt either by nationality or by being over the age.

Through a variety of complicated negotiations, it ended up that the Germans would take three more ministers to fulfill their requirement for the number to be deported. Two ministers had volunteered to go, leaving one space. On the list of those now earmarked to go to Germany, there was one minister ahead of Ord. Dunk was a Foursquare Gospel minister and a man with a young child who was very ill. And thus, Ord had his Garden of Gethsemane moment. He had experienced sleepless nights just dwelling on memories of his first imprisonment and "weighed down" with worry over his wife going through the same. Yet, he came to the decision that he must step in, should Dunk not be exempted, and offer to go in his place. At the last moment this cup was taken from him in the most surprising of ways. The Reverend Donald Stuart of Jersey made the surprisingly ill-timed decision to retire from active service and live on a piece of property he owned in Guernsey. When he arrived at the White Rock in St. Peter Port to move to his new home, he was stopped by the Germans. Examining his passport indicating English origin, the Germans announced that he would be going to Germany rather than to his retirement property in Guernsey. With this third minister providentially provided, Ord was freed from the sacrifice he had prepared himself to make.[182]

To compensate for so much bad news, a certain degree of gallows humor kicked in. At their regular Wednesday afternoon get-together, Winnie's friends greeted each new arrival with, "Are you wintering at Homburg or Cologne?" Despite there being a process for medical examinations, few exemptions were actually granted. The Friday after the announcement, the Medical Exemption Board met at Lukis House, forcing invalids to queue up outside in a dismal pouring rain. They had little success in proving their medical need, for they had to be 65 percent unfit to gain an exemption by the board. Even then, they had go before an unsympathetic German doctor to try and confirm their need for exemption.[183] Almost everyone was touched in some direct way by the deportation, even those personally exempted. As a widow, Elizabeth Doig was exempt, the deportation being directed at British males and their families, but her brother John and his family were not. So Elizabeth was left behind, knowing that she would miss her brother "terribly as it was on his act. [account] I stayed on the island & did not evacuate before the Germans came here."[184]

Unable to effect any substantive change in the situation, the Island as a whole gathered themselves to give the deported a good sendoff to internment camps at Biberach and Laufen. It would be a dramatic enactment of British spirit writ large, a mimetic performance of proper attitude, with the deported and those left behind serving as each other's audience. There was a tremendous "rush to have 'perms' done," according to Winifred Harvey, "and many girls have taken dance frocks and apparently think they are going on a Cook's Tour. I fear they will have a rude awakening but one feels proud of them and the way they have taken it."[185] Winnie and others saw this for what it was: an attempt to mask anxiety with cheerful gestures, a stance echoed by the farewells of "Goodbye, till this time next year," as if the deported were regular summer vacationers returning to the mainland.[186] Not all of these preparations for departure were symbolic, and some required bravery and commitment. Young Guernsey women who were engaged to Englishmen went quickly to the altar so that they could go to Germany together and share the same fate, whatever that might be.

The departure was just about as wearing as it could possibly have been. Torrential rain flooded down upon the Island as families, many with small children, struggled their way to the White Rock and the awaiting ships. Those not required to go turned out to see them off, with "handshaking at every corner & in every street" broken up by German police with their continuous orders to "Move on."[187] Quite of few of the young German soldiers and sailors were visibly upset and embarrassed, turning their faces away from the sodden parade of elderly, invalids, and children in their shabby clothes and drenched shoes, and remarking "Es ist farouk!" (It is outrageous). Winnie would overhear two officers talking later, one of them "gesticulating earnestly and saying, 'Aber die Kinder!'" (But the children!).[188]

The bottled-up emotions of the parting had to find some vent, and they largely came out in patriotic expressions, such as the miniature Union Jacks a few deportees held out to catch the wind as they gathered at assembly points.[189] Some of the crowds making their way to the White Rock started to sing "Good Old Churchill," "Rule Britannia," and other patriotic songs, with the Germans taking no notice of the singers (nor the singers of them).[190] And by the time they boarded the boats, they were singing "God Save the King" and "There Will Always Be an England," with some of the Germans singing along. It all made for, in Bill Warry's assessment, a "happy go lucky parting," at least on the surface.[191]

If Guernseymen now felt as though they were standing on sand and their Island home could slide from beneath them without warning, they had good reason for concern. Another "bombshell burst" during the first week in February 1943 when an order went out that all ex-army officers, including those who served in the first World War, would be deported along with Freemason officials and any criminals. It was at this point that the flouting of German orders, whether out of resistance, from simple misunderstanding, or from a scofflaw mentality, exacted its true cost. The Germans defined as "criminal" anyone who had served a prison sentence since 1923.[192] Those who had only just recently offended the German forces in some way were summarily deported. Bill Warry told of seeing a young girl of seventeen or eighteen deported (her two sisters seeing her to the ship "like red Indians with crying") because she sharply told off a German soldier. In Bill's estimation, the incident was the fault of the soldier. Nonetheless, the girl was reported and "got her ticket to go."[193]

So, barely six months after the first deportations, the entire process began again. The medical exemption was the same comedy it had been before, as Winifred Harvey reported:

> Mrs Barritt Hills told me the Doctor said to her, "How do you do, how are you?"
> She said, "Very well, thank you." And that was that.[194]

Even the weather repeated the pouring rain of the earlier deportation. And there were similar displays of defiance and patriotism. Capt. Jack Falla turned out to board the boats "looking like a tramp," only to discard his tattered coat and hat revealing his uniform from the First World War, replete with polished medals.[195] At this deportation, unlike the one six months previously, the German police made an attempt to control the crowds. They pushed the locals who had come to bid farewell "from pillar to post," only to have the crowd swell forward and push back. In a little boast seeking triumph out of powerlessness, Bill Warry claimed that "they got tired first."[196]

These events of the middle years of Occupation reset the relationship between occupier and occupied, as the German forces reached the height of their power in the Channel Islands. The evictions of Islanders from their homes, the ending of uncensored outside information by confiscation of the wireless, and the deportations of undesirables (in the German view) from the Island spoke of a widespread exercise of control. It should be noted at this point that, even with the iron grip of power in effect, no one in Guernsey had any inkling of the Final Solution or the depths of evil of the Nazi regime. The deportees went off to internment in Germany with the exact same concerns that they would have going to internment in France. They did not expect good conditions or excellent treatment, but they also had endured hardships at home under German control. The response to deportation, in the diaries and in life, would have been quite different had anyone known that death camps were operating in Germany. Without this knowledge, the Islanders left behind saw in the deportations a disturbing increase of German control, but nothing so ultimately sinister. Even so, with the heightened cruelty evinced during these years, Guernseymen and women felt the need for a new understanding and a deeper reading of these men who held power over them.

BEHIND THE MASK

The middle years of the Occupation presented a series of crises prompting a reassessment of the occupying forces. Spence et al. describe crises as "unanticipated events that throw off the everyday patterns of life," and as ones characterized by "high levels of potential danger."[197] By this definition, there could be few clearer examples of crises than the increasing slew of orders and resulting arrests, the ripping of Islanders from their homes, and the sudden deportations to an unknown future in Germany. Crisis events by their very nature increase the level of uncertainty in individuals and prompt a desire for information that could help them manage that uncertainty.[198] Reducing our uncertainty about the other party is a basic need in most early one-to-one encounters; thus, this process has generally been studied in the area of interpersonal communication.[199] Simple monitoring of the other is a "passive strategy" that is generally available when direct interaction and manipulation of a situation are not possible.[200] Uncertainty is generally uncomfortable,[201] but not always a negative feeling. A sense of uncertainty may actually have the positive attribute of buoying optimism in the face of threat.[202] The lack of solid information about the German internment camps was anxiety-provoking, but that void provided an opening for hope. The flip side of our anxiety about the future is the possibility that things will turn out better than we anticipate.[203] Yet, if the Islanders looked to a rereading of the occupiers seeking reassurance, they found very little to ease their minds.

As they examined the German forces for new understanding, occasionally the diarists were grudgingly positive about the self-styled young "Aryans" in their midst. However, this assessment was mainly about the physical attributes of these men who composed the enemy forces, and thus it was tinged with deep concern. Winifred Harvey described the eight hundred new troops of the 319th Infantry that had arrived recently: "very fine-looking men, tall and strong."[204] During that same summer of 1941, Jack Sauvary mentioned the Germans going bathing at the public beach pools at seven in the morning, at times with more than a hundred heading off together. Jack found it interesting that they never seemed to take a towel along and that they stayed undressed for most of the day.[205] Jack saw what other Islanders also sensed: the element of display put on by the German soldiers, a reflection of the Nazi cult of the body. Although the young soldiers were polite, mainly ignoring the civilians around them, they also did not cover themselves or retire to less visible parts of the public bathing pools. The message was one of power—a display of the very bodies that the husbands and sons of Guernsey were now fighting in the war—and the right to ownership of the area. It was a clear sign that they were "digging themselves in properly."[206]

One adjustment to the new imposition of Nazi power was an amusing tendency by Guernseymen to avoid speaking or writing of the German soldiers directly. Many of the diarists refer to Germans as an unspecified "They" or "Them" (at times underlined), as if a lack of verbal immediacy could distance the writers from the force that controlled their lives.[207] At times the indirect references drip with irony; the Germans become "our unwelcome tourists,"[208] the "visitors,"[209] "the gang,"[210] or "our 'Friends."[211] The Islanders also relied on synecdoche, or using a part of something to stand for the whole. The Germans become the "uniform," as when Dorothy Higgs declared, "They are stealing so much of our stuff and even our police daren't lay a hand on a uniform, no matter how mean the theft they catch it perpetrating."[212] For Kitty Bachmann, they were the "field-grey 'pestilence that walketh in the noonday' and stalketh by night to trap the unwary."[213] Thus, the German soldiers become an object, an "it," that must be treated with an undeserved deference. Winifred Harvey managed to combine all these forms of indirect reference when she described the Germans as "grey-uniformed uninvited guests."[214] And, of course, the residents of the Channel Islands, like all of the British, used the common nickname of "Jerry" for the Germans, a reference dating from World War I that likened the German helmet to a jeroboam or chamber pot. The combination of humor and contempt in such a nickname hardly needs comment.

The diarists also indulged in a series of metaphors, finding a commonality between the occupiers and the supposed traits of those in the animal world. Some of the references were essentially "dead" metaphors, ones so commonly used that they no longer function metaphorically. Thus, it is expected that Dorothy Higgs would call the Germans "swine,"[215] and Gertie Corbin would echo with the equally common "dirty swine."[216] Of more interest is a feline metaphor that occurred with an increased perception of danger as the Occupation continued. Very early on, Rev. Ord anticipated what would happen as the Island could not sustain the number of troops imposed upon it: "While they lapped up our cream they purred. Now that supplies are running short the true 'kulture' emerges."[217] Bert Williams described the German way of tightening police "beats," so that policemen were under almost constant surveillance, as being "watched like a cat watches a mouse."[218] However, the most operative sense of increasing control and danger came as the crises of 1942 and 1943 unfolded, leaving Dorothy Higgs to speak for many when she wrote, "We are just as helpless to defend ourselves as mice in a cat's paw."[219]

Rev. Ord maintained this sense of peril, simultaneously making a metaphoric switch when he described their unease: "And all the time a dog that may turn savage at any moment is roaming loose among us."[220] One of the major concerns was the increasing lack of food, and the ability of the Germans to confiscate what little there was at will. Thus, Winnie Harvey described the Germans with a mixed metaphor as "prowling" the Market with sacks, with "eyes like hawks" for any food they could claim.[221] And German thefts directly from the fields led Winnie to switch metaphors yet again, describing "what discouragement it is for the Guernsey people to plant their crops and have them all taken by these locusts."[222]

One means of domesticating, and thus taming, a threat is to liken it to something familiar and therefore more understandable and controllable. In their faceless numbers, the German troops were like bees, and Guernsey was "swarming with Germans,"[223] "swarming with Nazis."[224] Like a woman sitting among the bees in her summer garden, Winifred Harvey decided that even when an area was "swarming with troops," she would not allow their presence to worry her.[225] Rev. Ord was not so benign and dismissive, seeing in the surveillance of agents in the pay of the Germans "a regime which has bred a swarm of sneaks."[226]

Despite comparisons to the familiar, and some objective evaluation that was reluctantly positive, the Islanders' overwhelming assessment of the Germans highlighted contempt for their cruelty, pettiness, and immorality. The more that Guernseymen had contact with these "gentry," as Ord called them,[227] the more they saw the lack of a moral core in the men who held such power over them. Grae Ord learned that a friend's maid, a young and "very decent girl" who had worked for the family for some time, was overtaken on the street by a German officer billeted near the family. "Wouldn't you like a nice little German baby?" he asked the girl, with, as Rev. Ord recounted, "no trace of any sense of wrong." The girl hurried home very upset and indignant, but was followed to the house by the officer. He spoke to the girl's mistress and seemed surprised that, in Ord's words, "the girl had not seen fit to embrace so fair a proposition." The officer's sole consideration was a practical one: "The girl seems quite healthy and strong, too!"[228] Such instances, observed and reported widely around the Island, proved the much-vaunted "higher culture" of the German military establishment to be illusory.

Heedless cruelty, too, was on constant display. On a Sunday in early October 1941, Rev. Ord was walking up the hill towards Ville-au-Roi and came upon a girl cycling toward him. She was followed by an army lorry that held an officer seated next to the driver. After looking at the girl and grinning to each other, the two men steered the vehicle ever closer to her, nearly crushing her against the wall of the neighboring field. Leaving the girl pale and shaken behind them, they drove off apparently pleased with their "fine lark."[229] Because there were continual deaths of Guernsey cyclists and pedestrians in lorry "accidents," being toyed with by the Occupation forces had lethal implications.

Accounts of individual cruelty were so blatant and inexplicable that, unknown to the Islanders at the time, they proved to be a brief window into the same mindset that would fuel the Final Solution. During the final year of the war, a close friend of the Ords told them of being in the Rohais Road and seeing a German deliberately shoot a little girl's dog in the leg. The crying child picked up her pet, the dog's blood pouring down her dress. There was no option but to have the animal put down. Ord offered his conclusion to the story: "Is there any wonder the hatred grows? Difficult though it may be, one must fight against this instinctive reaction lest one lose the power of sober judgment altogether." Yet this assessment, couched as it was in the neutral parlance of academic morality, could not cover Ord's anger and disgust.[230]

The Islanders felt particular contempt for the obsequious nature of the Germans, and those having contact with the forces consistently noted the combination of bullying and fear that was on display. Bert Williams observed that "the average German soldier is terrified of the Officers and Under Officers,"[231] an atmosphere of fear that Ambrose Robin believed compromised the efficiency of the entire "German war machine." From his vantage point working for the Guernsey States, Robin noted the friction not just between units of the German army but also "between officers and men in the same unit."[232] Efficiency was compromised by the reluctance of German officers to put anything in writing, a tendency noted by Dorothy Higgs that she attributed to "fear of the next one above."[233] Some of this fear was apparently brought with the Germans from their homeland, where the same surveillance that they had imposed on the Island was a way of life.

In December 1941, Robin had a surprisingly frank talk with a German officer in a secluded office at the States. This unnamed officer had just come back from leave. While at home, he could not speak to his wife freely if the children were anywhere close by, because his son, apparently a member of the Hitler youth, would be sure to report him to the Gestapo. Despite his rank and his unsullied record of service, he believed that such a report by a child would spell his "finish"—whether of his life or merely his career was unclear.[234] As Rev. Ord, who was positioned to learn the inner workings of the German military, put it, "Great fear hangs over this delectable army. Spies and bullies hold complete sway."[235] Kitty Bachmann drew the comparison that she felt must be apparent to the Germans: "They find us unburdened by secret police; neither have we to resort to subterfuge and deceit between friends and relatives. We do not live furtively, like rabbits afraid to leave their burrows."[236]

The average Guernsey resident apparently found great humor in the obsequiousness, fostered by fear, of the German troops. The diarists' accounts are littered with a strong sense of schadenfreude, that useful German loanword that describes our unexpected pleasure at the misfortunes or suffering of another. One Islander told Rev. Ord of being in the Kommandantur and observing a German talking on the telephone. The German was apparently in a full toadying attitude, and by the time he hung up the receiver, he had actually saluted the person on the other end of the line (who was not, of course, there to see this gesture of deference). Whether this story was apocryphal or true, the pleasure of the mental image remains.[237]

By chance, Winifred Harvey saw the system of intimidation and response firsthand. On her way back from visiting Mrs. Clayton, by that point settled in the Mount Row Nursing Home, she heard "a roaring and a bellowing" from the direction of Queen's Road. When she came around the corner, she saw a thick-necked, crimson-faced old officer screaming in rage into the face of a small soldier. When the officer seemed to be done, the soldier saluted, marched off, and only made it about ten paces when he was pulled back by the officer for a "fresh dose." As the little soldier finally was released and passed Winnie, he grinned and tipped her a cheeky wink. It was then that Winnie realized that the officer was General Müller.[238] It was highly satisfying to watch the soldiers who bullied the civilians being bullied themselves.

And the pomp so cherished by the Third Reich gave ample opportunity for silent derision. Troops would tramp along the road accompanied by the spirited singing of martial songs. Yet, trailing in their wake, young boys would follow them, goose-stepping with great vigor and comic effect and also singing the more easily picked-up German verses. The Germans seemed to take no offense in these little mimics, perhaps because they so completely lacked a sense of humor. Quite likely, they read this total mockery as adulation and relished their ability to foster a generation of little British Nazis.[239]

When German high officials visited the Island, the symbolic trappings would be ratcheted up a notch. For example, on Sunday, December 20, 1942, a large German flag was flying at the Royal Hotel, and a continuous guard of two soldiers (their bayonets fixed) flanked the door. Islanders gathered silently to watch as the guard changed to much ceremonial goose-stepping. The observers were rewarded by the sight of one of the guards landing flat on his back mid goose step, a satisfying treat for those in attendance and a story that could be told with great glee around the Island.[240] Thus, the apparently simple act of *sousveillance*, or watching and assessment from "below," punctured the dignity of the occupiers and fostered a sense of agency that would support resistance.

DIFFERENTIATION

The final element of *sousveillance* that would influence the structure of resistance involved Islander differentiation of Nazi foe from potential anti-Party ally. In considering life under Occupation, one aspect seems to grip the public imagination. What would it be like during time of war to have contact with the enemy on a daily basis in a civilian setting? Over the five years of Occupation, the Channel Islanders encountered the occupiers in the Market, the street, the movie theater, at the communion altar rail, even (due to extensive billeting) in the bathroom, the hallway, the staircase of their own homes. Under these conditions, what would be considered proper behavior that would not "aid and comfort" the enemy or cross the indistinct line into collaboration? The fascination with this question has in some ways controlled discussions of the Occupation both in academic studies and in popular understanding.

This aspect is prominent, for example, in the Jersey War Tunnels exhibit, a beautifully designed museum set up in HO8, a former underground hospital complex constructed by slave labor in that larger Channel Island. In one of the primary exhibits of this examination of Occupation life, there are mannequins of German soldiers holding out an ice cream cone or laundry, or seated in an armchair, each with a video screen in place of his head. On each video screen, a young German's face appears, smiling and attractive and speaking directly to the viewer. One says, "How are you? Very nice to be here," and at his feet is a placard: "Would YOU . . . say hello to a German soldier in the street? If he shouted a cheery greeting could you ignore him?" Another "soldier" says, "But I very much like it. It is a very nice island. It has so much nature and sun and it is very beautiful." And at his feet is the placard, "Would YOU . . . invite a German soldier to your home? He speaks perfect English and shares your love of music."

The concept of putting the viewer in the place of the occupied is a strong one and obviously seeks to show outsiders that moral dilemmas were part and parcel of the Occupation. However, the situations described and questions asked were generally easy ones for the populace to answer. Most quickly developed a polite "game face" to present to the cheery greeting, some colder and more dismissive than others. In shaky handwriting appended to her diary, probably years later, Elizabeth Doig wrote, "I never stepped off the pavement for soldiers. I stood still & they had to walk round me."[241] The response to soldiers on the street had more to do with age and gender, "decent" young women taking particular care not to encourage the soldiers.

In an attempt to simplify for a general public, some of the questions in the exhibit may unconsciously foster false impressions. Inviting a soldier to your home, or taking in washing "for extra rations," another of the placard questions, might be viewed as collaboration, although the position of the person involved would be a mitigating factor. Just as a shoe-repair shop would be required to repair German boots, an individual working from his or her home in such a business would be compelled to provide services to the Germans or face serious repercussions. Such work would mean regular contact with Germans in the home. States officials or ministers might be viewed as having good reason for meeting with German officers in their homes, simply because it often signaled an informal intervention on behalf of a civilian.

The problem with the questions in the exhibit, sharpened by the underlined and capitalized YOU, is that they deal with relatively voluntary interactions. It is not difficult to come up with the patriotic, "correct" response foregoing the extra rations, or the pleasure of the nice German soldier's company and a stimulating discussion of music. Yet, Channel Islanders—in the case of this study those in Guernsey—had no choice but to interact with Germans. It was not a case of invitation into the home; a German soldier was billeted in the adjoining bedroom. Perhaps, as in Winifred Harvey's case, the family home was taken over entirely by Germans and contact was necessary, if only to monitor what was happening to the property. For the Warrys and Bachmanns as shop owners, both in the Guernsey Arcade, many of the customers crossing their doorsills would be Germans. For Ambrose Robin, Ken Lewis, and Rev. Ord, contact with Germans, particularly officers, came because of work with the States or in the course of the ministerial vocation. For those in certain positions, whether by vocation or standing in the Island, contact was handled on the basis of "keep your friends close and your enemies closer." The more that the Islanders knew, the more information informally gleaned of German reasoning and plans, the better for the civilians.

This matter of contact with the enemy was driven home to Rev. Ord one day as he sat typing an entry in his diary. Looking out the window, he could see a farmer's cart going into town as it did every other morning. Seated beside the Guernsey farmer was a German soldier who apparently had the job of purchasing for his battery and also had to make regular trips into town. Although Ord did not seem to know whether the German was also billeted on the farmer, the soldier had the right to demand transportation. In any case, Ord had watched as "week after week they go together," and contemplated the fact that sitting side by side for such a length of time would have to lead to some greater understanding between the two. Contact with the Germans was simply unavoidable, and in Ord's Christian viewpoint, "the only course is to judge a man as his character is revealed." Although, Ord wrote, "we 'see red' when a Nazi appears in his true colours or when we see the 'system' at work," Islanders also had opportunity to see "the Other Germany" of the anti-Party Germans, those who opposed Hitler and had been dragooned into the military, unable to resist out of fear for self and family. These were men "on our side in this struggle not of Empires but of ideas."[242]

There was relief, of course, for civilians whenever these armed men in their midst behaved in a simply decent fashion. Two aspects seemed to influence positive interactions with the Germans: the formal politeness that the more educated soldiers, particularly officers, displayed, and the youth of the soldiers in general. There was brutality, cruelty, and a cold Nazi pride on display as well, but that served to heighten the comparison when Islanders met up with the other type of German. When Jack Sauvary was introduced to the German staying with Mrs. Godfray, he noted that despite Jack's poor French, perhaps their only means to communicate, "being a polite officer" the man declared Jack to be quite fluent. When he saw that Jack was smoking a mixture of Lipton tea and bramble in his pipe, the officer immediately went upstairs and brought down a 2 oz. bag of tobacco ("very kind" mentioned Jack in parentheses).[243] These little interactions, unsought but unavoidable, and small kindnesses lessened some of the tension of contact.

Ken Lewis came across a German painter one Saturday evening as the man was trying to capture a pastoral farm scene down one of the charming Guernsey lanes. With his curiosity and total lack of concern about German contact, Ken spoke to the artist and discovered that he had been a professor at a Bohemian university during peacetime. Ken proclaimed him to be very good at painting and, despite being "only a private," to be a "very decent fellow."[244] As there was no benefit to the German war effort, artists, hobbyists, and intellectuals seem to have been appraised somewhat differently from the average German soldier. Bill Warry, who had studied for two years and passed the examinations at Kew Gardens, at times would go out into the field with a German botanist ("a good fellow") in order to show him a rare plant or a particular kind of Guernsey grass, the interest in the topic overriding the reality of their being enemies.[245]

As a shop owner, Bill Warry was in constant contact with German customers and seemed to have little difficulty in interacting with Germans, even to the point of some humorous baiting. When Bill and his wife, accompanied by a Mrs. Williamson and their shop assistant, went to Petit Bot to pick some ripe sloes in order to make jam, they found the area overrun with Germans. One German police officer fell into conversation with Bill. He asked if the Warrys liked the German people. "Yes," Bill replied, "but not their Government." He then asked, "When do you think the war will finish?" to which Bill replied that he knew, "but had been told not to tell." To this, the German responded, "Another 2 months then finished." Finally, the German remarked, "We like the English, you know," to which Bill dryly rejoined, "Yes it looks very much like it." Both men seemed to enjoy this back and forth, and neither seemed to fear repercussions. In fact, Bill finished recounting the exchange by writing, "Some of these Germans are very decent fellows & very polite."[246]

Of course, the social traits of politeness and decency, however that latter culturally charged term is defined, are easily assumed guises providing a convenient cover for all types of evil intent. Yet over five long years, the Islanders were observers of far deeper emotions in the occupying troops. Propinquity, simply being near another in time and place, provides an opportunity to see the soul of the other and to discover a common humanity that transcends our differences. This is the reason that propinquity is one of the key predictors of attraction in interpersonal relationships; we tend to be drawn to others as we get to know them, rather than being repelled by our greater knowledge.

Some interactions could not help but summon up thoughts of their own young men, serving with the Allied forces and out of contact with their homes and families. In January 1941, Ambrose Robin mentioned a temporary suspension of leave for the German troops and its impact on a young soldier who was his mother's sole support. He had not been home for four years and had been promised leave that very week, only to have it suddenly canceled. "He wept," Robin wrote with apparent sympathy, "like a child."[247]

Jack Sauvary witnessed this same rush of emotion when Goldie, the beautiful spaniel belonging to Elsie, Mrs. Godfray's maid, was run over by a car and killed. The family was devastated by the loss, and the German officer, the one who had been so polite to Jack at first meeting, actually cried because he was so attached to the dog. The officer had always brought in Goldie's meals, and took the dog for a drive with him in his car every day.[248] Even in the first month of Occupation, Kitty Bachmann learned through her husband that Germans in town were pathetically eager to show photographs of their homes and families "to anyone sufficiently interested to see them." She saw this as a tacit admission that the soldiers "had their fill of Hitler's Promised Land" and wanted little more than to return to their home and live their lives in peace.[249]

Humor, and a sense of the absurd, was a point of unity between some of the occupiers and the civilians under their control. Ernie Carre, whose brother owned the Bungalow Hotel in Sark, reported that the thirty or so men still in that tiny Island would spend evenings at the hotel. They would sing "Tipperary" and "There Will Always Be an England," and the loudest voices of all would belong to any Germans present, at least "when they have reached the stage when hats can be exchanged."[250] Not all the humor was alcohol-fueled, of course, and some was based on the personalities involved and their sense of the ridiculous. Two highly respectable Guernseywomen, Mrs. Sherbrooke and Mrs. Kinnersley, were put under temporary guard at their home while a charge that they had signaled to Allied parachutists from the upper windows of the house was being investigated. Neither woman seemed much perturbed by the situation, nor did their guard. When their friend Mrs. Brock went to visit, she was introduced by Mrs. Sherbrooke ("with much flicking of eyelashes") to "Our guard, Herr Gans." Whereupon the guard replied happily, "Ja, Herr Gans, Goosey, goosey gander."[251]

But let us state the obvious here from our position of knowing the full truth of Nazi atrocities. Hearing of these displays of humanity cannot help but trigger the response that Hitler, too, had a fondness for children and dogs but still was able to order the butchering of children and the poisoning of his own dog, Blondi. SS guards could have a rousing song at a *biergarten* and return to their work at the abattoirs of the concentration camps. It is important to point out that, even lacking information about the Final Solution, the Islanders were not fools, nor were they naive and easily won over by displays of emotion or humor. Still, they struggled often with how to properly behave so as not to collaborate, yet to encourage kind treatment of their own people, and even to foster questions within the occupying troops about the morality of the German cause.

This ethical dilemma was most intense from a Christian perspective, and many Islanders turned to their ministers for guidance. Rev. Ord, with his knowledge of German and experience as a prisoner of war, had urged his flock at the very outset of the Occupation not "to succumb to the facile temptation of hating," a Christian stance that he acknowledged to be increasingly difficult over the years. He developed and advocated a policy of differentiation, where Islanders would "do our utmost to distinguish between the régime and those who may have no way of open revolt against it. There is no inconsistency in hating the National Socialist system and those who exemplify its beastly features AND at the same time judging every man as we find him."[252] This proved to be useful advice, for as Hazel Knowles Smith so aptly put it, the Islanders saw "the full spectrum of violence and decency side by side in their topsy-turvy world."[253]

Some acts of German kindness were not without serious potential cost. In June 1942, a fresh warning came to the German troops forbidding fraternizing with civilians, more particularly stating that those giving bread to civilians would be shot.[254] Still, the gifts of bread, tobacco, or access to the wireless continued. It was a covert gesture of appreciation for help in a shop or an expression of affection to a family that treated a billeted soldier with kindness. Though the value to the recipient was undeniable, most Islanders did not considered such tokens as collaboration. In effect, accepting German bread was only depleting the resources of the Germans—an extra benefit, though not the motivating factor, for anti-Party Germans in giving the gifts and for Guernseymen in receiving them.

Rev. Ord provided an actual example of the exceptional German, who should be treated on his own merits, and the German who was not just a part of the Nazi system, but who embodied all that these British citizens despised. Eduard Lassauer was a young German soldier billeted on the Chilcotts, and one who seemed to win the affection of all who knew him. Courteous, thoughtful, he was considered "a delightful, well-educated young fellow." He was particularly considerate in allowing his "hosts" to use his wireless, banned at that point for them, and he brought them many small commodities from the army stores, all as a means to express his gratitude for the comfortable home they provided. Even when he went on leave, he took "snaps" to show his own family his billet and came back with a special message from his parents thanking the Chilcotts for the care of their son. He could, in Ord's opinion, be "easily taken for an English boy" and even reminded Ord of a particular relative.

The counterpoint came with the young NCO who occupied Eduard's billet while Eduard was on leave. Where Eduard was courteous, this young man had little in the way of breeding and very poor manners. Given to constantly performing what the Islanders called the Nazi "stretch" (the greeting done with a straight extension of the arm, literally the *Deutscher Gruß* or German greeting, but better known as the Nazi salute),[255] he just slightly outranked Eduard. Thus, any protest was futile, and Eduard was given another bedroom upon his return from leave. Although the Chilcotts tried to be even-handed "hosts" to both Germans, the new soldier began to complain that "those people" could listen to the wireless and that it would have to be moved to the bedroom. Under the advice of a higher-ranking sympathetic officer,

Eduard secretly took up carpets and linoleum and rigged the wiring so that the Chilcotts could still listen in on his set when the other billeted soldier was out. Eduard also ostentatiously removed a part of the set before going on his next leave, to reassure his billet mate that the Chilcotts could not use the set. He then quietly gave the part to the Chilcotts for safekeeping and invited them to use the set as often as they pleased.[256] With many such comparative examples before them, Islanders learned as one lesson of their unique experience of Occupation that all Germans were not alike and that the goodness of the individual could transcend the rotten nature of the larger system.

Rev. Ord developed deep personal contact with a series of anti-Party German officers, and this experience helped him to refine his general policy of differentiation. The first of these relationships came about in a fashion that would be remarkable under any circumstance but was doubly so in time of war. On September 2, 1941, Ord went to Rabey's bookshop and found John Rabey, the brother of the owner, in quite a state. He was attempting to help a tall, handsome officer, but having been left the shop to mind for his evacuated brother, and lacking any real knowledge of the trade, he was confused and made nervous by the German's requests. Spotting Ord entering the shop, Rabey cried, "Sir, this gentleman will help you," and introduced the two men. Ord helped the officer to purchase several English classics to take to his wife when on leave, and they passed a few words, Ord switching comfortably to German. "Oh, then you have been in Germany?" the officer asked, and on a sudden impulse, Ord replied that he wished for a magic carpet if only to visit Köhler's bookstore in Leipzig. The officer said that he would pass through Leipzig on leave and would be happy to bring a special book in appreciation of Ord's kind assistance. Ord replied:

> "That is very good of you. When there are so many, it is hard to decide. But perhaps, to name one scholar, I should be very glad to have a book by Hermann Gunkel, the distinguished . . ."
>
> [But here he interrupted in astonishment:] "But this is extraordinary! You ask for my Father's book! I am Hermann Gunkel's son!"

Thus, Ord met Dr. Gunkel, whose late father had been an Old Testament scholar very influential on Ord's interpretive understanding of the Bible. Both Rev. Ord and Dr. Gunkel were quite overwhelmed by this chance meeting, which sparked a relationship lasting until Gunkel was recalled to Berlin that December.[257]

During the time of their acquaintance, Dr. Gunkel proved to be a man of many surprises. He would visit Ord and speak with unusual frankness; in fact, Ord found that "his outbursts were almost staggering" for an officer of his rank. He was decidedly "no friend of the Nazis," and Ord encouraged him to "pour out his burdened soul."[258] Yet, Ord was not just offering a Methodist form of the confessional. He was more than willing to use this connection with the Occupation hierarchy to benefit the Islanders. This came to pass when Ord intervened in a court case involving one of his parishioners, Basil Martel. Martel had been arrested and charged with disrespect to the German army, because he challenged a young Guernseywoman, accompanied by two German officers, when she attempted to buy an expensive eiderdown without a permit. The girl, who had a questionable moral reputation and was a known fraternizer with the Germans, gave a colorful and blatantly false account of what Martel had said privately about the officers. When Ord found out, rather by chance, that his new friend Dr. Gunkel was the head of the Kriegsgericht, the "Judge for the Island," he wasted no time in sitting down with Gunkel to discuss the merits of Basil

Martel's case. Gunkel shared this information with the presiding judge who was coming in from Jersey. The upshot was that Martel was released at trial with no stain on his character, an unlikely outcome for a working-class Guernseyman.[259] Having found this "magic talisman,"[260] it is little wonder that Ord was sorry to lose Gunkel in December, realizing that "he might have been of use to us and to others."[261]

Other German relationships would develop to which Ord seemed even more personally attached. In February 1943, Heinrich Bödeker, a young German minister, came by bearing an introduction from a German scholar, a mutual acquaintance. Bödeker had been a minister in a German evangelical church until the day that Gestapo spies, planted in among the congregation, decided that he had stepped over the line in what he said. He had only ten minutes to report to the depot, at which time he was placed in the coastal guards. Through Bödeker, a man so strongly anti-Nazi that he was always in danger of being reported by spies and backbiters among the troops, Ord would be introduced to Hoffmann (another former minister of a parish in Germany) and to Reinhold Zachmann.[262] All three men would become close friends with Rev. Ord, bringing news about the war ("a precious window of escape from our narrow confinement")[263] and small gifts of bread or sugar, both at great risk to themselves. Ord never asked for this help or information, knowing the danger for his friends. However, these intellectual Germans valued a person with whom they could safely discuss their common loathing of the German regime, and they found small means to express that friendship.

The average Guernseyman would have difficulty knowing the Germans around them in the same way as Douglas Ord, with his knowledge of the German language and his ministerial position. Although they did see the difference in individuals among the occupying forces, these observations were tainted by suspicion that positive behavior was feigned rather than real. One story that went the rounds concerned the two men billeted on Leonard Guilbert at Saumarez Road. One young soldier was reserved and distant, but the other was very friendly, had a seat at the fireside throughout his stay, and became like a member of the family. All of this changed one evening when "the Gestapo" (a term used often in Islander accounts for men who were actually the Geheime Feldpolizei [GFP], or secret field police) came around and asked this young soldier, "Which is the door that is always kept locked?" whereupon the soldier indicated the pantry door. Guilbert was forced to open the pantry, as they suspected that he had a wireless, although only their meager store of food was kept there. When the GFP left, the young soldier tried to resume his usual seat and was told to go to his room and never to enter any other room as long as he was billeted there. Incidents like these made it "difficult to trust the best of Germans."[264]

With this carefully gleaned information about the occupiers garnered through their own countersurveillance, Islanders constructed a foundation on which to build their particular style of resistance. James Scott maintains that "discourses of resistance" must rely upon some network of cooperation among the powerless. There must be spaces that are sheltered from the watchful eyes of the powerful and beyond their control, where a line of resistant talk and practices can flourish.[265] Susan Gal provides a "nested" view of public and private that is a useful framework when seeking to understand the nature of Guernsey resistance. Gal points up the perceptual nature of the public/private dichotomy and seeks to find aspects of the "public inside a private or private inside a public." In Gal's example, the private home, set apart as it is from the public street, is further differentiated between more public areas (such as the living room) and more private areas (such as the bathroom or bedroom). Even these areas may be further broken into increasingly private distinctions by common usage.[266] As the Germans invaded the privacy of Islanders, imposing a surveillance of private actions that sought to restrict resistance, Guernseymen and women countered with a concept of resistance that confounded traditional notions of public action. In the newly hostile environment, public resistance would take on private shadings. Birthed in increasingly hidden locations and revealed in the private writings of Islander diaries, rhetorical resistance would be difficult to shoehorn into traditional notions of public resistance.

In the next chapter, we will see how interpersonal support among close family and friends and personal notions of defiance and patriotism, both generally considered private concerns, took on new public importance during the Occupation. Chapter 2 will first establish the strength of relationships among Islanders, and the networks of interpersonal care that grew up under the wearing and sometimes brutal conditions of the Occupation. These vital connections of support would be strained over the years as the physical and mental stresses of Occupation took their toll. Yet, these ties were the bedrock upon which common understandings of the situation and the spirit to survive were constructed. This sense of support would provide the first set of foundational elements necessary to the sustaining of a rhetorical resistance.

The second necessary component for fostering resistance was a reassurance that the majority of Islanders shared a common set of patriotic beliefs. Only with the trust that came from knowing the mindset of others could a common form of discursive resistance develop. It was an object of belief that Guernseymen and women should face their difficulties with the same "thumbs up" positive attitude that dominated stories of the British spirit. In the next chapter, too, I will discuss how identification with Britain became a primary influence on Guernsey mood and outlook. Although consigned by fate to the fringes of the war effort, Islander affiliation with the Allied cause reinforced their self-view as patriots and true Britons. Their concerns for their evacuated families, particularly children, and for relatives serving in the Allied forces were heightened by distance and the uncertainty of contact. Thus, a network for discursive resistance was constructed from common experience, mutual anxieties, and shared mindset, one so embedded in everyday familial, neighborhood, and occupational settings as to be "opaque to the authorities."[267] It was in these informal, everyday settings that the hidden transcript of resistance was written.

CHAPTER TWO

The Bedrock of Resistance

It was a Monday bank holiday in August 1941, but Jack Sauvary was hardly in a holiday mood. Midday fog had turned to windy rain, and Jack felt for those he watched set off with their ill-supplied picnic baskets and bathing suits in the morning. This attempt to carve out an illusion of past holiday-making ended with a slog home through the wild gales of early afternoon. All in all, it was a "dull day" for Jack as well, with "only the fowls and rabbits for company." When he had met that morning with Uncle Ned (in actuality, his brother-in-law) at the Bridge roadway and shopping area in St. Sampson, he found that Ned, too, was depressed and feeling deserted by his friends. It was, Jack mused, "the usual." When a person kept an "open house," as Ned did before his wife's death, then friends were sure to flock around; but when "you're down and alone you get nobody."[1] Jack fought his own battle with loneliness, especially in the evenings, when he missed "dear old Mum" the most. He would often visit a fellow widower and old family friend, Dr. Jones, until curfew, but in general, Jack wrote that he found little interest now in other people. With family and friends scattered and an unfillable void left by his wife's passing, he sometimes felt that "Life is very disappointing, very few people are sincere."[2]

If such a sociable optimist as Jack Sauvary could question the fundamental ties holding people together, then it is a clear indicator of the strains on interpersonal relationships brought by the Occupation. The interpersonal lives of the Guernsey Islanders during the period were integral to the development of rhetorical resistance because the situational constraints of the Occupation molded resistance into a specific form. Insight into Islanders' private living conditions, their concerns to protect certain members of the community, and their heightened sense of threat as the death toll mounted explains their choice of a symbolic resistance utilizing private resources.

This chapter will begin with examining some of these stresses, many of which developed in the enclosed, pressure-cooker atmosphere of new living arrangements. Widespread evictions resulted in a necessity for communal living, while at the same time, the nightly curfew, the lack of transportation, and the absence of evacuated/deported friends and family hindered broader socializing. What resulted was paradoxical in some ways: too much enforced proximity with others interwoven with feelings of isolation and loneliness. Stress over personal living situations often was traded for a more disinterested concern for several key groups considered particularly vulnerable: the young (particularly young girls and women), the elderly, family pets, and Guernsey itself as a physical entity. In a peculiar way, these more abstract worries lifted the Islanders out of their personal anxiety for self, family, and friends, providing an understanding that more was at stake than their own survival. I will also examine the deaths of Guernsey civilians during this time period, and the impact this ultimate interpersonal loss had on the Islanders' understanding of their situation. Recognizing the concerns that Islanders had for themselves, their families, and friends is important to understanding the unique experience of the Occupation, the nature of information flow, and the form that resistance ultimately took.

I will then discuss the two aspects that needed to be in place for the Guernsey populace before resistance could take place behind their collective mask of deference. Both elements are constructed through communication among members of a subjugated population, generally in those private areas of life away from the surveillance of the dominant. First, Islanders needed to feel supported by their families and neighbors in the basic necessities of life. The creative solutions to daunting shortages form a major aspect of the Occupation narrative, one already recounted in numerous books and articles. I am interested in the sharing of these necessities of life as a form of support and as a means of banding together. A society that degenerates into dog-eat-dog scrapping for survival has no energy to undermine the oppressive system. Knowing that others are willing to sacrifice for us, and that there is concern and support coming from others in similar circumstances frees us to focus our efforts against those in power. It also assures us that our society deserves our best efforts, showing itself to be basically sound even under the worst conditions.

The latter part of this chapter will explore the second aspect preliminary to resistance, the shape of the counter-ideology that was pitted against Nazi dogma during the Occupation. Resisters do not just oppose a dominant ideology; they also need "a counterideology—a negation," one that provides a common rallying point and shapes the resistant acts that are invented (often spontaneously) by the powerless.[3] For rhetorical resistance combined with creative acts of sabotage to flourish, there needs to be a sense of what life *should* be like, a common ideal of freedom and respect. If we know the goals and ideals of those who share our common position, then we can establish the trust that, coupled with support, is the necessary prerequisite to action.

In the case of the Guernsey Occupation, this ideology did not need to be constructed of whole cloth. Instead, the Islanders readily tapped into existing notions of British spirit that had bolstered the war effort since its advent. Through the diarists' exploration of their own feelings about England, it is possible to trace the importance of traditional patriotism to the unity and general mood of the Guernsey populace. It provided a foundation of trust among like-minded Islanders, and strengthening these feelings would be one goal of the evolving resistance. Under the particular conditions of the Occupation, where panopticism was a primary method of German control, Islanders needed "tacit or acknowledged coordination and communication"[4] in places safe from surveillance. The familiar images and catch phrases of patriotism served as a shorthand, easily and quickly exchanged under the nose of the occupiers. As the Occupation ground on and conditions became increasingly wearing, the "we can take it" attitude woven through Churchill's speeches and Londoners' response to the Blitz served as a barrier against both despair and numbed acquiescence to German control.

Guernseymen and women felt acutely their position on the fringes of the war, and their inability to do anything substantial for the war effort. At times they could not help but feel abandoned by Britain, and any attention directed their way refreshed their sense of connection to their nation and the war effort. Some of the British "attention" was not without its dangers, and a fascinating aspect of Islander patriotism was their coming to grips with the reality of what is now called "friendly fire." Finally, this chapter will examine the strongest tie that Islanders had with Great Britain: their relatives serving in the armed forces and their evacuated families, particularly the children. In a very real sense, the Channel Islanders had their greatest treasure under the temporary custody of Great Britain; this common interest helped to weave the net of trust among Islanders that was prerequisite to acts of resistance. The social lives, interpersonal communication, and deepest beliefs of Islanders are not tangential areas of idle interest, but necessary components to understanding the development of rhetorical resistance.

ALL IN THIS TOGETHER

The Occupation was a hurricane of dislocation that blew friends and family to the four winds through evacuation and deportation, and ripped the remaining Islanders from their homes through evictions. From the very beginning, new living combinations were tried as a means of support, or in an attempt to protect family homes. Kitty and Peter Bachmann "decided to throw in their lot" with the recently married George and Felicia (and briefly Felicia's mother, Allie) to live at La Guelle, the family home left empty by Kitty's parents upon evacuation.[5] This would leave Les Dunes (Peter and Kitty's home) open to confiscation, which actually did occur in 1942 when "some vagrant immigrants" (slave labor of the Organization Todt) were installed there.[6] Choosing which house to protect was a Morton's Fork decision, a choice between equally bad alternatives. But if only one place could be protected, it made sense to choose the larger and more valuable property. By June of 1941, a bungalow was being prepared for George and Felicia. At that point, both Kitty and Felicia were expecting, and the anticipated disruption of new babies (and one might speculate the natural tensions of two very pregnant women sharing household duties in the same kitchen) made a division into two households reasonable.[7]

Peter and Kitty's experience stands for the living arrangements made and remade by many throughout the Occupation. In writing her diary/letters in October 1940, the time when George and Felicia still shared La Guelle, Kitty admitted that she was sitting in her mother's old bedroom upstairs, despite the cold penetrating through the windows from a northeasterly gale. The only fire was downstairs in the kitchen, but the "stifling proximity of communal life is not conducive to lucid writing. Snatches of conversation, shufflings, wireless and the like, mingle with my thoughts until my brain feels like a mental stockpot."[8] Even a flexible and even-tempered person, as Kitty undoubtedly was, felt the lack of privacy and autonomy brought on by community life.

Subtle adjustments were tried to ease the strain, such as when Kitty and Felicia mutually agreed to do their own families' breakfasts and suppers. The ostensible reason for this agreement was that it gave them "all more freedom to come and go without being time-bound." Of course that would be true, but it also allowed the illusion of two wholly individual households occasionally overlapping their lives in the same space.[9] Yet, in the common view of the time, the ones to be pitied were not those thrown into too-close contact by the Occupation, but those bereft of their nearest ties. As Dorothy Higgs put it, "It must be terrible for people who are left here with no one."[10] With so many family members and friends gone, with a mercurial and cruel occupier who could deport more for any or no reason, the value of all personal relationships increased.

Kitty Bachmann believed that the most pathetic were those men who had "inveigled wives and children to go without them" and were now left stranded.[11] Their primary concern in those mad days of evacuation had been guaranteeing the safety of their families. Many had planned to secure their property/farms/businesses and also depart. But then the curtain lowered. Kitty saw three of these "grass widowers" sitting in the front pews of the church at George and Felicia's hastily arranged marriage on June 29, 1940, an event made all the more poignant because Felicia's aunt had been killed and her brother-in-law gravely injured in the air raid of the day before.[12] These newly single men must have been "painfully conscious," Kitty believed, that they were watching two young people enter the very state that they had "indefinitely relinquished a few hours before."[13]

Kitty and Peter adopted several grass widowers, almost like a project, making it a point to invite them over and to spend time with them—especially at Christmas, when they were most likely to feel alone. Kitty wondered how Stan Noel could get along without "Weazle," his highly competent wife, when Stan admitted that he had never even purchased a pack of cigarettes for himself. And she believed that Harry Marley was experiencing a "prolonged purgatory" without his American wife Martha, now in the United States with family for the duration.[14] Some of her contemplation of the loneliness of these men may have been balm for Kitty's concerns about remaining with Peter rather than accompanying their ten-year-old in evacuating to England. This type of social comparison was common, a means to rehearse the rationale for hastily made decisions and to gain comfort that those decisions were correct.

Clearly the odd situation of the Occupation forged new relationships and new forms of socializing. One problem was simply the means of offering hospitality. As food became scarce, a new etiquette developed to handle invitations to tea or dinner, and that was to Bring Your Own Rations. Jack Sauvary, developing into a keen observer of life around him, found it "amusing to see the couples and little families all along the Banques, all carrying their bags."[15] If not bringing individual rations, then a form of potluck was expected where each person was responsible for a dish based on whatever they had available to them.[16] As a sidelight to the new social rules of bring and share, it became a mark of privilege to be absolved of the need to provide one's own food. Thus there is a deeper meaning to Ken Lewis's proud comment that "Beattie told Mum today that when I went to her party I did not have to take any food whatsoever."[17] For some, this new etiquette did not seem like hospitality at all, and older Islanders still tried to marshal the resources to occasionally provide a true tea or full meal.

Food took on a new value as an expression of harmony. Months of scrimping and extra self-denial might go into a simple tea, but accepting such invitations held its own difficulties. During the 1942 Christmas season, Ken Lewis's family decided to invite the members of his Auntie Rache's family to tea and to spend a quiet evening. They planned, if possible, to provide some mashed potatoes, beetroot, and ("if we could get it") the rare treat of a slice of tongue each. The impetus for all this effort was simply that they had been hosted by others, and as Ken put it, "We did not like the idea of having been to all their houses and not returning the compliment." So, to accept hospitality brought with it the difficult pressure of reciprocity. That same holiday season, Ken's Auntie Rache frankly told Ken's parents that she was not having them over, although she was hosting the rest of the family on New Year's Day. She could not ask them without asking Ken's sister, Eileen, and she could not provide for so many.[18] The symbolic act of providing even a simple meal could convey the importance of some relationships over others, forcing difficult choices and risking hurt feelings and division.

Another of the major difficulties in maintaining ties to others was the curfew—always in force, but tightened whenever the Germans wished to punish Islanders in general for some infraction. Therefore, bridge parties and other social events in homes were conducted like middle-school sleepovers. Guests would appear early, armed with toothbrushes, pyjamas, and their own ration of food. Because the evening would barely be under way when the curfew (sometimes as early as eight o'clock) was imposed, guests would simply plan to spend the night.[19]

Some of these odd sleeping arrangements had the potential for misunderstandings. On August 10, 1942, Bert Williams reported on a two-month feud under way between his Mother, his sister Ivy, and his girlfriend Adele (who was often called Dell). Dell had not been in the Williams home since June 9, 1942, and Bert's family refused even to speak to Dell in the narrow streets of Guernsey, an awkward situation if ever there was one. Bert was having trouble figuring out why Dell was now "an outcast" and his family seemed to "hate the sight of the girl." He speculated that the trouble started on the Saturday before June 9, when his small band went up to Mr. Kramer's house to give a concert. With a curfew on and most likely a good time being had by all, they all "got stuck for the night." Dell, who had come along, stayed at Mr. Kramer's house with Joyce Turguson. The "boys" and Bert stayed at Villa De Rocque. "There was nothing wrong in that I am sure," wrote Bert primly. Communal living, especially with family, brought with it many watchful eyes and more than enough judgmental opinions. "But with all that," Bert stated, "I am sticking to the girl whatever happens."[20] And Bert was as good as his word. Almost exactly a year later, Bert practically crowed about the "red letter day in the Williams family," when he "led Miss Adele Sauvarin to the altar." All seems to have been long forgiven, for Bert could happily state that "Mum and Ivy were 100%, in fact it was a good day from start to finish."[21]

If upheaval served as an enabler for romance, it also brought a new closeness between family members with little previous contact. At Elizabeth College, where he had gone to receive some Red Cross messages, Jack Sauvary ran into his niece Mary Sauvary in March 1941. She was his brother Willie's fifth child and the only one left of her family in the Island. Although she had stopped by to see Jack once when he was out, they appear not to have had ongoing contact up to this point. This chance meeting, brought about because Mary was working at the Red Cross bureau, was the beginning of a very close relationship.

Jack and Mary seemed to delight in each other's company, and just as she became a substitute for Jack's children, he became a surrogate father for her. So, Mary brought Jack Red Cross messages and went with him to put flowers on his wife's grave (exploring the cemetery for other relatives' graves, which they forked and weeded). Jack took great pleasure in scaring up whatever tidbits he could to give Mary an occasional "nice tea," sending her off with little gifts of eggs or whatever was available.[22] The artifact of this newly close relationship is a charming picture taken on January 15, 1943, when Jack served as proxy for Mary's father and gave his young niece away in marriage. There is Mary, a pretty young woman in a blouse of French georgette covered in small forget-me-nots to match her bridesmaids' dresses (which Jack described as so thin he could have "put the lot in my pocket"), and a practical blue coat, suit, and hat. She towers a foot above her diminutive, smiling uncle, who appears proud if a bit drawn and thin.[23]

This is the dominant story of Islander relationships during the Occupation: a new closeness and interpersonal combinations that might not have occurred under other conditions. One surprise of this study is how little indication exists of "environmental spoiling."

Environmental spoiling, a term coined by Ebbeson, Kyos, and Konecni, refers to the stress engendered when people live in close proximity, often against their will.[24] It is a familiar concept to anyone forced to continue sharing living quarters with an uncongenial freshman roommate, or snowed in for a week with soon-to-be-former friends. I fully expected to find such strains in the tightened living quarters of the Occupation, aggravated by little food and by fear of the occupying forces. Such expectations, combined with the day-by-day revelations inherent in reading diaries, led to some amusing results. Bert Williams haughtily recorded on January 2, 1945: "Dell had a fit of temper, we are not on speaking terms." The reason for her foul mood came to light with his entry six days later, proudly relating Dell's trip to the Essential Commodities Committee to register herself as an expectant mother: "It seems that we are going to have an increase in the family next July."[25] Dell appears to be one whose pregnancy was marked by hormonal mood shifts, for Bert writes later, "Dell is in a raging temper, she often gets like this lately."[26] It would not be an easy pregnancy, coming as it did during the final year's starvation and bitter cold, but these temper flares were natural and temporary rather than indications of environmental spoiling or relational disintegration.

However, when things went south in relationships, they did so with a vengeance. Sometimes the loss of ready access to alcohol or tobacco, whether a true addiction or merely a pleasurable habit, added to the environmental strain on relationships.[27] Once relationships frayed, the tools for retaliation were readily available for those angry and heedless enough to use them. Ambrose Robin told of a family he sardonically called "the [Robinson] family of Saints."[28] Clive Robinson, it seems, had a sack of flour that was vanishing at a suspicious rate, so he called in the police to investigate. The guilty party turned out to be his sister Edna, and Clive was in the midst of having her called up before the magistrate. Before this could happen, Edna wrote to the commandant to report Clive for keeping a hidden wireless set. On her information, the German police came by and caught him listening to the nine o'clock news. At the time of Robin's writing, Clive was awaiting trial before a German court.[29] It is difficult to imagine relationships marked by such betrayals—mutual in the Robinson case—as recoverable when the war ended.

Knowledge of resistant actions could serve, in rare instances, as opportunity for personal retaliation. But more often, the need for privacy coupled with illegal activities to put extra strain on relationships. Throughout the Occupation, Ken Lewis is at everyone's beck and call to run errands; he is the one to remember to place flowers on his grandmother's grave; he is anguished when he cannot explain away the moral failings of others. Even when Ken and Ralph "dodge" a fellow their age, Dan Mahy, rather than have him walk around with them after chapel (mainly because Ken wanted to show Ralph his new wireless set), Ken felt "sorry for Dan and somehow all the evening I had a guilty conscience of having dodged him."[30] Ken is, in many ways, a pure soul. It is therefore a bit of a relief to see the preternaturally sweet-tempered and accommodating Ken have his brief moment of rebellion.

During the last April before Liberation, an argument occurred between Ken and his parents because Ken did not come in to be sociable when his Uncle Cliff dropped in unannounced. As Ken put it, "he always comes when we prefer to be on our own," and this time he appeared when Ken was listening to the family's hidden wireless. Considering how fast the news was changing with the war reaching its end, it is hard to fault Ken's preference. So, Ken remained where he was and only appeared when Uncle Cliff was in the process of leaving. Yet, this little show of defiant self-interest was short-lived, for "Mum was upset and Dad had a pain in his stomach" brought on by the resulting argument. "Therefore," a chastened Ken concluded, "I must try to put up with him coming."[31] An eighteen-year-old in 1940, Ken was now a young man of twenty-three. Living in close confinement with parents—frozen in time as adolescents in many ways—could not have been easy for many of the young people coming of age during the Occupation.

CRYSTALLIZED CONCERNS

Another interpersonal factor that would direct resistance toward a covert form concerned fear that overt resistance would harm a populace already at considerable risk. Anxiety was a constant companion during the Occupation—for oneself, of course, but much more acutely for one's family and friends. But there emerges in contemporaneous accounts a companion to this personal concern, and that was apprehension for those people and things deemed particularly vulnerable to the occupying forces. In an atmosphere already heavy with a sense of peril, resistance may have increased the threat to those dependent on their fellow Islanders for protection, particularly young women and the elderly. Foremost among these worries would be young women, whether unmarried or separated from their husbands due to the war. In the best of circumstances, the influx of young military men might be reason for concern, as can be seen in the British description of American soldiers stationed in England: "overpaid, oversexed, and over here." Because the occupiers were enemy soldiers, there was apparently an underlying fear that women might be considered spoils of war, much like the other resources of the Island.

This anxiety for young women was not misplaced, if one can believe a statement of witness given to the Guernsey Island Police on September 1, 1940, and now held in the Imperial War Museum archives. Wilma Bishop[32] was a nineteen-year-old woman, married since 1939 to a Guernseyman serving with the British forces. Home for a short leave right before the initial air raid, her husband was stranded in the Island and immediately interned as a prisoner of war in Castle Cornet. Wilma was informed that she could visit her husband if she could obtain a permit, so she went to the Royal Hotel, where she approached several German soldiers standing around. When told what she wanted, the men referred Wilma to a tall soldier in uniform with fair hair and a red face. When told that Wilma needed a permit to visit her husband, he said (in good English), "I will get one for you if you come this way." Leading her down the corridor and up a flight of stairs, he took her along a passage to a door to one of the hotel rooms, which he opened, pushing her inside. Holding her down on the bed, he tore off her knickers, dropped his trousers and—still pinning her hands behind her—he unbuttoned his tunic with his free hand. "If you scream," he said, "I'll shoot you." He raped her, then put on his uniform and left. Wilma straightened her clothing as best she could, and on going downstairs, she came across a Guernsey police constable whom she knew and told him what happened. The police constable informed Dr. Maass, who told Wilma, "I'm very sorry, I'll try and find the man who did it," and she heard him say to the constable, "We cannot let this go on in the Island."

When she visited her husband, Wilma also told him of the attack and, under his advice, she saw their family doctor. Six weeks later, she knew that she was pregnant. All of this was traumatic enough, although the most interesting aspect of the case is the report filed by Inspector Sculpher of the Island Police on the third of September. Dr. W. B. Fox had reported the incident to Inspector Sculpher on August 31, believing that this pregnancy, following as it did a sexual assault, was justification for an abortion (which Dr. Fox was willing to perform). Sculpher "differed from [the doctor] on that point," and it is clear that the inspector did not believe Wilma's account. Although Sculpher admits that Wilma reported the rape immediately to P. C. Tardif and that Dr. Fox examined her at that time, he decided that "her story of the procedure [the rape] is not convincing."

When the Inspector took Wilma back to the Royal Hotel, she could not positively identify the room where the rape occurred, although Mr. Mentha, the manager of the hotel, also confirmed the complaint being made immediately following the incident. Sculpher believed that he never would have learned of the rape if not for the pregnancy, and that finding the soldier should have been "a comparatively simple matter." Sculpher put forth his own theory that the pregnancy was the result of Wilma's relations with her husband before he was detained, and her desire for an abortion was simply an economic matter, since, in conversation with him, Wilma mentioned that she could not afford this new child. These documents are a window not just into the dangers women faced from the occupying forces, but into the skepticism most women encountered in reporting rape. It is difficult to know how many similar incidents occurred throughout the Occupation and how many children resulted from sexual assault.[33]

What is interesting in the contemporaneous accounts is the oblique way that this topic was approached, especially considering that concern over sexual assault was inescapable. Rev. Ord focuses on instances where young women stood up for themselves despite teasing and baiting from German soldiers. In February of 1941, Ord happened to be in a tobacconist's shop when he saw a young female assistant attempting to deal with "two swaggering officers." One officer picked up some trifling item, asking how much it was. When told the price, the officer teasingly said, "That's far too much," at which the girl tossed her head and "with thinly-disguised contempt" replied, "It's the price. I can't alter it." Ord believed that the officers could not see the "danger signals" in her flushed face and black eyes that "looked daggers," which was probably a good thing. "I greatly admired her pluck," wrote Ord, but the officers could easily have turned the girl in for disrespectful communication with the German forces.[34]

Maybe it was a youthful belief in their own invincibility, but some young girls seemed to lack common sense. Two servant girls were caught signaling with a bicycle lamp from the top floors of Ivy Gates, the Sherbrookes' house. When questioned, the girls claimed to be signaling to the Tommies, and told the Germans that they were meeting the Tommy parachutists in Cambridge Park to give them food and water. When the full story emerged, it turns out that this fifteen- and sixteen-year-old were signaling to no one; they merely sent the signals, and a message to the Germans to watch that particular house, as a "leg-pull." One girl appears to have skipped off with an apology, although the other girl was sent to prison in Jersey.[35] Perhaps had these girls read Wilma Bishop's account, they would not have so blithely put themselves in the hands of the Germans.

Equally heedless to possible consequences was the Guernsey girl who threw a bucket of dirty water over a German soldier at the start of the final year of Occupation. The lead-up to this aquatic encounter was not related, although Rev. Ord claimed that "great admiration is felt, and rightly" for the girl's action. The girl herself simply said that she had "always wanted to do just that." Ord believed that her escape with just a warning had much to do with her "frankness and cheerful good humour." Chances are that the soldier was unmistakably out of line in a manner that both the Guernsey and German authorities were invested in preventing.[36] In general, stories of plucky shop assistants, mischievous servant girls, and other young women who refused to tolerate "cheek" from German soldiers bolstered a sense of control and normalcy where none existed. As Ord put it, "When one sees young girls going about unconcerned, the Occupation seems an evil dream."[37]

Matching the fears for young women was a deep concern for the elderly left in the Island. The apparent number of "very old," a term now used for those in their eighties or nineties, left in Guernsey during the Occupation really is staggering when you consider that average life spans were shorter in the 1940s than today. It says something about the high quality of food and physical activity of Islanders during peacetime that so many very old were alive at the start of the Occupation. Granted, the percentage of elderly is skewed, because these were the very people who felt they could not make the evacuation journey into the unknown. Many had a sense that, coming as they were to the final portion of their lives, it was best to ride out the future in familiar surroundings. For some it would be a very short ride.

By August of the first summer of Occupation, Winifred Harvey noted that "several old people have died rather suddenly," among them "Old Dr. Collings" and Mr. Rose, the Presbyterian minister. Colonel Perceval Carey, who had been caught in the streets with Winnie and his wife Doris during the air raid of June 28, was on this short list. Doris came home from a trip into town and found her husband lying on the kitchen floor, dead of a sudden heart attack.[38] Winnie believed that the loss of private cars, leading to unaccustomed bicycling and carrying heavy parcels, combined with anxiety and grief over the deaths of his "lovely dogs" conspired to end the colonel's life prematurely.[39]

Such speculation over whether a natural death of older Islanders, often a heart attack or stroke, could be laid at the feet of the Occupation becomes a notable pattern throughout the contemporaneous narratives. Those who were ill had less opportunity to rest and recover, and some older Islanders pushed themselves, sometimes unnecessarily. During May of 1941, Jack Sauvary's good friend Dr. Jones had a heart attack while standing in the Market fish shop and was taken home by ambulance. By that afternoon, however, he was out in his yard chopping wood. One has to wonder why a doctor would do something so plainly contraindicated for a heart condition.[40] The Doctor, as Jack called him, had another heart attack in October 1942, but Jack ascribed this spell to the stress brought on by Dr. Jones's recent eviction from his home.[41] Jack lavished the Doctor with his concern and any resources that came to hand: picking up the Doctor's rationing coupons,[42] killing the last cockerel he had saved for himself, so the Doctor would have a good Christmas dinner.[43] But the Doctor gave as good as he got, having Jack over to Sunday lunch regularly,[44] and providing a little free medical advice along the way.[45] This was a meeting of minds and resources of two aging widowers and was the type of deepening friendship and mutual concern that older Islanders showed for each other in tenuous times.

In other instances, very elderly Islanders were effectively "adopted" by others in a way that masqueraded as simple friendship. Such was the relationship of Jack Sauvary to Miss Lihou, Mrs. Godfray, and Elsie (Mrs. Godfray's maid). Mrs. Godfray turned eighty-nine in March 1941, and Jack's diary shows how he quickly became her benefactor on the quiet.[46] Jack seems to have had Miss Lihou and Mrs. Godfray in mind much of the time, taking them gifts of flowers, or port (when possible), killing three fowl ("How cruel," Jack says in an aside), and even parting with one of his wife's 1938 Christmas puddings, all to ensure that they had a decent Christmas.[47] In giving them the smelt that had been given to him, along with the sultana cake Mrs. Rowe had baked for him, Jack admitted that he didn't "like to think of these old ladies being short of food at their ages (89 and a few years less)."[48] This was giving out of want, not plenty, for Jack was rapidly losing weight at that time, "a stone since January, *and* my 'Little Mary'," he wrote, using the British slang of the day for stomach.[49]

It was of great concern to Islanders that their oldest citizens were suffering under conditions that broke the health of those much younger. Bill Warry watched an old lady in the Market one day as she casually eyed a "rough-looking" bone lying in the sawdust of the floor. Apparently of little use, it might have been tossed in the direction of a starving dog when no one was looking. The old lady "pleasantly" claimed it for her own, slipping it into her basket. "All helps to make a meal," thought Bill, "but pathetic."[50] If it was heart-rending to watch a stranger suffer, lacking food to give an elderly relative in one's own home must have been emotionally draining. Such was apparently the case with Ambrose Robin as he watched the rapid decline of his eighty-two-year-old Uncle Phil in the summer of 1941. Thus, the simple note one Sunday morning that "Phil had BACON for breakfast" conveys strongly his feeling of triumph in finding a special treat for a loved family member.[51]

Deaths of the elderly often came in clusters, usually at the close of the difficult Occupation winters. Jack noted in January 1941, "We have had lots of deaths lately, old people between 85 and 95."[52] In actual fact, that January was one of the most deadly months of the entire Occupation, second only to January 1945, with a death rate of 41.1 per 1,000.[53] The following winter, which was very cold, there were 182 deaths in January and February alone.[54] Even before the starvation period of the final year of Occupation, malnutrition was taking its toll on older Islanders. Elizabeth Doig wrote in April 23, 1944, "Oh! how this war drags on, so many people are dying here from malnutrition, especially elderly people who cannot get about to find food."[55]

In losing their oldest citizens, Guernseymen and women could sense their history slipping away from them. This is one reason that the deaths of the elderly held almost as much symbolic as personal meaning. In one fortnight in March 1943, the Island lost two of its mainstays. Many of the diarists mention the passing at age eighty-eight of Mr. Gervase F. Peek, a man described, almost universally it seems, as "the grand old man" of Guernsey. Bill Warry carefully pasted in his scrapbook the funeral notice and a newspaper picture of Mr. Peek, noting that he was "an old friend & *one of the best*."[56] For Jack Sauvary, a more wrenching loss came hard on the heels of this death. On April 12, the Doctor passed away. Jack had watched as his friend faced his impending death with equanimity, slowly weakening until his heart finally gave out. Like Mr. Peek, Dr. Jones was a key member of the community, and as Jack put it, "All the old landmarks now seem to be dropping out."[57]

If human landmarks were disappearing, so too were the physical landmarks of their beautiful island home. The Island of Guernsey joined young women and the elderly as a major concern for the Islanders, seeming particularly vulnerable to destruction by the Germans. Kitty Bachmann watched with deep concern as the Germans dug themselves in and "the Island [was] slowly but surely being absorbed into their War Machine."[58] It was the "desecration of our 'Sarnia Chérie,'" she said, referring to the National Anthem of Guernsey ("Sarnia; dear Homeland, Gem of the sea. Island of beauty, my heart longs for thee . . ."). The concrete bunkers and fortifications that they built, particularly all along the coast, were "grotesque" and seemingly designed to be "as lasting as the pyramids."[59] Would the Island ever recover from what Jack Sauvary called the Germans' "concrete complex"?[60] This concern was justified, for the concrete fortifications, tunnels, and watchtowers are still much in evidence in the Island of Guernsey. Immediately following the war, Islanders may have wanted to remove these physical artifacts of the Occupation, but were in no position to expend the money and effort. Today's Islanders have melded them into the history of the Island with a relatively new initiative, Festung Guernsey, dedicated to preserving the fortifications and making them available to academics and historic societies for study.

What is absorbing history for later generations was simply pain and loss for occupied Guernsey. Kitty Bachmann could only pray that the end of the war would come "before the face of Guernsey is changed beyond recognition." And her use of the term "face" is appropriate, for the Island is generally described much like a person subject to disfigurement. It was, in Bert Williams's estimation, no less than the "mutilation of Guernsey."[61] Peter Bachmann came home one day to describe what he called "the Crowning Horror," a new expanse of road that would reach across the beautiful common land and stretch from Fort Le Marchant to Les Fontenelles.[62] The biggest problem was not what the Germans were constructing, but what they were destroying in their tendency to "knock down anything in their way."[63] Whether it was massive, ancient trees, the Weighbridge railings,[64] or the demolition of historic old homes,[65] the Germans merely plowed through anything that intervened between point A and point B.[66]

On December 7, 1943, came "the last straw,"[67] with the destruction of the Delancey Monument, a memorial built in 1876 to Admiral Lord de Saumarez, considered Guernsey's most distinguished sailor. The States were able to remove the bronze plaques on the plinth of the monument, although they were unable to prevent its destruction, because the monument was in the way of some big guns that the Germans were installing in the park. "But what destruction!" mourned Jack. "That beautiful monument and such a wonderful piece of work, all of Guernsey granite, and all done by Guernsey workmen."[68] There was general despair that such an important and historic landmark, so prominent that pilots used it to get their bearings when flying on the east coast of the Island, could be so irrevocably destroyed. As Jack put it, "Now it is no more."[69]

The final crystallized point of anxiety appearing often in contemporaneous narratives was the fate of the Island's animals, particularly the family dogs and cats that had not been euthanized in the pre-evacuation tumult. This was not a frivolous concern in a nation of animal lovers, and the absence of their children made many Islanders cling to their family pets. Winifred Harvey's grief and guilt over Rolf never fully abated,[70] and even when upset over the German destruction of the Island, Rolf was never far from her mind. She bemoaned the same road being driven through the Island that upset Peter Bachmann, in part because they "blasted right through the little old quarry there, one of Rolf's favorite walks in the happy days."[71] One year into the Occupation, Winnie counted her blessings that she still had food and was, at that point, still in her home. "Courage, Faith, and Endurance," she writes. Yet her next thought is, "Rolfie has been gone a year and I miss him still all the time, my dear little friend."[72]

In some ways, their animals stood proxy for all the constraints and deprivations that the Islanders were undergoing themselves, except that their pets' helplessness and dependency made every hardship that much more acute. Because the Germans were bringing dogs over from France, there was a new danger of rabies, something that did not normally concern Guernsey. In fact, Ken Lewis speaks of it as something totally unfamiliar, putting the term in quotation marks, as you might a foreign or slang term, when he described the fear that Guernsey dogs "might get 'Rabies' a continental disease." The order went out in December 1940 that Guernsey dogs were to be on leads, and that any dog running loose and entering a public thoroughfare was liable to be shot.[73] Since Islanders had adjusted to the lack of cars by riding bicycles with their dogs running beside them, this meant that the dogs would be tethered loosely on long leads to the bicycles, a dangerous proposition all the way around.[74]

Particularly aggravating to Ambrose Robin was the sight of officers and soldiers strolling about the town with their own dogs unleashed. In the meantime, Robin's dog, Tim, was forced "to remain tethered to me in a country lane. This makes me wild."[75] This anger at an order that had at least some basis in public safety points up the symbolic identification Islanders felt with their pets. Both animals and people were constrained in movement and liberty, and the orders for their own safety, whether leashing pets or forbidding Islanders from entry to mined beaches, were only necessary because of the dangers that the Germans themselves had brought to the Island. The occupied populace connected the fate of their pets to their own change in fortune, to the loss of their contented lives before the Occupation, and to their current position as prisoners in their own land. These mental links were best expressed when Ambrose Robin described his "painful decision to part with another chum," on the day in April 1942 when he walked Tim across the street to have him destroyed. His sorrow over this "miserable experience" was heightened by his angry certainty that "under normal conditions recovery would have been easy." Then, too, Tim was not only Robin's "faithful chum," but was considered "one of the links with the children," now so far away.[76]

Food was the greatest issue, for how could starving people, particularly in the final famine year of Occupation, justify feeding a family pet? Dorothy Higgs's two cats and Tim (seemingly a popular canine moniker) each found their own methods to make do. Tinker was a talented mouser, useful for their new rural location, and Tim scrounged for stolen scraps in the neighborhood. Dorothy believed he had good luck at "the Jerries' mess." But "poor old Bingo often cries almost all day. Gosh it's *beastly*—worse than being hungry yourself."[77] Animals were fed on scraps or inventive concoctions that humans had difficulty stomaching. So, Kitty Bachmann described the pungent and "briny tang" that permeated the whole house as she cooked dinner for their dog Kala. "The poor little blighter is clinging to life, as his present diet of limpets did before we prised them off the rocks."[78]

Although some forms of limpets (ormers, for example) are considered delicacies by Islanders, such was not their opinion of the common little limpets that clung to the Guernsey rocks. Generally they were just too smelly and tough for human consumption. This view changed for some as hunger set in, and soon the pet population had some competition for this food source. By February 1941, Jack Sauvary described the beaches on the Front, the local name for a section of the east coast, as cleared of limpets as they became yet another found food for the population. Still, most people gathered them to feed their pets, as did Jack's friend Miss Matthews, who had eight cats and (no surprise) was having difficulty feeding them. Jack, usually understanding of other's foibles, wrote, "There is one remedy?"[79] These cats, like most pets, had little chance of survival because they lived on skim milk, limpets, and the bread that came from Miss Matthews's rations. In Jack's estimation, "She has been mad to keep them so long."[80]

Many, over the five years, took the last loving step of ending the suffering of starving animals. Gertie Corbin wrote as early as February 1941 of seven neighborhood dogs being destroyed, "including Ranger," because there simply was no food for them.[81] Yet the decision to end a loved pet's life would be hard for all Islanders, especially those with evacuated children. Morale through these years was maintained by a belief that the war would turn, the Occupation would end, and the Islanders' children would return home. Part of the mental fantasy of that longed-for reunion included seeing their children greeted by the pets they left behind, the family circle restored once again as it was. Taking a pet to be euthanized was tantamount to abandoning this dream and the hope that it represented.

The dangers posed to those perceived as most vulnerable—young girls, the elderly, the Island itself, and even family pets—made the rest of the Islanders conscious of their role as protectors and caretakers. An unwillingness to further aggravate a dangerous situation made caution the watchword even when opposing the unpredictable occupiers in their midst. That these dangers were not chimerical was proven by the increased number of deaths during these years. Death caused either directly by the German forces or indirectly through the living conditions of the Occupation became the ultimate cost paid by some who had remained in Guernsey in 1940. For their families and friends, it was the fundamental tear in the fabric of interpersonal relationships.

THE ULTIMATE LOSS

Trying to achieve an accurate sense of the death rate directly attributable to the Occupation is not easy, but it is important to our understanding of the rending of human ties among Islanders and the impact on their lives. Hazel Knowles Smith does a nice job of trying to ferret out the mortality rate actually caused by the Occupation, a task complicated by the large number of elderly that had remained in Guernsey. Knowles Smith takes the four-year period from the start of 1941 to the end of 1944 and determines that out of a population of roughly 23,000 there were at least 1,810 deaths. There is a clear underlying logic to the choice of this four-year period, because it avoids counting the many deaths of the elderly and seriously ill that occurred during the first six months of Occupation. Some Islanders would have been too ill or frail to evacuate and could, in effect, be considered already dying in June of 1940. Although they might have lingered for a number of months, their deaths could not be attributed to the Occupation with any clarity. Also, during the relatively benign velvet glove period, the change in food rationing, although causing Islanders to lose weight rapidly, would be unlikely to affect the death rate substantially. The disadvantage in using this four-year period is that it obviously does not include the thirty-four dead from the violent air raid that ushered in the Occupation. Nor does it count the many deaths, violent and otherwise, that occurred from January to May of 1945. Knowles Smith mentions that January 1945 accounted for an additional eighty-plus deaths in that month alone.[82]

Knowles Smith and other historians are wise, however, to take this conservative view of the death rate in Guernsey during the Occupation. In any population of 23,000 to 25,000, there will be a natural rate of mortality, and this rate would likely be heightened by a population with a substantial number of elderly. Yet, the death rate was "consistently higher" during the Occupation than during the years prior to June 1940,[83] and this heightened mortality stretched across many demographics, not merely the elderly. Serious illnesses and deaths became major topics for consternation in contemporaneous accounts. In the bleak and bitterly cold winter of 1942, a number of people reported to the hospitals with the symptoms of starvation, only to be too far gone for the doctors to help them. "Why did they not come earlier?" wondered Ord. "Who, they ask, is to look after the others at home?" This was yet another example of the highest value being placed on relationships and the need to care for others. One of the sisters in the hospital ward told the reverend that five patients had "simply faded out" that week alone because they lacked food, and possibly could not have been saved even had they reported to the hospital promptly.[84]

In the spring of 1942, Dr. Symons told Winifred Harvey about the increased number of people dying with "the hunger oedoema," the swelling of the stomach that signaled malnutrition. Winnie saw for herself the terrible toll of starvation that April when she visited the hospital and saw four men dying of malnutrition, one of them apparently a young man whom she knew. In order to have additional fats provided through whole milk, as opposed to rationed skim milk devoid of milk fat, an individual had to appear before the Essential Commodities Committee and give proof of special medical need. Only pregnant women seem to have had an automatic right to these extra fats, and doctors had to choose from among those in the most need and support their case for special treatment.[85]

Malnutrition was the wedge that opened the way for disease, weakening Islanders and sparking some peculiar spates of nonfatal illness. Jack Sauvary mentioned in May 1942 that over 50 percent in his community of St. Sampson had developed shingles on some part of their body. This painful condition, a recurrence of the chicken-pox virus that attacks nerve endings, was apparently triggered by "poor food," in Jack's estimation.[86] Although vitamin deficiency led to odd mini-epidemics, dysentery during the Occupation was so widespread that it was simply called "the universal complaint." Even a minor attack could cause weakness that extended days or weeks, with Winifred Harvey describing herself as "dead tired" long after a brief bout.[87] A more serious attack like that suffered by Elizabeth Doig led to six days in the Emergency Hospital and two weeks in a nursing home.[88]

When a particularly widespread wave of dysentery sent many to the hospital in November of 1941, there were numerous operations performed for rupture at the same time. Chances are great that the repeated strain on stomach muscles was caused by dysentery.[89] Almost everyone had the "Guernsey Bug," and its embarrassing nature led to some management through humor. Kitty Bachmann described her family, always "grasping at straws for a chance of merriment, however ribald," as delighted over the conversation recounted by one "fastidious old lady." Suffering from the universal complaint, she asked her doctor to "restore her dignity." The doctor demurred, saying that he had no cure, not even for himself. "O but doctor," the old woman exclaimed, "it's so odorous!" Needless to say, this became a catchphrase in the Bachmann family, applied happily to any number of situations.[90]

What is not apparent in this humor is Islanders' knowledge that dysentery was the gateway condition for fatal disease. Even in today's climate of advanced medicine, it remains a devastating killer in much of the world. Existing health problems were aggravated by dysentery, and it proved often to be the tipping point. Peter Bachmann's father never recovered from the dysentery he suffered during the summer of 1941, and it combined with his long-standing diabetes until he simply "wasted away."[91]

The poor diet and dysentery were deadly for many, particularly in cases of diphtheria[92] and tuberculosis.[93] Death played by its own peculiar rules in who succumbed and who survived. So, in the final August of Occupation, Mrs. Godfray, then ninety-three, worked with Jack Sauvary to arrange the burial of her twenty-one-year-old niece who had died from tuberculosis.[94] Some Islanders evacuated in 1940 because they were aware of an existing health condition. Some did not but should have. So it was with the Bachmanns' good friend Tom Bennett, who died when his remaining good kidney failed. He simply did not respond to whatever treatment could be cobbled together in Guernsey, and Kitty counted him as one who should have accompanied his wife and children in the

1940 evacuation.[95] Yet no one could anticipate the serious illnesses that would develop over the five years of Occupation, many of which could not be handled in Guernsey but might have been treatable in England. More than one family was burdened with watching a family member die, believing that better treatment was tantalizingly near on the other side of the Channel.

Some of the violent deaths of the Occupation occurred simply because of the armed soldiers living amidst the civilian population. Where there are guns and young soldiers, there are bound to be fatal accidents. Gertie Corbin's Uncle Ernie Brouard died in November 1941 because he had the misfortune to have a German officer billeted on him in the bedroom directly above the sitting room. Mr. and Mrs. Brouard were having a quiet evening before their fire, unaware that the officer in his bedroom overhead was cleaning his gun. The gun discharged accidentally, and the bullet penetrated the floor of the bedroom and the ceiling of the room below, killing Mr. Brouard as he sat in his easy chair. The Brouards were not prominent in the Island, but the community rallied around Mrs. Brouard, seeing in her sudden widowhood the same threat that they all faced from armed, billeted men. When Quertier Le Pelley, the Guernsey magistrate presiding over the inquest, absolved the German of all blame, a brief flare of indignation swept the local community.[96]

The German soldiers also indulged in the habit of discharging their revolvers randomly in celebration of the New Year. The Guernsey populace learned to stay inside on New Year's Eve after an Islander was killed in 1941 by a stray celebratory shot.[97] Some of these shootings were not clearly accidental, and sheltering in one's own home did not necessarily provide protection. In January 1942, a man named Fisher watched as half a dozen Germans left his house after an impromptu party. Looking for a place to celebrate, they had earlier "gate-crashed" his house, bringing with them a number of bottles of liquor. As Fisher stood in his own doorway, watching them depart, a revolver bullet killed him. It is unclear from the accounts whether this was another stray bullet shot off in celebration or a deliberate act, perhaps after angry words were exchanged.[98]

The ormering season seemed a time of particular danger, beginning with the first spring of Occupation. On Easter Sunday, April 13, 1941, an ormering party of five men managed to convince two fishermen from l'Islet to ferry them to the outlying rocks of Saints Bay, an area in the forbidden zone. The fishermen dropped the men off on the rocks and left in the larger boat, leaving behind a nine-foot punt, a type of flat-bottomed boat. As the men headed up the beach, one of the German sentries warned them off with a shot and then a series of three rapid shots in warning. The men "lost their heads," in Ambrose Robin's opinion, and the five of them clambered into the flat boat, setting off into the middle of the bay. Swiftly, the small punt filled with water and overturned. Three men drowned and their bodies were never recovered. The fishermen who had dropped the men off earlier saw what was happening and returned in time to rescue the two remaining men.[99]

Although these men seem to have unnecessarily put themselves in harm's way (Ambrose Robin called it a "stupid business"), later deaths caused by the mines surrounding Guernsey were the result of more calculated, and desperate, attempts to augment the dwindling food supply. In February of 1943, Gertie Corbin, in her terse way, mentioned the death of "Elvina's nephew, nice boy 18, killed while ormering, a mine exploded."[100] Arthur Mauger elaborated on the details that it was a group of men from the Gallienne family who decided to take the risk to go ormering. On the way down to the beach, it was the father who struck a mine, the resulting explosion killing his only son and wounding all the rest in the party. By this time, the crisis in food was acute enough that these deaths were considered "a sad accident" rather than a risky gamble.[101]

That June, proof emerged that the mines surrounding Guernsey could be deadly to those doing their job in the correct way. The Quinain brothers were fishermen out in their boat off the Humps with two other men when they found themselves caught on some ropes or cords. Believing it to be a lost net, they were untangling the boat when they pulled up a black object. It was a mine, one that exploded immediately, blowing the boat to pieces and killing the two men with the Quinain brothers. The brothers managed to hold onto some floating debris and were picked up by fishermen who had been in a boat some distance away. It was not merely the tragic loss of life that affected the Island, but the loss of a large boat and skilled fishermen during a time when fish was so necessary to sustaining life.[102]

Mines also posed a threat for anyone who strayed into particular portions of the Island, and this was a source of worry for those with children or with elderly parents. On December 6, 1942, ninety-two-year-old Henry Robillard of Castel died of injuries sustained in a minefield. He had gone for a walk alone, so it was difficult to say what led him into the mined field, although his family had frequently reminded him about the dangers of that area. This did not seem to be a case of senile dementia, for Henry's mind was described in the newspaper account as "quite clear," and he still served as the primary cook for the family. Bill Warry confirmed this assessment in his comments beside the news article: "Old Harry was as game as a pebble right up to his death . . . & as lively as a good many young men."[103] A child's excitement or a momentary lapse in an older person could lead them into an area once open to them but now potentially deadly.

It was not simply German guns and mines that posed a danger to Islanders. The roads of Guernsey are narrow and treacherous still today; they definitely were not designed for large German lorries, sometimes driven at a breakneck speed by the soldiers. Often the lorries would come up quickly, sometimes around a curve, and strike a bicyclist from behind without warning. Even when civilians saw lorries bearing down on them, there was little opportunity to get out of the way because of the stone walls edging many of the roads.[104] Some of the stories of these deaths were particularly tragic, such as the six-year-old child crushed to death by a tractor hauling one of the gigantic German guns through Ville-au-Roi.[105] German soldiers often went unpunished for their reckless driving, which also meant that the same men were out again driving on the same roads.[106]

Rev. Ord experienced the horror of sudden death face-to-face on a day in September 1943. He and Grae had met two friends, Mrs. Pearsall and Mr. H. G. Jackson, in St. Peter Port for their usual cup of what was currently passing for coffee. The Ords walked their friends to the foot of the hill leading to Fort George and were standing talking when a huge Luftwaffe groundsman came careening around a sharp bend in the road on a bicycle, clearly out of control. Ord just happened to turn at that moment, a move that probably saved him, and shouted, "Watch out!" The bicyclist struck Mr. Jackson full in the face, breaking the Guernseyman's neck—an injury from which Mr. Jackson never regained consciousness. The Luftwaffe man was also injured and knocked unconscious. As the distraught Ords and Mrs. Pearsall waited at the scene for a doctor, a car containing Von Schmettow happened by. The four German officers walked over to look at the German lying senseless in the road, then silently returned to the car and left. They spared not even a glance for Mr. Jackson. That such a close friend could be lost so suddenly to the actions of a "drunken sot" devastated Ord, and the loss made Guernsey seem still more of a prison.[107]

The curfew imposed in Guernsey also took its toll, because it led to an extended period at night when medical help was difficult, if not impossible, to come by. An inquest was held into the death of a stillborn child in 1941 because the curfew regulations kept the husband from obtaining a nurse or doctor to attend his wife when she went into labor in the middle of the night. The husband, aided by "a rather helpless old woman," was forced to serve as midwife, with disastrous results.[108] Would the child have been stillborn under normal peacetime conditions? Quite possibly. However, the Islanders attributed this death and many others to the conditions imposed by their German masters, and these attributions became part of their sense-making process.

This search for an external attribution tied to the conditions of the Occupation can be seen in the death of George Dorey. On November 22, 1941, Rev. Ord was conducting services at Brock Road when he heard the sound of a chair overturning and a thud. When he looked toward the place where Grae had been standing, he saw that she had moved to help someone who seemed to have fallen. George Dorey had simply collapsed in place and was dead before he reached the ground. In letters to his wife, Winnie—some as far back as 1917—George had made clear that he did not expect a long life on account of his heart. Most people knew of his tenuous health, yet still attributed his sudden death to the Occupation. Jack Sauvary pondered whether the Doreys' recent eviction (coupled with the shock of the death of George's father and poor nutrition) might have caused his heart to fail. Rev. Ord believed the strain to have been from the loss of George's car, and his need to use a bicycle to get around. Even Ambrose Robin, who had known George since 1901, when George had slept in the next bed in the Number 13 dormitory of the Oxenford House School, cited the long walk the Doreys had to make that morning from Fort Road to reach the Brock Road Church. Despite George Dorey's chronic illness, Rev. Ord believed that these aggravating circumstances meant "this good man is another Occupation casualty."[109]

When Islanders affixed blame for apparently natural deaths on the conditions of the Occupation, they responded as people living "on the inside" of unusual circumstances. They could gauge their own level of tiredness, hunger, and physical strain, and this personal knowledge led them to understand how such factors could turn a serious health concern into a fatal one. Whether reacting to deaths caused by want or by violence, Islanders revealed their sensitivity to the perils caused by the German presence on their soil. They knew, too, that any acts on their part might lead to hostage-taking, executions, or long sentences and possible death in French or German prisons. Some aspects of interpersonal life in Guernsey were potential dampers on the cultivation of resistance: the lack of privacy in communal living, the concern over retaliation against the more vulnerable in the community, and the heightened sense of threat as the death toll rose. Instead of smothering resistance, however, these factors shaped subversive efforts into a covert and rhetorical form.

Other factors of interpersonal life enhanced the likelihood of resistance. For one thing, it was important for Islanders to meet the increasing crisis of food deprivation and to do so in a way that enhanced cooperation rather than competition over scarce resources. Stories of "making do," of a resourceful people meeting the challenges with cleverness and bravery, comprise many of the memories of those who lived through the Occupation. These stories are the primary focus of many of the published accounts of the period, nonfiction and fiction alike. More important to this study, an assurance of interpersonal support was the first component vital to finding safe spaces for the development of a resistant discourse.

THE SKELETON SOCIETY

Even a cursory reading of the diaries of Occupation challenges the concept that the Channel Islands were a safe and comfortable haven from the rigors of war. Rationing, of course, was immediate, and at first there were long, long queues for the last little luxuries such as cakes or scones.[110] But this quickly became far more grim, and the queues that were reported generally constituted a wait in vain: fifty people waiting as one dogfish was being skinned (and not enough, Jack believed, for a quarter of them),[111] or women trudging back in the rain from a long wait at the Market with only a head of lettuce in their baskets, their sole acquisition for the weekend.[112] One day, Jack came across hundreds of bicycles, a pile six and eight deep, at St. Sampson's Bridge. People had simply jumped from their bicycles, throwing them down wherever they happened to land, to join an endless queue in order to get sixpence worth of egg powder.[113] Elizabeth Doig described the "pathetic" sight of women standing in a street where potatoes were being delivered to the Germans, waiting in the hope that they could collect any that fell from the cart.[114] And once in a while, these long waits led to short tempers. There was a tussle one day in early 1941 in the fish market, and Mrs. Dredge, the local fishmonger, was slapped in the face with a whiting. There had been a long queue, and Mrs. Dredge simply did not have enough fish available to meet the demand. This shortage was hardly surprising since the Germans had a standing order for a certain quantity of the fish that came in. Bill Warry later estimated that the Germans took 25 percent immediately—more whenever they wished—and all of the best fish (whiting, mackerel, etc.), leaving only whatever was left for the locals.[115] Mrs. Dredge had no choice but to take these orders into account and leave the German fish untouched. All that the people standing in line knew was that they had waited a long time, and fish were still apparently available in the shop.[116]

What seems remarkable is how little actual disorder and panic there was and how people maintained the structure of society when, quite simply, they were "always feeling hungry."[117] Kitty Bachmann observed as early as 1941 that "those who kept their children here must be very worried indeed," as the bread ration plummeted, the milk was watered down to a blue sheen, and an egg was "more precious than gold."[118] Concern for family members could easily have fueled a desperation leading to widespread lawlessness. Instead, Islanders turned to old solutions such as gleaning in the fields after harvest.[119] Children also learned new means to forage for food—and there was some concern that in the odd circumstances under which they were growing up, they could lose their moral values. Rev. Ord described in 1943 how a grower caught several children raiding his flower garden, taking blooms to make into bouquets. The children had learned that they could trade these bouquets to the Germans for bread.[120] The fact that children went to such lengths, not for candy or some other superfluous treat but for a basic staple of life, gives some insight into the problem of hunger even before the final year.

Children actually looked better than the adults, simply because they took precedence when it came to food in the average household.[121] This did not mean that they were getting adequate nutrition, simply that their relatives sacrificed their own health to guarantee that their children had something to eat. And this was the story across the Island as individuals secretly slipped additional portions of food to those whom they loved. Douglas Ord was very plain-spoken about this issue of secret sacrifice: "I watch G. like a hawk lest she deprive herself of food in my favour."[122] Dorothy Higgs took a comical view of her own weight loss—"I have almost a pre-1914 figure now"—while at the same time fretting, "But I wish Frank would fatten up a bit."[123] And Kitty Bachmann also was concerned over her husband, Peter, a man of ample proportions ("generously upholstered" as Kitty put it) before the Occupation who was now discovering "bones hitherto concealed." Probably to ease her mind, Peter claimed that he felt better with the weight loss, but Kitty believed that the weight reduction was too sudden to be healthy.[124]

Particularly disturbing was the sight of their countrymen turning from "scarecrows" in 1942 to "skeletons only" by 1944. Bill Warry said that he often passed people in the street whom he knew well but didn't recognize because they had changed so much.[125] As the joke went, Guernseymen and women had their own version of the S.S., the "Skeleton Society."[126] Worse still, in Ord's view, all of these physical signs of hardship were juxtaposed against the comparative robustness of the German troops, who seemed to have "'fair round bellies,' if not 'with good capon lined.'"[127] Under these conditions, food became an obsession. Even during the benign first six months of Occupation, Winifred Harvey likened most conversations to those held on Antarctic expeditions, because they all revolved around food.[128] Dorothy Higgs suddenly interrupted her diary in mid-1943 with the expostulation, "BLOW! I WON'T talk about food!"[129] Of course, she was back to the same topic in the very next entry.

Although there was little of comfort food or drink available, Islanders did still use what they had as a measure of solace in difficult situations. It was only a month after Ambrose Robin had been so excited to give his Uncle Phil a treat of bacon for breakfast that Robin awakened in the night with pain in his blind right eye. He could see that the nurse who was in to care for Phil had the light on, and soon after four, the nurse called his name. Quickly he awakened his wife Amy and Aunt Adele, and they all "were just in time to see dear old Phil breathe his last." While the nurse and Amy laid Phil out, preparing the body as people had always done, Robin went down to the kitchen to make a cup of genuine tea for all, which they drank in Aunt Adele's room. Real tea, so rare as to be almost like medicine, was to be used under just this kind of duress, as the cure-all for shock and the means of comfort.[130]

More often, food was a means to communicate love. Islanders planned for months and scrounged what they could to show their affection for others, particularly on key occasions such as birthdays or Christmas. When Ken Lewis turned twenty on February 9, 1942, he received modest gifts. But, oh, what a birthday tea he had! Ken wrote with relish about the "boiled potatoes, tongue, golden plums in heavy syrup which had jellified, with a whipped Orange Jelly, pancakes crumbled in the pan, Barley Rolls and Auntie Ethel Le Page made a plain cake coated with choc. icing w/ K. L. in icing made w/ butter and sugar." This was a truly remarkable spread, and it must have been a concerted group effort of saving back rations and pulling out jealously guarded tins and jelly dating from before the Occupation. But Ken's delight is so apparent as he lovingly recounted the meal ("It was the best feed I had had in some time") that everyone must have believed it well worth the effort.[131]

The telling aspect to such stories is how pathetically rare they were. Any extra food that a family could obtain was more a source of guilt than of triumph. One thing emerges with clarity about the food situation during the Occupation: the hardship was not evenly distributed across the Island. It was much the same as during the American Great Depression; the advantage lay with those who could grow their own food.[132] As a rurally raised Guernseyman mentioned to me a few years ago, "For townspeople, it must have been hell."[133] This basic inequity was apparent to all, as the means of survival lay with having some land resources, perhaps even a decent back garden, or with having the possessions/money to augment one's rations through barter or the black market. The worst suffering would fall on those of average to below-average economic resources living in town.[134] "I don't know how people live," wrote Jack. "People like myself are lucky to have ground."[135]

Dorothy Higgs, whose entire day was made up of raising food, milking goats, and devising and publishing unusual recipes in the paper to help the Island cope with shortages, was doing well for her family. However, she worried constantly about those without the "private resources" of land. More than once she wrote to the effect that "It makes one feel so ashamed of having a bit extra."[136] At the same time, she was giving away goat's milk and then goats themselves to her sister Muriel (nicknamed Mu), who kept the sick in the neighborhood supplied with milk. When a hen was killed, there was meat and broth to be sent to the hospital.[137] Once in a while a particular need would come to light. The milk woman told Mu one day in the bleak March of 1944 of finding a seventy-six-year-old woman weeping by her empty grate because she did not have breakfast of any kind to give her nineteen-year-old grandson, and there was nothing to be had for his dinner that night as well. It was a Monday, and bread was not given except on Tuesday, Thursday, and Saturday. A weekly grocery ration was given on Tuesday, and it simply did not come close to lasting the week. Dorothy decided to send this woman carrots every Sunday and whatever bread they could spare to get her through Mondays, "but there must be hundreds more like her that we can't help."[138]

All of these little efforts were drops in the ocean, and the Islanders knew it. One March when potatoes were scarce, ten people came to Jack's door one day to see if he had any spuds to spare. He had given 10 lbs. to Martel, 15 to Tom Roberts, 8 to Pattimore and 4 lbs. to Miss Matthews, but, as he said, "I cannot continue at this rate." Although it was "awful to have to refuse," there was little else he could do.[139] Hunger was often kept a private issue, and in a land where all the civilians looked like ragged skeletons, it was difficult to tell who was in immediate danger of starvation. Many would not burden others with their suffering; if they were helped, they would be taking food out of the mouths of their benefactors. Sometimes the problem was not starvation but the more hidden danger of malnutrition. The tendency would be to "fill up," if at all possible, on anything available, and the person still might not get the nutrition needed to survive.

Thus, a reader can feel the palpable horror that Dorothy Higgs felt when her "little gnome of a gardener" died of starvation. This death actually occurred during 1945, when starvation was very high, but it still came as a shock. Dorothy had given him a good bowl of soup each day at lunchtime, and it can be assumed from her surprise at his death that he did not complain more of hunger or look thinner than anyone else. Dorothy had earlier described him as "definitely simple,"[140] and, trying to understand his death, she pondered that perhaps "it takes intelligence to manage the rations." She also knew that her gardener was a "feckless creature" likely to spend any cash he had (or trade any food) for tobacco, and his landlady was "a proper slut" who did nothing to look out for him. But all of this reasoning was to no avail; Dorothy apparently blamed herself for not seeing signs of his impending death, even though such signs probably did not exist.[141]

Another source of guilt over suffering that the Islanders could not prevent was found in the distant relationship between the populace and Organization Todt workers. These forced workers (slave labor) brought to the Island by the Nazis triggered both pity and fear in Guernseymen and women. Forced to survive on "sour German bread and watery soup," compared to which Guernsey rations were "luxurious fare,"[142] they were barely alive and "devilishly hungry"[143] all the time. Jack Sauvary learned from the sanitary inspector that these impressed workers from the defeated nations were dying at a rate of fifteen per month.[144]

Gertie Corbin wrote that "foreigners"—the general Island reference to forced workers, many Dutch and French, that differentiated them from the Germans—were constantly begging for food at their door.[145] The sight of these men tore at the hearts of Islanders. In November 1942, a group of Frenchmen were brought over, forced to camp out overnight in Havelet in the rain, and then "marched up Havelet by fat Germans; they were white and shivering; their thin coats soaked through." The scene that day at the Market, which Winifred Harvey went on to describe, was "tragic." People responded with a sympathetic outpouring, giving coffee or food from their own small rations to these poor men, many elderly or young boys of thirteen or fourteen.[146]

Through the treatment of the Organization Todt workers, Islanders could glimpse the dark cruelty of the Germans, an underlying evil that would only fully come to light with the 1945 liberation of the concentration camps. Their deepest fear was that their own men and boys would suffer the same fate. Many tried to help the OT workers, but were simply overwhelmed with the extent of the need. Kitty described how these "poor, half-starved slaves roam the streets in a ragged and filthy condition," going from door to door in the hope of finding food. Kitty would give a couple of them a bowl of soup, only to find a dozen waiting on the doorstep the next day. Just lack of provisions meant that she had to turn them away, distressed to know that they would find the same situation at the next house they approached.[147]

Yet there is another side to the Islanders' relationship with these tattered wretches whom they saw but did not know. They legitimately had much to fear from these slaves who seemed adept at slipping away from their captors to try to find food by one means or another. First, the OT workers were considered a health threat, spreading lice wherever they went, so that some Islanders would no longer sit on public benches, and they were believed to be the source of the waves of strange illnesses that seemed to sweep through Guernsey.[148] The outbreak of typhus, a disease vectored by lice and fleas, among the workers in early 1943 caused great concern, in part for the workers but also for the Islanders. Weakened by hunger, the average person would have difficulty surviving the high fevers of typhus, and an epidemic could be devastating.[149]

The Islanders did not blame the slave workers for their filth, disease, and need to beg, because these conditions were imposed on them by their German masters. They *did* blame them for situations where, as Kitty Bachmann wrote, "local benevolence towards these poor unfortunates has sometimes been rewarded with villainy." An elderly woman several doors up from Kitty had two Organization Todt workers visit her. As she answered the front door to the first of the pair, the other man slid around to enter her back door and steal her handbag.[150] Even sympathetic Islanders had an uneasy feeling around the forced laborers, fueled by accounts of assaults and thefts and aggravated by the workers' sheer numbers and any language barriers. Jack Sauvary wrote of passing a number of OT workers lined up for their evening meal on Christmas Eve, 1942. It was "dark as a grave," and Jack "was almost afraid passing as they might have bagged me in the lane and taken my bicycle." He could hear them talking all around him, but could not understand what they were saying ("Talk about chatter. It was like a lot of ducks"), an uncertainty that only heightened his sense of threat.[151] It was difficult to know how to respond to these slave workers, simultaneously so pathetic and yet so threatening in their desperate need to survive.

Whether through the suffering of the Organization Todt workers or the grinding hunger of family, friends, and neighbors, not to mention themselves, Islanders could readily see the effects of malnutrition throughout the first four years of the Occupation. They were worn down by a low caloric intake, a lack of vitamins, and a loss of calcium that made them subject to fractures. Even before conditions were at their worst, Islanders were unable to fight off disease, and the way was cleared for illness and early death. In the face of such deprivation, a dark contending for food could have emerged. This would have rent the community, negating any possibility of resistance and possibly leading to widespread collaboration with the simple goal of survival. Instead, what surfaced was enhanced cooperation, a determination that the whole community survive, and a banding together to find creative solutions. By taking this approach, Islanders established the first pillar on which to build resistance: the belief that they could rely on the goodwill and support of their neighbors. The second pillar supporting resistance would also be communal: the construction of a common ideology that Guernseymen and women could pit directly against the beliefs of their Nazi masters.

PATRIOT GAMES

It was July of 1940 at St. Sampson's Bridge, and three women were embroiled in a private battle. They had been involved in a discussion of the war situation when one woman innocently prefaced her remarks with, "If we win . . ." One of the other women immediately pounced on this phrase, shouting, "*If* we win, don't you say that. It's *when* we win." At that point, Jack Sauvary passed by the women, and the appeal was directed his way, "What do you think this awful woman is saying—If we win, IF we win. Of course we will win and don't say that again." Jack figured that it was just about time to laugh at this fervor, so he quietly took his departure.[152]

Even if the woman who accosted Jack was somewhat overwrought in her desire to impose the proper attitude on others, this process of "identity construction" was actually a necessary forerunner to the establishment of resistance. Granting that all of us must construct a "performed self" that conforms to the expectations of our culture, for those in a position of powerlessness, this construction is less likely to reflect the truth of their beliefs and self-concept. In other words, those who are living or working under the thumb of others must often construct a believable mask of compliance that will avoid trouble. The more onerous the conditions, the more likely it is that the mask will be designed to be impenetrable by those in power.[153] Simultaneously, the powerless develop their own subculture of beliefs and attitudes, sharing them in locations away from the surveillance of the powerful. This secondary culture carries its own normative pressures (as is clear from the women's exchange at the Bridge), but this is the level where true feelings are allowed to emerge and to be expressed. Such discourse, shared among the occupied population of Guernsey, provided a common page on which they could write their own hidden transcript. The remainder of this chapter will explore the British patriotism that Islanders tapped to form an ideological firewall during the Occupation. Easily and quickly shared, conventional symbols and slogans bound the Islanders together in a comfortable aura of mutual goals and beliefs, encouraging the trust necessary to develop a covert resistance.

Before the shock of the initial takeover had worn off, Kitty Bachmann looked back at the harrowing first three weeks, a period that seemed "more than three years" to her. The Occupation was "a heavy yoke for our British shoulders" and one that would need "a lot of traditional grit, humour and dignity" for the Islanders to rise above it and carry on. It is telling that Kitty continued on to describe the largely symbolic intrusions that the Germans were quick to impose. It was "the metallic ring of jackboots in our little cobbled Town, Swastikas floating in the breeze over all the main buildings, the clipped, full-throated singing of their marching troops, the heel-clicking and arm-raising; and above all, the shattering din of the German Band" that gave proof of Guernsey's "change of fortune." It was clear to the Islanders that the Germans felt they had actually secured the capture of Britain by their grasp on this small, triangular island. "If our little High Street were Whitehall," wrote Kitty, "they could not look more triumphant."[154]

No one reading these diaries, hearing the stories of the Occupation generation, or visiting Guernsey today can doubt the essential "Britishness" in lifestyle and identification, as well as fact, of the Channel Islanders. And Guernseymen and women did not keep their ties to Great Britain secret from their German captors. When Newlands was confiscated and Winifred Harvey in the process of being evicted, she had a polite but frank exchange with Professor Heinz Schlussrig, the German translator, who was overseeing her removal from her home. "Heinz" (Winnie's shorthand reference to him in her writing) turned their conversation to the task at hand of Winnie's eviction and the state of the house:

> On the stairs he said,
>
> "Madam, I hope we have not put you to too much trouble."
>
> "Trouble?" [I said], "well, if you call being turned out of your house no trouble, well, perhaps not."
>
> "Yes," [he said], "it is not pleasant . . . aber es ist Krieg [but it is war]. I do not know but I think in one year the war will be over and you can return."
>
> "Yes, I too think that in a year or a year and a half the war will be over but not in the same way as you think."
>
> "But you are not English. If you are Guernsey, how can you be English?"
>
> "I am Guernsey. My family have been here for two hundred years, but Guernsey has always belonged to England."
>
> "I do not know if the Germans will always be in Guernsey. If we are, what will you do?"
>
> "Much as I love my home and my island I shall not stay here."
>
> "Why not?"
>
> "Because I have always been English and all the men of my family have been and are officers in the British army and you cannot expect me to be disloyal now."
>
> Heinz looked at me and said, "I would think as you do."[155]

The average Islander shared Winifred Harvey's conventional patriotic feelings, but would find more covert means of expressing them.

What is doubtless clear is Guernsey's embrace of the "Myth of 1940" as it unfolded. By the term "myth," I am not referring to something necessarily untrue, but using the term in Malcolm Smith's sense as "a widely held view of the past which has helped to shape and explain the present."[156] The important myths of our culture transform specific events into something broader and more lasting, providing unifying commonalities and lessons to be learned. Sometimes we are only aware of the power of a particular myth when it serves as a later touchstone for persuasive appeals. As Smith maintains, the vital aspect of cultural myths is not so much their factual precision in every detail, but "that these myths are implicitly believed and that they help people to make sense of their lives, that they offer a popular memory which explains the past and the present and moulds expectations of the future." A mythology held in common is a unifying necessity in a nation's collective sense of self.[157]

The Myth of 1940 is actually the interplay of three specific narratives of that signal year: the "miracle of the little boats" in the evacuation at Dunkirk in May, the Battle of Britain starting in July, and the "Blitz," the bombing of civilian areas in Britain, stretching from September 1940 to May 1941. The Guernsey populace felt intimately involved in these events, and for good reason. It was the taking of France, culminating in the evacuation of Dunkirk, that had paved the way for their own captivity. They were unwilling spectators of part of the Battle of Britain, because as Winnie Harvey described it, they watched day after day of "roaring planes . . . in formations, wave after wave, ceaselessly backwards and forwards over the island, from the battles against England."[158]

The Blitz formed the largest point of commonality and concern between Channel Islanders and England. Guernsey had, of course, experienced a small taste of the cruelty of civilian bombing in the June 28th attack on the harbor. When parts of London and other civilian areas were bombed so mercilessly beginning in September, the Islanders reacted out of a familiarity with that particular horror of war. Early on, they could follow the news on the wireless and often reported with concern the worst of the damage. Winnie Harvey described the massive raid on the docks and East End of London; she knew the details that the raid had lasted twelve hours and that four hundred had been killed (with thirteen hundred casualties). She wondered if this would be the "peak" of the air war in Britain, and she went with many others to church on the National Day of Prayer to pray for the safety of the nation.[159] It is worth noting that these days of prayer for the nation, generally requested by the King, were imperative enough to lead some to churches they did not generally attend. When Kitty and Peter Bachmann attended St. John's Church in one such outpouring of common prayer, Kitty noted that it was their first appearance there since they were married in the church in 1928.[160] But these moments of simultaneously joining together as a nation in common purpose were uplifting and unifying for Guernsey, providing an outlet if only for symbolic action.

In the early days of the Blitz, Guernsey had the comfort, if it can be called that, of following the raids and damage on the wireless. The wireless sets were returned from their first confiscation just in time for Jack to follow the devastating raid on London of December 29th, admitting that "it makes our blood run cold here, to listen to such news."[161] This December 29th raid, when fires raged in the City of London, produced the iconic image of the St. Paul's Cathedral dome rising undamaged above the billowing smoke of the surrounding flames. Islanders could not see this photograph, but hearing news of St. Paul's escape reinforced in their minds—as in other Britons—the special protection God seemed to be granting their country. Winifred Harvey considered part of that protection to be in the hands of the RAF, the British fighter pilots whose exploits were followed ardently by those counting on their success.[162]

Islanders would continue to listen closely to the wireless—what Winnie called "the greatest treasure"[163]—for as long as they had it, and secretly once they were denied access. And they would follow the news of the air raids, torn between wanting to know and dreading the news they might hear. Jack Sauvary continued to fret about the ongoing Blitz in the spring of 1941, describing the reports as "too awful to be believed."[164] He was not alone in his sadness about the news in May 1941: "At last they have hit the Houses of Parliament, and how sad about the Abbey. All those beautiful carved stalls now, I suppose, in ruins."[165] These symbols not only of British history but also of the current church and state were considered by Islanders as their own cultural landmarks and prized as much as local buildings and monuments. More worrisome, naturally, was the fate of the people in the bombed areas, a population that could include, as far as the Islanders knew, their own children, other relatives, and friends.

In 1943, Gertie Corbin mentioned with deep consternation the news that went the rounds that a school in London had been bombed and teachers and children killed.[166] And that was often all the information that Guernsey heard, with little access to news of precisely which school was hit or the names of those who had died. A further twist of the knife came because Islanders had only spotty information about the location of their own children as the war continued. And so, Guernseymen and women listened as squadron after squadron of German planes flew overhead during the night. "We know," wrote Gertie, "when we are warm in bed, that they are going to bomb places in England and it makes us unhappy."[167]

Yet, all the airplanes overhead were not German, and following the exploits of the RAF in their occasional raids on the Island became part of occupied life. "How pleased we are to hear them overhead," Winifred Harvey maintained. "It is a tonic."[168] This unalloyed joy at the appearance of the RAF was an attitude that had to be cultivated for some in Guernsey. As is true for all civilians in a war zone, especially those in occupied territories, their saviors could well turn out to be their destroyers. Rarely is it possible to see someone grapple with these conflicting emotions as honestly as Dorothy Higgs did during the earliest days of the Occupation. It seemed so incongruous to Dorothy to merely serve as a spectator, watching the Germans prepare for what seemed an early invasion of England. But what she could not understand was the clutch of fear she felt at the sight of an English airplane. She likened it to the children's game "Nuts in May," where a child would be pulled over to a new team and suddenly feel conflicted over which side should win the game. This feeling of dread at the sight of the RAF, an emotion that flew in the face of conventional patriotism, seemed "inexplicable" to Dorothy. She pondered deeper meanings of having outgrown nationalism, or sensing the artificial nature of war and "taking sides" in an armed struggle, but finally she decided that it was the more "primitive" response of simple self-preservation.[169]

These conflicted feelings were very short-lived for Dorothy. By July 24, 1940, she had changed her lifetime attitude toward war in general, stating, "In fact, I have forgotten all about being a pacifist—I just want England not to be hurt."[170] And by September 24, a leaflet-dropping RAF "raid" drew an effusive gush of patriotic fervor: "Oh Phyll!!! We've had a raid—oh, and they dropped leaflets with a lovely message from the King. I could hug him! Before we knew about the leaflets we felt ten years younger—no, a hundred years younger!" More important than this excitement over the one-way contact with Great Britain was Dorothy's admission of a new sentimentality and more traditional patriotic feelings: "'Sfunny how primitive one becomes at these times. I even get wet eyes when I hear 'There'll always be an England' and 'Land of Hope and Glory,' though I hated their sentiment before."[171]

She was not done with exploring her own evolving attitudes and new willingness to sacrifice in war. There had been rumors that a German anti-aircraft gun would be located "on the Park," making it an inviting target for RAF aircraft and one sure to cause civilian casualties if it drew fire. But, unlike in July, Dorothy's feelings in August about the danger were now clear and unmixed: "Somehow it would be much better to die in an English raid than a German one."[172] The last step in Dorothy Higgs's transformation from theoretical pacifist to self-sacrificial patriot came by November, when her stance on the war was finalized: "This ghastly Naziism has *got* to be wiped out before the world can be a decent place and I know now that England was right to fight."[173] Experience was a tough teacher, and Dorothy now found her emotions (which were easily touched by injustice) leading her to embrace war and the British cause with a vigor that she had previously lacked.

On the evening of August 9, ironically exactly six weeks after the deadly German raid on the harbor, Kitty and Peter heard anti-aircraft fire and the sound of RAF bombing in an attack on the airport. Kitty wrote wryly that "We now have a new 'enemy' from which to take cover." Not that she could inveigle Peter into leaving the landing window and giving up his position as a spectator of the action.[174] Although Kitty and others were "not enthusiastic about this sort of thing," meaning the attack by their own forces, they were willing to welcome these potentially deadly "nuisance raids" if it made Guernsey a more difficult asset for the Germans to hold, and if the raids proved "a real headache to Hitler."[175] Bill Warry and his friends liked to watch from the windows at his club, which overlooked the Esplanade and the harbor in St. Peter Port, prime targets for RAF raiders. All calibers of guns "studded" the harbor front, and the Germans could be counted on to race to man them at the sound of the air-raid siren. "Yes," mused Warry with great satisfaction, "we've seen some great clashes from our windows & not too many to suit us."[176]

Islanders calculated their own nerve and bravery in the war effort by their attitude towards these RAF raids. It flies in the face of our common sense to heed the old military conceit to ride, or march, to the sound of the guns. In fact, much of military training is bent on retraining the natural impulse to respond to danger in a manner conducive to personal survival. It is surprising, therefore, to see through most of the diary narratives a willingness to chance being in the thick of battle, even as an unarmed civilian. The response to two relatively early RAF raids was notable, primarily because both involved civilian injuries and fatalities. The first came on Monday, December 16, 1940, in an attack on the new hangar recently completed at the airport. The hangar was disguised as a greenhouse, to blend into the actual greenhouses that surrounded it. The British seem not to have been fooled by such camouflage and made a direct hit on the hangar, turning it instantly into "a shambles." One of the Guernsey workers, a "youngish" carpenter named Anderson, was killed outright, and one man of the Martel family was injured. Ken Lewis reported that Anderson was actually decapitated ("his head being blown right off"),[177] the nature of his death making the friendly fire still more horrific. Winifred Harvey identified him as the only son of "Fuzzey's curtain and blind worker," a young man who had been married only five months.[178]

Although Winnie described Anderson's death as "sad," and Ken remarked that the incident "caused some regret in the Island,"[179] it is fascinating how others shifted the blame in some measure to the victim. Jack had been told that the civilian workers were not supposed to be in the hangar during the dinner hour, most likely out of a German fear of sabotage. However, four men had gone in to play cards; the remaining fifty or sixty stayed in the actual greenhouses as ordered and thus "came out safely" when the raid was over.[180] Dorothy Higgs gave Anderson even shorter shrift, calling the raid "marvellous," and mentioning Anderson's death in a dismissive aside: "Unfortunately one worker was killed—he should not have been there. 'They' were *most* impressed."[181] And that was the bottom line: the impact of the raid on German plans and morale far outweighed the death of one Islander.

The second notable raid of the first half of the Occupation came during January 1942. Three Beauforts flew low over St. Sampson's Harbor, Belle Grève Bay, and past the gasworks, swooping down out of the clouds to hit the St. Peter Port Harbor and the ships being unloaded there. Then they were gone, as Jack Sauvary put it, "like a shot out of a gun." Approximately sixty men were killed, most of them French and Belgian slave laborers. One local man—Tucker, the crane driver—was killed, having both his legs blown off,[182] and the unverified story went around that two horses that were in the crane crate in midair were obliterated so thoroughly that they vanished without a trace. The response to this raid, despite the casualties, was immediate and positive. Kitty called it "a very neat performance despite the tragic results for some local families." And Winifred Harvey—who considered the raid "beautifully done"—described how, as she walked down the Grange soon after, with ambulances and fire engines still on the way to the harbor, all those she passed were "thrilled and beaming." Thrilling, too, was the opportunity to listen to the BBC describe the raid that put Guernsey, however briefly, in the active war news. Winnie also maintained that it was more amusing than irritating to read the German account of the raid in the *Star*, with its entirely erroneous assessment of the Islanders' feelings.[183]

Many Islanders became inured to their own danger, sometimes responding like spectators at a sporting event. Rev. Ord described a group of youngsters at the La Vallette bathing pools, standing on the seawall and screaming to the pilots, "Give it to 'em! Give it 'em, Good old RAF!" as they watched a violent raid.[184] Even in the 1942 harbor raid described previously, Winnie Harvey stepped out of the glass greenhouse she was in at her old home when the raid started. She stood under an ash tree, watching the Germans pour out of Newlands at the sound of the bombs (the young Lieutenant Eiger beaming and grinning at her). But then, because she did not want the Germans to see her sheltering under the tree, she walked down the garden in the open. A friend later took her to task, with the obvious thought that had the RAF pilots seen the German uniforms of those so close by her, they might have machine-gunned the lot, including Winnie.[185]

It seems that the excitement of seeing "their boys" in action, combined with a need to show fearlessness and defiance in the face of the enemy, erased even reasonable caution from the Islanders' minds. The street demonstrations of approval during the RAF raids became so pointed that a new order was published in the *Press* in September 1941 demanding that civilians stay indoors and refrain from acknowledging the attacking planes.[186] This order was almost universally ignored. Perhaps this public response can be traced to the nonheroic nature of daily sacrifice demanded of the Channel Islanders during the Occupation. Standing tall in the face of guns and bombs, even if mainly that of friendly fire, was an opportunity to show visible courage and must have provided a satisfying feel of being part of the war effort.

What is also telling was the response to the news that the RAF had sunk supply ships coming from France. Most, like Rev. Ord, while acknowledging that British blockades were a primary factor in a spate of starvation deaths, described the widespread stoic attitude that "we would rather starve than see it relaxed."[187] If some Islanders secretly wished that Whitehall would act protectively toward their countrymen held hostage in the Channel Islands, most took Dorothy Higgs's attitude: "I don't mind being a lot more hungry if it helps Britain."[188] It is Dorothy who reveals the important point about the Islanders' view of English attacks. She maintained that personal danger was not on their minds, and everyone was "miles more cheerful" following the RAF strikes:[189] "Oh, it is such a lovely feeling that England is still interested in us. I bet the Jerries are jealous!"[190]

Being abandoned by Britain was a not unreasonable concern of the Guernsey civilians. When supply ships were hit in raids, there was no rationale provided by the British government for their actions. This only enhanced feelings that Whitehall viewed the Islanders as mere pawns in a game. Most were willing to play that role, although, as Dorothy Higgs noted, "If only Churchill would send us some kind of message explaining things, it would hearten people no end."[191] With such uncertainty and little means to obtain information, Guernsey clung to recognition from any quarter. When captured British airmen assured them that the Channel Islands' plight was known and that they were not forgotten, they embraced the information as true and comforting.[192]

It became apparent to Guernseymen and women that other Britons had little concept of the conditions of the Occupation. Sometimes this came through in the Red Cross messages, as it did in one message to Winnie Harvey. These messages were necessarily brief, and in the sign-off, a friend concluded with "Hope you flourish." This struck Winnie as particularly inappropriate, writing that "survive" would be a better term than "flourish": "The Town is tragic and the harbour desolation and we ourselves living, not knowing if, in an hour's time we may be turned out of our homes and lose all." Warming to her indignation, Winnie decided that her friend in England "must still be living in the Cloud Cuckoo Land of the pacifists. As Marie Louise said, 'Flourish! Our life is hell!'"[193]

At other times, the sense of disconnect was felt in the BBC programming. When wireless was available, the Islanders listened avidly for any sign that they were still remembered, and for any clue concerning the well-being of their evacuees. Yet, when a program was broadcast that spoke about the evacuated schoolchildren, much of the time was spent talking about Channel Islands produce and holidays. Still worse was a later broadcast that Guernsey widely considered "a travesty." Kitty Bachmann found it "provoking" that any mention of Guernsey portrayed them as a "nation of nitwits," still wearing poke bonnets, speaking patois, and mounted on donkeys riding to town. The BBC would drag out old Guernsey-French songs that no one recognized, when what the Islanders needed was current information about their loved ones and to hear the voices of friends and family. The one song universally recognized was "Sarnia Chérie," used widely as Guernsey's anthem from the time it was written in 1911. But that rendering struck a bit close to home, being in Kitty's opinion "a trifle too evocative for our good, if we are to tackle the job at hand in philosophical manner."[194]

The seeming insensitivity of the BBC had deeper consequences for those attempting to listen secretly once the wireless sets had been confiscated. Rev. Ord wondered at the judgment of the BBC, as they continued to introduce their stories with martial music such as Purcell's "Trumpet Voluntary." It seemed as though the BBC believed the world to have unfettered access to their broadcasts, and the notion of people listening in secret, and at great peril, had never occurred to them. Loud martial music that could be overheard was an unnecessary story enhancement in Ord's opinion, because "it wastes precious time and no one could doubt it was British music." He pondered on how many secret listeners had been given away not only in occupied territories but also in the Reich itself. It made him want to write to the BBC or the *Times* to "remind them that we no longer live in a civilized world of liberty."[195] This seemingly small issue, though of great importance in some quarters, illustrates a continued disconnect between the lived experience of Occupation and perceptions of that experience from the outside.

THUMBS UP!

Like any occupied people, individual Islanders would fight an internal war to maintain their spirits. Stephen Ash, writing of the occupation of the American South during the Civil War, described the common attitude of Southern civilians: "Until their liberators arrived, the people were determined to uphold the faith." Ash continues on to describe the communal nature of this mental attitude, and how both morale and the ability to resist, in ways large and small, "were not just matters of private faith and individual conscience." Instead, the internal moral compass that gave guidance as to right versus wrong actions, and provided powerless individuals with a sense of their own intrinsic worth had much to do with community beliefs.[196] Resistance cannot flourish in an atmosphere of individual and collective despair.

There was much to drag down the spirits of Guernseymen and women over the five years of Occupation, and by the middle point in May of 1943, Elizabeth Doig could describe the general feeling as "war weary," worn down by hunger, evictions from their homes, and most especially by isolation from their family and friends.[197] As early as the week of October 21, 1940, Jack Sauvary was so down over his late wife's birthday and some recent deaths that "even the sea and the islands don't seem the same. I hardly look at them now."[198] Jack chalked up this early depression to a sense of isolation, something that would only grow over time and made even a beautiful prison unbearable. Dorothy Higgs felt this constraint acutely. It was "depressing to have no control," because their efforts to maintain the health and welfare of the Island did nothing to move them toward freedom.[199] In fact, all the heartfelt work to ensure the survival of their Island, neighbors, and way of life for the day of freedom seemed "only to help the wrong side," because it did nothing to dislodge the enemy.[200] In May 1943, the same time when Elizabeth and Jack wrote of their depression, Dorothy also described her own "claustrophobia from being shut in physically and from spiritual isolation." Although she believed the first year was the most difficult adjustment, she found "so little joy in this perpetual scrounging existence."[201]

Islanders were beginning to appreciate the very real dangers of a downturn in mood. Ambrose Robin, so intimately concerned with the welfare of the community in his work with the States, saw weariness with the Occupation as part of a larger public-health issue: "Depression, lack of food and fuel knock people right out when they fall ill."[202] The deeper concern was that mental depression might well prove fatal as people increasingly despaired of an end to the Occupation and a reunion with family. By June of 1943, there was a spell when reportedly there was one suicide a week.[203] Suicides had increased beginning quite early in the Occupation, and the reports are sprinkled briefly throughout the contemporaneous accounts: Nicholas Edward Hotton, a seventy-four-year-old who hanged himself in his coach house in December 1940;[204] a friend of Bill Warry who hanged himself in January 1943;[205] Sidney N. West ("Buskin"), a reporter for the *Star* who committed suicide in April 1941.[206] West's death was most likely on Rev. Ord's mind when he wrote that same April, "The death is announced of a man whose loneliness was greater than he could bear."[207]

Just as with other Guernsey deaths during these years, instances of depression or suicide cannot all be attributed to conditions of the Occupation. It is difficult to know why Ralph, Ken Lewis's friend, went through a spell of being noticeably quiet, seemingly detached, and uninterested in any of his usual pursuits. Ken did not quite know how to handle this new situation, but found himself having to work at conversation with his friend so they did not just lapse into silence.[208] Young men on the cusp between adolescence and adulthood are often subject to intense mood swings, and Ralph's sudden pensiveness, though of concern to his mother and Ken, might have been little more than typical of his age. But when, only months before Liberation, Ken's Uncle Arthur was found drowned in the Bathing Places, the family seemed shocked but not completely surprised. He had acted strangely lately and had just been in the hospital for an operation. But, other than his misery over a lack of tobacco, his depression and suicide might have had any number of causes not directly tied to the Occupation. It is impossible to know what was in his mind, and whether, had he stuck it out until May, the improved diet, not to mention the sudden joy and new prospects of Liberation, might have made any difference.[209]

At other times, the link of a suicide to the Occupation seemed inescapable to contemporaneous writers. One case mentioned by more than one diarist was that of Edward Roussel, who drowned himself in the family well on a July Sunday in 1941. He had been cared for at Vauquiedor Hospital since the advent of the Occupation and had only been released for three weeks at the time that he took his life. One of his sons had stayed home to watch his father while the rest of the family went to chapel, but Roussel managed to slip away and fling himself down the well.[210] The coinciding of his hospitalization with the start of Occupation seems to indicate a link with his depression, and that is certainly the way Jack Sauvary saw it. Uncle Ned came to see his brother-in-law, seeking a little nip of "O be Joyful" that Jack generously provided. Jack and Ned discussed the Roussel case, with Jack expressing his relief that he did not experience that suicidal level of depression. For his own part, Uncle Ned was not surprised at the uptick in suicides, because the small amount of spirits that he was cadging from Jack was his own way of fighting depression.

Jack seems to have been the go-to source to raise the spirits (literally) of the elderly. Much later in the Occupation, he mentioned taking a little of "the necessary" to old Miss Lihou, because that was the "only thing that keeps her up."[211] Others had their own ways of coping with depression and the difficult living conditions that lacked a certain end. For some Islanders, even the church that had always sustained them ceased to be a comfort. Ambrose Robin, generally very involved in the Methodist church, found that by the middle of the Occupation his "old attraction for church and church services" was "withering." He was unsure whether this feeling was "right or wrong," but it certainly seemed shared by others, especially in the colder months. One February Sunday in 1943, he counted the entire afternoon congregation at Brock Road to be forty-four, with only nine men in attendance. Despite a good sermon by Rev. Ord, it was "very cold in church—a miserable place."[212]

With the lack of body fat in the congregants and the inadequate heat in the churches, this inability to withstand a full service seems reasonable, although the length of the service appears to have been a matter of perception. On February 13, 1944, Robin described the afternoon sermon by Rev. Ord as "very long and uninteresting," while Rev. Ord noted in his own diary on that date, "Because of the cold I make the services as brief as possible."[213] Ken Lewis was quite distressed when his father declared near the end of the Occupation that he had lost all interest in going to chapel. "We had never heard him speak in this manner before," wrote Ken. "I think a shortage of tobacco makes him like that."[214] So, while the church served for many as a point of unity and hope, it only became another drag on the emotions of some whose spiritual resources were at low ebb.

Thus, a universal need existed for Islanders to raise their spirits, even if the effort was patently artificial. Jack repeatedly sounded a note of determination to overcome every trial, giving himself and others little pep talks along the way. Was a friend worried about the German destruction of the Island? She cannot do anything about it, "so why worry." It was best to "just let things take their course . . . just to live is all we can expect."[215] Were the Germans turning the confiscated houses into derelict ruins? Well, Jack just refused to "bother about mine . . . what's the use of bothering as long as we get through with our skins?"[216] Was his garden such a waste that it almost made Mrs. Rowe cry, leaving her at a loss to understand how Jack still smiled? "Crying and worrying won't make it any better," he told her.[217] This was Jack's nature. He was generally sunny at heart, although the past few years since his wife's death had brought little cheer. Even when confessing to his diary about having "the humps," he covered his melancholy for the sake of others in an attempt to bolster their ability to see the Occupation through. Jack firmly believed that "while people can keep their spirits up they prolong their lives."[218]

The majority of Guernseymen and women adopted the "smiling through" attitude that had long been presented to them as the proper British approach to adversity. Although Winnie Harvey referred to being uplifted in difficulty by "the Americanism, 'I can take it!'" most Islanders proudly characterized this as a British trait.[219] The concept of the stiff upper lip long predated the war, but new versions of it served as the rallying perspective of Londoners bombed out in the Blitz. As Islanders followed news of the destruction in the capital city, they were proud that "England is wonderful and sticking it well."[220] Soon, this became an ongoing theme, where a particular hardship or looming problem would be mentioned, but accompanied by a description of civilian cheerfulness and the hopeful appendage of "We can stick it!"[221] Such verbal affirmations served also to reinforce the Islanders' natural identification with Britain.

Far more interesting was Guernsey's initial foray into a resistance tactic that would develop throughout the Occupation, one that could be described as a form of "subversive affirmation and over-identification."[222] "Subversive affirmation" is actually a term recently coined to describe very specific resistance tactics developed in socialist Eastern Europe during the 1980s in politics and arts. Key to this method is what appears to be an affirmation of the very beliefs, identities, and culture of those in power. The discourses of the powerless, whether verbal or nonverbal, apparently support the controlling forces, even to the point of overidentification with their agenda. Some of the more amusing examples of this tactic could be found in the Polish Orange Alternative activities. When an official Day of the Police and Security Service was declared in 1987 to honor the police "doing their duty with a smile," youth of the Orange Alternative relentlessly "showered" police and their patrol cars with flowers, trying as often as possible to hug these symbols of oppressive power and thank them for their service.[223]

What is important is to differentiate this tactic not just from covert criticism but also from irony. For Guernsey, resistance by subversive affirmation was a simple matter of the cheerful smile. One of the primary themes early in the diarists' writing was the perception that the Guernsey populace was "very cheery," and, as Winnie put it, "the frightfulness has quite failed thus far."[224] So many people mention the confident mien and happy faces of Guernseymen at this time that it was undoubtedly true that special efforts were being made to show a game face when out in public. It started slowly, because in the early days, Kitty tells us, there were "very few sunny faces in the streets and byways, as though all gaiety had dried up at its source."[225] Soon, however, a strong "esprit de corps" developed as those walking among the Germans in town sought some level of comfort from each other:

> Words are not necessary to convey the unity of spirit in the nod, wink and smile exchanged behind the German uniform as they pass between us. In this fashion we greet and are greeted by all and sundry, as though a lifetime of detached recognition has ripened overnight into a mature friendship.[226]

Jack was also taken with the ability of the people on Victoria Avenue, so recently evicted from their homes, who would "brighten up, laugh and whistle, and find the humorous side," or those who queued up at the Market with precious little to buy, yet could "laugh and joke about it." This was, in Jack's estimation, a manifestation of "the spirit that built England."[227]

Yet, over time, an element of conscious subversion filtered into this display of a cheerful countenance. Smiling acquiescence to German orders, however repugnant, seemed to flummox the occupiers. While fellow civilians could read this bright, rather than sardonic, smile as displaying, in Ambrose Robin's words, "a strong feeling of hope reflected in the minds and faces of our population," the Germans had more difficulty with their interpretation.[228] How could one punish those who followed orders with facial expressions reflecting a compliant spirit and possibly even agreement with German actions? The subtlety of double meaning seemed to be beyond most German observers, and Rev. Ord often reported on Islanders who reveled in their ability to keep the Germans guessing. When the food supply was so dangerously low in the final year, a girl at the bread depot said to Ord, "Well, it's bad, but we mustn't let THEM see how hard hit we are!"[229] Many of the Germans were incapable of penetrating the guise of subversive affirmation, and in Ord's opinion, "German psychology is at fault. They just do not understand us, and it has often been said that the British are mad."[230]

Even the Germans who caught on to this approach were helpless to do anything about it. One day in May 1943, Ord was out visiting around the Bailiff's Cross area and paused to talk to some men who were conducting repairs on a water main. Because the men worked in essential maintenance, they often had contact with Germans, some of whom had expressed irritation with the cheerful smiles on Guernsey faces. One of the workmen characterized the attitude of those Germans who understood what the smiles meant as, "We'll take them bloomin' grins off your faces one of these 'ere days!" And, to Ord's delight, the workman went on to say that he expected the coming years to be a bit thin, "But we can always tighten our belts and grin a bit 'arder, Sir, can't we?" Ord saw this determination as a sign that "the spirit is sound as the garrison will one day find," a belief that behind the acquiescent smiles lay a determined resistance that could be tapped if the opportunity arose.[231]

Despite the symbolic defiance of the impenetrable smile, and some pleasure it provided in confusing the occupiers, the Islanders felt acutely their forced acquiescence to enemy demands. It was appalling to many in time of war to become "a sadly unmilitant body, waiting in the wings like actors without a rôle."[232] Still, this was a frustration they would have to master if they wanted to control overt defiance, channeling it into forms that served some actual purpose and would not result in the deportation of all civilians. Alderney had already been cleared of civilians and turned into a slave labor camp. The same fate could as easily befall Guernsey, and the Islanders had to come quickly to a realization of their purpose in the war.

First, they had to acknowledge that they were in no position to help the war effort. "If in England," Jack lamented, "we could have done war work and helped the cause," but now they were "in camp and able to do nothing."[233] Their removal from a direct role in securing Britain's survival was the great regret for all who stayed by choice or by chance in Guernsey. Elizabeth Doig could claim in 1942 that everyone she knew was "weary of the isolation" and regretted staying: "How very much help we would have been able to give Britain in her hour of need."[234] While they clung to the hope that they were "too small and unimportant" to benefit the enemy,[235] Dorothy Higgs worried that they were "just stagnating in a backwater."[236] Though the hope was often expressed that Guernsey would one day be key in the invasion, and they would take their proper place on the frontlines, Islanders came to accept a less heroic role and to seek some value in it.

Coming to grips with this reality was most difficult for young men like Ken Lewis who came of age while the Occupation wore on. What seemed exciting when the Nazis first arrived yielded over time to Ken's concerns over their "seemingly uselessness in this island." Ken was pulled between "I would like to be doing my bit for the war effort" and the more philosophical "Someone had to stop behind . . . What is to be will be . . . All this may be for our good, time alone will tell."[237] The grand adventure that war seems to be to young men (until they experience it) was passing Ken by, and he knew it.

Over time, Guernsey redefined its role as a player in a game of endurance, a war of attrition as opposed to action. Kitty defined quite well her understanding of the Island's purpose in the larger conflict:

> Our war effort seems to consist of holding down a couple of German Divisions and, by our presence here, to prevent the R.A.F. blasting Guernsey to pieces in order to annihilate our enemies. We remain tethered here with a sizeable slice of the German Army, all fellow-prisoners, they in exile and we in isolation.[238]

In an odd way, they were holding a piece of ground in the war, preventing its destruction in any way they could and lessening its value as a resource of the enemy.

Once it became apparent that Guernsey would not serve as a staging ground for an imminent invasion of England, the cost to the enemy of maintaining German operations so far from home gradually became apparent to the Islanders. Resources expended fortifying Guernsey against Allied action were resources denied to the rest of the German war effort. The Occupation had saddled Germany with a civilian population to tend, and tied down German forces to defend this relatively useless, from a strategic standpoint, territory. Kitty found it "comforting . . . to be indirectly useful to the War Effort even in a microscopic way, and in a fuller sense to be the preservers of our Beloved Guernsey."[239] This was a vital realization, and one that would structure Guernsey self-understanding and actions. Just as Britain was fighting to protect and maintain her land and way of life, Guernsey would do the same, although by different means, with different numbers, and under far different circumstances. It might be "easier to feel heroic and uplifted when one is at the heart of things,"[240] as Guernseymen and women felt during even violent RAF raids, but their destiny would lie down a quieter if equally determined path.

DON'T KNOW WHERE, DON'T KNOW WHEN

The strongest tie to Britain and the continuous reminder of the Islanders' isolation was that unavoidable empty space once filled by their evacuated children. Daily they were met with reminders of this absence by the quiet streets and the silent playgrounds and bathing pools. True, there were children who remained, whose parents could not part from them, but the vast majority of homes had desolate children's rooms and empty chairs at the dinner table. Kitty described the sudden change that summer of 1940 this way: "Guernsey is almost childless as though a modern Pied Piper has enticed all the children away."[241] Early tasks, such as collecting Diana's schoolbooks, took Kitty to Elizabeth College, where the memories of evacuation were still raw. She walked the quiet halls, seeing in her mind's eye the "phantom" figures of children rushing past, and hearing the echo of their singing and laughter. As she went down the school drive, she could see again "the streams of parents bringing their children like lambs to the slaughter, to be deposited and labelled for transport."[242]

Most Islanders were slow to realize the length of time that they would be separated from their children, and this delay served as a psychological buffer against despair. During evacuation, Jack had gone to wish his second daughter, Kit, "many happy returns" for her birthday, but she already "had flown," answering a call to help with the evacuated school. The decision to leave had been an agonizing one for Kit, but both she and her father considered her work an opportunity to help the war effort. So, Jack went to town one Saturday in August to buy her gifts of lavender water and French talcum powder to save for their reunion. "I often wonder," he mused, "if you will ever get them."[243] But why would any sensible person foresee a five-year separation? The Bachmanns certainly did not. Peter liked to tease Kitty with what she considered "such inanities" as predictions that Diana would have finished school and entered a job by the time the war ended. "Our ten year old!" Kitty wrote in 1940. "I refuse to believe it."[244] Diana would be fifteen before they saw her again.

With the many restrictions and delays of Red Cross messages, Kitty and the other Islanders lived in a world where they could agree, "all is conjecture" when it came to the fate of their loved ones in Britain.[245] The void, which should have held solid information about their children, was rapidly filled by a steady supply of worry, particularly over the Blitz. Ambrose Robin called the poor communication with the British mainland the "biggest bugbear" of the Occupation, far outstripping the lack of food, clothing, soap, and other necessities.[246] Because information came in short bursts spaced many months apart, trying to picture the current lives of their evacuated families was like reading under strobe lights. Robin received in December 1941 a message from his daughter Marie dated August 14th, telling him that his son David had sat for his library exams.[247] Yet Robin had already received news of David leaving college before the close of the school year. What did that imply?[248] By the next August (1942) there came the anticipated news that David was serving in the military, although his earlier message telling them so had been altered by censors from "serving" to "working." So, even when news came through, there was little guarantee that the message remained unaltered. "More food," Robin maintained, "for murky thoughts."[249]

Part of the problem for Islanders lay in the bizarre rules controlling the receiving and sending of Red Cross messages, a form of communication instituted quite early in the Occupation and the only means of contact with evacuated family and friends. At first, Islanders could not initiate a message, even when they had a known recipient's address in England. No method existed for finding their relatives, who could be spread all over the British mainland. Therefore, those in Guernsey could only reply once someone in Britain sent a message to them, leaving the power to make first contact in the hands of others. It is easy to imagine the consternation and self-doubt that could occur as time passed and no attempt at contact was forthcoming from family. Therefore, when in April 1941 the news came that messages could be sent from Guernsey to relatives in England who had not yet made contact, Ken Lewis came across a queue stretching all the way across the Elizabeth College playground. Over eight hundred messages were sent on that day alone.[250]

Messages, and their response, were paid for by those on the mainland. Once a message came, Guernseymen and women had to reply to it on the spot, a situation not exactly conducive to intelligent response. The one compensation was that Islanders had 25-word limits for their response, while those in mainland Britain were initially restricted to 10. This need for spur-of-the-moment creative writing resulted in some unintentionally comical messages. Rev. Ord, excited over the news of the arrival of a new grand-nephew, drafted as his first response, "Thrilled by news. TRY AGAIN!" At least, Ord wrote, the censor "took it I meant thrilled by getting a Red Cross Message!"[251] Dorothy Higgs, like others, seems to have adjusted to these rules by preparing 25-word messages months in advance—doubtlessly updating them over time—just in case she heard from a particular family member.[252]

The messages from Guernsey back to England went through in a somewhat timely fashion compared to those making their way from England to the Channel Islands. Sacks of mail were held up in Granville, France, on their way to the Islands and allowed to sit out in the rain until the letters within were rotten and unreadable.[253] Reportedly, at least one batch of mail was left lying under meat and had to be destroyed.[254] The Germans could not be bothered tending to items of no importance to their war effort; transporting supplies, building materials, and troops to the Island took precedence over messages to ease the minds of the occupied. More space would be available to transport messages leaving Guernsey, explaining the uneven and frustrating call and response of communication between evacuees and their relatives still in Guernsey.

Ambrose Robin, with his usual precision, tried to keep track of personal messages starting with the date they left England, their receipt and acknowledgment in Guernsey, the date when the acknowledgment reached England, and finally when news of that receipt reached Guernsey. Charting out the messages from Marie in 1941, he came up with an average of 13⅞ weeks from England to Guernsey, 12½ weeks from Guernsey to England, and 18 weeks return message from England back to Guernsey. Thus, a simple three-part round of a single message (initiation of message exchange, acknowledgment and response, receipt of response, and return message) took nine to ten months.[255]

And that was just it: the fact that Red Cross messages, the one connection to their families, often came to a halt or were just "dribbling through"[256] caused concern for even the most strong-minded. When others received messages from family and the Ords did not, the reverend admitted that "the silence makes us wonder if our people have survived the Blitz."[257] While Peter Bachmann read in bed each night, Kitty lay awake beside him, far too preoccupied with her thoughts of absent loved ones to sleep. Instead, she listened to the incessant droning of the German surveillance plane that all had dubbed "Minnie the Moocher," making the nightly round of Island reconnaissance. Each of Kitty's absent family members had a place in her "maze of thoughts," although Diana held the top place in this endless "labyrinth of conjecture."[258]

The gravest news could be held up for many months or possibly never delivered at all. In September 1941, the Robins tried to send news of Uncle Phil's death to Marie through a reply to an evacuated friend's message. Yet, in mid-March 1942, they received a reply to their monthly message of August 1941, reading in part, "Delighted fourth message . . . Going Vic's home Christmas. Hope Uncle Phil better."[259] So, at the time of this message dated the 6th of December 1941, news of Phil's death in September had not reached his evacuated family. Even when in contact, the delays in transmission led to some eerie results and bolstered an overall fear that Islanders were praying for and worrying over relatives who were long dead. Perhaps it was a presentiment of pain to come that led Kitty Bachmann to write about her sister on July 27, 1942: "Audrey's third Birthday in exile . . . I have to persuade myself that Pam's allusion to her condition was not a gentle warning of impending disaster. It is unthinkable!"[260]

Kitty Bachmann's sister Audrey had evacuated with the rest of the family, a wise choice considering her chronic heart problems. Because she did not dwell on her own health, it was easy to lose sight of what the family all knew: that Audrey's life would be a short one. But even with this past knowledge and Kitty's little flash of insight on July 27, it was still a shock to learn just days later that Audrey had been dead for two months. The Giraud family had received a message from England that included an expression of sorrow at Audrey's sudden death. Peter received the news through a friend on a Wednesday evening and, needing to verify that the news was accurate before telling Kitty, he left the house to visit the Girauds and see the message for himself. He constructed a story of seeing a business associate before the man left for Jersey in the morning, and left the house only fifteen minutes before curfew. Unaware of the actual purpose of Peter's mission, Kitty worried that he would be caught on the streets after curfew and held in prison. Peter made it back home without incident, but still kept the knowledge of Audrey's death to himself until after a long-planned outing on Thursday (which Kitty enjoyed "in blessed oblivion" of the blow to come).

When Peter finally broke the news that evening, it was as though all the claustrophobia of being confined to Guernsey came in on Kitty at once. Despite the curfew, she had to get out of the four walls of the house and into the field across the way, just to be able to breathe. For days afterward she experienced the same "wild ideas" that others had on receiving bad news through the unreliable grapevine of the Red Cross messages. Perhaps it was simply a rumor, a misunderstanding by the person who had expressed sorrow to the Girauds. Perhaps, with so few words allowed to compose a Red Cross message, everyone was misinterpreting the message itself. There was no means for immediate confirmation, and a family message with firsthand information might be months in coming. As it turned out, a message from Kitty's mother came only two weeks later, ending Kitty's hopes for a different outcome but also allowing her to grieve fully. To sharpen the pain, messages from Kitty to her sister were still en route to the family. And Kitty actually hoped that messages from Audrey might be on their slow path to Guernsey, "painful but treasured souvenirs."[261]

In lieu of actual contact with evacuated families and friends, the Islanders substituted a rich fantasy life of dreams and imaginative projection. Kitty still met her daughter Diana in dreams, "frisking along the Esplanade with Kala bounding ahead." The war was over and Diana was home for good. Running to her and hugging her tight, Kitty asked if she had missed them, but Diana assured her that she had not had time.[262] Such almost nightly dreams held a "wonderland of reunion" for Kitty where she could be with her family, although there was always the "crude awakening" to the reality of their absence.[263] When messages came steadily from Diana at the time of her twelfth birthday in mid-1942, they imagined a new "adult tone" to her writing, mining each brief message for a greater sense of their child growing up at such a distance.[264]

Yet, for a relationship developed largely in imagination, it would be difficult to top the fantasy love affair that Ken Lewis conducted with Brenda Parker,[265] a girl of his age who had evacuated before the Occupation commenced. The special nature of this one particular girl becomes clear very early on in Ken's diary. In November 1940 a broadcast from England mentioned that all the evacuated intermediate boys and girls were safe and away from the bombing of the Blitz. Ken's response to the news ("This meant that [Brenda Parker] was safe") cannot help but raise a smile as it makes unmistakable the special nature of this one particular evacuee.[266] Apparently, Ken had never acted on his schoolboy crush while Brenda was still in Guernsey, though he seemed aware of the details of her life, making note of her birthday in the spring and the June anniversary of her leaving Guernsey for England.[267] And now, through a new closeness with Brenda's mother, who must have found his willingness to run errands and endless interest in her daughter's welfare both charming and transparent, Ken obtained Brenda's address and sent messages of his own to her.

Then came May 26, 1942—one of those days when the angels seemed to smile on Ken Lewis. Ever devout, he had "prayed continually" for a reply from Brenda to his message, and without warning his prayers were answered. There it was, in Brenda's own handwriting no less, and only just over two months in transit: "Well. Shorthand typist. Delighted received your news. Always thinking of everyone at home. Glad contact parents, writing them frequently. Keep smiling. Love to all, [Brenda]." On his way home to dinner the next day, Ken stopped in triumph to see Mrs. Parker and share Brenda's message with her family. It was the first that they had in Brenda's own hand, the touch that verified the authenticity of the message, as it seemed to bring Brenda closer to them. Several days later, Auntie Ede added a pleasurable extra fillip by telling Ken that Mrs. Parker had been "so overjoyed to see Brenda's handwriting that she could have cried with joy."[268]

Ken's prayers often seemed to tend toward Brenda, and his great petition was to receive a message (and, could he even dare to hope for a photograph?) before his twenty-first birthday. He considered his prayer at least partially answered when a message came on the 4th of February in 1943. A simple message, filled with cheerful chat (such as about Ken's use of Brenda's old bicycle to ride to chapel), this letter actually came at a time that threatened Ken's entire link to Brenda. Only days later, Ken stopped by the Parkers' on his way to work to say goodbye to both of them as they left in the deportation of the English-born to Germany. And as they left, much of the easy connection to Brenda and extra information about her life went with them. Still, the personal messages came back and forth, carefully mined for any clues as to Brenda's location and work conditions. When she wrote that she was "always eating pasties," and the "Spring flowers are out, climate like home," Ken knew she was in Cornwall, just across the Channel and so very close.[269]

There were many bumps in the road for this ephemeral, and likely one-way, relationship. Ken knew that Brenda had passed her physical and joined the Women's Auxiliary Air Force in May of 1942.[270] By December, word was coming through from some of her relations that Brenda "looked very smart" in her uniform. Such news made Ken wistful ("I only wish I could be in Uniform in England"), though he stoutly maintained his certainty that doing his "share over here to keep things going" had its own value in the war effort.[271] Still, the greatest obstacle to this affair of the imagination was that Ken was a flesh-and-blood young man and there were young women his age in Guernsey. Occasionally they would flit across Ken's mind, but always filtered through the unattainable standard of Brenda.

In 1943, Ken's heart appeared to be ripe for the picking by Vera Lloyd,[272] a girl at work who served as a secretary for the States. Soon after he first really started thinking about Vera and the pleasant walks home they took together, Ken was thrown into "a quandry," and one that caused him to do "some hard thinking." He started to wonder if all this thought and effort to make contact with Brenda was worthwhile. After all, she was thrown into the wider world of the war effort, surrounded undoubtedly by young soldiers, and "as she is good looking they must have been attracted to her." She answered Ken's messages and always mentioned that she longed for a reunion, but maybe she would look down on Ken, not in uniform and so much a part of the world of her past.

Ken pondered two conflicting idioms that have always puzzled long-distance lovers: would absence make the heart grow fonder, or would it be a case of out of sight, out of mind? "On the other hand I have discovered that [Vera] is a very nice girl and seems to like my company." But was it right to shift affections to a girl who was so different in nature to himself, especially when these differences were apparent to Ken from the beginning? Vera liked to go out to dances, freely mixed with all sorts of people, and was not shy about mentioning other boys that she talked with regularly. During a slack week at work, Ken and Vera talked to while away the time, and many interesting stories were related. Vera described a time when she had been drunk and, upon being taken home to her parents, covered the fact by saying that she had fainted. Ken appeared quite ready to accept her account that she had simply lacked willpower and followed the crowd that one time. She claimed that the incident was "a lesson to her and that she would never drink again."[273] How could such a party-loving girl compete for dutiful and moral Ken when compared to Brenda, absolved of every flaw by time and distance? Then again, how could a phantom like Brenda compete with a girl like Vera, who was warm, alive, and (most important of all) actually there?

For hopeful lovers, for parents and their evacuated children, and for all of the many families and friends divided from each other by Occupation, reunion was uppermost in their minds for five years. The fate of their loved ones in the British armed forces and sheltering on the mainland was bound up in the fate of Britain as a whole. Proud of their British identity and unique history before the war, the Islanders developed a new sense of what patriotism meant during Occupation, and what they could accomplish with their limited resources and in their marginal position. This was a vital revelation for any chance of resistance, or any hope that they could be of use in the war effort. They had to come to grips with the concept that their task was survival, that they served a purpose by holding their own land for Britain, preventing its destruction, and returning it, and themselves, whole and intact as possible at war's end.

But, with that said, Islanders also started to develop a sense of worthwhile risk, a belief in forms of resistance that were necessary to maintain their spirits and their separation from their German occupiers. They developed the resources to bolster those worn by deprivations, and the trust needed to act in ways counter to the ideology that their Nazi masters wished to impose upon them. As they honed a common perception of support and trust, Guernseymen and women reached for their first inkling of control over specific Islanders, particularly those in positions of trust and those who appeared to be complicit with the enemy. This control would be exercised through discursive means, and through the gradual development of a complicated structure of subversion.

In many ways, a resistance of some kind was inevitable for Guernsey. There is no sign in the diaries or elsewhere that Islanders shared in the Nazi ideology. Even the known collaborators and fraternizers appear to have been motivated by a desire for financial/resources benefits or the need for entertainment/love/sex. With a lack of ideological agreement, what functioned in the relationship between occupier and occupied was the imposition of raw power. As Michael Huspek simply puts it, "Where there is power there is resistance."[274] Huspek argues for the intimate relationship between power and resistance, claiming that power itself brings resistance into being by necessity. Resistance then emerges as the "other" to the power that created it, serving as a limitation on that power and a means of determining the boundaries beyond which power cannot go.[275]

There is, in other words, a natural desire for liberty and self-determination that develops when power is imposed upon us. It is such a compelling feeling that only intense threat coupled with ongoing surveillance, of such a type as was found in this panoptical Occupation, can serve to drive it underground.[276] The problem for the more controversial descriptions of the

Occupation has been in mistaking a necessarily covert and sheltered form of resistance with a weakness of underlying determination. Instead, resistance without the means to express itself fully can smolder for a long period and only burst out occasionally in small flames. It would be a mistake to underestimate the intensity of the heat of such a fire, or its ability for general conflagration under the right circumstances. The military power of the Third Reich, its determination to control the occupied populace, and its imposition of extensive surveillance to further those efforts set up the ideal situation to trigger "a reaction that may lie in wait."[277] The next three chapters will outline the shape of that reaction and the rhetorical resistance that emerged in the Guernsey Occupation.

CHAPTER THREE

Reaching for Control

It was Easter Sunday in 1941, and as Reverend Ord left church on his way home after services, he found himself with an uncomfortable escort. A German submarine was currently in the St. Peter Port harbor, and some of the men from its crew happened to be heading in the same direction as Rev. Ord for part of his journey. Ord could guess where the "filthy wretches" came from simply by their unwashed faces and the state of their uniforms. As they all reached the steep road leading up Monument Hill, the men apparently decided to have a little fun at the expense of this British reverend gentleman whom they had now encountered. The Germans fell in on both sides of Ord and entertained themselves with some rude comments at his expense. Ord walked in silence for some time, allowing this little comedy to proceed, before he spoke in their language himself and had the pleasure of watching the German faces fall. He later speculated as to the German soldiers' reaction: "Had this cleric understood what they had been saying about him?"

As this "little cavalcade" passed some of the Guernsey passersby, Ord could observe the sympathy on people's faces and their deep concern to see him flanked by German soldiers. It dawned on him that news would quickly travel all over Guernsey that Reverend Ord was under arrest! Sure enough, later in the day a phone call came to his home anxiously seeking confirmation that he had been detained, and Ord had the pleasure of answering the telephone personally to put the caller's mind at ease. But what, he pondered, would his wife, Grae, have thought had she been alone and answered the call herself?[1]

On that Easter Sunday, Ord was able to experience himself as the subject of the extensive network of rumors that served as one counterpoint to official German-controlled information. It is an exploration of such shadow methods of communication that will compose this chapter and serve as a first foray into understanding the hidden transcript of the Guernsey Occupation. Now that we have a rough outline of the events and shifting character of the first four years of Occupation, a sense of the panoptical style of German control, and a feel for the support and trust that the majority of the Guernsey population carved out for themselves, it may be possible to understand the rhetorical nature of resistance in its many forms. Those outside of the experience of Occupation (particularly when writing decades after the events) have had difficulty acknowledging and appreciating this resistance for one very good reason: outsiders, just like the Germans in authority, were never intended as the audience for these acts. One clear aspect of other studies of subordinated people is the specificity of intended audience for the hidden transcript. It is only meant as communication to "those in the know," that is, to those sharing a position of powerlessness, and therefore it has "to costume itself and speak more warily" in the presence of the powerful.[2]

This necessarily restrictive audience has sometimes led to deep frustration in the Channel Islands with modern interpretations of their history. Our rapidly dwindling survivors of the time of the Occupation, modest as that generation tends to be, have recently opened up and shared their best anecdotes of clever thwarting of the German will, only to have these efforts dismissed as minor and unremarkable, or worse yet, viewed as some cover for mass collaboration. This is not a unique interpretive problem. Subordinated populations know intimately the aggression behind symbolic and coded discourse, and the use of these subtle means to affect the conduct of the powerful.[3] Those outside the situation of powerlessness often only see the "façade of the public transcript" and are unable to see through a discursive guise that was, after all, designed to be "cryptic and opaque."[4] It could be said that the public transcript of the Occupation was metaphorically written in German, just as the official story of American slavery and post–Civil War Reconstruction was for so many years only written by whites, many of them slaveholders and their descendants. The story of most corporations and large businesses is written not by the many lower-level workers, but by the few in the front office. Thus there is a tendency for the shadow discourse of those without power (the hidden and the coded) to be viewed not as true subversion, but as a simple popping off at the mouth, as pinpricks easily ignored by the powerful, or as "empty posturing" that takes the place of actual resistance.[5]

The concept of the "safety valve" is a potentially valid one that I will discuss later, but for now there is a basic rule of thumb that can be followed in assessing the subversive power of acts found in the hidden transcript. We should keep our eyes on the Germans. When they, the "elites" of the Occupation, view even small acts as important and react toward them with shows of force and with countermeasures, it is a sure sign that these acts possess some ability to undercut the power differential.[6] By keeping German reactions in view, it will aid us in avoiding the key mistake of perceiving open resistance as the only resistance. As James Scott puts it so clearly, "Each realm of open resistance to domination is shadowed by an infrapolitical twin sister who aims at the same strategic goals but whose low profile is better adapted to resisting an opponent who could probably win any open confrontation."[7] The next three chapters will profile this "twin sister" as she emerged during the Occupation. The remainder of this study will show that rhetorical resistance took three primary forms: alternative discursive channels and the flow of information, narrative sense-making, and subversion of the dominant through acts of symbolic defiance.

Information was a nexus of power and a basic need for both the Germans and the Islanders. Chapter 3 will examine the secondary channels of private discourse that ran parallel to the occupier-controlled public channels of information. Rumor and gossip, despite their reputations as problematic hindrances to communication, are actually effective means of control when exercised by the powerless. Although rumor and gossip have their own narrative content, which I will discuss, they also provided a stream of information that wended its own path around the Island. Chapter 4 will present the mental game that was played through propaganda and counter-propaganda in the Island. The Germans were on a constant drive to control the narrative content of information, just as the Islanders were always on the alert for means to circumvent that control. In that chapter, too, I will discuss the way that narrative sense-making took place through common, and deceptively harmless forms of communication such as jokes and stories. Chapter 5 then takes us to the heart of the matter with an examination of more active resistance during the Guernsey Occupation, acts that clustered around symbolic expression. I will seek common threads uniting the various covert means of standing up to German control, and the points where these means erupted into public view.

In this chapter, I will begin the examination of the first form of rhetorical resistance during the Occupation, with the role of rumor as a shadow means of discourse. Rumors, which swept the Island and were seemingly the least controlled by anyone, including the Islanders, actually served a distinct function of expressing the deepest hopes and anxieties of those passing them on. There were points where rumor transcended simple expression, and attempts were made to manipulate this informal channel for distinct purposes. On the other hand, gossip—rumor's fellow traveler—had a far stronger ability to check the actions of others. Gossip became the one method that the vast majority of patriotic Guernseymen and women had to protect themselves against the bad players in their midst. This chapter will consider the function of gossip as a rhetorical tool, one that instructed on acceptable norms and values at the same time that it sanctioned those outside the pale. Because of the natural connection with gossip, this chapter will also examine one of the points of controversy in the historical record of the Guernsey Occupation: the role of informants, collaborators, black-marketeers, and those willing to fraternize with the occupying forces. Just as hardship brought out the best in most of the Island, it brought out the worst in a certain part of the population. The Islanders were well aware and contemptuous of any quislings and rogues in their midst. A further complication arose from the fact that these were neighbors, with whom they often had interpersonal relationships before the Occupation.

There developed, particularly as the war moved toward its end, common fantasies of postwar retribution, when the guilty would receive their just desserts. This projection into the future provided an outlet for aggrieved feelings and prevented retaliation during the Occupation itself, actions that would have been dangerous for the entire population. Although appalled by those lacking basic morals and/or patriotism, some Islanders found themselves weighing the seriousness of offenses, discovering a measure of forgiveness for human weakness. Islanders also worried about the *appearance* of fraternization. Even setting the line dividing acceptable versus unacceptable behavior is difficult in unstable times, when situations are unfamiliar and the rules of the game are not always clear. Thus, these accounts provide an opportunity to explore self-concept and our justifications for personal behavior when the lines of honesty and proper action are not clearly drawn.

THAT LYING DAME

For such a familiar aspect of our communicative lives, rumor can be surprisingly elusive to define. Most researchers agree that rumor is unverified information, usually put forward as a claim intended to be believed, that passes from person to person and involves events and issues of public concern.[8] Important in such definitions is that rumor, by its very nature, is unsubstantiated, although that does not mean that it will prove false as events unfold. The unreliable nature of rumor, its lack of solid grounding in fact, fuels the contempt most intelligent people have for rumors and for those who spread and believe them. In the introduction to his diary, written after Liberation, Ord refers to the traditional personification of rumor as "that lying Dame" and admits that any record of the Occupation would be incomplete without an account of the rumors that swept Guernsey. He also quotes E. F. Benson's view that a study of World War II could be composed simply from the wild rumors of the time, a psychological portrait of "the effect of jangled and excited nerves on our capacity for credulity."[9] All communities trade in rumor as part of their everyday currency of discourse, and rumor was not new to the Island as simply a product of the war or the Occupation. It did, however, take on a new importance as other means of obtaining information were restricted.

It is no mystery why rumors grew in number, and the tendency to pay heed to them also increased during the Occupation years. In recent years, Ralph Rosnow predicted the construction and transmission of rumors based on four conditions: an overall sense of uncertainty, the importance of the rumor topic ("outcome-relevant involvement") to those involved in transmission, a state of individual anxiety, and credulity (whether the rumor appears trustworthy).[10] It is easy to see how the first three of these factors were in almost continuous play during the Occupation, simply based on conditions already discussed in this study. What is particularly interesting is the contemporaneous viewpoint concerning the last factor: the level of believability when it came to the many rumors racing from person to person across the Island.

Kitty Bachmann remembered that the "first of a record crop of rumours" came to her hearing before the Occupation was even under way, when Miss Ross came to tell her that ocean liners were coming to take the entire population to Canada.[11] The uncertainty of the evacuation period meant that rumors of highly questionable origin were given credence as people sought any information that would help them to decide whether to stay or go. But rumor never settled back down to the typical level of normal Island life, and Ambrose Robin shared Kitty's metaphor when he described the "tremendous crop of rumors that circulate from day to day." His theory for this harvest of questionable information had to do with the "meagre" quantity of local news in the papers and the "official German Communique" that passed for news of the outside world. No one knew what was happening even on the other side of the Island, so there was considerable room for speculation to grow.[12]

Our diarists, as a whole, might have been less credulous than the average Islander, simply because the process of keeping a diary reveals some verbal ability and a mind that sifts through experiences. Sometimes Kitty became exasperated with the Guernsey populace, as when the "alluring fable" went around that a BBC broadcast was planned with some Guernsey schoolteachers. What could be more desirable to parents than word of their evacuated children? When this broadcast turned out to be a discussion of the Alderney evacuation, Kitty expostulated, "Alas! Just how gullible can we be?" She believed that it was "wishful thinking" that made the populace naive, and it was wiser "to leave truth and rumour to do their own winnowing."[13]

The person apparently most interested in rumor as an Occupation phenomenon was Rev. Ord. Part of this fascination was simply the wry viewpoint of a highly educated and perceptive man now in the position of leading a flock that was far more gullible. Occasionally, he would record some of the more outlandish stories making the rounds, and simply appended, "O sancta simplicitas!"[14] as a passing assessment of those likely to believe such tales. Other times, he was drawn unwillingly into the rumor itself, as with the report of his "arrest" that opened this chapter. The combination of these factors was irresistible to Ord's sense of the comic. In that first Occupation July, a woman, "one of the more simple type" of his congregation, passed along a rumor about the war to another lady. The story was improbable enough that the hearer expressed doubt about the tale in no uncertain terms. Whereupon the first woman responded, "Oh, but it's perfectly true. I have it ON THE HIGHEST AUTHORITY. In fact I don't mind telling you it came from the Reverend Ord." Ord related this little event with relish, calling his role in this rumor "pure imagination," but rather "pleasant to be thought to be in the know."[15]

Ord's true interest in rumor and its attribution was based in the psychological impact that he could see in his congregation. An elderly man stopped Ord on the street in September 1940: "Just hear— nasty bit of news from a most reliable source!" ("Always a reliable source," dryly observed Ord to his diary.)[16] That same fall, Ord described the considerable distress caused by a "petty official" (he does not say which one) indulging in some "idle chatter" that all church services were soon to be canceled. This casual prophecy was merely this particular official's interpretation of the newly imposed ban on meetings, but "one old lady wept inconsolably when she heard it." With a rare display of anger, Ord considered it "intolerable" that this official, "with the glint of superior information in his eye," should add to the fears of an innocent population trying to be brave in the face of uncertainty.[17]

What prevented the dismissal of even absurd stories were the times that rumor preceded reality. Although Rev. Ord bemoaned the fact that they were "beaten from pillar to post in this land of rumour," he also had to grant that few could afford to reject such tales wholesale when "so many have turned out to contain a modicum of truth." Ord seems embarrassed by this need to rely on unsubstantiated stories, noting that "outsiders may laugh," but under the current conditions "this is the air we breathe."[18] Indeed, many of the rumors reported by the diarists turned out later to be true, at least in part, and these "hits" more than justified closer attention to rumors despite the many "misses" when they proved false. At times rumors preceded reality because they were based on hidden facts.

In September 1941, a "vile rumour" swept through the Island, upsetting everyone. It was said that in reprisal for the Nazi agents being seized in Iran, all non-Guernsey men (some said between eighteen and forty-five, and some all the way up to age sixty) would be deported. The basis for the rumor had been the request German authorities had made for detailed reports concerning anyone not born in Guernsey. According to Rev. Ord, it was "indiscreet chatter" by States clerks complying with this request for information that had launched the rumor. Once under way, it started to grow as rumors do, and soon came to encompass women and children.[19] But a glance behind the scenes proved this rumor to be based on a very real threat. It was true that British authorities had interned a group of German nationals in Iran, suspecting them of illegal, subversive activities. Hitler was furious and, seeking a means of reprisal, ordered ten British subjects deported from the Channel Islands for every German detained in Iran.[20] Ken Lewis, who might have been one of the clerks responsible for a little "indiscreet chatter" about the German plans, "heard the Germans wanted 700 men to take away. As a result I worked all Thursday afternoon till 8:30 all day Friday till 7:15pm" compiling the demanded lists.[21]

It would seem that this planned deportation was an ill-kept secret, because the rumor spread very quickly to anyone with connections to the States. Winifred Harvey heard of the threat through Mr. Dorey—although in the version she received, a thousand men were to be impressed into forced labor and sent off the Island.[22] At the same time, a counter-rumor emerged to give a positive spin in the opposite direction. Ord reported that in this version, it was the Royal Navy that was planning to come on the weekend to ferry away men of military age. These men should be prepared to go on the given signal! Ord considered it "a pity that there should be such gullible folk—and not only among the ill-educated either!" Throughout the rest of September 1941, the deportation rumor stayed the primary topic of conversation, and the newspapers were opened anxiously each morning in anticipation of the worst. Even Ord, who believed that many of these rumors came from the Germans, admitted to feeling the anxiety. Perhaps it was not "alarmist" to heed some of the most sensible members of the community who were saying, "No smoke without fire."[23]

The combination of a rumor that just would not go away, and occupiers who were always unpredictable served to heighten the suspense. It was only in October that the deportation rumor died. Ken Lewis got wind of this possible change of fortune early on, because of his position in the States. He wrote, "On Monday morning I heard that the question of deporting men may die out altogether and every minute of the day prayers were being offered to God in order that nothing may come of it."[24] Then, exactly one year later—seemingly out of the blue—came the deportation of the English-born from Guernsey. As Ord's neighbor said, "Here it is at last!"—handing him the order published in the *Evening Press.*[25] Perhaps the deportation would never have happened had it not been for humanitarian efforts by the Red Cross in the late summer of 1942. A proposal to exchange seriously wounded POWs was expanded by the Swiss to include Channel Islanders who might need to go to England. Unfortunately, this proposal, made for all the best of intentions, brought to Hitler's attention that his order of 1941 had not been carried out.[26] For that reason, the deportation of 1942 was both anticipated and abrupt. It actually was a plan long postponed, but existed for the Islanders as a series of apparently unfounded rumors. When distressing rumors occasionally proved true even after a long delay, it is little wonder that Islanders were left not knowing what to believe and what to dismiss.

Research on rumor, much of which started immediately after World War II because of the astonishing number of rumors during that conflict, emphasizes its spontaneous rather than strategic nature.[27] The truth that, as Jean-Noel Kapferer maintains, the "public is the main actor" when it comes to rumor transmission has sometimes been sheltered by attempts to give rumor more weight and importance. When defeatist rumors cropped up in the United States during the war, the government attempted to counter them with a propaganda campaign attributing such rumors to the "fifth column," the enemy within. These murky confederates of the Axis were supposedly listening in at the grocery store or the street corner for any rumors that would reveal military plans. They also were portrayed as the source of any negative rumors about conduct of the war, supposedly sending these rumors around to damage morale.[28] Believing there to be a dark force behind the transmission of rumor might make those taken in by an absurd tale feel better and, at least in theory, could aid in squelching destructive or morale-damaging stories. Yet it is the average person hearing a rumor who has the power to pass it on or to allow it to die unreplicated. The decision to speed a rumor on its rounds through a population tells us quite a bit about the psychology of a people in a given situation. As Hans-Joachim Neubauer puts it, a rumor is "a mirror in which society catches sight of its hidden self."[29]

Rosnow provides an oft-repeated metaphor for his view of rumor transmission. He likens rumor-mongering to loading and firing a gun, with the gun being the public audience for the rumor, and the bullet being the rumor. Rosnow believes the gun to be loaded in situations where there is anxiety and uncertainty, and the gun fired (the rumor spread) when "the bullet will hit the mark," that is, when the rumor will be viewed as credible.[30] Ord seemed in tune with this notion of a hidden psychological purpose to rumors, believing that they may help "some mercurial spirits over times of depression," and therefore even the most far-fetched positive stories could be "patriotic and helpful." Still he was wary of the impact of negative tales.[31] This rough division between positive and negative rumors has been studied as the difference between "wish rumors," those predicting consequences desired by the rumor public, and "dread rumors," those that speak of consequences to be feared.[32] Even a brief examination of Guernsey Occupation rumors uncovers this same rough division.

When it comes to wish rumors, almost all tended in the direction of imminent release from Occupation. This theme of rescue confirms James Scott's observation that all subjugated groups read into rumors "promises of their imminent liberation" from their position of powerlessness.[33] The world *will* turn upside down, and the last shall be first. Some of the wish rumors of the Occupation involved positive (if unlikely) war news. In July 1941, Ord reported that the rumors were flying "thick and fast," including the British invading France "any time now."[34] This liberation-any-day-now rumor never died, and the Pollyannas of the populace had ample time to embroider on the tale.

The problem with wish rumors and relying upon them for a shot of hope was the speed at which they could be deflated. As Dorothy Higgs put it in September 1942, "The place is full of lovely rumours again. When they fly around, we feel on top of the world but it is an awful flop when they fizzle out!"[35] At that point, prior to the tremendous blow of the English deportation, the rumor was that the Germans would hightail it off the Islands in advance of an invasion. The advantage to this version of the liberation myth was that its scenario promised freedom without the military engagement that could destroy Guernsey.

Dread rumors also followed predictable courses during the Occupation, generally clustering around the fear of further deportations or of a German invasion of mainland Britain. In light of the deportations, first of the English and then the announcement of the plan to deport ex-officers, it was not surprising that Jack Sauvary and others believed a rumor that all Freemasons would also be sent to Germany. As Jack wrote, "That will mean my turn next."[36] This rumor was not unreasonable considering that the Germans had banned Freemason and Oddfellows meetings in 1941 and seized their property.[37] And this is the way that dread rumors tend to operate: the person paying heed to the rumor and passing it on often falls into the category that will be negatively affected should the rumor prove true. This was Rosnow's point when he described "outcome-relevant involvement" as one condition of rumor transmission.[38]

When Winifred Harvey was on a brief visit to Sark in 1942, the rumor at the Dixcart Hotel was that fifteen hundred men from Jersey, a thousand men from Guernsey, and a hundred from Sark were to be deported to work on the Continent. This particular dread rumor was given weight by the co-rumor that multiple gun emplacements were to be built in Sark, turning that tiny and quaint island into a virtual weapon itself. One evening, in promoting the veracity of this rumor, a Miss Duckitt told them that she had been to see the German commandant about an unrelated matter and, while there, saw that he had a map of Sark unrolled on his desk. As she talked to him, she looked over his shoulder at the map and could see red crosses at various points on the map. Realizing that she was studying his map, the commandant shouted, "Dat is not for you to look at!" and he abruptly rolled up the map and stuffed it into a drawer.[39]

Now, this little story of Miss Duckitt, told on a dark evening at a quiet hotel, when the travelers had been temporarily stranded in Sark and refused passage back to Guernsey, illustrates an alternative view of rumor and its transmission. Bernard Guerin and Yoshihiko Miyazaki associate the passing of rumor not with anxiety reduction or the rumor's sense-making properties, but with the social spotlight it provides for the speaker. The relating of rumor and gossip—much like jokes, stories, and urban legends—is a form of entertainment, exciting to tell and enjoyable to hear. Even in the case of dread rumors, which tend to heighten our level of anxiety, there is some psychological amusement in contemplating the worst that could happen. Rather like hearing a ghost or horror story, the considering of a worst-case scenario gives a chill up the back that has a peculiar aspect of pleasure to it, but only when the threat is a remote possibility and not an inevitable fact. For the teller, being first to relate a rumor has "conversational cash value," guaranteeing a place at the center of attention.[40] This desire to be first with the engaging story works against any reasonable attempts to verify the truth underlying rumor or gossip, and means that the embroidering of the tale (to make it more thrilling) is increased.

The very traits that Rosnow identifies as key to rumor transmission (anxiety, uncertainty, personal importance, and credulity) are precisely what makes a story "interesting and attention-grabbing."[41] It is also possible to sense a different approach to rumor by those diarists with more of the raconteur about them. So, Jack Sauvary, Bill Warry, Bert Williams, Dorothy Higgs, and Kitty Bachmann seem more interested in rumors and the chit-chat that made up the informal communication links of the Island. "Chewing the fat" with others seemed to be part of their personality and social makeup. Some, such as Elizabeth Doig and Arthur Mauger, were in such a poor position to differentiate rumor from fact that these stories were more of a source of anxiety. And for those more in the know (by position, education, or nature), rumors were interesting as a phenomenon, but ready belief in them was viewed as the product of a subpar mentality or a lack of solid information. Thus, Reverend Ord, Ambrose Robin, Winnie Harvey, and (making allowance for his age) even Ken Lewis wrote often about the rumors of the day, but generally looked askance at them, gauging such stories against the more solid information to which they were privy.

Although a rumor may appear uncontrolled, it is clear that during its transmission "the process of embellishment and exaggeration is not at all random." It expands and contracts as it moves from person to person, adding and deleting details to bring it more in line with the underlying worldview of the tellers.[42] For example, one of the more amusing and popular rumors was that "a very big personage" was visiting the Island. Based on such evidence as the doubling of sentries at the Royal Hotel (and conveyed, at least to Winnie, by "Dora-at-the-Royal," who said that the staff had to prepare a special luncheon), this unknown high-ranking Nazi was first considered to be next to Goering, maybe even Goering himself.[43]

By the next year, the same rumor was circulating of an important, secret visitor to the Island. Some were saying that it was actually Hitler (!) and based the importance of the supposed guest on armed sentries, an unusual number of airplanes (supposedly an escort for the great man), and the foul tempers and frayed nerves (again, according to insider Dora-at-the-Royal) of the German command. By then—with actual news of Rudolph Hess's flight to England circulating—it was put forward that the visitor of the previous year was actually Hess.[44] In this rumor as it morphed over a year's time, it is possible to see the sense-making function of rumor (Oh, it must have been Hess getting as close to England as possible to plan his later flight . . .) and the underlying need this rumor expresses of viewing Guernsey as an important player, on some level, in the war.

In addition to what they tell us about the mindset of those passing and receiving them, rumors perform distinct functions in the hidden transcript. First, rumors provide a means to convey interpersonal trust and the assurance of shared interests and goals. Beneath their chatty, friendly narrative of the latest news, however bogus, lies an unspoken test of commonality. Kitty Bachmann provides an insight into this role of rumor in her perceptive description of everyday talk:

> So we live from day to day. We see friends and exchange rumours grave and comical, credible and bizarre. We seldom reveal our innermost thoughts, but we know just as surely as though exchanged by word of mouth that the next person's feelings are identical with our own, thought for thought. What a mess we are in! How will it end? And the inaudible cry goes up: "How long?"[45]

In addition to its role in solidarity and a subtle feeling out of others, rumor has a practical value as a warning device. A story circulated early in the Occupation, when new orders and restrictions were almost a daily matter, was that an unnamed girl had been electrocuted when she went near one of the local bays. "Serves her right, if it is true," was Winifred Harvey's response. "We have been warned."[46]

Warning messages are often those conveyed through the "grapevine," a term coined in America sometime in the late 1840s or early 1850s to compare the twisted nature of rumor and gossip (the "grapevine telegraph" of distorted talk from person to person) to the straight lines of the new electric telegraph that was considered such a marvel.[47] Some rumors seem to have such a clear purpose that they appear to be planned and sent abroad with a goal in mind. Warning rumors, such as the one about the girl electrocuted when she trespassed, seem particularly structured around a desired outcome. When there was crackdown on black-marketeers, with some men involved given five years imprisonment, Elizabeth Doig reported a rumor at the same time that there was powdered glass in some of the sugar that was being sold, and chalk in some of the flour.[48] This rumor may have developed spontaneously—Elizabeth seized upon it as an explanation for her own bout of gastric upset—but its timing seems to indicate a conscious hand at work.

An equivalent rumor had been passed around earlier in the spring of that year (1943) that a number of Germans had died from poisoning in the food, wine, and spirits that had been imported from France, purportedly because they were tainted with arsenic and iron filings. Winnie Harvey gave some credence to this particular rumor, saying that the States were testing food being imported for civilians' use, and noting that the chocolate and cheese intended as an "Easter treat" for the Islanders had been discarded. Now in analyzing a rumor such as this, it is important to note that Winnie uses the phrase "we hear that" as the lead-in to her explanation. Thus, she is employing rumor to verify rumor. In effect, this is an unsubstantiated discarding of hypothetical treats due to a rumored poisoning.[49] Such a story, if sent around on purpose, would warn civilians away from items that might have been sabotaged by the French Underground. It would also make anyone contemplating collaboration in exchange for German food or drink think twice about the wisdom of such a move. Such apparent practical and ideological benefits for the Islanders point to the important rhetorical purposes that rumor could provide in a time of oppression.

TITTLE-TATTLE

By August 1940 multiple social feelers had been sent out by German officers, still laboring under the belief that a pleasant new relationship could be established with the Guernsey populace. The occupiers had arranged for several dances for Germans and civilians to be held at St. George's Hall, and must have been delighted when not only did some Islanders attend but also several civilians held reciprocal events in their own homes. What pleased the Nazi elite outraged the Island as a whole, who sharpened their tongues to mount a blistering attack on these "turncoats" who were quickly "suitably ostracised." Kitty Bachmann wrote to her mother that the names of those entertaining the Germans would come as no surprise, particularly one man—an Englishman not all that long a resident of the Island—who now was broadly being referred to as "Herr Blank."[50]

An odd little battle erupted among those telling this tale. Kitty was flabbergasted when a mainlander had the temerity to say to her, "This sort of thing would never happen in England," leading her to retort that every person identified thus far as entertaining Germans had been an English transplant It is rather remarkable to see this small tension over comparative loyalty crop up early in the Occupation, only to be echoed at the end of the twentieth century by those seeking evidence of Islander collaboration. At the time, although staunchly defending the "overwhelming loyalty to the British Crown" of her fellow Guernseymen and women, Kitty wisely predicted that the Island would "produce her own crop of traitors, they infest every sizeable community the world over."[51]

Kitty was less concerned over those making a conscious choice to fraternize with the enemy, and more worried about friends put in an untenable position by German overtures. Faced with "a dearth of dance-partners," the Germans directly issued invitations to the daughters of some of the Bachmanns' friends. This situation was more awkward than it might first appear. The offers in this case were "declined, firmly," but with the knowledge that the family ran the risk of antagonizing men with the power to do them harm. It was, Kitty maintained, a "precarious" place to be, for it was difficult to know how these German officers—who considered these invitations a great honor that they were conferring—would react to such a rebuff.[52] It was not merely that the "honored" family was refusing to fraternize with the enemy; they were, in their refusal, insulting that enemy at a time when the reaction could not be predicted.

Very early in the Occupation, Islanders had to grapple with the fact that some among them were willing to ease their way through the new circumstances undeterred by thoughts of patriotism and untroubled by ethical scruples. For those who were already thieves and rogues (and every population of 25,000 has its share of those), the Occupation presented new ground on which to operate. For any woman who had always, as the charming old phrase goes, sailed through life on her bottom, the influx of handsome German officers and men must have seemed like a unexpected benefit of war. Kitty Bachmann was right that her mother, to whom her diary entries were directed, would recognize the names of early welcomers of the enemy presence. Yet, she was also correct in predicting that over time, and under wearing circumstances, some Islanders would very consciously put their patriotism, even their fellow feeling with their neighbors, on hold and seek whatever personal advantage could be gained through fraternization and collaboration. Still others could be said to accidentally overstep the invisible and fuzzy ethical line that separates clever survival tactics from unacceptable actions.

The modern fascination with this minority population of quislings, informers, and other rogues is far out of proportion to their actual number. So many recent books (not just supposed "exposés" by journalists, but mysteries like Elizabeth George's *A Place of Hiding*) and television shows (like the British *Island at War* series) cannot resist the easy plot device of secret collaborators, or the forbidden love between Guernsey maid and dashing German soldier. Considering that such individuals did exist and provide a dramatic fillip to the norm of Occupation life, not to mention a dangerous counterpoint to Guernsey resisters, it is difficult to blame these authors and dramatists for their focus on the exception rather than the rule.

Also, the need at the close of the war to decide on whether there would be war-crimes trials for certain named collaborators shifted the emphasis to those who had failed their country, rather than those who acquitted themselves with honor.[53]

The truth is that it will always be impossible to put a number on the bad players of various stripes in Guernsey, though every reasonable assessment is that the percentage of the population was quite small. Kitty speaks at this early point in the Occupation of the "99% who do not fraternise with the Germans."[54] She asserted that, despite certain exceptions "in the woodpile, Guernsey's attitude towards them [the Germans] is correct."[55] On the other hand, you have Madeleine Bunting, who, typical of her style, indicts everyone in a blanket statement that "islanders compromised, collaborated and fraternised just as people did throughout occupied Europe."[56] But if a person looks at the evidence cited by Bunting, rather than her conclusions, a different picture emerges. She mentions a letter by an anonymous Islander, one that was smuggled out by an escapee and published in the *London Times* on December 5, 1944: "The only people who can get any food now are the collaborators [described later in the letter as "the black marketeers . . . the informers and quislings" that should be "dealt with"] and the jerrybags and there are a few hundred of each kind."[57] Yet, if this number is read in reference to Guernsey, then "a few hundred" (300?) of each kind would combine to be somewhere between 2 to 3 percent of the population. Even in a letter written by an Islander aggravated enough to send communication through an escapee, and thus subject to exaggeration, a 97 to 98 percent majority managing to do the right thing on a daily basis seems to be a reasonable estimate.

Yet what damage even a small percentage of nest-feathering in a population could cause, and what a shock it was to most Guernseymen and women that *any* Islanders would forego ethics to get by or thrive financially. Jack Sauvary, who makes a pretty fair model of the average Guernseyman, was "stunned" at the lack of sincerity he found in some of the civilian population. Although he does not give details or name names, he speaks of those who could "run with the foxes and hunt with the hounds," shifting with the circumstances to play the side that benefited them in the current moment. This revelation was actually depressing for Jack, who took it much to heart, claiming, "Life is very disappointing."[58]

Jack wanted to see the better side of people and was like many who could forgive those who "kept friendly" with the Germans for a "little food." But by 1944, he had come to the conclusion that the great motivator of fraternization was "money, the great curse." By that late date in the Occupation, it was clear to him that there were those who "would sell their own relations or country for money."[59] As it became clear to the Islanders that some of their neighbors were no longer to be trusted, an old and readily available means of control was honed to deal with the problem. If rumor served as a means of sense-making and the expression of common interests, then gossip provided a far more directed and powerful method of self-protection and constraint.

Although rumor and gossip are sometimes blended in the public mind, they are actually two very different discursive moves with distinct purposes. Sarah Wert and Peter Salovey provide the cleanest definition of gossip when they describe it as "informal, evaluative talk about a member of the discussants' social environment who is not present."[60] This definition rings true with our common understanding about gossip: it is the process of talking behind the back of another specific person. Unlike rumor, which may be highly generalized, gossipers are telling stories about a particular target who is known to them, and quite often, although not always, with whom they have a personal relationship. If rumor has sometimes been viewed as the proof of a gullible mind, then gossip is often treated as mere tittle-tattle, an "indirect form of aggression, akin to teasing" and of little public importance.[61]

Slowly, such views of this type of informal discourse have given way to an understanding of its strategic value, especially when more formal channels of communication are blocked.[62] Gossip, in particular, serves as an efficient weapon for those who have in other ways been disarmed. One aspect that has emerged in recent studies of gossip is the dramatic upsurge in the amount of gossip within a society under external threat from a more dominant society.[63] In some more commonplace situations, the ability to gossip about our bosses and our peers at work gives an illusion of power where none exists. Yet, in a situation of high stakes, gossip can be wielded with controlled intent, far more than is seen in rumor transmission.

Although gossip has multiple functions, there are two purposes that emerge as particularly important during the Occupation of Guernsey. First, gossip has power as a teaching tool. It is a means whereby peers are able to pool their knowledge, information, and beliefs in order to understand which actions are permissible and which actions are beyond the pale. By gossiping about the other's failings, and less commonly about the other's successes and positive actions, a society transmits a sense of cultural norms and the expectations of moral conduct. Baumeister et al. say it best when they describe gossip as "observational learning of a cultural kind" and maintain that in learning of "the misadventures of others, we may not have to endure costs to ourselves," simply because we can avoid similar mistakes.[64]

There is considerable power in storytelling, or as some would say, telling tales out of school, because the narrative form has a far stronger impact than any list of rules and regulations. The use of purportedly true stories of the failings of others functions much like fables and fairy tales. Through admonishment and disapproval, and perhaps even a satisfying ending of the guilty party's fall from grace, gossip is well structured to teach lessons even to the young.[65] Although some gossip is actually positive, we tend to think of gossip as derogatory. This negative form may be more useful during times of hazardous oppression, as in war and occupation, because of the heightened need to learn about dangers.[66] But gossip has the advantage of traveling in disguise; when we speed gossip on its way, we often know only the most recent stops on its journey and not its point of origin. And this tale told of another will continue to be spread only so long as it fulfills some need of the tellers. It is for this reason that we say that gossip, like rumor, may die down given time.[67]

One of the needs fulfilled by conveying gossip resembles the social spotlight provided by passing rumors. Although passing a negative tale about someone we know is an occasion for guilt and is disapproved of by most religions, it is also enjoyable, much like all storytelling. As with rumor, we hold our audience by being the first to convey new gossip. Our interest in the story is often enhanced because the teller and hearer both share a relationship with the absent subject. The audience for gossip is thus encouraged to comment and speculate on the story, making gossip "a shared and collaborative experience."[68] By relating a story tinged with malice about another, we also enhance our own status as someone who knows the rules of society. It is a move of moral superiority, because it subtly implies that our own behavior could better pass the inspection of others.[69]

In fact, Wert and Salovey maintain that social comparison is a factor in all gossip. Often, the comparison is with peers, those who are similar to us in their position in life and subject to the same temptations, opportunities, successes, and failures. Other times the gossip is about someone in a position of less power and fewer resources ("downward social comparison"), or someone of greater power and in a position to access more extensive opportunities and resources ("upward social comparison").[70] In all of these cases, gossip provides a method of mutually determining and sharing the "shoulds" and "oughts" of a society.

Perhaps even more important in understanding the role of gossip during the Occupation is to understand its second purpose as a means of control over others. It has aptly been described as a "policing device . . . a low-cost method of regulating members' [of a given society] actions."[71] It is for that reason that gossip becomes an important topic at this point when I am considering those who failed to acquit themselves honorably during the Occupation. By establishing an Occupation constructed through panoptical control, the German occupiers hoped to encourage the kind of lateral surveillance where civilian would spy on civilian, being rewarded for denunciations made to the authorities. Yet, the more important story of the Occupation was the marshaling of lateral surveillance by the majority population as a means of self-protection and a means to resist German control. In effect, by heightened watchfulness and the use of gossip, the Islanders were often successful in "belling the cat," whether the threat came from above or from their peers.

As James Scott tells us, within powerless subordinates there is a high level of policing of speech and actions, and a considerable social pressure for conformity. This type of control may be "painful and often ugly," but it is undeniably effective.[72] When the common good seems to be under attack by individuals, gossip provides a discursive means of offering punishment. Because, most commonly, the gossip is malicious, it links a specific person's name with a tale of scandal or error. Dealing in local character assassination, this "stereotypical village tyranny of the majority" is more often directed against our peers and serves as the democratic voice of condemnation.[73] Yet, it also serves as a critique of those immediately above us, particularly those middle managers who serve as the liaison between the powerless many and the powerful few.

In both cases, during the Occupation, gossip became a vital means for Islanders to warn their compatriots and block the actions of those whose loyalty and ethics did not measure up. In the following pages I will consider some of the ethical conundrums of these years, the many who strove to maintain their sense of morality and patriotic action, and the minority who played the conditions of the Occupation for personal gain. Throughout, my emphasis will be on the role that informal discourse played in the Islanders' collective understanding of the ethics of survival, and in their structuring of means of self-protection and resistance.

BARTER AND BLACK-MARKETEERS

One legitimate method of survival that appeared quickly during the Occupation was the ancient practice of barter, a direct swapping of goods and services without the exchange of money. This means of finding value in whatever is ready to hand may be the oldest method of surviving during times of scarcity and want. It has generally been as simple as the trade of a pair of outgrown children's shoes for a joint of meat or basket of vegetables. The willingness to part with an item is based on the greater personal value of the item to be gained. Therefore, we barter out of both our excess and our want.

This innocent form of barter is precisely the way that it began in Guernsey. Dorothy Higgs was quite the mistress of effective and legitimate barter. Although rurally based with enough land to raise hens, rabbits, goats, and to lay in a decent small garden, her positive food situation did not protect her from want in other areas. One perpetual problem for Islanders was a lack of soap, particularly important not just in terms of hygiene and health, but key to the preservation of the few clothes that they had. For some time, Dorothy had a good store of soap (the pre-Occupation kind, not the "lump of clay" that was rationed but rarely bought). Yet she "gave it away too freely," as was her nature, and soon was completely out of washing (laundry) soap, though still with a few small bars of personal-care soap. In May 1943, she was thrilled to obtain a full one-pound bar of washing soap in exchange for a dress length of linen.[74] Any discovery of such a stray, unneeded item as this linen sent imaginations scrambling to consider its value in trade for some desired necessity. Kitty Bachmann found amusing this universal hunt for "clothes and oddments ferreted out of drawers and cupboards," items that might have remained where they were had not the general emergency brought them to "the light of day."[75]

Quite soon a barter column appeared in the *Press* where practically anything was offered, "cigarettes, roller skates, gramophone records, vases, fur coats,"[76] in exchange for food. This was one of the few ways to augment the diets of those living in towns and lacking land for gardens—particularly those also lacking the prewar wealth needed to purchase food at the current exorbitant prices. Soon barter shops opened up all over Guernsey, though particularly in St. Peter Port. As a shopkeeper and small businessman himself, Bill Warry liked to paste into his scrapbook/diary ads from these establishments, more than one of which appears to have been named "Barter Mart." The copy from one of these ads gives the gist of them all:

> ROLL UP AND BE SATISFIED
> and have a SQUARE DEAL at
> BARTER MART
> 16, Fountain St.
> Clothing Bought and Exchanged.
> I also buy GOLD, SOAP and
> TINNED FRUIT, or anything
> you have to sell that's of no use to
> yourself. So———
> ROLL UP AND DON'T BE SHY[77]

The last line of this advertisement seems to point to some hesitancy on the part of a proud and independent people, now forced to part with both "junk" and family treasures in a bid for survival.

There was more than a tinge of humor to some of the items proffered. Rev. Ord found great amusement in one ad: "A large Family Bible . . . quite untouched, valued at 45/- for one pound of tea." Was this, Ord pondered, "the modern equivalent of Esau's 'mess of pottage'?" And, besides, "who did the valuing"?[78] Most common barter was on a one-to-one basis and quite satisfying on both sides. Bill Warry believed that he had received the best side of a "good deal" when he traded a quarter-pound tin of Players Navy Cut tobacco and received 15 pounds of Guernsey wheat (then valued at 8 to 10 shillings—each shilling worth 12 pennies—per pound). Bill considered such deals as "few & far between," but the smoker with whom he was dealing was probably just as happy with the outcome.[79] The same joy of the *bon marché* could be sensed in Elizabeth Doig's news that she had "bartered 3 packets Virginia cigarettes for 10 lbs desert [*sic*] apples."[80] It is casy to see the impact of an ingrained smoking habit on the bartering process: those who could part with tobacco were in a much stronger position than those who could not.

All such barter had to be conducted with the careful caginess for which the Islanders were famous, yet soon a dark issue with barter emerged. Shop windows seemed to be full of available goods that could be obtained by a trade, generally food or tobacco.[81] But where did this bounty in hard goods originate? By mid-1942, the States were attempting to crack down on barter, because the temptations surrounding the practice were simply too great for thieves. Anything stolen, whether from a shop or a private home, could be brought to a barter shop, which would end up serving as a—presumably—unknowing fence for the goods.[82] Those houses of evacuees and deportees, perpetually unguarded, were picked clean. Winifred Harvey wrote at this time of some furniture stores as full of fine objets d'art, china, linen, and art sold to the Germans at very high prices. Rumor was widespread, and believable, that this was "loot" that had belonged to fine homes.[83]

At Christmas 1942, the States were keeping especially close watch on the shops for very good reason. During this particular Yuletide, such a spate of thefts occurred that almost all of the diarists discuss it from their various vantage points. November saw a remarkable number of robberies, most of them consisting of break-ins when a home or shop owner was conveniently away. The hairdresser, Langlois, had his house broken into when he went out with his family one December night to Central Hall.[84] Similarly, the States supervisor Mr. Marquand and his wife were out for tea and came back to find their home looted of a wide variety of items, even the linens taken straight off the beds.[85] Ambrose Robin long felt that some organized foreign gang was at work, because every three days or so, half a dozen houses would be broken into on the same night (with one night having ten robberies). The robbers were so highly trained that they could break in and rob a house while the occupants were asleep.[86]

All of this speculation reached a satisfying conclusion when the police arrested a number of men working with a French laborer named Jean Binet. Ken Lewis mentioned that Binet was only eighteen, but responsible for most of the thefts that had occurred recently.[87] Dramatically, Winnie Harvey described the capture of a "Frenchman and his gang," and referred to Binet as a "well-known international cat burglar," a depiction somewhat at odds with his reported youth.[88] More worrying was the news that Binet had evaded capture initially because he was aided by a local man. Ken could hardly believe this, finding it "incredible to think that any local person would assist foreigners in robbing his own countrymen."[89] The most disturbing aspect for Winnie Harvey was the revelation that old Harvey, Fuzzey's packer, who had helped her with her removal to Grange Terrace and was a man she had trusted with her valuables for thirty years, had "stolen wholesale."[90] After so many years as a simple workman handling the beautiful possessions of others, the temptation to fortune provided by the Occupation may have made out-and-out thievery look like simple opportunity.[91]

Much like barter, the black market in Guernsey was a necessary means of survival for some, an oddity that was a simple matter of choice for others, and an invitation to greed for a few. A flourishing black market erupted quickly in the Island, becoming known as the GUT (the Guernsey Underground Traffic). The ethics of the black market were not the same in mainland Britain as in the Islands, where, as discussed earlier, death from malnutrition was a persistent threat. This difference was mentioned by Kitty, who could hear over the wireless the BBC's condemnation of black-marketeers and repeated urgings for the general population to refrain from black-market purchases. "Practised here," she noted, "it is a far more hazardous, not to say, heroic procedure."[92]

Some civilians bought directly from these traffickers, often German soldiers, who offered good prices to those willing to buy in bulk. From the soldiers' standpoint, unloading the stolen goods quickly was key. The civilian fences then sold from their bulk supplies in smaller quantities to the public, running the risk of "the dreaded knock at the door." The fences then made a comfortable profit margin off of their own neighbors. Herein lay the ethical issue. Had the fence conducted this traffic as an attempt to provide necessities to the population, even with a small profit taken for the time consumption and considerable risk being run, then the GUT might widely have been viewed as patriotic as well as necessary. Of course, this is where greed enters the picture, and these civilian links in the black-market chain were generally in it for all the cash they could extort from their customers.[93]

Considering that rations were inadequate and the resources to grow or raise supplementary food uneven across Guernsey, Islanders did not generally condemn those who felt the need to buy on the black market. Necessity, especially for those aging or in bad health, made exorbitant purchases on the black market a regular occurrence. Jack Sauvary was one who readily admitted that he would spend what little he had on whatever was available. The prices were completely outrageous: 2s. for each egg (though they were generally unobtainable), 35s. per pound for butter, 6s. for flour. But Jack justified such purchases with his usual practicality: "Better a poor man alive than a rich man dead, and the majority about here seem to feel as I do. Some of course won't pay the price. I say fools if you have the dough."[94]

Elizabeth Doig was another who agreed with those paying the high prices for black-market food, believing that "it keeps one in health & saves in the end doctor's bills." Her real concern was for those without the money to supplement their diets and who were in a bad way for lack of nourishment.[95] Not that Elizabeth was sanguine about the black market. She had traded a gold brooch to black-marketeers for two and a half pounds of flour (although it made her ill after eating biscuits made from it), and one pair of silk stockings for one pound of Guernsey butter.[96] So when men working in the black market were caught and given five years' imprisonment, she could only say, "& they deserve it."[97]

By the summer of 1944, Elizabeth was effectively priced out of the black market. She turned down tea at £7 per quarter ounce, refusing to pay "these famine prices," even though some of her friends were willing to do so. And this is an important point about the black market from the civilian perspective. There was no shame involved in needing to turn to this secondary source of nutrition, though perhaps some embarrassment in having to yield to prices that were thievery in disguise. It appears to have been normalized as an extension of life before the war in a capitalist culture; those with money, jewelry, or goods to exchange simply were able to purchase more. What they did with their money was their business, as long as they were not the ones extorting money from their countrymen.[98] It might not be fair, but those with money had always had the advantage.

Quality of black-market items was an issue, since these goods were in no way regulated. Black-market goods were often shoddy to the point of potentially dangerous for health. Desperate for a bit of meat, Bill Warry broke down and bought two pounds of pork (and in his diary he puts a question mark at this point) from a Dutchman, paying 22s. 6d. per pound, and notes, "Some job to masticate."[99] As a businessman, Bill had a sense of humor about the black market, mentioning that the government was down on this underground traffic ("& rightly so"), but that the States were busy buying whatever they could for the Island—at times utilizing the black market in France.[100] And in reading his diary, hints appear that it is the bit of meat that could tempt Bill into underground transactions. After writing about the black market and pasting in stories cut from the newspaper about those caught and fined, he mentions the "good Xmas dinner" they had managed to prepare of "baked potatoes, cabbage, a nice joint of young veal which I scrounged (silence)."[101]

Any theory claiming that had all the Islanders just refused to buy, the prices would have come down and the black market would have withered does not seem to hold up well. The German soldiers had money to spend, and some growers were willing to sell directly to them in order to make a profit. Rev. Ord excoriated those whose "sheer lust of money" kept them from making things easier on the general population. His overall opinion is worth noting, because it reflects the common view:

> The Germans they fleece by exorbitant prices—"fair game," they call them. The Townsfolk must buy at controlled prices, if purchase be at all possible. Such prices, though far above the normal are yet too low to touch the seller's patriotism or humanity. People die for want of eggs: peasants may easily make a mark an egg from soldiers. Indeed that figure is ridiculously low as prices go. No appeal moves these stony hearts.[102]

That "these miserable Shylocks" could see such deprivation among their neighbors and still only focus on "their chief end in life: the acquisition of money" deeply angered even Reverend Ord, normally forgiving of other's faults.[103] The only recourse for Islanders was to differentiate those running barter and black market activities that helped their countrymen to survive from those focused solely on profit. Positive gossip could laud those legitimate (in Island eyes) members of the GUT, just as negative gossip could marginalize those of suspect motive.

WATCHING AND JUDGING

In March 1943, Ken Lewis was surprised and concerned when a Mrs. Cortvriend, who claimed to be writing a book about the Occupation, dropped by the States office. His supervisor Louis Guillemette gave her considerable information and went so far as to let her look at the Controlling Committee minutes. Ken was a little shocked that President Leale would allow this to happen, considering that the minutes were meant to be confidential to the Committee and "one or two of the Staff including myself." This led Ken to consider Mr. Leale "very slack" in issues of security as compared to Sir Abraham Lainé, the former acting president, whom he considered "more methodical and efficient."[104] Now, as it turns out, Ken had no reason to be concerned, for V. V. Cortvriend did write a book on the Occupation, *Isolated Island*, which would be published in 1947. But that lay in the future, and how was one to know who could and could not be trusted with sensitive information?

In addition to security and a need for self-protection, heightened watchfulness during the Occupation was often based on the desire for fairness in the distribution of the few resources available. One of the primary triggers of malicious or negative gossip among subordinates is an uneasy sense that some of their peers are "first among equals." Even when there are few rewards to be had and power is negligible within a dominated society, any sense of injustice, any hint of unevenness in the distribution of benefits, will serve as an impetus for gossip.[105] The heightened lateral surveillance that the Germans hoped to establish as a means of control, pitting neighbor against neighbor in an atmosphere of denunciation and distrust, did occur in some quarters. Yet much of this increased watchfulness among the Guernsey populace turned to a control over those hoping to take advantage of their particular positions for personal gain.

It seemed a matter of common understanding that some Guernseymen and women would be in a better position to take advantage of little extras that came their way. When Rev. Ord and his wife were able to take a rare Sunday off, they were hosted for dinner by the principal wholesale and retail butchers, people whom Ord described as having "ways and means." The Ords' hosts were "conditioned" to a richer diet than the Ords could handle, and so Grae was quite ill during the night.[106] Most likely, the Ords' hosts had long been principal butchers before the Occupation and just continued their position under the new circumstances. Yet, it is generally understood, too, that access to such positions can be utilized by those in control for their own purposes. Elites in power are constantly on the watch for members of the subordinate population who can be used as "the loyal retainers, 'trustees,' and informers" necessary to control the larger mass. One technique to acquire such trustees is through "individual strategies of preferment," tempting defections from the subordinate group with positions of responsibility at higher pay, additional benefits, or simply opportunities for under-the-table extras to which those in power will turn a blind eye.[107]

Subordinates are not powerless in this equation, and they are constantly assessing the loyalty to those "below" still held by former peers who rise to middle-management posts. Often those in such positions are never fully trusted by the powerful or the subordinated and thus open themselves to heightened surveillance and critique. From the perspective of the Islanders, those in positions of distribution or control of food were particularly important and could garner goodwill simply by passing on little benefits to others outside the immediate circle of their families and friends. Sometimes it was simply a matter of turning a judicious blind eye to the actions of former peers that could earn one a reputation as a good fellow of the right sort.

Far more of the gossip surrounding those in enhanced or trustee positions will be malicious or at least rooted in suspicion. Part of this negative assessment is purely a matter of self-protection for those left behind in the subordinate population. The most important question is that of loyalty to the larger group, and who might be prone to defection.[108] Wert and Salovey point out the role of gossip as "an inquiry into the backstage lives of others: What is this person really about? What is motivating him or her? Where do his or her loyalties lie?"[109] Such concerns are familiar in a business setting, but they obviously are not stray questions in a situation of war and occupation when the stakes are considerably higher.

There is a level of gossip aimed at those in favored positions that is based more on envy than on any concerns about loyalty or safety. Sometimes this is simple grousing, a heaping of scorn and contempt on those who violate the social norms of the one making the comparison. Of course, these kinds of comparisons to those who may be our "betters" in terms of position, but our "inferiors" in terms of morality serve the purpose of making us look better in our own eyes. We can take pride in our superior moral strength simply by talking about those who are taking advantage of their position in unacceptable ways.[110] The king of such backbiting had to have been Bert Williams, who continuously turns a sardonic and critical eye on anyone appearing to do better under Occupation conditions. When he sees the long queues of women at the Market, endless lines that started at 6:30 A.M., he moves to a further observation that "you never see any Heads in these queues . . . so the only conclusion people come to is, that these Heads are getting their goods from other sources."[111]

Whether this is the conclusion of "people" and widespread, or primarily Bert's belief, is difficult to say. The long Market queues were (as he observed) largely composed of women—housewives specifically—and it is doubtful that the heads of departments would have the time to wait hours in line and still fulfill their jobs. Bert's focus is on the presumed advantage of the well-placed and wealthy as opposed to the common man, and this is a continuing theme—along with basic unfairness, graft, and corruption—throughout his diary. When the meat controller, Mr. Chilcott, searched the baskets of the slaughtermen to make sure that they were not illegally taking bits of meat home to their own families, Bert fumes, "This in itself was a dam dirty trick. But of course Mr. Chilcott is meat controller and that means that he doesn't want for anything."[112]

Sometimes he turns his ire on those running Market stalls and their tendency to value certain items for barter over money. Bert puts the following incident forward as typical of "what goes on every day":

> I go in the Market I want a crab, I ask a stallholder if he has any, he says he has'nt, [*sic*] but (I know he has as I have seen them come in) I hang about & presently someone comes along with a parcel, gives it to the Stallholder & lo & behold out comes a crab and away goes the customer well satisfied, & so is the stallholder as he now has something to smoke, whereas I have got money on me but it cant buy that crab.[113]

This was an ongoing problem of barter, and one that the States tried to control.

But Bert was just winding up his complaints about those he viewed as taking particular advantage. Were the raspberries and strawberries in season, but completely unaffordable at 10s. and 10s. 6d. per pound? The growers would have been fined in England, "But not in Guernsey, you see these fruits are grown by members of the States. Nuff Cedd."[114] And this is the way that gossip often functions: the gossiper crystallizes responsibility for a perceived social wrong on a distinct individual, or set of related individuals, and shares that theory with others.

Two incidents during the Occupation appeared to strengthen beliefs that some were using their position for personal gain while simultaneously proving the power of gossip as a normative teaching tool. If there is one marker scandal that appears in practically every account of the time, it is the Police Theft case. This one incident roiled the Island, making many question the loyalty and goodwill of those in one of the highest of "trustee" positions. It also provided one of those "valuable lessons about . . . how *not* to behave" that Wert and Salovey see as the comparative power of gossip.[115] The facts of the Police Theft case are deceptively simple, but the actual story of what happened and what the principals of the case intended are still debated today. The case involved eighteen policemen and one civilian who were accused of thefts from the German army stores, and from the civilian stores as well.

According to Rev. Ord, commodities valued at £60 had been found in the home of one of the accused, while another had been caught with butter hidden up his chimney.[116] And Ord provided the more dramatic account of the Gestapo coming to admire one of the suspected policemen's "tidy horticultural efforts all nicely weeded and dug," complimenting him on his gardening prowess, then barking, "Bring your spade and dig a trench here!" And there were the stolen tins underneath the newly laid-in cabbages.[117] Inspector Sculpher was suspended—"a thoroughly upright and honest man" in Winnie's estimation—not because he was implicated in the crime, but because he was unaware of the actions of the men in his charge.[118]

It is at this point where events become less clear and ongoing questions are raised about this case. At first, sympathy of the Islanders lay with the accused, and many saw this as a resistance tactic to undermine the German occupying forces. Winnie seemed to set store by Wilfred Poat's view that this was an answer to Colonel Britton, the personified BBC creation calling for sabotage and symbolic resistance in all areas occupied by the Nazis.[119] This, too, is what the police have claimed, that their actions were intended as the type of sabotage and pilfering that was a response to Colonel Britton's call to action. It was for that reason, and not just the interrogation beatings that they endured, that they signed confessions to the thefts not only to German stores but also to the stores belonging to the States. To be found guilty of theft only of the German stores as a form of sabotage would be to open themselves to the death penalty. The police were represented by Ambrose Sherwill, who had already been imprisoned by the Germans and who was determined above all to save the policemen's lives.

These considerations give additional weight to the claim that this was a strategic move rather than accurate confessions. Constable Fred Short later said that they were forced to use the excuse of hunger as motivation for the thefts in order to avoid the charge of sabotage.[120] But what saved their lives destroyed their reputations. The German-controlled press in the Island had plenty of time between arrest and conviction to convince the public that crimes had occurred against the Island in general. The trial itself added further details that the policemen had stolen from the Island's stores "twenty pounds of meat at a time, ten pounds of dripping, wine, our butter, grain and other commodities," as Winnie reported the news.[121]

And the effort to divide the policemen from the support of the public was quite effective. In an attempt to show that this was theft against the Guernsey people, and to turn the populace against the policemen, the Germans took a theft at the States Dairy back in 1939 and claimed that the police were responsible for this incident as well. This was duly noted by Jack Sauvary, who wrote, "It's an awful disgrace for the Island and this game has been going on since 1939, before the German Occupation."[122] The police were not in a position to deny any charges if they wished to be treated as common criminals rather than saboteurs, and they were also not in a position to control the official transcript (or even the hidden transcript) of their own story. Jack was scathing: "They have lost their jobs, pensions, some had 20 years service. What fools!"[123]

Rev. Ord wrote that the Island population felt "terribly let down," and described the response from the common man thusly: "If they had pinched the stuff to share with the starving people it wouldn't have been so bad, since the Germans probably pinched a lot of the rations to begin with."[124] Winnie considered the general opinion to be that there was no harm in stealing from the Germans, but that "the police should be above suspicion." Some of the concern was the fear that the Germans would use these thefts as an excuse for a crackdown, or to limit the civilians' already meager rations.[125]

The trial was, predictably, a show trial in the Royal Court, with the German-controlled *Press* milking it for all the propaganda value it could muster. Bill Warry pasted much of the account in his scrapbook. The men were brought from prison—where they were already serving a sentence imposed by the German Court—to be tried by the States. Constable William Burton was acquitted, as PC Pill had been at an earlier stage, but ten of the men were given additional sentences, ranging from three months to sixteen months of hard labor. In an address that had all the earmarks of one constructed for the official transcript, the Bailiff dressed the men down severely when imposing sentence:

> You have brought shame and humiliation to every single soul in the Island . . . I am filled with shame. It is revolting to think how you have abused your position. I cannot imagine what all the foreigners in the Island—brought up, as they are, to look upon the British policeman as an example to the world—think of you.[126]

Considering that Ambrose Sherwill was the policemen's attorney, and remembering the careful dumb show he performed when negotiating the surrender of Nicole and Symes, this performance of collective shame and apologia seems carefully designed to avoid general retaliation.

Low-level pilfering and financial sabotage are primary means of retaliation by which those in subordinated positions strike back at their rulers. It takes the form in business of beleaguered "temps" removing office supplies, "till-tapping" by convenience-store workers, or overpouring (slipping customers double shots instead of singles) by disaffected bartenders. Yet, pilfering must have compliance from peers, who usually are in a position to know what is taking place and choose to look the other way in a display of solidarity. Otherwise, the acts are viewed, in the hidden as well as the official transcript, as theft by an individual rather than acts of resistance by subordinates. Thus, it is important in "settling scores" with those in power that the form of resistance be "satisfying to peers and appropriately provoking to superiors."[127] This is an awkward position for the resister, who must seek approval by peers and trust that none among them will curry favor with the powerful by giving the game away.

Assuming that the later accounts by the police involved that this was resistant sabotage are true—which can never be firmly established[128]—they may have been caught in a trap between the civilian population's desire to discipline profiteers, and the need to keep the theft and its rationale private, as protection against discovery. Later accounts described how some Islanders gathered to send off the policemen with upbeat remarks and gestures of support.[129] Some further sympathy, simply on a human level, accrued when exactly one year later, one policeman, Percy Smith, died in solitary confinement on the Continent. Questions immediately grew over the likelihood of natural death in a thirty-nine-year-old. As Bert Williams put it, "He is said to have died of heart failure, but was it?" Bert and others believed that there was much of this story yet to be revealed.[130] Overall, however, it is the official version of the entire saga of the Police Trial that has survived.

If "tales of misdeeds may be taken as more morally instructive than tales of virtue,"[131] the Hill-Cottingham case definitely proves the point, perhaps more so than the Police Trial. The case was best described by Winnie Harvey, who knew the Hill-Cottinghams quite well and worked with Mrs. Hill-Cottingham at the Trinity Air Raid Precautions. Some sacks of flour turned up missing from the Vauvert Flour Store, so the police were set to watch and stop all lorries that carried sacks appearing suspicious. When one lorry stopped at a baker's, unloading all the sacks but one, and started to drive off, the driver was stopped and asked where he was going. He refused to answer until taken to the police station, whereupon he admitted that the sack held flour for the "Boss," meaning the flour controller, Mr. Hill-Cottingham. As it turned out, the sack held fifty-six pounds of flour, what Hill-Cottingham called "sweepings" from the flour-store floor and intended for his chickens. He paid 5 shillings for the sack. Yet, when analyzed, the flour was reported as of better quality than the usual bread ration.[132]

While the case was still pending, little was talked about in the Island except the Hill-Cottingham affair, and there seemed to be some sense that his social standing and position would put him above the law. HILL-COTTINGHAM? was chalked up on some of the public buildings and the hoardings around St. Peter Port.[133] Hill-Cottingham was tried and found guilty before the Royal Court, fined £200 in lieu of three months in prison, and relieved of his post.[134] Bert Williams pasted the account of the trial and sentence in his diary, labeling it "A Law for the Rich." On the next page, he pasted a press cutting describing two States Dairy workers who took pots of milk from the dairy and were given six month's hard labor. Over this account, Bert wrote, "And One for the Poor."[135]

Even as a friend, Winnie could not raise her voice in Hill-Cottingham's defense, although she was personally sorry for his "fall." And, Winnie wrote, "The word 'sweepings' is now a byeword in the island."[136] Ambrose Robin read public opinion as believing the sentence given to be "perfectly wicked" and a "grave miscarriage of justice." From Robin's perspective, the common view was that Hill-Cottingham had a lapse in judgment as opposed to criminal intent.[137] So, even though this case ended in the courts, it first played out in the so-called court of public opinion, as people weighed with each other privately their beliefs in his guilt or innocence. Such incidents provide gossip's "parables . . . third-hand lessons about what can happen if one commits a certain behavior," which provide a primary teaching tool and method of normative control.[138]

JERRY-CHASERS

In considering those peers who were of particular concern to the resisters of the Occupation, the fraternizers and collaborators, I will start with the girls and women who formed attachments to various degrees with the German occupiers. These women have received far more consideration in recent accounts of the Occupation than their numbers would warrant, but the fascination with "forbidden love" is universal and understandable. Almost every fictional account of the Channel Island Occupation (book or film) weaves in a story of a brief encounter or an "eternal love" connection between an Island woman and a German soldier. In some of the storylines, a pregnancy results and the response of fellow Islanders to the offspring enters into the plot. Increasingly, as with the *Island at War* television series or the publishing sensation of *The Guernsey Literary and Potato Peel Pie Society*, the young woman in question is actually the heroine of the story.

The Guernsey Islanders anticipated the probability of some female fraternization with the influx of handsome young soldiers. It is for that reason, as well as worries over sexual assault, that so much concern was expressed for young women in general, as discussed earlier. Winifred Harvey, old enough to have seen much of the world, took a wry and biblical approach to the issue. She was reading about the old prophets and "the invasion and occupation of Palestine by the Babylonians" and enjoyed the parallels to the current Occupation. For example, there was "they shall eat their bread with carefulness." But even better was the report that Jewish women were castigated for chasing after the Babylonian officers, "*all of them desirable young men!*"[139] There were, of course, levels of this fraternization, and some women played the dangerous but lucrative game of coquetry that has long been part of the female arsenal. Stephen Ash, in his study of the occupied American South, listed among "feminine survival strategies" such skills as "coquetry and flattery, feigned stupidity or innocence."[140] Setting aside "loose" women and good-time girls, who made a practice of plying men for gain, there would certainly be a temptation to some women left alone in the Island to play up to German officers without carrying the game too far, hoping that chivalry would ease the way through the Occupation.

In October of the first fall of Occupation, Rev. Ord mentioned "an unpleasant report" making the rounds that a "wretched woman has been holding cocktail parties to which German officers and local girls are invited. The sequel may be guessed."[141] Particularly appalling to Bert Williams and many others was the fact that some of these girls and women had "their menfolk in the British forces which makes matters worse." They were consorting, therefore, with the very men dedicated to the deaths of their male relatives. "We in Guernsey know them all," Bert claimed, "and I personally have played at some of these parties & so have seen what goes on."[142] Oddly, it was not only single women and those with absent husbands who seem to have been noticed in German company. Ken Lewis found it "annoying" to see girls and women "from age 15 upwards" in the company of Germans on the roads, "despite the fact that many of them still had their husbands living in Guernsey." This would indeed be odd if the fraternization was of a sexual nature. Instead, this might indicate a couple, both of whom had an ongoing collaborative relationship with the Germans and were therefore to be seen in their company whether separately or together.[143]

For all of his understandable disgust at quislings and fraternizers, Ken is careful in his estimation of young women who were quite simply bored and wanted a good time. In other words, Ken seems to understand, as a young person himself, when "fraternization" was not a matter of patriotism and politics, but a matter of youth and a desire by some young women for parties and excitement while they were still young. This is what ultimately turned Ken from any interest in Vera at work and kept his mind on the distant star of Brenda Parker. Despite trying to see Vera as simply a lively girl who learned from her mistakes, in March 1944, Ken had to admit:

> [Vera] is definitely what is called nowadays a "Jerry chaser" and she is always with them. She has on her own admission stated that she has been out with them and recently she became drunk in their company and had stated that despite this she would be ready to go again. I do not for one moment class her with some of the other girls who go with the Germans and sleep with them &c.[144]

While Ken's naiveté may be apparent in this entry, as a product of a good upbringing and a positive nature, he is right about many of the young women who "went with" the Germans. They were missing their youth stuck away in the Island, and simply wanted to go to parties and dance.

There seemed to be little need to bell this particular cat, because the "jerry-chasers" were rather heedless with their reputations. Not only were they seen about the streets flirting with the German soldiers or at dances with the same, the privileges granted by the occupiers marked them as fraternizers. At the time of the D-Day Invasion, Winifred Harvey went over to Newlands and found the house shuttered and the blinds down. With the Germans gone, Winnie had a lovely day in the gardens, feeling free for the first time in years. Later in the afternoon, she saw a pretty young woman hovering near the gate, and Winnie asked her if she was looking for someone. The girl wanted to get into the German office because some of the clerks were developing film for her. Of course, cameras had been called in at the start of the Occupation, so the only Islanders taking pictures, except in secret, and having the films developed were those taking holiday-style snaps of their German friends. Winnie describes her response to the young woman: "'I'm afraid you're too late,' I told the pretty Miss Quisling, 'the house is shut up and they are all in the cellar. I think that sort of thing is at an end.'"[145] Because these girls and women were so apparent, they became part of the humor of the Island. Kitty Bachmann joked about local women "of low degree, who had taken too literally the Divine exhortation to love their enemies."[146]

Although some treated the women willing to run with the Germans as part of the side-show of the Occupation, they often posed a danger for the noncollaborating majority. Ken acknowledged the difficulty of being around Guernsey girls and women of uncertain morals. There were some who were not simply playing the Germans for their own comfort, but who had forged an allegiance to the German cause. As Ken put it, "Some of these girls or women had no scruples about telling the Germans what you said, especially if it was detrimental to the Dritte Reich (Third Reich)."[147] If willing to trade their reputations or their bodies for the advantages the Germans could supply, trading information on others would have been an easy next step. Islanders also knew that many of the foreign girls working in the Island before the Occupation (Hungarians, for example, like Winifred Harvey's Rosa and Maria) had flocked to the Germans and were not to be trusted. There also quickly developed some distrust of Irish-born Islanders. Ireland was neutral, and although most Irish Islanders were loyal to Guernsey government and sympathizers to the British cause, there were exceptions, willing to work privately with the Germans, and not to be trusted.

Winifred Harvey had a serious run-in with just such a woman in the Red Cross office on January 29, 1944. Winnie was serving as a volunteer, showing messages received to the recipients and typing replies. A woman named Kathleen Torode attempted to send a Red Cross message that ended, "We are very well treated by the Germans." It was strictly forbidden that any message be sent that was general and not personal. Winnie pointed this out to Mrs. Torode and requested that she change the final sentence. "No, I will not," replied Mrs. Torode haughtily. Winnie then suggested that she send the rest of the message and simply leave out the final line, and here is where Winnie made a mistake that could have been tragic. In a burst of frankness, she said to Mrs. Torode, "Everyone is not well-treated by the German authorities. People have been turned out of their houses and we have not much to eat." Mrs. Torode demanded her message back, angrily saying that she had just come from the German authorities and they had proclaimed the message to be perfectly all right. As Mrs. Torode sailed out the door, her message unsent, a fellow volunteer, Mrs. Baker, leaned over to Winnie and said, "Wasn't she in a rage! I believe it is a put-up job and she has gone straight back to the Germans."

Winnie, too, worried for several days that the incident would come back to haunt her. Kathleen Torode, as it turned out, was an Irishwoman who worked for the German Schmidt-Walkoff as his "housekeeper," a euphemism used by Winnie to indicate that Torode was his mistress. Sure enough, several days later, Winnie was summoned to appear before Herr Kraft at Grange Lodge (headquarters of the Feldkommandant) with Mrs. Torode present. Soon they were in the presence of the Feldkommandant, Major Kratzer, a "short, bald, podgy little man with a roar like a bull." Kratzer began to bellow at them in German, which Winnie could follow quite easily. The issue of the message itself was quickly dispensed with, and Kratzer declared it appropriate to send.

The topic then turned to the more dangerous one of Winnie's words on the treatment of the Guernsey people. Mrs. Torode claimed that she had written Winnie's words down as "into the bargain, we are not well treated by the German authorities, and we have nothing to eat." Winnie wrote that there was "silence at this exhibition of treachery," because it became clear to all that Mrs. Torode had planned to denounce her and had taken her words down as evidence. Winnie provided what she had actually said and apologized for saying such a thing in a public place: "I regret gentlemen, that I said those words, I realized immediately that they should not have been spoken." Winnie's polite and calm demeanor—not to mention her standing in the Island, important to the snobbish Germans—meant that she was let off this time, although with warnings that a future incident would require "treatment." She noted that Major Kratzer gave her the Nazi salute on leaving and Herr Kraft shook her hand as she left, politenesses not extended to Mrs. Torode. "Jerry-bags" willing to denounce the Guernsey populace were useful to the Germans, but not generally respected by them.[148]

So, some female fraternization was definitely taking place in the Island, and the Islanders used gossip about these women to protect themselves from possible denunciations. But how prevalent were these affairs and how often did they result in pregnancy? The reason for this question lies in the fascination in the British press with the topic of German-fathered births during the Occupation. Marriages between Islanders and German soldiers were not allowed, and so German progeny would show up in the illegitimate births. The exception, of course, would be in a birth to a married woman—though unless her husband still was in Guernsey, a birth would signal an affair with someone. Some of the more comical estimates made by journalists include 2,000 (and even 3,000) illegitimate births in Guernsey alone. Consider that much of the roughly 25,000-member population of Guernsey consisted of men and boys, elderly and middle-aged women past childbearing, girls under twelve, and married women. This would mean that the limited population of single women and married women with absent husbands, the only members of the population whose births could have been recorded as illegitimate, would have been very busy indeed. The official estimation of illegitimate births was 285, although Ralph Durand sets the number at 196, and both of these numbers appear far more accurate simply from a logical standpoint.[149]

That girls and women were not flocking to sleep with the German soldiers may be seen in the need to import "professional women" from the Continent for that purpose. But dread rumors of massive numbers of illegitimate births began to filter across the Island. Rev. Ord heard a startling rumor that before Christmas of 1943, five hundred illegitimate babies had been born in Guernsey. It was disturbing enough that he consulted the matron and sister for their own estimate, which turned out to be under 120 for the Occupation to that point, which was more in line with later official numbers.[150] Yet, unquestionably there were women and teenage girls in the Island left with a permanent souvenir of their indiscretion.

As word of an increase in illegitimate births got around, many Islanders responded harshly. Bill Warry noted that several girls had been in the Emergency Hospital, and that there "will be & is a lot of new blood (German) in the coming generation. Some of these girls should be put in the pillory."[151] Bert Williams, too, thought that "we have got the German blood here alright, that will want some getting rid of." He was particularly scandalized at the mothers who seemed proud to "have had a child for a Jerry." And Bert stated that there were quite a few married women now with a baby by the occupying forces, and that most would never be able to trace the fathers: "What a lovely thing for the children themselves. The single girl's parents are to blame in a large degree for allowing the girls to knock around with the troops. It is a proper disgrace to the Island & strong measures should be taken at the earliest opportunity."[152]

Bert was on point when he criticized the fact that some parents allowed their girls to "knock around" with soldiers, because these were not sophisticated young women. They were quite likely not to know how to protect themselves either from sexual assault, which undoubtedly happened, or from the flattery and charm of soldiers who were usually older and more experienced. In April, just before the close of the Occupation, Ken Lewis reported that two of Vera Lloyd's friends were both expecting babies from the German Panzer troops recently in the Island. Vera's mother was concerned that a slur would attach to Vera and her sister Jane (particularly because Jane had been in the hospital to have some teeth out and thus was not "about" and visible).[153] But this shows the oddity of the situation; Mrs. Lloyd knew that both girls flirted with the troops and went to dances with them. One would think that the damage to their reputation would have already taken place, and it is difficult not to see Mrs. Lloyd as negligent where her daughters were concerned.

Of course, some of these illegitimate babies had mothers among the foreign girls who left their positions with Guernsey families and worked for the Germans. Again, if Rosa and Maria are any indication, what you have are some naive country girls from the Continent with romantic notions and surrounded by young soldiers. Another factor that is too rarely considered is that the fathers of many of these illegitimate babies may not have been German.[154] In January 1943, Ken was surprised when a young man he knew, only twenty-eight years old, died one morning, apparently of natural causes. Ken pondered this untimely death: "He had never lived what one could call a good life and he always went about with other girls despite the fact that he was married."[155] Thus, Ken reminds us of what we already know: that the Occupation did not put a moratorium on the illicit affairs that go on in any community. In fact, war itself heightens this tendency toward casual affairs, and we can see this acknowledged in the popular culture. After World War II, there was a spate of movies that touched on this issue and the need to forgive and forget any indiscretions.[156]

The Occupation could only have been more difficult for married couples now separated by the English Channel, because it would be five very long years without any leave to ease the strain. Kitty Bachmann wrote often in the early days about the number of "grass widowers" she knew, now separated from their wives who had evacuated with the children before the Occupation. Kitty was all sympathy for their loneliness. Then, in early 1944, she writes, "A number of deserted husbands have sought 'solace' elsewhere. This staggered us at first as we clung to the tenets of our Victorian up-bringing." Peter, it seems, took a more "liberal" view, acknowledging that it was hard to be judgmental when "four, or perhaps five, years is a long time to be lonely." So, not only were there the usual single Guernseymen to get a girl "in trouble," but an entire new population of deserted married men seeking comfort where they could find it.

Some of the married women, also alone and with husbands in the British forces, would find themselves with a new baby to greet their husband's arrival after the war. The volatile combination of lonely-though-married Islanders who knew each other and socialized together increased the odds that many of these babies were not German-fathered. Kitty overheard two brothers talking about this turn of affairs, so to speak, as they were working to repair a shed in the Bachmanns' back garden. Bill was "most scathing" about the lack of marital fidelity among the people they knew. John replied, "Go on! If, when Betsy returns from England you find she've been unfaithful, you'll forgive 'er." "Eh," Bill replied, "Never! I'm pure and I expects 'er to be pure!" Kitty wrote that it really took hearing the Guernsey-French accent to do the exchange justice.[157]

Before leaving this subject, I want to touch on one aspect not always acknowledged when discussing young women who did have affairs with, and occasionally babies by, the German soldiers. This action is often treated as traitorous in some way, as a form of fraternization that was unpatriotic and a matter of "sleeping with the enemy." We need to be careful about reading anything political or pro-Nazi into the average liaison between a young girl who might have been thirteen or fourteen at the start of the Occupation and eighteen to nineteen by its close. She did not have to go and seek out the soldiers, nor did she have to be a wild girl who liked to drink or dance and was heedless with her reputation.

A young nineteen-year-old soldier might well be billeted nearby, where she would have learned to know him as an individual. She would have met these young men in the shops or on the streets or on a country walk along the cliffs (occasionally even seen them at church). Over time, they might have shyly spoken to each other for one reason or another and have practiced exchanging a few words of German or English. Many of these young men were apolitical, with no interest in the war except to see it end, and some would be anti-Party. It does not take much imagination to see how an attraction would result. And anyone familiar with teenaged girls knows that the added fillip of a Romeo and Juliet love—one opposed by parents and community—would only add to the appeal.[158]

If time has given some perspective on these women and their motivations, the response from Islanders during the Occupation was anything but forgiving. Plans for retaliation against all quislings and traitors became part of the fantasy life of the Islanders—particularly against those who sent anonymous letters to the Germans denouncing Islanders with hidden wireless sets. Winifred Harvey wrote about this last group, "The behaviour of such cads is shameful: they are traitors and deserve to be shot by the British when we are free."[159] Such collaborators who "'sold' their own countrymen to the enemy" through betrayals were high on the list of those targeted for retaliation after the war. "Hanging is too good for them," wrote Bert Williams.[160] Bert extended his desire for revenge to growers who sold to the Germans, hoping that they would be "rounded up after the war & either deported or branded."[161] Even the mild Rev. Ord had a flash of these thoughts: "For quislings it is quite appropriate to cage them in the zoo!" although this is swiftly followed by "But allowance must be made for overstrain after these years."[162] But women who fraternized with the Germans came in for more than their fair share of retribution fantasies.

As is typical of the stream of consciousness of diaries, Ken mentioned on September 5, 1944, that he had washed his hair that evening, abruptly making the mental leap to write that girls who had gone with the Germans would have their hair cut off after the war. A post office worker told Ken that postcards had been sent to some girls, "You are No. ——— on the list for a hair cut," with the cards signed, GUB (Guernsey Underground Barbers). Reportedly, a young dancer whose baby had a German father was number one on the list.[163] Just a few days later, Kitty confirmed this report of the GUB and its inspiration in the attacks on women with German babies in post-Occupation France. Rumor was going around that a local woman had already been "scalped," as Kitty put it, not for having a baby but for revealing the location of an Islander's hidden wireless.[164] Had punishment been based on such betrayals, and Kitty's report appears to only be a rumor, then the GUB might have garnered widespread support.

Yet, many people feared being falsely labeled as fraternizers. That same September, Winifred Harvey described how she was pushing a heavy cart up St. Julian's Avenue, an exceptionally steep road, when "two hands descended over mine on to the handle," and a German soldier—unbidden—started to help her push. Once they reached the Grange Club, Winnie worried that watching eyes would see her German helper and she would "earn the attentions of the G. U. B." The fact that the GUB was rumored to consist of young men, who had set themselves up as judge and jury over the women of the Island, evidently rankled Winnie. "But they themselves are in a doubtful position," she noted, "for why are they in the island at all and not in the army?"[165] This was not fully fair on Winnie's part, because many of these young men, now of fighting age, were trapped in the Island four years earlier at a time when they were too young to enlist. But Rev. Ord, too, saw the sexual politics being played out by the GUB and proclaimed it "lynch-law." As he put it, "There are people who might well be taught a lesson—and they are not all of one sex." Ord wisely believed that any punishment for sexual indiscretions were already natural to the situation, and "Girls who have had children to Germans will have their own burdens to carry long after public feeling has cooled."[166]

Young women were not the only ones who had to guard their reputations against claims of fraternization. Only young men like Ken Lewis and his mates seemed to have no thought about appearances, probably because of their age. They cheerfully would talk to Germans whenever and wherever possible, seeing little but an opportunity to learn something new. This was not the case for most adults. For example, Winnie Harvey was a woman deeply interested in music. The loss of the wireless and her regular musical evenings of concerts in her home were both great blows to her. Of course live concerts were available to her at Candie Gardens and other venues, but these were concerts held by the Germans. Would going to such a concert be a form of fraternization? In March 1941, Winnie was firm in a principled stance. A concert of top musical artists from Berlin was being presented at the Regal Theater. The concert was free, and the opportunity was a rare one to hear some world-class music, but Winnie chose not to attend. "Why did you not go to it?" Winnie's friends asked her. "Music is an international thing." While Winnie agreed with these sentiments, she saw the concert as little more than propaganda "turned to the use of the war machine. And I am not accepting *their* invitations."[167]

But music was an irresistible draw for Winnie. When a friend was spending a week with Winnie, they took their "courage in both hands and went to hear the German band at Candie." Winnie described the scene on that sunny Sunday in June 1942 as "truly Continental, "filled with German officers, soldiers, sailors, and a small number of Islanders. Rather than intermingle with the Germans and be an obvious audience for the concert, Winnie and Miss Caparne simply strolled around the lower gardens to look at the flowers and found an "inconspicuous bench" tucked away at some remove to rest and hear the music. She obviously was conflicted about visiting the Gardens when the German band was playing and being seen there.[168]

Kitty and Peter had their own difficulties avoiding the appearance of collaboration, especially just after D-Day, when "on the whole, the Germans are as eager to fraternize as we feel eager to remain quietly aloof." One German officer began stopping by the house during the times when Peter was at the shop in town. Kitty was careful to leave the door shut and locked and would talk to the man at the open window, a wise precaution on her part. But this was not acceptable in the long run, as his repeated visibility at her window could end, Kitty feared, with her being "branded as a collaborator." Just as Kitty and Peter had decided to run the risk of directly insulting him by reminding him that their shop was in town and telling him not to come by their house, his visits stopped.[169]

The Bachmanns' son, Peter-John, was a German magnet, for it seems that many of the soldiers and officers saw in him the children that they had left behind. But this was a problem for Kitty, who was sensitive to what people thought, and determined to get through the

Occupation with the Bachmanns' good name intact. When P.J. turned two, Kitty was out with her son picking flowers, only to look up and see a German officer kneeling close by with his arms outstretched. P.J. who had a great fascination with the Germans (calling them all "Oys," a reference that Kitty and Peter never could figure out) rushed happily into the man's arms. So, here stood Kitty in sight of "the possible raised eyebrows in upper windows along our lane," her son happily fingering the epaulettes and hat of a German who was grinning broadly and showing his gold-filled teeth. Summoning up a mixture of "good nature, firmness, and aplomb," Kitty said to her son, "Say good afternoon," which P.J. did happily. "Now say good-bye," which P.J. did more reluctantly. The German took the hint, set her son down, clicked his heels, "Heiled Hitler and departed, seemingly unoffended and quite unabashed." When she told Peter of the incident later, her husband simply said, "The poor devil—he is probably missing his own youngsters." Kitty was left feeling that she had maintained her honor without unnecessary offense, and "in case of possible witnesses, only the most gossip-starved could have made anything of the incident."[170]

SMUDGING THE LINE

Reputation with their fellow Islanders was particularly important for those who represented the civilian population. Those who were tapped by the States government to serve as liaisons with the Germans were in a particularly vulnerable position. Winifred Harvey had a chat with two friends after the Occupation had been underway for just a few months, and the topic turned to Smith, a man who served as "general factotum to the Germans and who, everyone says, is too friendly to them." Smith had actually asked Winnie's friends about the gossip going around concerning his relationship with the occupiers and was trying actively to let people know that the stories were not true. According to him, he had taken steps to try and give up the position entirely, but Sherwill (still Procureur at that point) prevailed on him to remain in the post. According to Smith, Sherwill was having great difficulties with the Germans by then; indeed, Sherwill would not be in his position for much longer and needed all the help he could muster.[171]

Yet it did not take a special position that required contact with the Germans to have one's reputation threatened. If we want to understand how outward deference could be combined with resistance under the Occupation, a vital concept is the notion of "performed compliance."[172] In situations where all of the power is in the hands of others—be it in a workplace, a family situation, or in the larger historical loci of slavery, indentured servitude, or military occupation—direct and total refusal to comply is a rare and risky gamble with few rewards. For every nineteenth-century woman who defied her husband and convention, there were thousands more who, unwilling to risk losing their children, homes, and finances under laws that gave parental and financial rights only to the husband, learned the game of outward compliance and covert manipulation. For every Nat Turner or "troublesome" slave, thousands more wore a neutral or even cheerful mask of compliance for fear that their families would be sold away from them. It is the nature of performed compliance that it is a survival device—a way around hostile conditions for the powerless, but one that leaves the underlying identity intact.

This Janus-headed approach of overt compliance and covert impeding/resistance is unlikely to be understood based on a reading of the public transcript of speech and acts. Only those outside of the coercive situation are fully free to express their opinions about that situation publicly. One must be naive to look at African Americans suffering under slavery or living in the Deep South under Jim Crow and expect them to be the clear voice of public opposition to their servitude. Southern slaveholders often pointed to the "happy" and compliant slave majority as proof of their benign ownership, conveniently ignoring the number of slaves who attempted or succeeded in escape. It often took many years of effort constructing the perfect mask to gain the trust and privileges that put a slave in a position where escape was even possible. Then again, any individual resistance held a likelihood of punishment for the entire community, so those who did escape or rebel knew that they could make conditions worse for others. And this threat to the larger community became a further mechanism for the powerful to prop up the status quo.

Thus, the prudent stance of those in a position of powerlessness is to adopt a blanket public deference to those in power. When a hierarchy is extreme in its power differential and marked by oppression, the need for a believable performance of deference becomes more serious, particularly when it covers acts of personal and collective subversion. James Scott makes several points about deference in situations of pervasive imbalance of power. First, many deferential acts are "highly routinized and shallow." The Guernsey police continued to preface their reports, as they did before the Occupation, with "I beg to report," a standard acknowledgment of their position in serving the larger community and their superiors. This did not reflect any actual respect toward their new German masters any more than did their opening a car door for a German officer whom they were required to chauffeur to some destination. Second, deferential acts are learned behavior, and Scott uses as an example the need for slave mothers to train their children in deference and conformity for their own safety.[173] The kabuki of averted eyes or the attentive but nonchallenging gaze, honorifics of titles and "sirs and ma'ams," and all the other small gestures of respect and deference are still a part of social education in any hierarchical society.

It was important to the solidarity of the Islanders that they were able to sort out necessary deference and performed compliance from true collaboration. For the most part they became adept in knowing those for whom compliance was a protective pose versus those who conformed willingly to German dictates. Compulsory work for the Germans became one of the gray areas during the Guernsey Occupation, and one that could spark charges of collaboration in some quarters. In effect, as mentioned earlier, any work that sustained the Island and kept it intact for the day of liberation could be characterized as "working for" the new German owners. Most people at the time, and in later assessments, have understood the unfairness and basic illogic of such a critique. Still, it was difficult even for the Islanders to sort out when work was compulsory and when it was not.[174]

In March 1943, Winifred Harvey wrote of a German announcement that the number of foreign workers would be drastically reduced, due to the disease and filth that these poor men brought with them. Instead, Island men were to be impressed into work for the Germans. A form was being sent around to various offices and businesses that accounted for the activities of men and women. This then was "followed by a quick round-up, especially from the shops," where the unemployed, the underemployed, and older men were apt to congregate. The men would then be put to work driving lorries or working to move ammunition (a perilous job).[175] By June, she described yet another German "round-up of labour" where men and women from banks, shops, and offices were pulled away from their regular work and set to packing up produce for shipment. Sympathetically, she described Ruth Ferguson being pulled from her pleasant job at Hirzel House, the headquarters of the Controlling Committee, and forced to do physical labor for thirteen hours at a stretch. She "saw poor Mrs. Ferguson looking completely exhausted," dragging sacks of food through the wet weather to feed the Germans' rabbits.[176] Obviously, this was not work that Mrs. Ferguson chose for the temptation of larger rations and pay.

Yet, even knowing the compulsory nature of impressed work for the Germans, Winnie was oddly torn on the issue. In early 1944, she could not get workers to help her head gardener Moullin in his upkeep of the Newlands property. In Winnie's view, the men were "all working for the Germans at a high rate of pay, with extra food," and growers and Islanders such as herself could not compete. She did find a man to work for her from St. Martin (Mr. Dorey) who was "steady and respectable and no lover of Germans." It is interesting to note that as she needed to hire men herself, her understanding of the forced nature of German work, or at least the difficult quandary the workers experienced, went out the window. Somehow, only the men free to choose to work for Islanders were not "lovers" of the Germans.[177]

Many wrote about the ongoing impressment of Islanders for German work. For example, Bill Warry described a new German order in late March 1943 that followed a census of everyone's occupation and number of hours. Around fifty-eight people were given notices that they had to appear at the German Kommandantur, whereupon they were told to resign their jobs in order to work for the Germans. The next day another batch of workers received notification of their date to appear (and others were sent word that they would be asked to appear when notified). Bill reported that the ages of men subject to these notifications ranged from sixteen to sixty, and women up to age forty-five. From the general "state of excitement" caused by this order and the notification to appear at the German Kommandantur, the implied threat makes work for the Germans appear far from voluntary.[178]

But most interesting of all is Bert Williams's account, because he was one of those on the second day who received orders to report to Summerland House for compulsory work with the German forces. He described this summons as "a blow to everyone." It is really fascinating to gauge Bert's reaction because, simply by chance, he was assigned a plum job. Having some skills, he was set to work as an electrician at the main German hospital, previously a mental institution. However, others who were summoned had far worse jobs of trench digging, driving horses, or working in the German kitchens. Bert admitted that one good thing about this work was the increased wages, "very much higher than local rates," particularly important to him since losing his position as a policeman.

Bert then reported that some had managed to gain exemptions from the work, among them a particular man from the Pollet. "I always thought he was yellow & and this has proved it," expostulated Bert. "I glory in the fellows who have taken their medicine & gone to work as ordered. They wont get us down this way. We can take it." It is pure speculation on my part, but the intensity of Bert's reaction may have been because of flak he received after being assigned a good job at higher pay. This does not lessen the compulsory nature of the work; it was simply the luck of the draw that he was not digging ditches. However, his better position may have looked like a collaborative choice to others. Bert therefore wreathes compliance with the German order in elements of patriotism, of doing one's duty and not being "yellow."

It is difficult to see someone managing to wriggle out of the German net as cowardly, and Bert grants that some of the jobs would have been difficult for "the chaps who have never done a hard days work in their lives." Even Bert, having landed a lucky—if unchosen—position, voiced the "real snag" noted by others that once the Germans had impressed a person as a worker, "you never know what they will do next." His theory was also that this compulsory work was instituted to allow the Germans to send younger soldiers away from Guernsey, presumably to augment the fighting forces at the front lines. Thus, Bert saw that his being shanghaied into German labor could indirectly bolster the German war effort, and he called it a "dirty trick."[179]

There were those, too, who watched and judged whether their fellow Islanders were following the rules laid down by the Germans. In conditions of domination, it is when the powerless attempt to skirt the onerous conditions established by those in power that lateral surveillance by peers becomes a disadvantage. As a professional in shoe repair, Ken's dad found it to work to his advantage to set up a subtle system of the barter of his talents. Civilians were hard-pressed to get their shoes mended, and Mr. Lewis would have been forced to take on official repair duties (often for the German officers) during his normal business. The order commanding that Germans were to be attended to first and to be treated with respect by shop owners and craftsmen was clear. So, Mr. Lewis occasionally went by the Market on his own time, where he "was kept supplied with fish in return for mending the various stall-holders shoes." Ken described it much like a game where Mr. Stead, the new fish controller, "was continually on the look out for persons cheating the law but the fishmongers fooled him all the more."[180] Trustees in the middle-management positions, such as the fish controller or meat controller, were viewed as carrying out laws that would not exist but for the hated German presence. Although the controllers were not viewed as friendly to the Germans—after all, they technically worked for the States—they became fair game when it came to circumventing these Occupation laws and orders.

Bert Williams becomes a case study in this civilian effort to undercut the rules imposed by the Germans but administered by the States. When I described Bert's diatribe against Mr. Chilcott, the meat controller who searched all the baskets of the slaughtermen, I did not reveal the trigger for his anger. Bert had developed a habit of going to the slaughterhouse on the days that cattle came in from France, and hanging about "to get a bit of meat for the dog." Bert's friend (one of the butchers) slipped Bert a skull bone "to make a drop of soup with." But this little under-the-table gift was spotted by Mr. Chilcott junior, the son of the meat controller. It was this act that had prompted the search of the slaughtermen's baskets. Bert was furious. "These skull bones are only offal and the public don't see a lot of them as it is," he fumed. Bert clearly felt no guilt in skirting the German-enforced rules, and viewed himself as a representative of the common man kept at a disadvantage: "I often wonder where they [the skull bones] go after leaving the Slaughter House . . . The man in the street has'nt [*sic*] got an earthly chance with all the graft that is going on at the present time." The meat controller and his son were not men doing their jobs, but the enemy, ripe for vilification: "And the son that reported my incident is always scrounging around the Slaughter House for brains. I imagine he wants more brains than a cow or Bullock can give him."[181]

Then one of the little ironies of the Occupation occurred during that final spring. On Sunday, April 1, 1945, Mr. Stead dropped by Bert Williams's house with the news that Bert had been appointed a deputy fish controller! He started his job that Tuesday, and Bert thought that it would suit him well with its flexible hours and decent pay of £3 a week.[182] The reader of Bert's diary cannot help but feel a sense of anticipation. Bert has spent his diary castigating the States, the controllers, and anyone in a position where he (or she) might game the system. He rails constantly against graft and corruption; he awaits the day when the Occupation ends and the common man can take revenge on anyone using position to violate the rules for personal gain. Will this be the opportunity for Bert to take a trustee job and enforce the rules that are in place? Then again, he plainly believes that trustees should help the common man skirt the onerous laws laid down by the Germans. Which side of his complex character would emerge when he found himself in a middle-manager position?

On his first full day as deputy fish controller, Bert "okayed" four boats in the evening as they came in with their small catches after a day of ormering. In mentioning the small catch, Bert writes, "Needless to say I did'nt [*sic*] get any," an early glimmer of what was in his mind. But dearth of advantage shifted quickly, as he was given two whiting on April 20; two dogfish, a whiting, and seven spider crabs on May 2; a spider crab, a dogfish, and a whiting on May 4; and seven spider crabs and a whiting on May 5. So, now we apparently see Bert take the same type of advantage of position that he has condemned in others throughout the Occupation. Yet before we judge his actions, it is good to consider two competing explanations for Bert's acceptance of the fish.

The first possible explanation is that Bert lacks the ability to hold his own actions to the same standard that he holds others', even when the actions are identical. This is so much an aspect of human nature that those who examine attribution theory (the study of how we interpret events and assign different motivations to our own and others' behavior) consider this part of the "fundamental attribution error." Attribution theory tells us that when assessing a potentially negative action of another, we tend to see that action as motivated by a character flaw in that person. It is a stable aspect of the personality of that person; they are dishonest, or greedy, or selfish. When we seek the causes behind our own negative acts, even when they are the same actions, we emphasize the external situation in which we find ourselves. We were hungry or desperate, or are simply righting a prior wrong or disadvantage.[183]

The fact that we do not use the same yardstick in measuring our own, as compared to others' actions may be seen in the common saying that we want justice for others, mercy for ourselves. We therefore provide ourselves with that mercy by the way we interpret the situation, shifting our assessment so that we remain the hero in our own eyes. Few people living under famine conditions would turn down a freely offered gift of food if it meant an opportunity to feed their families (and Bert has the care of a pregnant wife and an elderly parent). His good reasons for accepting the fish are important to Bert, and he carefully documents when he gives three spider crabs to Fred, or a whiting or dogfish to his mother ("I have given my Dog fish to Mother she likes them & it will do her good"). But he is equally aware that not everyone would be happy for his windfall, for he also writes, "I could get a lot of fish but the difficulty is getting them away as there are always the jealous element of Guernsey people on the watch."[184] Like those who worried about being falsely viewed as fraternizers, Bert is conscious of the judgment of others and wants to keep his reputation unblemished. He now sees the negative side of lateral surveillance, viewing those who watch and judge as "jealous" types, a basic character flaw.

Yet before we make any decisions about what this incident reveals, we should consider another explanation that sheds more light on Occupation resistance. Bert's acceptance of the fish occurred only days before Liberation, but during a time when the Germans still could enforce their standing order for the first of all fish that were caught. It is quite likely that we are witnessing the type of semi-organized resistant pilfering from the Germans that we have seen elsewhere in the Occupation. If the fishermen had decided to bypass the Germans and slip as much fish directly to the Islanders as possible, it would be natural to use a fish controller "of the right sort" as their confederate. In a situation of extreme want, the first Islanders to benefit might be the controller's family and friends, but the circle of beneficiaries would broaden quickly. Certain pieces of evidence seem to support this reading of the situation.

There is no sign at all that Bert used pressure or requested the fish; they seem to have been freely offered and gratefully accepted. The fact that he anticipated that fish would come his way may indicate an awareness of an ongoing system of pilfering, possibly already involving the man that he replaced. And during these same weeks, Bert expressed anger at growers who still sold to the Germans for personal gain, advocating that they should be "hung in public" or "rounded up after the war & either deported or branded."[185] Even granting a tendency to ignore our own flaws, Bert's disgust at all those who seek personal gain seems wholehearted and not tinged with personal guilt. This second reading also more closely matches Bert's consistent view that "trustees" should help in siphoning resources from the enemy and placing them into the hands of average Islanders.

Speculating about such small incidents and whether they involved smudging of the ethical line or constituted a form of resistant pilfering makes clear the moral achievement of Islanders over five years of Occupation. The diarists are forthcoming about ethical dilemmas and were obviously determined to see the Occupation through with a clean reputation in their own and others' eyes. When Madeleine Bunting claims that "each individual faced moral choices" during the Occupation, she is absolutely right. But when she adds, "and only a few could claim a calm conscience by 1945," she could not be further from the mark. I cannot find in the contemporary accounts any basis to her belief that "the Occupation compromised almost everybody who lived through it," if she is considering compromises of any serious weight.[186] And in the Islanders' pride in their history, I do not read some murky undercurrent of suppressed guilt and shame.

The reason Bunting sees Islanders as almost universally compromised and sporting uneasy consciences is largely because she conflates small ethical conundrums with major moral failings. Perhaps this indicates a different level of expectation between Bunting and myself when it comes to human perfection. The majority of Islanders do not have to be viewed as plaster saints in order to know that they were not collaborators, fraternizers, or dishonest agents hoping to profit off of their situation. Their very intolerance of the minority who *did* fall into these categories reveals the strong ethical values that were part of their Island heritage. They developed the discursive means described in this chapter in order to protect themselves from the bad players in their midst. And we will see later how this moral strength and self-protection were needed to avoid a collapse of civilized society during the worsening conditions of the final year.

Although not necessarily developed in temporal order, the first aspects of rhetorical resistance that we can identify occur through shadow channels of discourse emerging when other means of communication and information flow are restricted. Rumor as an alternative discourse carries with it a sense-making capacity and the ability to transmit the hopes and fears of the community. The value of gossip is in its function as a mechanism of normative control and self-protection. Part of the resistance to domination involves lateral surveillance and the ability to identify those in collaborative relationships with the powerful. Fantasies of retaliation unite a subjugated community, and dreams of a future made right serve to sustain resistance. Yet, all members of that same community face issues of their own need to comply with power and the proper limits of that compliance. It is a tricky discursive task to skirt the borders that might bring down retaliation from above, while still communicating solidarity with the community of the dispossessed. As I will discuss in the next chapter, this need, and a desire to lay claim to their own story of the Occupation, gave birth to a second form of rhetorical resistance in the detailed construction of an oppositional narrative.

CHAPTER FOUR

Understanding the Story

IT WAS THE KIND OF FUNNY STORY THAT MADE THE ROUNDS PRACTICALLY EVERY WEEK during the heart of the Occupation. In this case, we will allow Reverend Ord to do the honors:

> A German propaganda film was being shown in Jersey, featuring British and American soldiers dying by the hundreds in battle. Not so much as a single casualty was sustained by the Germans! It was a stirring narrative. It was finally rounded off by a special "shot" of a German Military funeral, for—one supposes—not even Germans live forever. A hero's honours were accorded. The coffin was borne slowly past amid, at least, the respectful silence of the audience, when a sepulchral voice from the pit broke the spell of amazement: "That man died of indigestion"! Immediately the house rocked with great gusts of laughter. Swiftly the Germans reacted. They stopped the performance, locked the doors and made valiant efforts to identify the culprit, but in vain.[1]

In this one little tale we can find many of the narrative elements that helped Islanders understand their own experience of Occupation and construct the second element of rhetorical resistance.

Ord's story begins with the German propaganda that surrounded the civilian population, permeating their newspapers and serving as the required prelude to airings of popular films. Islanders were subjected both to German propaganda and British counterpropaganda to such an extent that it almost seemed as if the successful outcome of the entire war hinged on the hearts and minds of this small population. The story swiftly moves to recount the execution of a resistant joke, one successfully pulled off because of the cleverness of the perpetrator and the determination of his neighbors not to give him away. The act itself, as well as the humor behind the comment, would have been appreciated by this truly "captive" audience, both in the theater and in life.

Finally, the incident continued to exist as a story, one to be heard and then relished in the retelling as it passed from neighbor to neighbor. It was a tale laced with humor, and one that had much to say about life in the Island community. Such stories—along with jokes, metaphors, puns, and other discursive artifacts—still survive as remnants of the hidden transcript of the Occupation. Too often ignored by historians in favor of the official documents and proclamations of the public transcript, the stories and other shared "chat" of daily life provided a "web of interaction" for the common Islander, and an informal means of constructing a shared worldview.[2] They also constitute an underestimated narrative form of resistance to power.

This chapter will examine the discursive life of the occupied population of Guernsey, and the view of reality that was constructed by this shared narrative. Common narratives serve as a vital sense-making process and are key to resisting the mental control exerted by the dominant. I will begin with competing German and British propaganda, in relation to which the civilian populace served more as an audience than as active participants. Not only did the Islanders become adept decipherers of German propaganda, they constructed counter-readings by comparing the narratives found in the local press, and in films of the Channel Islands constructed for German consumption, with the daily reality they could view for themselves. The hunger for trustworthy information on the conduct of the war would make them a ready audience for the counterpropaganda of British leaflets and newssheets occasionally dropped over the Island by the RAF.

It should not be assumed that Guernseymen and women were naive readers of the British presentation of the war, as they were in a position that occasionally made them critical recipients of the hopeful messages from the mainland. Still, this ability to compare the patently deceptive war news and anti-Semitic nonsense of the German official press to the British worldview put forth in leaflets and through the BBC only strengthened the Islanders' psychological ties to the Allied cause. Second, this chapter will consider some of the many stories, jokes, metaphors, and other narrative elements that the Islanders utilized as one of their few available means of resistance, and one they learned to mold to their own purposes. The final portion of this chapter will examine the diarists' understanding of performed compliance and of their own Controlling Committee, and the small triumphs, grave miscalculations, and other difficulties inherent in powerless leadership. As their leaders in the highest levels of Island governance constructed their own resistance based on a mask of outward compliance, their audience consisted not simply of the German command but also the common Islander. It was a mimetic performance that created its own narrative, one that could be read—and misread—during the Occupation and by subsequent generations. All of these largely discursive elements provide a window into narrative resistance, one that would be vital in the construction of the hidden transcript of the Occupation.

A CRESCENDO OF HARD LYING

Our understanding of propaganda and the general response to its use has shifted considerably since the term's origination in 1622 in Pope Gregory's establishment of the Congregation for the Propagation of the Faith. "Propaganda" was simply derived from the Latin (meaning "to sow") and intended "to propagate" an understanding of Church teachings, thus clarifying Catholic doctrine for the people and resisting the persuasive goals of the Reformation. Now, the meaning is clearly pejorative, summoning to mind a dark art of lies and distortion bordering on brainwashing.[3]

"Black propaganda" is, quite naturally, the form we think of when dealing with fabrications, lies, and "all types of creative deceit."[4] In this case, the propaganda is covert, concealing often the source of the propaganda and the intentions behind its use. And the gold standard for the widespread and intensive application of this form of propaganda was the Nazi Party, from 1933 under the minister for propaganda, Joseph Goebbels. Goebbels pioneered a highly coordinated and media-centric style of propaganda that was, at its best (or worst), finely crafted and devastatingly effective in its psychological impact. One element that has remained as a historic artifact of his work is the concept of the "Big Lie," what Ted J. Smith calls "the paradigm instance of the craft" of deception.[5] Hitler and Goebbels both propagated a concept of the Big Lie (*Große Lüge*), a falsehood so large—perhaps so fantastic—that few would believe anyone to be impudent enough to create it out of whole cloth.[6]

The Nazi propaganda machine would be the force to control information in the Channel Islands during the Occupation, and Goebbels's reputation had preceded him. Islanders anticipated that a change in the ready flow of information would come just when news of the outside world was so vitally important to them. Initially, the change was delayed. It was November of 1940 when Ord decided that Goebbels (whom Ord liked to call "the little Doctor") had "at last discovered that we have newspapers in Guernsey" and ordered that subsequent issues would be "special 'cooked' versions of the news." Unwilling to just accept Goebbels's propaganda as news, Ord noted in his diary that he would now call the papers "the Front Page," for they would be little more than "German communiques."[7] Local Guernsey news remained in the papers, but only encompassed silver and golden anniversaries, mundane police blotter and court cases, and the usual accounts of accidents and obituaries. Ambrose Robin believed that by early 1941, not even one in ten people continued to read the outside news.[8]

Even this narrow window of information closed further in the spring of 1942, when the *Evening Press* and *Star* began to publish on an alternate-day schedule,[9] and even more so in early 1944 when the newspapers were reduced in size. By then, not that many missed having the full salvo of "contradictory news and Haw Haw's effusions," according to Robin.[10] Even granting their loss of control over war news, the editors often lost the battle for the remaining small portions of the papers. In October 1943, Gartell, the editor of the *Press*, was suspended because of his desire to publish a Red Cross message from the King and Queen congratulating a couple on their golden anniversary. It seems that it was more the "tone" of his protest over this relatively inconsequential issue that led to his fall, a reflection most likely of intense frustration on a daily basis. It is noteworthy that Gartell lost control of his mask of cooperation under the heady combination of emotion for an elderly couple and a sentimental patriotism.[11]

Although there was irritation with what Rev. Ord called "the crescendo of hard lying on the 'Front Page,'" there was a degree of amusement in reading the more obscure or imaginative German propaganda offerings.[12] It was, for example, "with deepest sympathy" that the Islanders were informed that "President Roosevelt is either ill or insane," in one press offering,[13] and that a Churchill speech was reported under the banner headline "CHURCHILL OUTLINES PROGRAMME OF TERROR." This last offering gave details of Churchill's receiving the Freedom of the City of London from the Lord Mayor of the City, described as "presenting a magnificent figure in his resplendent robes." The account of the ceremony was improved upon by the description of Churchill's pledge of obedience to the Lord Mayor and the German commentator's assertion, "I had now wonder at the deeper meaning of the words, for the Lord Mayor is a Jew!"[14]

If such blatant twisting of information was amusing to Ord, he also grew heartily tired of the "wild propaganda statements" trumpeted by *Press* and *Star* headlines: "Britain Ready to Forget her War Heroes," "Jews Have a Firm Grip on Britain" (according to Ord, this was "a regular stand-by").[15] Ord seemed particularly to relish the crazier stories given major news treatment in the *Evening Press* and *Star*, perhaps because the ludicrous propaganda twist relieved some of the despair inherent in bad news. He related a tidbit from Dr. Goebbels, whether directly or by implication, describing "the King's visit to the smoking ruins of Coventry." According to the "Front Page," at the close of the visit, the King turned to the local dignitaries and said, "I am glad that everything went off so well." Ord could only respond, "Oh, Doctor!"[16]

More fascinating in its own way was Islander awareness of their starring roles in an entire series of propaganda offerings designed for the German home front. This particular campaign would probably be best described as a specialized type of black propaganda called "disinformation," even though the word was not coined until 1955. Still, the term well suits the highly targeted efforts to frame the taking of the Channel Islands as a triumph of German will, and the relationship of occupied to occupier as a cozy meeting of minds. Disinformation is less broad-based than general propaganda, and a more subtle tweaking of the details of a larger news story, designed to show adversaries in a negative light and thus to weaken them.[17] Civilians reading these accounts had lived through the actual taking of Guernsey by the Germans, an event that was a combination of the mass murder of civilians in the bombing and strafing of the harbor, and an anticlimactic final takeover of a demilitarized population incapable of offering armed resistance. The introduction to a publicity film being shown in Germany made the rounds to the amusement of Islanders in its description of the Germans' "daring and sudden attack" that allowed the seizing of Guernsey, or as the film described it, "Tomato Island." The film was obviously structured to appeal to Germans under wartime rationing in its description of the greenhouses of Guernsey supplying "tomatoes, bunches of grapes and melons," now to be diverted to Germany.[18]

By a year later, various versions of the occupying of the Channel Islands were filtering through to Guernsey, revealing just how the Germans had embroidered the account for home consumption. Rev. Ord came across a German periodical that published stills from a film account of the capture of Guernsey, a fictional pitched battle complete with British dead strewn about the streets and "no German dead noticeable."[19] Winifred Harvey inserted into her diary a translated account from *Der Durchbreche*, July 3, 1941, that was a pastiche of comical (and irritating) distortions. According to this version of the advent of Occupation, when abandoned by the British the Guernsey civilians left the streets and closed their businesses as they "awaited the cruelty of the barbarians." The shops then reopened the next day, and the shopkeepers were very willing to serve the German soldiers. To the astonishment of the populace, the Germans paid for everything, and they found that "the lies told about the Germans were not to be believed!"[20]

This propaganda happy-talk, an account that left out such uncomfortable details as the murderous initial air raid and slave labor camps in Alderney, closed with assurances that there was now universal "praise of the Germans' conduct." Highlighted was the relief of the Islanders in knowing "that the German power cares more for them than their fellow countrymen were willing to do."[21] To Guernseymen and women, the news of their gratitude for the tender ministrations of the occupiers was laughable. However, they became accustomed to having their feelings, whether about RAF raids or German orders, mischaracterized in the German press and took it no more seriously than the other factual misstatements and overt lies that composed Nazi propaganda. Little could they know that their attitudes, as falsely filtered through German disinformation, would sit like a little narrative time bomb, only to emerge in the revisionist 1990s as part of the "newly uncovered" story of the Occupation. Although accompanied in the German public transcript by easily debunked historic "facts," German characterizations of Islander beliefs and attitudes have sometimes been accepted in surprisingly uncritical fashion.

Guernseymen and women were undoubtedly aware of their propaganda value to the Germans, who lumped the stories of a welcoming populace together with the photographs taken of supposedly helpful citizens. A perennial favorite seems to have been a German soldier asking street directions of a uniformed Guernsey policeman. A photographer would be standing by to capture the policeman pointing the way or, failing that, merely standing listening to the soldier's request. Either type of photograph implied chumminess, but was unavoidable from the policeman's perspective. Still, the populace had to learn hard lessons of how the most innocent contact with the Germans could pull them into propaganda efforts against their will. The Reverend Hartley Jackson, vicar of St. Stephen's, was presented with an invitation to write an article on Christmas for the *Star.* He quite willingly accepted this opportunity to reach the Island with an encouraging Christian message at the holy season, only to find that the "press führer" had seen fit to improve his offering with a final ending that "The recognition that Christ was born into the world to save the world and to bring peace on earth is the need of Britain and her Bolshevist allies!"[22]

A propaganda piece from 1942 that Bill Warry appended in his diary shows the technique that helped install the perception of cozy familiarity between German and Islander into the public transcript. It took the form of a retrospective piece on the "German Occupation of Guernsey," written from the vantage point of two years into Occupation. Written as if by a Guernseyman, it lauds the German soldiers who "are still with us" as "friendly and honest, generous and understanding." Instead of the "arrogance which we had been led to expect," the great surprise for the Islanders was "the fact that fundamentally the German is closely akin to themselves." As to fears of atrocities, the soldiers had, since coming to Guernsey, "conducted themselves immaculately." Although the wording, which is only slightly off from standard English ("immaculately" having the stilted formality that marks German English), gives a hint of foreign authorship, it is generally seamless to a modern reader. But in no way could it sucker contemporary Islanders such as Bill Warry for long, who wrote at the bottom of the article: "The above appeared on front page of our local paper today. Who wrote it? Not the Editor!"[23]

Islanders found some forms of German propaganda to be particularly amusing, especially those that substituted local pictures as scenes from London. One German newsreel had the caption "bread queues in London," but showed a short queue for cakes early in the Occupation in front of the easily recognizable exterior of Maison Carré in Guernsey's Commercial Arcade. A German officer showed a local family a German periodical with another London bread queue, which was actually a photograph of the queue in Smith Street at Collins Sweet Shop, again from early in the Occupation. Reportedly, the German officer refused to believe that this was a picture from Guernsey until he went into town and could see for himself that the shops in the background were Cecile Shoes, Stonelakes the Chemist, and a small part of Lloyds Bank.[24]

Such silly propaganda attempts made Rev. Ord ponder the effort that went into their creation. Before English films were occasionally shown in the local cinemas, a German propaganda film would be aired. Islanders would delay arriving at the theater until this preliminary film was over, so the Germans added a caption that said, "See all or see nothing." Despite the law against expressing criticism or emotions during such entertainments, it was impossible to sit through these propaganda offerings without laughter and response. One film, for example, showed scenes of the Grand National, with the commentator saying it was "held this year in Paris, AS USUAL, under the patronage of the German authorities." Yet the crowds were togged out in "the very tip-top of pre-war fashion, but NOT A GERMAN OFFICER TO BE SEEN!"

The audience simply roared with laughter. To Ord, it was "a mystery that so much German intelligence or cunning should be put at the disposal of this futile propaganda which even the bairns see through."[25]

The young, anti-Party Germans that Ord came to know well during the Occupation gave intriguing insights into German disgust with Goebbels's form of propaganda. Ord barely knew the young German minister Heinrich Bödeker before Heinrich was talking about his father's habit of listening to London on the wireless. At Heinrich's battery in Guernsey as well, all of his messmates listened to the news from London (broadcast in German). Each new soldier posted to the billet was "sounded out" to see if he was genuine in his desire to subvert the ban on listening to the British news. It was "as good as a play" to watch the process of testing that each new man went through "before being admitted to this 'wireless fellowship.'" But even after one and all had passed the test, the entire group listened at the same time, so that a spy or turncoat would also have violated regulations and could not slip away to report them in the act. This move brought out the Shakespeare in Ord, who sarcastically added, "We few, we happy few, we band of brothers!"[26]

Ord's other close German friend, Reinhold, told him that his father in Germany also listened to the BBC every night at 9 P.M., feeling safe from spying eyes simply because of the isolation of his home. A friend of advanced years visited Reinhold and his family and related to them all the actual news, which they had already heard in the British broadcast. Reinhold confronted the man with "You heard that from London," and lectured him on the danger of talking about the news, for "even good friends may make a mistake." Still, Reinhold gave an indication of the increasing desire for accurate information among the Germans, particularly among workers and soldiers who bore the brunt of the war.[27]

On the Islanders' part, being subjected to an ongoing twisting of information did little but depress them and add to the monotony of a seemingly endless situation. So, Guernsey was a willing and eager recipient of the counterpropaganda provided by RAF leaflet drops. An early drop in September 1940, "No. 1 English News Leaflet," contained photographs of the King and Queen (Winnie Harvey reported it as the iconic photo of the King and Queen examining the Blitz damage at Buckingham Palace),[28] the King's speech, and miscellaneous other news.[29] This first drop appeared to be targeted toward the morale of Guernseymen, although the second leaflet, titled "News From England, No. 2, September 30, 1940, Distributed by R.A.F., Leaves and News," had a more blended purpose.

The lead story spoke of autumn leaves falling (as well as the copies of the leaflet) and put this forward as "far more ominous" to the Germans. The leaflet reminded the reader of Kaiser Wilhelm's promise to the German troops in 1914, "You will be back before the leaves fall," and Hitler's promise of a victory parade through London in August—both promises, of course, now unfulfilled. The leaflet predicted that Germans huddled "in air raid shelters through the coming winter nights" would realize that conquest was a fleeting dream and that the reign of "Nazi gangsters" would be brief. And this article ended with a simple "Cheer up." Although purportedly directed towards the morale of the captive Guernsey civilians, this general message appeared aimed at the German soldiers who would gather the leaflets and read them, or have them translated by friends. As it boosted hope for Islanders, it was designed to make German soldiers consider their families at home and question the promises of Hitler.

This secondary German audience makes the follow-up article on the leaflet all the more inexplicable. It detailed the escape from Guernsey to England of eight men in a 20-foot boat. It was an exciting account of German flares dropping close to the boat, which somehow remained unseen, and engine breakdown that took four hours to repair. All well and good in that it told friends and family back home that their escapees had made it to England safely. But this easing of anxiety had to be weighed against the possibility that the Germans did not know of the escape, and that this knowledge could easily trigger reprisals. But then the British did something that is difficult to fathom in that they identified each of the escapees by name and position: "Mr. Frederick Hockey, 47, a signalman employed by the harbour administration at St. Peter Port, three of his sons Frederick 25, George 21 and Harold 16, who were engaged in tomato growing and Mssrs. William Mahy, Percy du Port, William Dorey and Herbert Bichard, independent growers."[30]

This giving of names was completely gratuitous, considering that family and friends would know of the escapees' absence already. Indeed, word had been out among civilians about the escape since early in September. Winnie noted that nine men had escaped (although the leaflet said eight and gave the names of seven), that they had taken donations with them for the Spitfire Fund, and that they were going to inform the British government about conditions in Guernsey.[31] The plan, according to Winnie, was that the BBC would simply note a large contribution to the Spitfire Fund as a means to let those left behind in Guernsey know that the escapees had arrived safely. The changed plan shows questionable judgment by the BBC and British government. They could not know whether hostages would be shot in reprisal for the escape, and by giving up the names of the escaped fishermen, they made the escapees' family members a convenient target for reprisals. Indeed, it was tantamount to taunting the Germans to note that Frederick Hockey was part of the harbor administration, a move so mocking as to court a response. As it turns out, reprisals did occur, to be discussed in the next chapter.

It was not just specially designed leaflets that were dropped on the Channel Islands by the RAF. In September 1941, a bundle of newspapers, including the *Times*, *Sketch*, and *Daily Mirror*, was dropped at Vazon, to the delight of Guernsey. Because the papers were plainly marked "Not to be taken away from the messroom," this drop appeared to be a spontaneous "free gift" courtesy of the pilot. But it was quite a pleasure for a print-oriented people to see actual British newspapers rather than to read a recap or to hear an account from the wireless. Rev. Ord was one who had the opportunity to see one of the papers, having been summoned to a banker's private "sanctum" to take a look.[32]

It would only be a matter of time before the Germans decided to use these leaflet drops as part of their own propaganda efforts. Goebbels functioned on the notion that anything genuine could also be faked as a form of disinformation. Ambrose Robin described one of these efforts that furthered an ongoing Nazi theme of supposed dissension between the United States and Britain. In Jersey, the Germans sent around a story of a drop of leaflets by an American airplane over the town. In Robin's view, the authors of this piece of propaganda gave the game away in two substantial ways. First, the leaflets strangely enough only "landed" on the right-hand side of Queen and King Streets, somehow avoiding even one falling on a roof or into a backyard. This evidence was augmented by eyewitness reports that a German staff car was observed "disgorging" the leaflets at dawn. But Robin believed that the simple fact that so many leaflets were found in a restricted area would be enough to make the public say, "I am not deceived." Second, the discourse found in the leaflets was a dead giveaway of the source for a people now well-attuned to Nazi rhetoric. Clearly, in Robin's estimation, there did not exist an American printing press anywhere, especially in the government or military service, likely to "use such crude and filthy adjectives againt [*sic*] the British.[33]

The occupied population of Guernsey navigated past the German propaganda that was intended to function in multiple ways. Some was designed to plant doubts about the veracity of British information, and thus to foster the conclusion that *all* information is slanted and not to be trusted. If, as Ted Smith frames it, "a lie and the truth are equally probable, or that all parties to the discussion are lying," the result can be paralyzing for the audience. Lessening belief in British information—planting that kernel of misgiving—could slow the response to any call to action that might come.[34] Primarily, of course, the German propaganda that filled the Island newspapers was calculated to influence the emotional perspective of local readers. Over time, the drumbeat of German self-congratulation and the constant reiteration of the Nazi worldview were meant to seep into the reader's consciousness. One of the key concepts to differentiate legitimate advocacy from propaganda is rationality, because the tendency of propaganda is to function solely on a gut level. However, when reasonable people can, as the Islanders did, approach propaganda with a degree of "critical scrutiny," its persuasive force evaporates.[35] Guernseymen and women developed a fine contempt for German propaganda. And, as will be discussed next, tales about propaganda would form part of the hidden transcript of stories, jokes, and metaphors used by the Islanders to make sense of their Occupation experience.

A TALE TO TELL

The theory of symbolic convergence provides a useful means of dissecting the rich legacy of stories, jokes, and metaphors that remain from the Occupation years, and provides a window into how such discourse has a purpose in resistance. According to this concept, during communication with others, our "private symbolic worlds" begin to converge, providing a common vocabulary by which we share our experiences and give meaning to our existence.[36] In other words, we construct our reality through the symbols we use and the stories we tell.[37] Although Symbolic Convergence Theory is useful in understanding some rather bizarre groups whose common narrative worldview does not always seem to comport with reality, its general purpose is more prosaic and thus more helpful. It focuses upon actual messages to discover the "common perspective" unique to any particular group,[38] the "meeting of the minds" achieved as group members "chain out" an account of their experiences in narratives (stories, jokes) and word play.[39]

Out of the communicative interplay within a group emerges a series of "fantasy themes," a term that does *not* mean that the stories told are imaginary. Usually our fantasy themes deal with actual people or events, with real heroes or villains, with projections into the future or common understandings of the past.[40] To give a simple example, a group of professors might meet over coffee and chain out stories of their students. Through these narratives, the professors "make visible (understandable) a common experience and shape it into common knowledge."[41] They develop a shared understanding of each new crop of students, sometimes in positive and sometimes in negative ways. Of course, the students are simultaneously developing their own fantasy themes concerning their professors. Particularly fascinating are such "mirror image fantasies," where the "heroes of one account are the villains of the other, the laudable actions in one becoming the deplorable actions in the other."[42]

What Ernest Bormann calls the "fossilized remains" of these fantasies continue to exist as these stories are shared with others. What are left behind are remnants that can be read to understand a group's sense of "social reality." One interesting aspect of fantasy theme important to understanding narratives of the Guernsey Occupation is the "inside joke," where speakers (or writers) reference a shared fantasy by a gesture, coded term, or other symbol.[43] Often such inside jokes remain mysterious to those outside the original group, leading to misunderstandings and false readings.[44] Average Guernseymen and women, excluding the minority of collaborators, fraternizers, or profiteers who functioned outside the mainstream, formed a "rhetorical community"[45] of shared values and common perceptions. In their stories, jokes, and metaphors are the traces left behind of a sense-making process used to give meaning to their confused and stressful experience of Occupation.

To capture the mindset of Islanders and understand the narrative they constructed informally, it is important to seek clusters of stories that portray recurrent "fantasy types." Sometimes the same story or joke appears, with only slight variations, in more than one account. More often, the fantasy type is composed of narratives that vary somewhat in their characters and plots but nonetheless possess an essential similarity.[46] Not surprisingly, given all the control over information, one cluster of stories that made the rounds dealt with propaganda and the German use of the Channel Islands as a propaganda device. One story conveyed early on by Winifred Harvey also took the form of a warning narrative, a major fantasy type that appears in a variety of settings.

Winnie introduced this tale with "The story goes . . . ," an indicator that she did not necessarily accept it as true, but perhaps recorded it as instructive and fairly widespread. At a German concert in Jersey, the commandant stepped forward to speak to the crowd, asking who among them could speak German. Only three or four raised their hands in response. With such a small response, he switched gears and asked those who did *not* speak German to raise their hands. Of course, the hundreds in attendance raised their hands, and at that moment, the German photographer took a picture. This, then, was published in Germany "as the Jersey people 'heiling' Hitler." Winnie concluded that the moral of the story was "keep away from crowds."[47]

It is fascinating to see a variation of this story appear in a modern recollection by Maurice Green, a man who was a schoolboy in Jersey during the Occupation. As recorded by Madeleine Bunting, in Green's memory the Germans gathered together elementary schoolchildren, and a German officer said, "Hands up all the children who would like to have a bar of German milk chocolate." Film was then made of the children purportedly doing the Heil Hitler salute. In Green's account, he did not want the chocolate and did not raise his hand, thus making him the one not caught in the propaganda. There are multiple difficulties with this story that, assuming the sincerity of the interviewee and the accuracy of Bunting's report, point to it as a false memory. However, even if such is the case, this simply highlights that the story was so common as to become embedded in a child's mind, later to be recalled as a personal event.[48]

This story in its various iterations reflects Islanders' awareness of their potential usefulness to further the German cause, if only as unwitting players in a German propaganda script. Hearing this tale when it was making the rounds in August 1940 would only strengthen Guernsey's resolve to avoid contact with their new masters, avoidance being one of the most basic levels of resistance to power. While many narratives portray Germans as duplicitous, the outward friendliness sheltering negative intentions, some of the stories passed around as true possessed a tinge of sympathy for the common German soldiers as co-victims of the Nazi regime. Such stories of revelation, of Germans forced to confront the truth of either their own nature or that of the regime they supported, were prevalent throughout the Occupation.

During the fall of 1941, after a series of evictions and confiscations of Islander houses, Rev. Ord wrote of one German, adept at colloquial English and dressed in civilian attire, who had entered Miss Gaudin's shop. She knew perfectly well his country of origin, but Miss Gaudin asked, "Are you a Frenchman?" The German's reply was phrased, according to Ord, "with a grasp of Shakespearian English that shewed what a good school he had attended." The man answered, "No, I'm one of your bloody Germans." His "thoroughly crestfallen and ashamed" manner, Ord believed, reflected his awareness of the newly stigmatized reputation of Germany.[49]

If there was the occasional story that differentiated a particular soldier from the mass or portrayed them as unwitting dupes of the Nazi regime, these tales were far outweighed by warning stories. As mentioned previously, the warning story was a preeminent fantasy type and often dealt with the need to see through the friendly and polite guise of the Germans to the dark heart beneath. One story was shocking enough to have been repeated broadly. It appeared in the diary kept by Kitty Bachmann in November 1941 and then was repeated as a complete story in Violet Carey's diary in October 1942. It is worth examining in its entirety as an indication of the function of warning narratives, and as an insight into how oral stories "morph" as they are passed from person to person over the course of a year.

I will start with Kitty's version of the story, which she introduced with the common device of "the story goes," and without indicating by whom the story had come her way. The story involved a "certain family who entertained the Germans" and who had a young son that was a great favorite of a particular German guest. This German soldier "would dandle the child on his knee and make a great show of affection." The father of the child decided, for unspecified reasons, to test the German and asked, "If you were ordered by the Führer to destroy this child, would you do so?" The German soldier replied without pause, "I would have no choice but to obey!" Shocked by what Kitty called "this admission of weakness," the parent told the soldier to leave the house and never return.[50]

Now let us turn to the version recorded by Violet Carey the following year. In Violet's version, the incident occurred in a "family who has a soldier billeted on them and with whom they have become very friendly." This time the child who had become a favorite of the German soldier was a little girl. One day, as the soldier was stroking the little girl's hair, he said, without prompting or questioning, "If Hitler ordered me to shoot this little girl I would shoot her." Violet reported that she was "glad to say they [the family] had the spunk to turn him out of their room and to have nothing more to do with him."[51] The differences in these warning stories are notable. Kitty's version involves a family with whom few Islanders would have been sympathetic, for they had chosen to entertain the Germans voluntarily. In a sense, these quislings got what they deserved in the shocking revelation that their houseguest was not a fond uncle to their little boy, but a thoroughgoing Nazi. It is a story that implies that those foolish enough to have voluntary contact with the Germans would rue the day when the evil nature of their new friends emerged in full force.

Violet Carey's version was told after a period of intense billeting and confiscation of Islanders' homes. In this case, the innocence of the Guernsey family is heightened in a number of ways. First, the German is not a voluntary houseguest, but a soldier they were forced to billet in their home. Even the child in question is made more vulnerable and innocent by the change from a boy to a girl. The mistake made by the family pointed to an error possibly being made by many now forced to billet German soldiers: to see these young men as friends, much like their own sons serving in the British forces, and innocent of attachment to the Nazi cause. As discussed earlier, this actually was the experience of some of those billeting German soldiers. In this case, the German, unbidden, dramatically reveals his Nazi fanaticism hidden under the guise of friendliness. This is a version that is far more chilling, and one that allows the Guernsey family to win the day by showing the "spunk" necessary to avoid further close contact, despite his continued presence in their home. Anyone hearing this story would put a new frame on the pleasant young man now housed in the bedroom down the hall.

And that is the important aspect of warning narratives; they reframe something that the teller and listener have in common and thus provide both admonitions for past behavior and implied advice for the future. Some early stories related to the dangerous combination of armed soldiers and a language barrier. One apparently true tale from the first month of Occupation involved E. H. Ogier of Duvaux Farm, who fell asleep in his armchair before night had fallen. He was awakened at 2 A.M. by a pair of German soldiers knocking on his front door. The German soldiers did not speak English and Mr. Ogier did not understand German, so there seemed to be an impasse. That is, until one soldier pointed to the electric light and fired off two rounds. Both missed the target, but "Teddy Ogier then understood what was wanted and switched off the light."[52]

In this story, Teddy Ogier could be considered the target of the humor. In most of the stories and jokes, however, we generally see this same designation of the "butt of the joke" as someone other than the average Guernsey Islander, and thus as someone other than the person relating the story. Self-deprecating humor is a luxury of the powerful, or at least of those with some modicum of control over their own lives. Among those with limited to no power, the humor is often at the expense of others, generally based on a comparative that makes the teller feel momentarily one-up on another person or group.[53]

Stories about propaganda generally implied superiority over the Germans, particularly in Islanders' ability to obtain British information despite the German ban. Of course, many of these stories involve the civilians' ability to retain and read leaflets. One classic reversal story was related by Ambrose Robin on October 10, 1940, and involved a Guernsey special constable impressed by German soldiers into collecting leaflets dropped by the RAF. The soldiers and constable went door to door together for a while before coming to a neighborhood with houses on both sides of the street. The German corporal directed the special constable to take the houses on one side, while the Germans approached the houses on the other. At the first house, the constable, as he had been directed, asked the homeowners, "Have you any leaflets—if so, you must give them up." When the occupants replied, "No," the constable said, "Well, here's a couple," and handed over several leaflets collected earlier in the day.[54]

This story was similar to a pair of matching tales related on the same day by Rev. Ord. The first involved a young lad in Grande Rue, St. Martin. He was walking along the road reading a dog-eared copy of "Comic Cuts," or "some similar literature," when he was stopped by a large German soldier. The soldier examined the paper the boy was carrying, satisfying himself that it was not a British leaflet, and then let the boy go with an admonition to turn in any leaflets he might find. The boy went home and told his parents about his conversation with the German, and his father took the opportunity to tell his son to be very careful. The boy agreed readily and then, "diving into his inner pocket," produced the leaflets he had been carrying the entire time he was questioned by the German.

The second incident occurred in a field where a farm worker was milking cows, each tethered to her own rope, taking advantage of the lush grass. A German soldier came by looking for leaflets, and the farm worker truthfully told him that he had seen none. Having milked

"Mabel," he went over to "Susan." When Susan got to her feet in preparation for milking, it turned out that she had been "lying on a thick wad of leaflets." Thus, the worker had many leaflets to distribute to those who had yet to read one. And it was all because the German "had not been sufficiently 'efficient' to question" Susan as well![55]

What makes these three stories work as a fantasy type is the juxtaposition of force, as represented by the Germans' power to commandeer, question, and confiscate, with either cleverness or a complete innocence that manages to thwart that force. In the latter stories, the German is outwitted first by an innocent child and—the greater insult—ultimately by a cow. It could be expected that stories about the Germans would show them up or portray them in a state of discomfiture. It is a desire for "negative reciprocity, a settling of scores when the high shall be brought low and the last shall be first."[56] What cannot be achieved by counterforce can easily take place in narratives, some factual and most fictional.

Other factual stories provide a clear one-upmanship for the Guernseyman in encounters with the Germans in charge. Following a hurricane and intense storms in November 1940, Captain Henderson had to go to see Dr. Brosch of the Feldkommandantur. He took great pleasure in relating the ensuing conversation to Winnie Harvey:

> "What weather! What weather!" said Dr. Brotsch.
> "Weather? *We* like it."
> "Like it!"
> Captain Henderson said, "Oh, well, it's only autumn yet, we haven't had the winter."
> "Autumn! Winter!" exclaimed Dr. Brotsch, "What is it like here in winter, then?"
> "Oh, winter! In the winter we have *storms*."[57]

This actual conversation has the same rhythm that builds to a punch line as that mainstay of American folk humor, the Farmer and the Stranger joke ("Say, Farmer, you been living here all your life?" "Not yet.") In this case, the story pits the Guernseyman as the Farmer, steeped in local knowledge and common sense, against the German as the clueless, effete Stranger passing through.

Jack Sauvary related another purportedly true story of native wits confounding endless rules and regulations. Early on, farmers were allowed to keep half of their own pigs when they were slaughtered, the rest having to be surrendered. One farmer, on slaughtering a pig, cut the animal across the back, sending in the front part and keeping the back portion for himself. Jack heard that the authorities "made a little fuss," but the farmer maintained that he had only done what the law demanded by sending in half. His technical compliance was indisputable, but the law was quickly changed to specify that the pig must be divided down the center of the spine. In relating this story of clever circumventing of the powers-that-be, Jack put in parentheses, "Trust a Guernsey farmer to be cute."[58]

Some of the one-upmanship stories about the Germans were brief and likely apocryphal. A common tale (Robin called it "the tale of the day") from October 1940 was that a German officer stopped a Guernseyman in the Grange, asking in broken English, "Heil Hitler—Which is the way to the Regal?" Whereupon, the local man supposedly replied, "God save the King—first turn on the left."[59] Other jokes at the Germans' expense were throwaway lines, *bon mots* made in the company of friends. An example of such witticisms would include a running joke in Kitty Bachmann's circle. During the time when so many private homes were being seized by the Germans, La Guelle remained untouched for the time being. Kitty claimed to be tempted by an unidentified friend's advice to "rename the house 'Stalingrad' because it had not been taken."[60] This is the humor found in difficult circumstances that binds a subordinate group together in common viewpoint and understanding. It finds a "chink in the armor" of those in control and exploits that flaw to diminish perceptions of their power and competence.

Before leaving the stories and jokes told at the expense of the Germans, it is interesting to examine more formal jokes, ones that are presented as purely fictional and structured to build to an actual punch line.[61] These jokes have a particularly subversive potency. One such joke is found in both Ambrose Robin's diary and in the diary of Violet Carey, their accounts appearing only a week apart. Robin worked for the States, and Violet Carey was not only related to the Bailiff but was also married to a jurat of the Royal Court. Thus, they would have heard many of the same jokes that were passed around the States offices and then filtered through to the homes of States officials. Both indicate that the joke is from German sources. The joke starts with Goering believing that London had been bombed to the ground. Eager to see his handiwork up close, he flew in a plane to London. After he had been in the air for an hour or so, he passed over a city that was completely flattened. Leaning out to look, he rubbed his hands together saying, "Gut! Gut! My Luftwaffe has done well indeed." The pilot became very red in the face and said, "I am sorry your Excellency, we have half an hour more to go, that town is Wilhelmshaven!"[62]

Told first as an acknowledgment of weakness by the Germans, this joke would likely continue to make the rounds long after its origin was forgotten. Some German jokes had a more sinister purpose, as Rev. Ord learned from Reinhold Zachmann. The joke Reinhold told Ord went like this. Hitler, Goering, and Goebbels were taking a drive to try out the new Volkswagen when they passed a farm that had posted a notice, "Pig for Sale!" When inquiries were made about the pig, the farmer asked for 185 marks. The three leaders each put down that they would give 15 marks, carefully writing down:

$$\begin{array}{c} 15 \\ 15 \\ \underline{15} \\ 185 \end{array}$$

The math was based on the new Nazi accounting method: 5 and 5 and 5 make 15. Put down the 5 and carry on from column one, counting "fifteen, sixteen, seventeen, eighteen" and put down the 18. "Ah!" said the farmer. "Now I see how you compute the British naval and merchant shipping losses." Reinhold then said that to repeat this joke in Germany could literally cost a person his head. It had been devised specifically to serve as a trap for those disloyal to the Third Reich.[63]

F. K. M. Hillenbrand has written about the speed with which anti-regime jokes traveled through Germany, and the ongoing rumors that these jokes originated with Goebbels as a test of loyalty among the German people. The fear involved in the covert passing of such humor, and the subversive nature of joking may be seen in the habit that developed of scanning one's environment before delivering the joke. The term coined for this act was the "German glance" (*der Deutsche Blick*), and when combined with another term, "the whispered joke" (*Flüsterwitze*), the role of covert joking in undermining panoptical power becomes clear.[64] For our purposes, the fear in being caught passing anti-Party humor indicates that Germans viewed narratives (stories or jokes) as accurately reflecting the teller's internal beliefs, and as powerful enough in their effects to be treated as treason.

Humor directed at the Germans—whether stories based on contact with them or more formal jokes—met Sigmund Freud's definition of the "tendentious joke." This kind of humor makes the target appear small and foolish, easily thwarted by circumstances and at the mercy of his/her own shortcomings. Significantly, Freud saw tendentious humor as a substitute for violent action, as a means of besting an enemy when physical action is impossible or unwise. Freud claimed that "by making our enemy small, inferior, despicable or comic, we achieve in a roundabout way the enjoyment of overcoming him."[65] Such humor during the Occupation provided an outlet for aggression during a time when direct attacks would put the actor and the community in danger for no good purpose. At the same time, by diminishing the Germans, this humor also taught the Islanders not to live in fear of them. This control over how the powerful are perceived is vital if those under their control are ever to take effective action. So, we would expect to (and do) see the use of tendentious humor prior to, and in the early stages of, great social movements. It is a mainstay of the hidden transcript of the powerless, not just because it effectively paves the way for later action, but also because of its own subversive power.

Although Germans served as the object of ridicule for most jokes told by Islanders, the other most common form of structured, narrative humor might today be called the "idiot joke." Various versions of this joke were put forward, basing the humor on the person too unintelligent or too out of it to understand circumstances the way they were. Rev. Ord related a classic of this genre of humor in the story of the simple-minded man whose wife had evacuated in 1940. Now, this "grass-widower of three year's standing" received news via a Red Cross message that his wife had just delivered a baby. With the pride of a new father, the man told this happy news to a friend, who was having some difficulty concealing his surprise. "You're surprised," said the simple-minded husband. "There's no reason to be. You see, there's a good five years between my brother and me!"[66] Like many "idiot" or "moron" jokes, this humor may have been based on the simplicity of the slow of wit, but it pointed to a common anxiety. Only a fool, this joke argues, believed he had an accurate picture of what was happening in the lives of evacuated spouses.

The other butt of Island stories and jokes was the elderly woman, a staple of humor throughout history. Although modern eyes read into these stories an unpleasant ageism and sexism, the fact is that some were based on true incidents. One story told by Winifred Harvey, a woman over fifty herself, occurred while she was in the post office. The "old countrywoman" in front of her was drawing some money from her savings bank account and requested that her book be sent up this month, presumably to the London bank headquarters. The clerk said that it could not be sent now and would not be sent until after the war. Whereupon the woman replied, "Then they not settled the war yet?"[67] Rev. Ord had a true weakness for such stories, loving the blend between the rural innocence of some of his parishioners and the perceived dottiness of elderly women. He told of an incident following a raid made by the RAF in July 1941, when the fire brigade had been summoned. When some of the brigade went to a country cottage for water, they were greeted by an old woman who took one look at their uniforms, mistook them for British parachutists, and exclaimed, "I knew you'd come some day!"[68]

Ord managed to combine a classic joke at German expense with some follow-up humor provided by elderly women. The formal joke involved Hitler staring out at the Straits of Dover in 1940, angry over the obstacle that the Channel presented to his invasion plans. A staff officer (toadying for credit) said that he knew of a great Führer who conquered just such a barrier:

> "Who was he?" asked Hitler.
> "A man called Moses, my Führer."
> "Ah! A Jew! Nevertheless, how did he do it?"
> "Sir, he waved his rod and the waters parted."
> "Where is that rod now?"
> "My Führer, it is in the British Museum!"

But Ord continued that he told this joke to an acquaintance, who then related it to "two elderly maiden ladies of most retired habits." When Ord's friend reached the end of the joke, one of the elderly women looked up and said with great interest, "That is a very nice story. But IS the rod really in the British Museum?"[69] Thus, this joke functions in two standard ways. The first part is the typical joke of diminishment, with Hitler as the stooge, and is told with clear contempt for the principals. The addendum, which would join the original joke in subsequent retelling, is of a different nature entirely. It embraces the target in its gentle humor and is the type of story that we tell on ourselves or on one that we love. In a nostalgic way, it argues for a return to innocence, for a time when elderly women could be of "most retired habits," untroubled by Nazi occupiers and a world at war.

In addition to full stories and jokes, another way to read fantasy types is through examining wordplay, particularly narrative equivalencies such as similes and metaphors. Not surprisingly, the primary metaphor that emerged in contemporaneous documents compared the Island to a prison and the Guernsey population to prisoners. Jack Sauvary, immediately after the Occupation, began to refer to being "in Camp." In a light vein, Jack maintained, "Our camp is not barbed wire, but surrounded by water, and it's too far to swim the Channel, and these days too cold!"[70] And Jack was right that there was little need of barbed wire considering Guernsey's location and the inherent difficulty in escape. Ambrose Robin felt acutely the restrictions of this "miserable cramped existence" and believed that it combined with wide-spread illness, unhealthy diet, and generally depressing conditions to make Guernseymen and women feel "interned good and proper."[71]

Other metaphors bolstered the concept of imprisonment. Bill Warry described how the final seizing of wireless sets left them "cut off from the world," with no concept of "how the war is going on at all or what is happening to our & other people." It was clear to Bill that "*We are rats in a trap proper*."[72] Many commented on the transformation of the Island under Nazi control into a foreign, almost bizarre place. It was not merely the presence of German troops crowding out the civilians, but the deserted streets of St. Peter Port after dark. Newly forced by eviction to move to St. Peter Port, Ambrose Robin found it lonely to walk the streets with Tim in the evening; with the hotels and shops closed and the streets deserted, "I am a stranger in a strange land."[73]

If some of the common talk among civilians described a desolate and empty landscape, other fantasy types emphasized the danger inherent in their new world. Kitty Bachmann described how a particularly bleak piece of war news filtering through the Island, or the imposition of some new German order would "descend upon us like a pall." It was then that Islanders realized "how narrow is the towpath, how deep and swift the torrent on either side."[74] Kitty was often aware that Islanders now lived "on the edge of a volcano which may erupt at any moment."[75] All of these metaphors and similes emphasized the precarious nature of life under Occupation, the belief that they were walking a narrow ledge with destruction a simple misstep away.

Dissecting narrative constructions is key to seeing the Occupation through the eyes of the occupied rather than through the official viewpoint of their captors. The most pressing need was to understand those in power over them. It is not that these stories told average people something new, for they had ample opportunity to experience German duplicity and strong-arm tactics. However, warning narratives served to heighten wariness as Islanders faced new situations, such as German billeting. Stories and jokes also provided a satisfying means to overcome an enemy who, in reality, held all the cards. Other stories gathered their humor from fellow Islanders who just did not get it, usually due to age or some other infirmity. And they defined their world in common through language that captured the barrenness, the danger, and the twisted new reality that they lived.

So it was in casual conversation—in sharing among themselves jokes and stories, small turns of phrase, colorful metaphors—that Islanders wrote their own account of the Occupation. Most of this narrative has been lost to history, although its echo exists in the stories of the Occupation generation, who at one point were very forthcoming in sharing narratives pulled from the hidden transcript. They quickly found that the far more vast remnants of the public transcript overwhelmed their simple story of courage and resourcefulness. This result, while frustrating to the Islanders, was hardly surprising, for it is the self-congratulatory narrative of those in power that is designed to live. The hidden transcript is neither structured for public consumption nor likely to survive its creators in its full form. In the final portion of this chapter, I will explore one small aspect of this hidden transcript, seeking contemporaneous perspectives on an Island leadership tasked with guiding Guernsey through five years as an occupied people.

BUFFERS

Following an evening service in St. Sampson on May 2, 1943, a very prominent States official sought a private word with Rev. Ord. The prospect of an impending cut to the already meager civilian rations was anticipated around the Island, and this official wanted to fill Ord in on the negotiations taking place behind the scenes. On the previous Friday, the Controlling Committee had a German order thrust before them that would reduce the bread ration to 2 lbs 5 oz. (from the current 4½ lbs.) per week. The meat ration would go from 4 oz. per week to 2 oz., and cooking fats would be reduced to 1¾ oz. The Germans insisted that this plan be placed in effect "AT ONCE." The Controlling Committee was horrified, believing this to be tantamount to a death sentence for very many in the Island who were barely clinging to their physical health as it was. The Committee protested vehemently and began a process to "play for time."

Telling the Germans that some parts of the order were unclear and implementation would take time, the Committee requested a conversation with their opposite numbers in Jersey to discuss how best to put the order into effect. To their great surprise, this request—made often but never previously allowed—was granted. Buoyed by contact with the "strong-minded Bailiff of Jersey," the Committee decided to continue stalling and to submit an appeal through the Swiss ambassador in Berlin. If the rations were cut to the extent ordered, the Committee insisted to the Germans, only the intervention of Red Cross supplies could prevent disaster. And now they had to wait to see how this move to bring in the protecting power (Switzerland) would play with the Germans.[76]

This conversation with Ord was not merely to provide information but also to solicit his aid. According to this States official, the Germans had refused to allow the papers to publish the States' position on this anticipated ration cut. What would likely appear would be the usual order and explanation that implied, or directly stated, that this cut came from the Controlling Committee, or at least was readily agreed to by them. This official wondered if Ord could "circulate the facts as discreetly as I might."[77] The actual story of a determined pushback against Nazi orders would never be allowed in the press, so the truth must be sent word of mouth among the civilian population. This account gives a clear description of the subtle battle for control between the dominant and the subordinate that occurred regularly during the Occupation. More important for the purposes of this study, it highlights the resistant role of the hidden transcript as a parallel construction to the public transcript.

When the Bread Rationing Order (1943) came out on May 7, it was a victory for the Controlling Committee. Male heavy workers would receive 4¾ lbs. of bread (female heavy workers would receive 4¼), and all other adults would be reduced to 3¾ lbs.[78] According to Ambrose Robin, the Controlling Committee also managed to gain a cancellation of the fat and meat reduction at least temporarily.[79] Ord lauded the grit of the Island authorities: "The courageous stand of the Controlling Committee has thus won for the Island a concession which may make all the difference."[80] Yet who would be privy to this story of playing for time in desperate circumstances? The public transcript of the newspapers and official documents—all controlled by the occupiers—would give an account of collaboration, or at least cooperation, between the Germans and Island authorities.

Although most later readers of the Guernsey newspapers could see through the propaganda that littered their pages, the same could not be said of the official documents. When many of the internal documents from the Occupation were released in the 1990s, they fueled a view of the States as at best weak-kneed, and at worst collaborative. A new frame needs to be introduced in reading these documents. Even a verbatim transcript of a meeting between the Controlling Committee and the German authorities would only record the carefully couched language that committee members used in negotiation. The true opinions and intent of the speaker, the steps taken behind the scenes, and the efforts to circumvent authority are not to be found in these official documents.

In the final portion of this chapter, I want to examine briefly the Islanders' view of their own Controlling Committee and some of the positive outcomes and identifiable shortcomings of its tenure. Knowles Smith's account of the Occupation, as well as the many books written by those in the Islands, has moved the historical discussion forward on this complicated question. When it comes to the particular controversy of the treatment of Jewish Islanders, especially the three women from Guernsey who lost their lives in German concentration camps, the combination of Knowles Smith's general account and Frederick Cohen's fair and detailed *The Jews in the Channel Islands during the German Occupation, 1940–1945* provides new understanding of the way these events unfolded.

I am interested in related questions that seek an understanding of the Committee's actions from the perspective of rhetorical theory. How did average Islanders read the actions of their leaders, and was the Committee's mask of outward compliance understood by those whom they represented? At what point did this tactic—the most common and perhaps the only option for a subordinate population—break down, leaving the Committee unable to protect its people and subject to the condemnation of a history based on the public transcript? What do the discursive games played by the Committee with their German masters tell us of narrative as the second form of rhetorical resistance?

An overall examination of the workings of the Controlling Committee supports the contention that they took a "utilitarian approach" to their work, attempting to gain "the greatest good for the greatest number of Islanders."[81] This was a reasonable general perspective for men thrown suddenly into the task of ruling without power, under the watchful gaze of a ruthless master. However, there is no evidence that the States officials consciously made a choice to "sacrifice the few to save the many."[82] The members of the Controlling Committee spent the five years of Occupation playing it by ear. None of them were trained for anything even slightly representing their new situation; indeed, what type of training could there be? John Leale, who stepped into Sherwill's position as president of the Controlling Committee, after Sherwill's early ouster, later accurately said that they were merely "pitchforked" into their new roles.[83]

Once formed and operating as the only voice for the people of Guernsey, they adopted a common perspective of how best to play the hand that they were dealt. In doing so, they came to the same conclusion that other subordinate groups have reached: that a "blanket rejection of compliance seems poorly reasoned and potentially harmful."[84] They already saw that even a crack in the mask of compliance had led to the removal of Sherwill, giving them reason to fear that the entire Committee could just as easily be dissolved, and the Island run directly by the Germans as an enlarged prison camp. Piecing together hints from insider views and fragments from the hidden transcript with an examination of the Committee's actions, it seems clear that the States in general worked to perfect their "performance of deference and consent."[85]

It might fairly be asked when we can know that such deference is a performance and not an expression of wholehearted collaboration. Those who adopt this strategy are at a distinct disadvantage in proving that their mask of compliance does not reflect the actual contours of their own faces. We have such documents as Sherwill's memoirs and the report of John Leale made during May 1945, but any documents made after the fact are easily dismissed as justifications or window dressing to disguise collaboration. Even during the time that the strategy is unfolding, those who take this stance run the risk of alienating their peers if the mask is too impenetrable, or if there is no alternative means regularly to reveal their true intentions and feelings. According to John Jordan, those who take the stance of performed compliance, being privy to their own intent, often find it "liberating" and see it as "a different means of resistance . . . the performance of a role rather than a crystallized identity."[86] They are often frustrated to find that they are misunderstood by their fellows and condemned by history for their compliance.

Despite the risks inherent in such a stance, and the unlikelihood that it is, in any sense, a cure for powerlessness or some ticket to a "utopian existence," it may allow not only survival but also a subtle means to subvert the most onerous of situations.[87] On both sides of the power divide, we can see how the Germans and the Islanders, especially the Controlling Committee, engaged in a "dialectic of disguise and surveillance," both trying to maintain a mask of competence and command while attempting "to peer behind the mask" of the other.[88] One clear purview of the powerful is the ability to maintain their own privacy while stripping away the privacy of those under their control. In an Occupation structured on panopticism, thwarting the penetrating gaze of the Germans was an initial step towards regaining some measure of secrecy for the States officials. Few masks are as impenetrable as that of ostensible compliance, or a better disguise for the covert manipulation of the powerful.[89] As practiced by the States of Guernsey, it was a tactic that yielded both gratifying success and unintended, sometimes devastating, failure.

Although we can never penetrate the States offices and listen in on the opposition and negotiations made by the Controlling Committee, there are hints as to what took place. Leale, in his overview of the Occupation provided in his May 23, 1945, address, mentioned that it was unfortunate that there was no record in the early period of the Committee's protests, which were limited "to those of a verbal nature." It was only as time passed, as the strain of governing and limited nutrition began to take its toll, that the Committee members realized that they would no longer be able to trust their memories of what had been said in these negotiations. At the time, they were not focused on postwar justification of their actions, but on proof in later dealings with the occupiers that certain opinions had been expressed, specific representations had been made, and precise agreements had been reached. Increasingly, the Committee began to write more letters and to have Mr. Guillemette take notes if an interview with the Germans seemed particularly important. The Committee members would immediately read and sign his minutes before fading memories could muddle a perception of what had happened.[90]

Fortunately, there are two contemporaneous reports that give hints of the functioning of the States officials in their role as buffers between the Germans and the Guernsey populace. In October 1940, Ken Lewis had an informal interview with Mr. Sherwill and started to work in his office, remaining as a clerk in the States offices throughout the war, doing all sorts of jobs. He spent considerable time, it seems, typing in German, a difficult job until he got the hang of it.[91] He gives a good sense that any and everything fell to the lot of Sherwill (and later Leale) to be examined and negotiated with the Germans. For example, a letter came through the office from a POW named Beresford Pezet addressed to his parents in St. Peter Port. Amid the chat about family and friends came these lines: "I don't suppose I will see you again . . . You know how quick tempered I am well I got myself into a mess and now I got to take the punishment for it, so will understand what I mean, you can't live forever. So goodbye my sweet lots of love and kisses." This information slid blandly between the lines (likely to foil the censors) must have terrified his parents. Ken mentioned that Leale was taking the matter up with the Germans to find out the nature of the crime and punishment and to try to intervene at a distance.[92]

Ken gave hints of the life-and-death importance of such interventions and the deeper level of tension involved in continuous negotiations with the Germans. In his postwar address, Leale described the options when the Committee received an order:

> We could carry it out without demur or could risk doing nothing in the hope that this would be the last we would hear of it; or try by arguments to get it reversed; or accept as a fait accompli, that something unpleasant was going to happen and to make the best of a bad job by suggesting alternative proposals which, though unpleasant, would be less burdensome than the original order.[93]

Ken described many of the Committee's moves as typical of "the 'go-slow' policy in Guernsey."[94] And such work slowdowns are classic forms of resistance under a general veil of compliance. After all the arguments are made against an action, if arguments are allowed at all, a smiling, vague willingness shelters a molasses-like pace of completion. It is little wonder that powerless populations of all kinds earn reputations as lazy, inefficient, and incompetent; these are disguised strategies of obstruction.

From Leale's report and from the contemporaneous diaries, it is clear that the Committee attempted to push back whenever they felt that opposition would yield results. At other times, the Committee bided its time, believing that delay would put them in a better position to make their case. The ability to read those in power, a sensitivity to the nonverbal cues of those in control, has often been noted as an adaptation of those in subordinate positions. It is posited by some that women's "intuition" is tied to centuries of reading nonverbal signs, because pleasing others was integral to fulfillment of their subordinate role. Even children develop a sense of the danger signals when approaching a parent with a request would be an unwise move. Whereas those with the ability to enforce their own will often remain insensitive to the emotional cues given off by those in their power.

It is clear that the Controlling Committee made the decision to serve as "middle management" for the Nazi occupiers whenever orders affected the life and well-being of the Islanders—a sweeping decision that has been treated by some in the late twentieth century as conscious collaboration. It is also clear from Ambrose Robin's and Ken Lewis's accounts that the Controlling Committee lacked any discernable collaborative intent—in fact, quite the opposite.

As Leale himself stated in his report given only two weeks after Liberation, "The apparent motives for the actions of an administration are by no means always, perhaps they are seldom, the true motives. To discover these one has to penetrate more deeply."[95] There could be few better descriptions of performed compliance and the thickness of a carefully sculpted mask of subordination. Yet, how did the Islanders see their own States leadership at the time? If properly veiled, performed compliance is as mystifying to those below as it is to those above. Did the average Guernseyman and woman "get" the intent of the Committee in their role as the overseers of German policy?

The answer is sometimes. There are moments when the diarists reveal an Islander understanding of moves by States officials that met with criticism at the time and would become controversial in later years. Let us just take as one example Sherwill's recording of a speech on August 1, 1940, that was meant to assuage any fears that evacuees would have concerning the fate of their friends and families left behind in Guernsey. He started his speech, "I imagine that many of you must be greatly worried as to how we are getting on," and he went on to extol the courtesy with which the German military authorities had treated the Island officials. He continued to include the key statement, "The conduct of the German troops is exemplary." This proclamation describing the occupier as the model of restraint and civility, broadcast over Radio Bremen on August 8, was a gift to Nazi propaganda.

So why would Sherwill allow himself to be used in this manner, one that could not help but imply a cozy relationship with the enemy? There were practical reasons behind what Knowles Smith called "the façade of bonhomie" evident in this speech. Considering what he was up to behind the scenes, Sherwill was rather like a duck, all calm to outside appearance while actually paddling frantically. At the time, Sherwill was fully embroiled in the Martel and Mulholland affair.[96] It was also during this time, according to John Leale's report and backed by other witnesses, that the Germans had threatened to shoot twenty leading citizens if they discovered that Islanders were harboring members of the British armed forces.[97] Considering that these hostage shootings had taken place in occupied areas of the Continent, it was a threat to be taken as real.

In many ways, this speech was pure Sherwill in its tactics, and was consistent with other moves made during his brief tenure as president of the new Controlling Committee. Sherwill seemed perfectly willing to schmooze the occupier, as we would say today, and later described some of his letters to the Germans as "a bit smarmy."[98] He played to German vanity, to their sense of having a higher culture, and to their desire that other nations ultimately acknowledge the superiority of the German race. It is one of the oldest rhetorical tricks during times of tyranny to laud the oppressor in advance with the aim of structuring their actions in a positive direction.[99] How much harder would it be for the Germans to shoot civilians when they had just been complimented before the world as the beau ideal of consideration and restraint? Of course, behind-the-scenes machinations and Sherwill's rationale for such a thick coat of varnish were sheltered from the average Islander. Still, they were all eager to send a general message to allay the fears of displaced Guernseymen. Evacuated relatives were painfully aware of the bombing raid that had ended evacuations in such deadly fashion. Also, prior to the Occupation, there had been fearful speculation whispered through the Island that women left behind would be subject to wholesale rape by German forces.

So, despite the heaping of approbation on a hated occupier, and even acknowledging that the propaganda benefited the Third Reich, response to the broadcast to England through Bremen was met with "great excitement" according to Rev. Ord. The text of the address was published in the Guernsey papers, so Ord could accurately describe how the message spoke to "the courtesy of the German authorities, of the efforts being made to re-start the economic life of the Island after the severance of communications, and of the exemplary conduct of the troops." Quite likely, a man with Ord's training and earlier experience of Germans during his years as a prisoner of war could sense exactly what Sherwill hoped to accomplish. Just taking his words at face value, however, Ord saw the speech through the lens of his calling as a pastor, as a balm and strengthener in time of trouble: "If this message is allowed to go through as it stands written, and if our people believe it, it may comfort troubled minds."[100]

Others had a different, although still positive, response to the speech. Dorothy Higgs took the motives behind the speech to be of a more personal nature: "Mr. Sherwill, who made the record, has three children away. Everyone envies them being able to send love even by such a chancy method."[101] Far from worrying about the praise of the Germans, Dorothy viewed the speech rather like a modern hostage recording: as simply an opportunity to allow relatives to hear the captive's voice and know that he was alive. The intelligent listener might be expected to take the veracity of the message with a grain of salt. Others, and among them the British government, considered Sherwill's actions as "unwise" and even naive.[102] A more accurate critique might have described the move as shortsighted, for Sherwill's eyes truly were focused on immediate, at the expense of long-term, effect.

The Islanders seemed to understand the States' interposition between German orders and the Guernsey populace. Scott posits that tactical compliance is unlikely to "affect the face of the actor" unless such compliance is viewed as an "uncoerced choice."[103] The coercion under military occupation was clear to those living under similar conditions, and they could ask themselves just how often they were personally forced to comply with demands of a German soldier or to hold their tongues to avoid reprisals. Still, there were plenty of times when States officials received the fury often reserved for middle management under oppressive conditions. It has already been discussed how the States chose to take responsibility for requisitioning, out of fear, as John Leale put it in his postwar report: "To say to them: 'You must do your own requisitioning,' was tantamount to saying: 'Go and help yourselves to as much as you like.'"[104] But the communication to let Islanders know how hard the Committee fought for them was spotty at best.

So, even though the German *Bekanntmachungs* were published in the newspapers, it would be the States that would oversee the demand for a person's bicycle, or the amount of milk to be rationed to children. When things went wrong, it was the States officials who received the blame for their inability to stop the Germans. Even fair-minded and knowledgeable people could lose sight of the Controlling Committee's lack of recourse. When, for example, a harvest of haricot beans was stored in a single location in the fall of 1941, the Germans simply located them and took the lot. Winifred Harvey, already exasperated over the loss of tons of potatoes carried off in much the same manner, wrote, "The States hand everything over without a protest. There is a great deal of dissatisfaction about."[105] Bert Williams provides a sense of the "armchair quarterbacking" in which some Islanders indulged. He firmly believed that many food shortages and rationings could have been avoided entirely "if the Powers that be had been efficient & listened to people who knew their job." The primary problem was sheer incompetence, and simply that "there isn't one man in the right job."[106]

Perhaps it was critiques from some Islanders that led to one piece of plain speaking by John Leale after the fact. Apparently stung by criticism from those not forced to face up to the Germans and negotiate for the well-being of the Island, Leale stated bluntly, "It is easy to talk big when you have no responsibilities on your shoulders. We all met the type whose fierce hostility to the Germans varied in inverse ratio to their proximity to Grange Lodge." Those attitudes might earn the critic some "undeserved reputation for heroism," but there was real work to be done by men who could not spend time "adopting histrionic attitudes." Leale answered not just contemporary critics unaware of the facts behind the scenes but also the journalists of the future seeking dramatic "last stands" of defiance from the very men charged with their countrymen's survival: "We were facing real life not acting in a melodrama."[107]

The States decided that the Hague Convention was the best overall safeguard and their partner "through thick and thin." It was clear from the Convention and the establishment of International Law that occupying powers had the right to requisition the service of tradesmen, bakers, butchers, etc. But could they force growers to raise food for them, fishermen to fish for them, and other men to do a variety of work? A close examination of International Law made clear that the men could not be forced to work on entrenchments and fortifications, though that seemed to be the extent of refusal allowed. The States pushed the point with the Germans, who, in their turn, pointed out that on the back of the call-up notices, it distinctly said, "Service of labour is not demanded for work of any kind against your own country."[108]

So, this dealt with the technicalities but not with the feelings involved. Leale was frank that this conclusion reached under the Hague Convention "seemed unpatriotic." He told of a grower who was informed that he would have to comply with the German demand for his services. The grower simply looked at Leale, and in that stare, Leale could see what the man was thinking: "You're not much of a Briton." And in one sense, Leale said, he agreed with this silent condemnation, for "truth to tell, I was not feeling particularly heroic at the moment." With more thought, Leale knew this to be "a very superficial view," for the Hague Convention was a protection worth following, even when the results in a given instance were not to their liking. All they really had to fall back on, considering that they were under the control of an armed belligerent, was the balancing of rights and responsibilities of both the occupied and occupier under this neutral document. Whenever the Germans sought to stray outside the bounds of the Convention, the Committee would play to German vanity, claiming that "they [the Germans] were setting a lower standard than the British." Rather smugly, Leale noted that the Germans "were always susceptible to arguments of this kind."

At times, the Controlling Committee used the Hague Convention to great effect, although it could not prevent the general order that Islanders must work for the Germans. Ultimately, the Controlling Committee interposed itself in the work question as it had in requisitioning and rationing, clarifying to Guernseymen that they must comply with the hated order. They could not stop it, in their view, for fear that the Germans would simply send the Island men "to France to build bridges or to the Rhine to clear away the debris left by the bombers," replacing them in the Island with Continental workers already impressed into slave labor. All the States could do, once again, was to try and verify that all tasks fell within the guidelines of the Convention, and to intervene on behalf of Islanders asked to do work that seemed directly tied to the German war effort.[109]

Before I consider the final area where the States interposed themselves between occupier and civilian—one that would be the source of much regret, soul-searching, and later recrimination—it is worth a pause to consider the response to the array of public documents from the Occupation that were released in the 1990s. Why did a revisionist reading catch hold so strongly, one that accepted these public documents as the "truth" of the Occupation and largely ignored the evidence readily available in the hidden transcript? I believe that here we can see the power of a public transcript that is "systematically skewed in the direction of the libretto, the discourse, represented by the dominant." It is very difficult to know, simply based on the public transcript, whether "a performance is genuine or not."[110] The greater the disparity of power, the more onerous the situation; the fewer the options for escape or improved conditions, then the more survival, and whatever level of resistance can be mustered, must take place behind a dumb show of "humility and deference."[111] And if we hope to understand the reality of certain historical periods, it becomes more important to penetrate the "display and public theater" inherent in domination,[112] and peer behind the scenes.

One example will have to stand as a call for a more complex reading of the public transcript. On August 7, 1940, the first full Occupation meeting took place that brought together members of the Guernsey States with Major Lanz and Dr. Maass. It was at this meeting that Sherwill made a speech outlining his view of how the Occupation should proceed:

> May this occupation be a model to the world. On the one hand, tolerance on the part of the military authority, and courtesy and correctness on the part of the occupying forces, and on the other hand, dignity and courtesy and exemplary behaviour on the part of the civilian population . . . When it is over, I hope that the occupying force and occupied population may each be able to say: of different nations, having different outlooks, we lived together with tolerance and mutual respect.

This statement has been highlighted repeatedly and was of such importance to Madeleine Bunting that it provided the title of her book *The Model Occupation.* Often, it is treated as somewhere between a Vichy-style offer of collaboration and a simple toadying to German authority. Bunting, for example, takes it at face value: as a sincere statement of principles of "scrupulous obedience," "meek gratitude" for anything positive offered by the Germans, and "a rejection of any form of resistance." She goes on to describe this as a policy of "peace at any price" and one that very nicely "suited German interests" as it reduced the Committee to only the most "timid" of protests in their policy of continuous appeasement.[113]

It is time to appreciate this little speech for its rhetorical aptitude and the way it encapsulates Sherwill's strategy of charming insincerity, even as he attempted to structure the Germans' occupation for them. Much like the recording made on August 1, it cannot be read separate from the knowledge that barely one week earlier, Martell and Mulholland had appeared at Sherwill's door. Sherwill spoke on August 7, fully aware that he was guilty of conspiring after the fact with these British raiders and had been instrumental in taking steps to protect them from being shot as spies. Even as he spoke, he was waiting to see what the fallout would be for the families that concealed the young men. And, most notably, he was working every angle to encourage leniency by the German authorities. Those who would take this display of deference as anything more than a manipulative performance should be reminded that Sherwill would provide similarly illegal aid for Nicolle and Symes two months after this speech promised "exemplary behaviour." This little address was a performance of cool nerve and serves as a reminder that there is an art to acts of subordination when they shelter subversive intent. Scott uses a wonderful simile for such performances of "deference and a smile" as being "like the normal walk of the fleeing suspect when he encounters a cop on the beat."[114]

Yet even separate from the knowledge of events behind the scenes, this speech performs the old trick of proposing ground rules in advance, and ones that are favorable to the powerless. *We* promise to be on our best behavior (at least on the surface), displaying a minimum level of deference and a show of cooperation, and *you* will show toleration in dealing with our actions (especially if we are caught) and treat us with the same respect you would grant to your equals in power. It is easily imagined, with freedom not in the offing, that this proposal could appeal to many oppressed populations, particularly when held under force of arms. Sherwill and, in his turn, Leale evidently took "dignity" as the watchword of their performances, rightly assessing that this would be the best stance in dealing with the German preference for formality and hierarchy.

Suitable to their natural personalities, Sherwill coupled dignity with a bluff friendliness and Leale with a cool practicality, and both carefully guarded their chosen guise of compliance. Subordinate groups in other settings, one example being women in the occupied South, choose to "play dumb," using a stance of artificial naiveté and ignorance as a veil. Sometimes a combined "fool and trickster" persona provides the same cover for exercising the "guile of the underdog"—as captured in the saying of Jamaican slaves, "Play fool, to catch wise."[115] If successful and believed by the powerful, these carefully honed performances join other aspects of the dominant worldview and are woven into the public transcript. There the performances continue to live, becoming part of the stereotype of the subordinate group.

The subtle art of subordination and the need for a parallel transcript to cue peers in on actual intent become apparent when a performance is awkward or the actor oversteps the compliance acceptable to the community. In 1941, in response to the call from "Colonel Britton" for symbolic resistance, a spate of V's were chalked up all over Guernsey. This episode and the response by the Germans will be discussed at length in the next chapter, but the Germans' vehement determination to stamp out this particular resistant act took the Island, and certainly States officials, by surprise. On July 4, 1941, a "WARNING" was published in the paper stating that these acts were "regarded very seriously" by the Germans. It warned that the broader population might be "penalized in the same way as in the case of acts of sabotage." The notice ended with an appeal against "these foolish acts, which accomplish nothing but merely bring grave consequences in their train," and the warning was signed by the Lieutenant Governor and Bailiff Victor Carey. The response to this first warning was minor in the community; Rev. Ord used the formula that the notice "appears over the signature of" the Bailiff (the same wording chosen by Ken Lewis), an acknowledgment that the message came from German authorities.[116]

Then, on July 8, a second notice appeared with the heading "REWARD of £25," offering this amount to the first person to give information leading to conviction of anyone marking a public place with the letter "V" or with "any other sign or any word or words calculating to offend the German authorities or soldiers." This notice, too, appeared over the signature of Victor Carey.[117] This time, the response by the Island community was quite different. Ord underlined the word "calculating" in the notice, which he took to "betray the hand of a German," but he still found it "hard to believe that the Bailiff agreed to this notice." It was a move that would earn the Bailiff considerable flak at the time and would haunt him after the Occupation. It is, along with Sherwill's August address, the prime piece of evidence against States officials pointed to by later seekers of Island collaboration.

In fact, Carey was questioned about this notice in June 1945. He took full responsibility for appending his signature, stating that it followed "a very stormy interview with the Feldcommandant." The threats made at that meeting combined in Carey's mind with his knowledge that a list of eighty potential hostages (for execution or deportation to a concentration camp in Germany) had already been gathered. Eager to prevent widespread reprisals, he agreed to sign, later stating his belief that "the majority of the civilian population realised that though these notices bore my signature they were really German orders."[118]

But the frail Bailiff overestimated the ability of Islanders to see through this particular performance of subordination. Response was instantaneous and widely negative, even though some thought the Germans had simply put the notice in the paper using the Bailiff's name. Why did the first warning pass without concern and this second one call down the wrath of the Bailiff's peers? As we have seen in earlier chapters, trust was the coin of the realm among the loyal majority of Guernseymen and women. The tendering of a reward placed the temptation of money as a possible wedge between neighbors. Even with faith that the majority would turn up their noses at such an offer of cash for betrayal, Islanders were well aware of that minority element who would not hesitate to make accusations (false or true) if they could line their pockets or curry favor with the occupier. As Rev. Ord responded to the notice, "Only Quislings need apply!"[119]

Although the Bailiff apparently foresaw only a chilling effect on the chalking of V's rather than wholesale betrayal of one neighbor by another, others saw a danger that could strike at the heart of the Island's sense of community. The offer of money for lateral surveillance played directly into the panoptical nature of the Occupation as the Germans were choosing to conduct it. It is little wonder that a cartoon was reportedly passed around showing Victor Carey as Judas Iscariot dangling from a noose in a tree.[120] As Rev. Ord put it, "At present the Bailiff's name is 'Mud' with many."[121] Although there is no evidence that anyone attempted to claim this reward,[122] the incident reveals the limits to a strategy of performed compliance.

States officials appear to have learned certain lessons from the negative reaction by the community. Ken Lewis maintained that when notice of the bread ration cut was published in

May 1943, Abraham Lainé signed only after the words "By order of the German authorities" were added.[123] And on February 19, 1944, John Leale signed a notice published in the paper that read:

> I am directed by the Feldkommandant to warn all concerned that he has ordered that Members of the German Forces must be given prior attention in all shops and other establishments frequented by them and that severe punishment will be imposed on any who disregard this order.

This notice may have appeared over Leale's name, but the careful wording left no doubt but that he was "directed" to warn the populace of an order made by the Feldkommandant, and that punishment would come from that quarter.[124] Still, there is no formula for determining the actions that a subordinate community will find acceptable and will understand as cooperation retaining the hardened kernel of resistance within. The challenge is not merely to avoid detection by the powerful, who could then short-circuit tactics of obstruction and institute reprisals, but to court detection by peers. The porous nature of the hidden transcript often makes it an inefficient ally in this endeavor.

THERESE, AUGUSTE, AND MARIANNE

With a better understanding of the way the Island officials chose to handle their newly subordinate position, and the strengths and weaknesses of this strategy, it is time to examine the most heartbreaking event of the Guernsey Occupation. Much that has been written about the Occupation of Guernsey focuses on the fates of three young Jewish women: Therese Steiner, Auguste Spitz, and Marianne Grunfeld. All would be identified as Jews, deported to France, and subsequently murdered in the extermination camps of the Third Reich. They are only three of the innocent victims among the millions to die in this way during the Holocaust, so why are we fascinated with their fate? I believe that our deep interest is natural, for these women domesticate a monumental tragedy, bringing it down to a size that we can feel on a personal level. They look out at us from their identification photographs, and through this artificial immediacy, we can at least try to put ourselves in their place: scared, defenseless, and doomed at a point when life should hold such promise. When the Holocaust seems both too large and too staggering to grasp, these women—like Anne Frank and her family—help us to recover the individual suffering of those who died at the hands of monsters.

Born in Vienna, Austria, Therese Steiner was a dental nurse who had traveled to England to work with Edgar Potts, a dentist in Kent. With the outbreak of war in 1939, the entire family moved to Sark, and Therese went along to serve as nanny to the Potts children. Although Dr. Potts returned to England to resume practicing dentistry the following year, Mrs. Potts took the children and Therese to Guernsey. Then, as rumors of a possible Occupation spread, Mrs. Potts returned to England with the children, forced to leave behind Therese (who, as an "enemy alien," could not travel). Auguste Spitz shared many similarities with Therese Steiner. She was also born in Vienna and had come to Guernsey to work as a nanny in September 1937. During the years leading up to the outbreak of war, the Aliens Office in England had closely regulated the comings and goings of aliens to the Channel Islands. As the Occupation drew closer, and as dictated by British policy, "enemy aliens," including Therese and Auguste, were interned from early May until June 25, 1940. Thus, Therese Steiner and Auguste Spitz were also among the twenty-eight names of enemy aliens placed on a list compiled a month before the Occupation began.[125] Upon their release from internment, both women went to work at the Castel Hospital. Auguste, who went by the nickname "Gustie," served as a domestic at the hospital, and Therese was employed as a nurse.[126]

Marianne Grunfeld's path to Guernsey was somewhat different and actually took more determined effort. She was born in Poland and had traveled to England in 1937 to study horticulture at Reading University. It was through an agricultural magazine that Marianne was connected to E. H. Ogier, a sixty-five-year-old farmer in St. Sampson who was seeking replacement for a worker who had joined the British forces. At first, Ogier's request for a work permit to bring Marianne to Guernsey was declined. The Bailiff was concerned about violating policies designed to prevent an influx of alien farm laborers to the Island. Armed with a glowing letter of recommendation from a woman on the *London Times* editorial staff, who happened to be a friend of Marianne's mother, Ogier prevailed. Marianne came to Guernsey in early May 1940 to begin work and registered as an alien.[127]

After the Germans arrived, one of their earliest requirements was a list of all resident aliens, including information on each person's nationality and religion. Because of their known status as resident aliens, Therese, Auguste, and Marianne appeared on this list of 407 names. It is interesting that the States provided all the information the Germans requested, with the notable exception of religion, an early indication of their use of selective compliance.[128] Narrowing this list considerably, Dr. Brosch ordered Police Inspector Sculpher to contact all Germans, Austrians, and Italians on the list. They were to come for an interview at the Feldkommandantur on October 21.[129]

Three days later came "The (First) Order relating to Measures against the Jews," registered on October 23, 1940, in the Royal Courts of Guernsey and published in the local press. This First Order attempted to define what it meant to be Jewish according to the German standpoint, and required those falling within the criteria to register with the inspector of police in Guernsey.[130] Inspector Sculpher was informed separately by the Bailiff that the Feldkommandantur had designated the inspector's office as the location for registration, and therefore, Sculpher would have to provide by October 29 a list of the Jews who registered. Although Sculpher had been aliens officer before the Occupation, this was a very different task; the only saving grace was that any Jews in the Island would have to step forward voluntarily to register themselves. Four people appeared at the office in response to the order, among them Therese Steiner and Auguste Spitz. The other two women who came to register were Elisabet Duquemin, a woman born in Vienna and married to Henry Duquemin, a Guernseyman, and Elda Brouard, born in Florence and a widow of a British citizen. Both women listed their religion as Church of England.[131]

This First Order, defining the degrees of what it was to be Jewish and requiring Jews to register, was only the first of a series of Orders against the Jews in the Channel Islands. These early orders were promulgated by the Germans only four months into the Occupation, at a time when the Controlling Committee was still finding its feet, and when most interactions behind the scenes were oral. Therefore, what exists from this vital period are formal letters to the Germans, and documents produced by the Germans detailing events from their standpoint. To say that such documents are sanitized versions of the public transcript would be an understatement, because the Germans in charge of the Island were trying to fulfill the requirements of Hitler in the area of his great obsession, the treatment of the Jews.

To have any sense of what may have happened in the hearing where members of the Royal Court were required to register this first key Order against the Jews, we have to turn to Sherwill's unpublished memoirs. This is a poor instrument, because this document was written in the 1960s and based on the memories of an older man who now knew the ultimate outcome of all his actions (positive or negative). Still, there are insights here about his reasoning that appear to make sense. First, Sherwill does not claim to have stepped forward to protest the registration of this First Order, although he was present and a senior advisor to the Court. He treats his own silence as something of which he was "ashamed," not because it would have made any substantive difference but because "a vital principle was at stake." Instead, he uses his own failings as a means to highlight the bravery of Abraham Lainé, who "openly and categorically refused his assent and stated his grave objections to such a measure."[132]

Why did Sherwill see this order as merely an issue of principle, and not as a real threat to actual people? Sherwill claimed in his memoirs that he believed all the Jewish residents of Guernsey had evacuated before the Occupation, and this tragically incorrect notion he remembered as having been "conveyed to the Bailiff and Jurats in private, as they assembled for the sitting." The belief that the Orders against the Jews "would harm no one on the Island"[133] because any resident Jews had evacuated in advance of the Germans' approach was a mistaken notion shared by others. On October 29, 1940, Rev. Ord wrote, "The anti-Jewish laws have now been promulgated here. Thank God the few we had are safely in England, including the kindly Dr. Montague. With grim humor the Order forbids Jews to re-enter Occupied Territory if they have already fled therefrom! . . . Every Jew must register."[134] One reason that Sherwill and others believed that all Jews were safely off Guernsey may well have been the prominence of Dr. Montague and his evacuation. Ken Lewis attached to his diary a copy of a letter sent by Ambrose Sherwill with Dr. Montague when he evacuated in 1940. Ken was aware that Dr. Montague was Jewish and "therefore liable to persecution by the Germans." Sherwill's letter read, in part:

> The bearer of this letter, Dr. W. J. Montague is for racial reasons being directed to proceed to England and not to return until after the cessation of hostilities. I much regret losing him for he is a very able doctor, a close personal friend and a man of the most sterling character. He had volunteered to remain regardless of the consequences to himself. Will you please arrange that he be given an opportunity to make a report on the medical aspect of the whole matter.[135]

The fact that Sherwill and Dr. Montague were close friends, and the special favor of writing a letter of introduction, explains why the doctor's evacuation would loom large in Sherwill's mind. Dr. Montague was truly beloved in Guernsey. When word came of his death in England in 1944, it was widely noted, and a memorial service was held in his honor.[136]

Perhaps Sherwill and others' initial belief that these were symbolic, toothless laws—simply because no one remained that they could harm—is understandable. Dr. Montague was not the only prominent Jewish Islander to evacuate; others joined him, including Louis Cohen, Mr. and Mrs. William Middlewick, and David Rudnidsky.[137] Even had Sherwill, for some reason, perused the enemy aliens list from before the Occupation, there was no indication of the religion of those listed. Therese and Auguste were not prominent citizens, but single foreign women living and working quietly at the hospital; Marianne was an agricultural worker tucked away on a farm. They were among the other foreign women living and working in the Island. Elisabet Duquemin and Elda Brouard were, according to their later registration information, practicing Anglicans. In a population of nearly 25,000, these five women would have been easy to overlook. Had they been aware that any Jews remained in Guernsey, perhaps more of the jurats would have joined Lainé in making an oral objection to these orders, not that it would have mattered.

The German record of the Royal Court simply omits any reference to Lainé's protest and presumably would have cleansed the public transcript of any other objections. While it is possible that Sherwill, our only alternative to the German official record, made up this story of Lainé's principled refusal, this is highly unlikely. Sherwill tells it as a story of his own failure to speak, and as a regret that he would always have in hindsight, at least for its symbolic value. He was convinced that his speaking out would have been no more effective than Lainé's in preventing the orders. Also, his reasoning for not speaking, that he was particularly "anxious at that time to avoid a collision with the Germans," rings true. Nicole and Symes had surrendered two days previously, and Sherwill knew himself to be on thin ice.[138]

It often sounds from some accounts that Inspector Sculpher, when ordered to turn in the names of Jews in Guernsey, went to ferret out any hidden Jews who might have remained. Instead, he merely turned in the list of four people in Guernsey who came in and registered voluntarily. On this list, Brouard and Duquemin are clearly listed as Church of England. Dr. Brosch was not satisfied with Sculpher's report, because the Germans were aware of Julia Brichta, a Hungarian woman who had been in and out of various types of trouble and was known to the police. When ordered to investigate Julia Brichta, the inspector reported that Brichta was now a cook employed by the Germans and that she attended the Church of England. Dr. Brosch considered Sculpher's report to be evasive (which it was) and required him to ask directly whether Brichta was of pure Aryan blood. Sculpher questioned her and reported that she had no known Jewish background.[139]

And thus, the first of the Orders against the Jews came to Guernsey. Far from sharing in anti-Semitism, the response by the diarists to these laws show a clear contempt for this aspect of the German mentality.[140] Winifred Harvey described how all the regulations against Jews "made me feel quite sick." There was no uncertainty in her mind about who was responsible. She described how they "had to be passed and registered by the Royal Court," clearly indicating the involuntary nature of the jurats' role, but they were "signed by the Commandant of the German forces in France."[141] In late November, she would describe a period with a "new Bekanntmachung every other day, with death penalties attached." Now the identity cards were "stamped with Swastikas." And amid all of this bad news, still more "new anti-Jew orders are out."[142]

In Winnie's account, we can see how the Orders against the Jews were subsumed by small floods of onerous new regulations. At this point everyone had to fill out a form to get an identity card, and one piece of information required was each person's relationship to British officers. News also came out at this time that, like France, Guernsey was now subject to trial by military law. Amid all of these orders, ones that required registration by everyone, the Orders against the Jews still stood out. If the Germans hoped to numb the Islanders and have these particular orders pass unremarked, they failed in the attempt. Although many forms of racial stereotyping were widespread in England and America at this time, the constant flood of anti-Semitic propaganda in the *Press* highlighted the Germans' racial hatred as something peculiar to Nazi ideology. Ambrose Robin described this propaganda as "becoming more and more strained and stupid. Their outpourings against Jews alone are sufficient to place the German nation in a category of racial maniacs."[143] The Germans seemed to believe that repeated anti-Semitic diatribes or screenings of *Jew Suss*—a film rather like *Birth of a Nation* in its portrayal of a damsel in distress struggling to flee from intended rape, although in this instance the assailant is Jewish rather than black—would bring Islanders around to embrace the anti-Jewish orders. In Rev. Ord's estimation, this proved to be another German failure. On November 28, 1940, he wrote, "With regard to the Order against the Jews, there is a feeling of relief that it falls flat in Guernsey. Decent people look upon it as the result of diseased imagination, and think of it with fathomless contempt."[144]

Julia Brichta, or Julia Barry following her marriage in 1942 to Jeremiah Barry, was the one case where anonymous letters denouncing her to the Germans contained references to her supposed Jewish heritage. On September 16, 1943, the Feldkommandantur received a letter signed "Fair Play for All," which denounced numerous suspected black-marketeers. The letter referred to "Mrs. Barry, a Hungarian Jew, just married for a business affair to escape your jurisdiction on Jews, carries on a very large bartering trade at her house in Mill Street." Other anonymous letters also denounced Brichta and her work in the black market, including one dated September 30, 1940, which read, "She is truly a bad tongued Jew and an awful cheat."[145] These references to her Jewish background seem geared toward the prejudice of the recipient, an attempt to cause Brichta trouble in terms the Germans would understand. Brichta was known in Guernsey as the "Black Market Queen" and was finally caught in January 1944—after numerous searches of her house—and deported to France.[146] She ended up at Ravensbrück Concentration Camp, but survived the war. These two letters show that at least some, whether broadly anti-Semitic or not, were willing to utilize the Germans' racial hatred in order to rid themselves of a troublesome woman. But there is no sign that anti-Semitism was part of the average Islander's makeup.

Ord even had a little fun with the German censor and the ban on all things Jewish. On a November Sunday in 1943, the reverend announced, "with some show of innocence," that the next Sunday they would "listen to Mendelssohn's 'Hymn of Praise,' which is the work of a great master known the world over. I am not however permitted to tell you who wrote it." And Ord ended his account with a cheerful "THAT went home," and enjoyed the crowd that packed the church the following week.[147]

From November 1940 to March 1942, the subsequent series of orders did not directly affect the four women who had identified themselves as Jews. The Second through the Fifth Orders largely concerned further details on what it meant to be Jewish in the eyes of the Third Reich, or dealt with Jewish-owned businesses.[148] But then came the Sixth Order of March 21, 1942. This order decreed that Jews could not change residence without permission and imposed a curfew of 8 P.M. to 6 A.M. for Jews. Further, the order stated that violators could be "interned in a camp for Jews." With hindsight it is easy to see the noose tightening, as it is apparent that at this point the women were being monitored. On March 17, the Bailiff received an instruction that the registration cards of Jews be marked with a J.[149] Inspector Sculpher was notified, and he reported carrying out the marking of Therese's and Auguste's cards. Interestingly, however, Sculpher did not mark the cards of Elisabet and Elda, although he noted their existence. Perhaps this was an example of Sculpher taking refuge behind a hyperscrupulous compliance with the exact terms of the instructions. These two women, even though they came forward as falling within the criteria of being Jewish, listed their religion as Church of England, and Sculpher could respond to the letter, rather than the intent, of the order.[150]

It is to be remembered from chapter 3 that as of September 1941, a list existed of all English-born men over the age of eighteen, gathered as part of planned reprisals for Allied actions in

Iran. Also, on September 22, 1941, the Bailiff received a demand for a further list including all foreigners who were nationals of a broad list of countries large and small (everywhere from Russia and the United States to the Congo, Sudan, and Ruanda-Urundi mandate). The list was also to include those without nationality, emigrants from Germany since 1933, emigrants from Czechoslovakia since 1938, and all Jews. To this last request, Sculpher provided the now-familiar names of the four women who had registered in October 1940. Next came a request for the names, ages, and addresses of former British officers now residing in Guernsey.[151] As described in the last chapter, the expected reprisal did not materialize in 1941, but the master list was now in place. What the Germans would do with it, if anything, was anyone's guess.

The answer was apparently nothing for now, and States officials must have taken a deep breath. However, before the first deportation scare was past, the Germans requested a list of "Key persons" to be submitted, chosen from the previous list of aliens. This list would be an opportunity for the States to indicate workers whose services were particularly necessary for the Island. Prominent on that list forwarded by Leale in October 1941 was the name of Therese Steiner in her position as a trained nurse. Also, under the longer list of those key aliens employed in agriculture and horticulture, a primary area of need for Guernsey, was the name of Marianne Grunfeld—at this point, because she avoided stepping forward to register, not known to be Jewish.[152] So, the extensive master list and an initial request for exemptions existed from September and October of 1941, and the following year the German military authorities made use of it.

In April 1942, the Germans cherry-picked from this list an initial group to be deported to France. Mrs. Millicent McGahy, Therese Steiner, Auguste Spitz, and Marianne Grunfeld all received a notice signed by Rittmeister von Oettingen that they were to be deported from the Channel Islands, and they were ordered to report to St. Peter Port harbor on April 21.[153] Let us take a pause and look at some of the names on this short list. Millicent McGahy was married to Arthur McGahy, and both were Guernsey-born, although they had emigrated to the United States in the twenties. They became United States citizens and settled in Boston. Before a scheduled move to California, they decided to take a short vacation to visit relatives in Guernsey. The visit continued longer than originally planned, and the McGahys ended up being trapped by the Occupation. Reportedly, Arthur was noted for arguing directly with the German authorities, using his American citizenship as a shield against retaliation. He seems to have been quite a nuisance, trying to wrangle various benefits for other people. But then America entered the war, the neutrality shield disappeared for Arthur McGahy, and the Germans were swift to pounce. Although a key worker in charge of a vineyard, the Germans contacted him on January 2 at 10:00 in the morning and told him to pack for France. He was picked up at his home at 4:30 to stay in the Royal Hotel—not for luxury's sake, but because this was the German headquarters in Guernsey. He was taken to Jersey the next day to cool his heels in jail until taken to internment in France on the 7th of January.[154]

It is easy to see that Mrs. McGahy was on the list to join her husband in France to close the loop on one deemed a troublemaker by the Germans. Therese Steiner, Auguste Spitz, and Marianne Grunfeld were deported to France quite simply because they were Jews, although Elisabet Duquemin and Elda Brouard were not included. But Marianne Grunfeld had not stepped forward back in October 1940 when Jews were ordered to register, so how did her name come to be on the list for deportation? There has always been speculation that she must have been denounced by a neighbor or fellow worker at the farm, but there is no evidence to support this.[155] It seems unlikely that her Guernsey neighbors knew her to be

Jewish, because her pictures show her to be fair and almost stereotypically "Aryan-looking." Of course, her name was on the list of 407 aliens and also on the list of key aliens, but in no place is her religion given. One possibility, as pointed out by William Bell, was that E. H. Ogier (her employer) was under investigation, along with fourteen fellow farmers, for "unlawful trading in foodstuffs." The investigation would have brought the Germans into direct contact with the Ogier family and all of the workers on the farm.[156]

The answer to this little mystery may be more mundane. Frederick Cohen points out that Grunfeld ("Greenfield") would have stood out to the Germans as an unmistakably Jewish surname.[157] While Grunfeld has little meaning to non-Germans, the equivalent ability to read supposedly "Jewish names" appears in such American popular culture as *Gentleman's Agreement.*[158] Marianne's identification as Jewish, her deportation, and her subsequent death may have simply been a matter of her name being spotted by the Germans on one of the many lists they demanded.

There is no indication that any of the four women on the list for deportation attempted to escape or to seek a hiding place. Escape off of the Island was only undertaken by a few people over the five years, because it was a dangerous option that took months to plan and relied heavily on weather and tides to accomplish. Finding a secret location in which to hide for many years undetected would have likely been impossible in an island the size of Guernsey and with a ratio of slightly more than one soldier for every two Guernseymen.[159] In any event, the Germans utilized the advantage of surprise in this first deportation. Just considering the order of the previous month, it seems clear that the Jewish women, at least, were under close surveillance. The timing also seems to indicate a desire to shorten the window during which the targeted women could plan some form of escape, for they were warned for deportation on the 17th and left the Island on the 21st.

If the deportation was a surprise, various forces stepped in to attempt intervention in these few days. Some of these attempts at intervention were written and therefore survive as an indication of the efforts of States officials and private citizens. John Leale provided E. H. Ogier with a letter of introduction to the Feldkommandantur on April 18: "The bearer, Mr. E. H. Ogier (Duvaux Farm, St. Sampson) is a well-known and respected Guernseyman . . . He wishes to discuss the possibility of retaining in his employ Miss Marianne Grunfeld. I would be obliged if you would grant him an interview on this subject."[160] Ogier did attempt to intervene on his employee's behalf, and the outcome happened to be witnessed by Rev. Ord. That evening, Ord wrote in his diary:

> This morning as I passed down the Grange, a friend stopped me outside Grange Lodge, the Civilkommandantur, to vent his rage and sorrow. He had gone to appeal for a girl employee who is only just within the forbidden degrees of Jewish birth and is to be carried off. The officials listened to the arguments he put but were powerless to resist the inhuman decree of the Nazi Frankenstein.[161]

This attempt to prevent Marianne's deportation was not the sole attempt to intervene.

The fact that Therese Steiner and Marianne Grunfeld were already on the "key aliens" list made it unlikely that the States would let them go without renewing the argument to retain them. A trained nurse like Therese would have been a particular loss, and the entire concept of indispensible workers was at stake. According to Sandra James, John Leale made an appeal on Therese's behalf along the lines of "key worker," but it failed, just as had the plea made for

Marianne. The hospital records recorded "an expression of regret at losing their [Therese and Auguste] services as their work had been of the highest order."[162]

It seems that Rev. Ord had contact with Therese Steiner during this period between her notification and her departure. A year later, in March 1943, he wrote that when they spoke, possibly at the hospital where his work would have taken him, she had received "orders to go to France. She was in great distress and seemed to feel that her feet were now set upon her Via Dolorosa. I did what I could to comfort her but what can one say."[163] Although too much should not be made of Ord's term "Via Dolorosa," since he could not anticipate the full extent of the tragedy that awaited her, it is clear that Therese expected discrimination and an uncertain future. While to some she maintained that she would be all right, and at least one friend described her as "in good heart," Ernest Plevin, who was a police clerk sergeant, remembered her "bursting into tears and exclaiming that I would never see her again."[164] Elisabet Duquemin also described the anxiety of both Therese and Auguste when they came to see her the night before deportation to say goodbye and borrow a suitcase.[165]

The departure of the four women was quiet because they reported separately to the St. Peter Port harbor. Barbara Newman went with Therese to the Weighbridge and spent about half an hour with her and the other women before the deportees entered the departure area. This was an area guarded by German soldiers where only the deportees could go, and from there they were sent to France.[166] As Cohen points out, nationality played a major role in this first deportation. Millicent McGahy was deported in part because she was an American citizen. Elisabet Duquemin and Elda Brouard gained a certain level of protection from having married British nationals. They would be the only registered Jews left in Guernsey to be subject to the Eighth Order, demanding that Jews over six years old wear, attached to the left side of their coat, a six-pointed yellow star with "Jew" written on it in black letters. The Ninth Order banned Jews from locations of public entertainment, and designated their shopping hours as only between 3 and 4 P.M. Of course the Ninth Order depended on the yellow star of the Eighth Order before it could be easily carried out.

Although the names of Elisabet Duquemin and Elda Brouard were known as the only remaining registered Jews, the stars never arrived, and Guernsey officials, shopkeepers, and the general public never were faced with participation in this Nazi performance of racial discrimination.[167] Ultimately, Elisabet and Henry Duquemin (along with Janet Duquemin, their eighteen-month-old daughter) and Elda Brouard were deported along with former British officers, high-ranking freemasons, those with criminal convictions, and communists in the February 13, 1943, deportation. Although Henry Duquemin wrote a letter of appeal about his family's deportation, the German authorities turned him down, the Nebenstelle affixing to his written appeal a curt "Wife is a Jew."[168] The Duquemins and Elda Brouard were treated much like the majority of the Guernsey deportees; in fact, Elisabet was a "Barrack Leader" in Biberach.[169] All survived the war.

Such was not the case for Therese, Auguste, and Marianne, who would be deported from France on July 20, 1942, along with 821 other Jews. Crammed into cattle cars, they suffered the full horrors of a journey that has been documented many times, arriving at Auschwitz-Birkenau on July 23. We do not know whether they survived the first "Selektion" or were sent immediately to the gas chambers. We do know that they did not survive the war, although word of their fate would not come quickly to Guernsey. Pathetically, the Ogiers noted in their farm visitors book on Christmas Day 1942, "Toasted our dear Marianne Grunfeld . . . and all other evacuees."[170] By then, all three women were most likely already dead. A year after the women left Guernsey, Rev. Ord would have their initial deportation confirmed, and even had knowledge of the further deportation to Poland, although with no idea of what this meant. On March 4, 1943, he wrote, "In hospital today I learned that that bright and universally respected little nurse Steiner had been taken to France for internment. A letter had come from her saying that she and another girl like her were being taken to Poland."[171] Frederick Cohen, in discussing this diary entry, makes a note that the pretext used by the Germans with the French government for this second deportation was that a new "Jewish state" was being established in Poland.[172] It is difficult to know if rumor of this chimerical Jewish state came to Guernsey, easing the minds of those who knew of this further transfer of their friends to Poland. It would only be in April 1945, with the shocking news of the concentration-camp liberation, that the Guernsey Islanders would learn the truth.

As is clear from this account, States officials took the same position toward deportations that they did toward requisitions, evictions, and rationing, imposing themselves as middlemen so that the Germans would not carry out their orders directly. In Leale's postwar report, he stated that in most situations, the Committee was "given every liberty to state our case with the utmost frankness and to argue about it." Then the Germans' decision was made, and the consequences for the population of noncompliance by the Committee were made clear. As Leale put it, the Germans "were always at the right end of the gun."[173] In this same report, Leale described the deportations as the "cruellest" problem that they had to face, and clearly all the deportations haunted him. Again, the decision was whether they "should cut ourselves completely adrift on the grounds that the thing was unclean," or whether, considering that they could not prevent them, they should remain in the middle and seek the maximum exemptions and the easiest path for those affected. Leale and the other officials believed that they only would have achieved "a little notoriety" by refusal to cooperate, losing any influence on the process that they might have had.[174]

Even as Leale spoke, he could have no idea of how much the entire history of the Occupation of Guernsey would later be judged by the fate of Therese, Auguste, and Marianne, although not by the other deportations. Rather than focusing on the failed attempts to exempt the women, later writers have sometimes implied that officials were willing and eager to sacrifice the three for some other gain they sought for the Island.[175] Yet, we have seen that the only Jews officially identified in Guernsey were the four women who stepped forward to register. Even on the day of deportation, the women reported to the harbor without being arrested or "handed over." It is a fair question to ask why States officials and the general public did not anticipate the different fate that awaited Therese, Auguste, and Marianne than lay in store for the other deportees, including the Duquemins and Elda Brouard.

Numerous people have pointed to the fact that although genocide of Jews had taken place earlier in certain locations, the systematic Final Solution was still in the planning stages at the time of the April 1942 deportation. The Wannsee Conference, chaired by Reinhard Heydrich, who had been tasked by Reichsmarshall Göring the previous year with devising a "solution of the Jewish question," had only taken place on January 20, 1942.[176] This means that Therese, Auguste, and Marianne were among the first Jews to be transported from Western Europe to the Auschwitz-Birkenau extermination camp in the summer of 1942. It would have been unlikely, therefore, for Guernsey to know in April 1942 what the future held for the Jewish women transported to France, for the formal policy was not yet in operation.[177] With the restrictions on outside information coming into Guernsey, Islanders were not even in the position to hear substantive rumors concerning such organized genocide.

Our problem is our post hoc awareness of the Holocaust, a knowledge that has come to plague our analysis of events as they unfolded. Popular histories derive some of their interest from a writing style incorporating "narrative backshadowing." Narrative backshadowing allows us to view the past from our vantage point in the present, with all paths seemingly leading to an unavoidable end. According to Gary Saul Morson, such backshadowing implies that the signs pointing to that end were as visible in the past as they are now in retrospect.[178] Narrative backshadowing is a writer's tool that gives the little frisson of irony to the mundane statement, and historical fiction makes great use of the technique for dramatic effect. "What are they going to do?" says a Jewish passenger in the movie of Katharine Ann Porter's *Ship of Fools*, with a philosophical shrug. "Kill all of us?" The viewer feels the chill of superior knowledge, but also marks the unsuspecting passenger as naive or a blind fool.[179] So even those who attempt a fair analysis of the path that took Therese, Auguste, and Marianne to the gas chambers end up playing defense, explaining why the Controlling Committee, or Islanders in general, did not see an end that seems so obvious to us now.

The only way to shake free of backshadowing and to identify clear mistakes in judgment, ones where the consequences were discernable at the time, is to posit other outcomes. Everyone knew that Jews would face discrimination under the Nazis, but the four women initially deported were sent to France, where many had been sent for various reasons and had returned unscathed. Yes, France was occupied by the Nazis, but, we seem to forget, so was Guernsey. As far as anyone could know, the three Jewish women were deported to face the same discrimination in France under the Nazi occupiers that they were likely to face in the future in Guernsey under the Nazi occupiers. A second factor to consider is that Islanders were also not able to prevent the September 1942 deportations of the English-born to Germany. How much more threatening would it seem to be slated for a camp in Germany, the very heart of the enemy state?

If there had been *any* knowledge, or even solid rumor, of death camps operating in the Third Reich, there were enough people slated for deportation to Germany in September 1942 that some pockets of physical resistance (or mass attempts to flee the Island) would have been likely. But even private accounts anticipated only separation from loved ones, and the bad food, isolation, and other rigors of a prison camp—rather than mass execution. And what if Hitler had, in retaliation for the bombing of Hamburg or other events during the war, systematically executed English and Americans from Biberach? Would we make an assumption of anti-American and anti-English feeling, as some do of anti-Semitism, among the States officials as a factor in the deportations?

Debate is certainly warranted as to whether a policy of performed compliance, where middlemen serve as "buffers" between the occupier and the populace, is superior to a last stand of defiance and blanket refusal to cooperate even in minor ways. The tradeoff is between the ability to obstruct and gain small advantages for the occupied by ostensible compliance (at the cost of an appearance of collaboration in the public transcript) and the clear, symbolic patriotism of having no cooperation with the enemy whatsoever (at the cost of ceding all governance to the occupier and forfeiting any influence over events). It is reasonable to discuss which would have been the better path. What is not reasonable is to accept the sanitized German documents and carefully worded States' replies of the public transcript, using them to imply that there was voluntary Vichy-like collaboration on the part of States officials, without seeking insight from contemporaneous, nonofficial sources into the States' actual strategy and motivation.

Perhaps we should also question our strange, bifurcated view when it comes to the Germans themselves. On the one hand, we expect the States officials and public to know, because *we* know, the full extent of the evil heart of the Third Reich, and to anticipate the horrors of the Holocaust. At the same time, we pretend that this same Nazi regime that could butcher millions without compunction would have been cowed into changing their plans for Guernsey had the Controlling Committee just stood up to them forcefully enough. As John Leale said, in obvious frustration, after the war, "Full marks for wishful thinking should be given to those who pathetically clung to the idea that the Germans would shudder if we showed our teeth and snarled."[180] Mistakes and miscalculations were natural for all in Guernsey, who were often deprived of full information and always lacked unfettered choice. But neither the Controlling Committee, the Guernsey populace, nor—for those who prefer to blame the victims—the women themselves were responsible for the deportation and subsequent deaths of Therese, Auguste, and Marianne. The responsibility falls squarely at the feet of the German occupying forces.

Narrative facility, whether found in the deconstructing of propaganda, construction and spreading of subversive stories and jokes, or exercising the conscious duplicity of performed compliance, is a necessary skill in the undermining of power. As an aspect of rhetorical resistance, it is a wielding of the resources at hand through language and improvisation to shift the ground under the dominant. As we will see in the next chapter, it is also a natural ally for other symbolic forms that emerge as tools of resistance.

CHAPTER FIVE

A Subtle Resistance

It may have been a poor choice of bookshop for one of the many plain-clothes Germans to frequent. Run by Miss Gaudin, a woman noted locally for her uncompromising spirit cloaked beneath a façade of cheeriness, the bookshop on Smith Street was also known by customers as a place to obtain forbidden war news on the QT. On this particular day, the unfortunate German entered and requested a guidebook to Guernsey. Miss Gaudin sailed up to him with the book, chirping gaily, "Here you are! But you're the first tourist we've had this season. It's rather a pity because you won't be able to get any fishing or bathing—the Germans have put a stop to all that!" To the delight of the Islanders present, watching and enjoying this little performance, the German was at a loss for where to look and what to say.

Miss Gaudin specialized in more than the discomfiture of individual Germans. Behind the counter, she kept a box with the day's news typed out and available to her customers, an information service aimed at "encouragement and enlightenment" during the period when wireless sets had been confiscated. According to accounts at the time, a small crowd of Germans piled into the shop one day, parading all over the store, upending things and making their presence very much known. Just as one German was about to open the box containing the forbidden news transcription, Miss Gaudin snatched the box right out of his grip, with a cheerful, "That's no good to you. Look at this! This should interest you!" Rev. Ord expressed the opinion of many in Guernsey when he wrote admiringly, "She has the pluck of a regiment."[1]

Personal actions such as the ones taken by Miss Gaudin, whether conducted in private or public, are an integral part of the shape that resistance took in Guernsey during the Occupation. Some have found it challenging to develop an appreciation for the potential of such acts to undermine a power differential. For good reasons, history has a distinct preference for the overt moments of active resistance—for Nat Turner, Alice Paul, Emmeline Pankhurst, Rosa Parks, and Martin Luther King, Jr. Their exploits do not require double readings; they are what they appear to be, and clear intentions are embodied in distinct actions. The phrase appended in the 1970s to some whose powerless condition led to adoption of a mask of deference and covert obstruction was "participating in their own oppression." It is only recently that academics have sought an understanding of the more subtle forms of resistance sheltered beneath the disguise of cooperation. After all, what has been called "Uncle Tom behavior . . . may be no more than a label for someone who has mastered the theater arts of subordination."[2] Beneath this mask of deference lay a "history of foot dragging, false compliance, flight, feigned ignorance, sabotage, theft, and not least, cultural resistance," adopted as the appropriate—indeed, the only long-term effective—means of resistance to the violent enforcement of slavery and Jim Crow.[3]

In our understanding of the Guernsey resistance, it is now clear that we need not choose between the false dichotomy of collaboration and willing consent versus armed resistance and overt rebellion. Under a situation of armed tyranny, the Guernsey Islanders developed what many oppressed populations have sought: a "practical" means of resistance, and one suited to the unique demands of their situation.[4] I have already discussed the first two aspects of rhetorical resistance: the use of a shadow discourse as a method of control, and the utilizing of narrative construction and interpretation. This chapter will detail the shape of the third prong of rhetorical resistance in Guernsey, an active and generally more apparent resistance clustered around communication, symbolism, and the flow of information. First, I will consider the three primary forms of communication that constituted active rhetorical resistance: defiant speech, the coding of messages, and physical resistance or "body rhetoric," including various forms of self-exemption from German orders. In the remainder of the chapter, I will examine one particular aspect of resistance in depth: the role that hidden wireless sets played in the movement of information and the undermining of German control. This form of resistance to German edicts made subversives of average people, opening them to the danger of lateral surveillance by collaborators and retaliation by Occupation forces.

In their willingness to take these risks, the Islanders displayed their uncompromising desire for psychological involvement in the British war effort, and their heightened determination to seek control over their own lives. In this chapter, I hope to challenge the view that has confined true resistance in Guernsey to sabotage or other "exceptional moments of popular explosion." The political territory of a subjugated people is far broader and often occupies a space somewhere between resigned acceptance and overt demonstration. There is a danger that in acknowledging only the dramatic, unmistakable act, we will "focus on the visible coastline of politics and miss the continent that lies beyond."[5] Instead, active resistance often may be found in what James Scott calls "weapons of the weak,"[6] the subtle, personal, and often discursive means that come to hand when other tools are unavailable.

A NEED FOR SUBTLETY

The need for wariness and a subtlety in resistance was driven home early to the occupied Islanders as their new German masters made their intentions to enforce the new reality unmistakably clear. Even without knowing about threats to hostages behind the scenes in the early days of the Occupation, the average Islander now was aware of the distinct possibility that resistance would lead to the murder of innocents. The general attitude about resistant acts came to resemble Kitty Bachmann's feelings, ones that she expressed during the "velvet glove" period of the fall of 1940. Worried by the failed landings of British servicemen on Guernsey and the reprisals against their families, Kitty wondered when the Germans' "august patience" might end. She further pondered:

> There is always the risk that some fiery character might go berserk and carry out some of the things we all feel the urge to do at times. If such acts would assist our cause in particular, and the war effort

in general, no doubt many attempts would have been made long ago, with the full blessing of us all. But one must be wary, even with the pen.[7]

Kitty's concerns make a pretty fair summary of Islander attitudes when it came to resistant acts.

First, the spirit to resist was widespread and bubbled up in ways that were difficult to tamp down at times. The danger lay in the "fiery" among them who might throw caution to the wind and conduct an act on the spur of the moment, rather than with the cool calculation that resistance under armed occupation requires. Even so, despite the dangers and the possible reprisals against other civilians, any act that helped Guernsey, or could definitely help the war effort, would find support in the Island. But wariness was the watchword under the current conditions, and blatant or poorly calculated acts would be generally dismissed as foolish and unproductive. In a broad sense, these would remain the ground rules for acceptable resistance until the combination of desperate circumstances and renewed hopes for liberation changed the feelings of Guernseymen and women during the final year.

In addition to threats against nonparticipants, early punishments for resisters had an influence on the evolving form that resistance would take. In September 1940 one of the more notable of these warnings came with the news that "The mechanic, MARCEL BROSSIER of Rennes, has been sentenced to DEATH . . . for having cut German telephone cables . . . Brossier has been FUSILATED."[8] This rather odd term (based on fusillade) for a firing-squad execution was marked as German phrasing and stuck in people's minds. In February 1941, Ambrose Robin learned that "Nelson Le Breton (probably drunk?) attempted to escape from the island on Saturday," and Robin's first thought was "will he be fusilated?" As it turned out, this escape attempt simply amounted to Le Breton being found drunk and passed out in a boat moored in the town harbor. He would spend some extended time in prison rather than face a firing squad, but the repeat of German phrasing shows that the warnings of counter-resistance punishments in France took hold in Robin's mind.[9]

It seems very likely that the François Scornet case also heightened the sense of threat for Guernsey. Scornet, along with fifteen fellow Frenchmen, had sailed from the Brittany Coast in early 1941 with the hope of joining the Free French Forces. The weather during the voyage was intensely rough, so after sailing for hours, they believed that they had reached the Isle of Wight. Instead, they sailed into Vazon Bay, Guernsey, triumphantly singing the "Marseillaise," only to be immediately captured by the Germans. The young men were transferred to Jersey for trial, and three were given the death penalty (with the others given varying lengths of prison sentences). His two compatriots later had their sentences reduced to life imprisonment, but Scornet faced the firing squad at Saint Ouens Manor in Jersey during the early morning hours of March 17, 1941.

Touching words from his final letter to his parents ("I believe the end of my existence has come, I will die for France, bravely facing the enemy. In an hour it will be finished . . . be assured that I will die a good Christian . . . for the last time I embrace you") are proudly displayed on websites to his honor. His stalwart demeanor at his execution and final words of "Vive Dieu! Vive La France!" revealed him to be an unusually brave twenty-one-year-old and made him a natural hero to the Channel Islanders.[10] Knowles Smith is correct when she describes news of this event as summoning up Islanders' emotions similar to ones experienced in the initial air raid, and diminishing their "trust in German standards of human justice, and of their respect for the Law."[11] It also drove home to all their need to tread carefully and find means to resist that would lessen the opportunity for retaliation by their German captors.

TALKING BACK AND SIDEWAYS

The power of expression, whether embodied in speech, writing, or other symbolic forms, has not always been fully recognized for its "dynamic, creative, change-making, history altering" potential.[12] Andrew Smith makes the important point, one that has been apparent throughout this study thus far, that efforts against domination are more opaque than transparent. They travel, by necessity, in disguise and function by "foiling the dominant other's game in singular instances."[13] In other words, only rarely is rhetorical resistance overt, group-organized, and unmistakable. It is for this reason that many analysts miss both the "human drive to counter injustices"[14] and the potential for a powerful collective effect in acts that seem individual and spur-of-the-moment. Nowhere is this underestimation of the power of rhetorical resistance more apparent than in discussions of individual verbal confrontations during the Occupation. Therefore, this is the first form of a more active rhetorical resistance to be considered: the many instances of verbal opposition to the enemy that became noteworthy parts of Island lore during and after the Occupation.

In his Berkeley lectures on "fearless speech," Michel Foucault addressed the ancient concept of "parrhesia," or in its English translation "free speech," as a counter to power. In parrhesia, the speaker values frankness over safety and views the speaking of truth as a duty to the larger community. Two aspects of parrhesia link this concept to the verbal confrontations practiced by the Islanders as a means of resistance. First, the "parrhesiastic game" is played in a situation of unequal power: "The parrhesia comes from 'below' as it were, and is directed towards 'above.'" Second, the exercise of parrhesia is "linked to courage in the face of danger: it demands the courage to speak the truth in spite of some danger."[15] Both of these defining attributes of parrhesia were clearly present in the oppositional speech that emerged during the Occupation.

The Germans (and we must always, as suggested earlier, look to them to gauge the impact of resistance) were well aware of the danger if they allowed verbal confrontations to go unremarked and unpunished. It is to be remembered that one of the very first concerns of the Occupation, as early as July 1940, was the need to curb speech viewed as insulting by the Germans. Part of the concern was that an interpersonal confrontation might cause simmering resentments and a natural antipathy for the enemy occupier to explode into violence.[16]

The tendency to verbally confront the German forces in Guernsey was apparently shared across gender, although men seemed to be also on the edge of a more physical opposition. Frank Mallett, who specialized in automotive repairs, had been kept busy building and repairing German lorries. But according to Jack Sauvary, one day at his works on the Banques, he "had a few words with one of them and showed his fists." He was summarily arrested.[17] Because reports of arrests for various confrontations are so common in the contemporaneous accounts, details are often omitted. It is difficult to know, for example, what was the exact nature of the term "insult" that accompanied Gertie Corbin's terse entry that Nico Le Prevost and Bill Russel were "in prison because they insulted soldiers."[18] It is not always apparent whether such insults were verbal, a matter of offensive look and manner, or blended with a more physical confrontation. After all, some Germans considered it insulting not to be given preferential treatment in a store, or for a civilian not to yield the sidewalk. Thus, the type or level of "insult" could be fairly wide-ranging.

Some descriptions of arrests are more definitely for speech, and they begin very early and extend to quite late in the Occupation. So, for example, Rev. Ord mentions in August 1940 that two girls were sentenced (one to six months and the other to nine months in prison) for "unguarded speech."[19] Only three days later, Winnie Harvey records that the still-room maid at the Royal Hotel (the German headquarters) had been interned for "speaking against the German troops." For working-class women who needed to earn their living, positions working for and around the German troops were almost inevitable.[20] The dangers of juxtaposing plain-spoken Guernsey women, who did not suffer fools gladly, with young German troops seems clear. The inevitable result of enemies living side by side continued, and Bert Williams could say of the prisons in May 1944, "One has only to say anything a little out of the way, and in you go."[21]

Of course, the ability to express an opinion without reprisal varied based on the position of the speaker and the context of the exchange. Winnie Harvey had the standing, as a member of the upper class, that appealed to the snobbish Germans now in possession of Newlands. In her contact with the lesser members of the contingent ensconced in her home, such as Eitel the interpreter and Paul the batman, she could slyly get her point across. One afternoon in the spring of 1942, she was in the Newlands back lawn, despite the presence of some of the men who liked to sunbathe there whenever the officers were away. Winnie found this to be "a nuisance," but as the men were "very civil and polite," she could use the absence of the officers to check on her property.

On this day Eitel (and Winnie puts in parentheses "I don't like him") was chatting about the beautiful spring weather, how much rain was needed, and asking about the Guernsey summers. Eitel said, "I tink it is so beautiful for us, everything is always just right for *us.*" To that, Winnie looked up and replied, "Perhaps, yes, for now, but I think a *change* is coming soon." Winnie added in her diary, "He understood what I meant."[22] A similar exchange occurred when Paul, the batman, gave Winnie the war news following the battle of Dieppe. He happily came "dancing down the garden" to tell her that there were 1,500 British prisoners and ninety planes shot down. "And how many German?" asked Winnie to the suddenly "crestfallen" Paul, who replied, "Ach, I do not know. Perhaps twenty." "Perhaps twenty thousand!" responded Winnie.[23]

There were several elements that protected speakers who shared opinions counter to the German perspective, and we can see them operating in Winnie's exchange. First, the relative standing of the speaker mattered. Winnie seemed to carry with her the sense of being mistress of the manor, even when she was dispossessed of the property. The German officers treated her with a respect that her bearing demanded, and lower-ranking Germans, serving as support staff for those officers, were unlikely to report her regardless of what she said. This was not always the case, of course. So, second, Winnie was careful to shelter what she was saying, so as to give no opportunity for trouble. Eitel would have been hard pressed to report any insult in her words, and even the words with Paul, while a little closer to the line, could have been easily defended. But third, and most important, was the private nature of the exchange. A speech act that seems wholly interpersonal—a private exchange between a specific Islander and a German—takes on symbolic weight as it is observed or discussed by others. Much of the power of spontaneous verbal insults and challenges comes from the collective effect these confrontations can trigger.[24]

The difference in what could safely be said, and who could say it, may be seen in the sad case of John Ingrouille. John was born in Vale, Guernsey, in 1920, an only child who worked as a laborer like his father. He was working on a farm in Jersey at the start of the Occupation and returned to Guernsey soon thereafter. Because work was difficult to obtain, John started work as a cook for a group of Luftwaffe air-sea rescue signalers who conducted their observations from the top of Vale Mill and lived in an adjoining house. For a short time, the position went well, but then John—with the bravado of young men—started talking about having eight hundred men ready and willing to shoot the Germans. He also took home a knife and fork belonging to an officer.

At this point, the account is somewhat muddy. His mother clearly believed, and gave a postwar deposition to the effect, that John was denounced by a woman, who along with her daughter worked in the same place. According to Mrs. Ingrouille, when the Germans came to the Ingrouilles' house searching for guns, this woman accompanied them on one occasion. Then again, Mrs. Ingrouille also claimed that John brought the knife and fork home for safekeeping while the officer was away. By other estimations, John, who had a "quick temper," may have done a little boasting about his threat against the Germans and this tiny bit of resistant pilfering. Whether denounced or overheard by the Germans, John's actions were taken very seriously.

On December 31, 1940, two Germans came to the Ingrouille home, took John aside into his room, and apparently searched thoroughly. That afternoon, they took John away with them. As he prepared to enter the Germans' car, John turned back to his mother and said, "So long Mum, I won't be long. I have not done anything or said anything." It was the last his parents were to see of their son. John was tried in Jersey and sentenced to five years for treason and one month for stealing the knife and fork. Simply the structuring of the charge against him as "treason," as opposed to a milder charge along the lines of "dangerous talking," seems completely out of proportion with the incident. After all, there was no sign that the threat of having eight hundred armed men waiting to strike the Germans was anything but unbelievable talk.

It seems clear that a young man of fighting age was considered a particular threat, and the Germans were eager to send a message that such talk would not be tolerated. John's story would have a tragic end. He spent four years in French prisons before being transferred to Brandenburg Prison in Germany. When the British took Brandenburg in May 1945, John was discovered to be very ill. He was taken to a hospital in Brussels, where he died on June 13, 1945. His body was returned to Guernsey in 1946 and buried at the Domaille cemetery at St. Michael du Valle church.[25]

It could easily be claimed that John Ingrouille's case was an oddity and not representative of most of the resistant speech in the Island. It was, after all, a threat of violence, however unlikely, which in the German mind would heighten a desire to smother it in the crib. If we are seeking the most common form of confrontation, the kind Andrew Smith describes as "individual, often voluble engagements" where one of the powerless speaks "like a citizen rather than a subject,"[26] then Mrs. Winifred Green might prove a better example. Different versions of the Winnie Green account appear in local histories of the Occupation, but the most complete may come from her cousin in an article written after the war. Winnie's children had been evacuated to Scotland, and "to fill the void," she started work as a waitress at the

Royal Hotel. This hotel, of course, became the German headquarters in Guernsey, so Winnie was surrounded by Germans and their support staff, a situation that was ripe for possible missteps by someone as patriotic and outspoken as Mrs. Green.

The Swiss chef was a great admirer of Hitler, and to the same extent, Winifred Green was an ardent admirer of Winston Churchill. A "teasing" relationship developed between the two, with the chef greeting Mrs. Green each day with, "Good morning, Mrs. Green. Heil Hitler!" and with Winnie retorting, "Good Morning, Chef. Heil Churchill!" The staff lunches became a lively tit for tat, with the chef crowing over any positive German war news: "Have you hear the news Mrs. Green? Germany has taken Yugoslavia (or Greece, or Crete)." On one day, it was "We've got the battleship *Hood*!" to which Winnie came back days later with "Heard the news? We've got the *Bismarck*!"

The danger for those in a subjugated position of such "joking" exchanges is apparent. In this case, the chef and Mrs. Green were commenting in areas involving patriotism, war, and matters of life and death, all uneasy areas for humor. Any levity in the back and forth with the chef wore away quickly, and the comments became more bitter and freighted with meaning. Finally, one day the chef asked Winifred, "Would you like some rice pudding, Mrs. Green?" "Yes, please," she replied. The chef baited her: "Only if you say Heil Hitler." After a few seconds' silence, Winnie burst forth with, "To hell with Hitler for a rice pudding—and one made of skim milk at that!" For this exchange, one she defiantly verified at trial, Winnie Green would receive six months in the Caen prison. To relieve the boredom of her sentence, she secretly embroidered a bed sheet with "Heil Churchill, RAF, Caen Prison 1941, V," smuggling it out in the lining of her coat .[27]

The response to this colorful but small incident in studies of the Occupation has been interesting. Most treat it simply in passing, and Madeleine Bunting appends a dry, "She became a folk heroine," to further her argument that the dearth of true resistance made Islanders bolster even miniscule acts to prominence.[28] Of course, upon her release from prison, Mrs. Green *was* quietly lauded by Islanders who teasingly called her "Mrs. Churchill," and the bed sheet was displayed for many years in a guest house the Greens operated after the war. What the Islanders and the Germans understood, and what has largely been missed by later analysts, is the importance of such verbal eruptions as that of Winifred Green. It is little wonder that the Germans reacted harshly to such speech acts, for "when suddenly subservience evaporates and is replaced by open defiance, we encounter one of those rare and dangerous moments in power relations."[29] The Germans saw such incidents not as "pinpricks," as so often they are described, but as serious disruptions to the seamless functioning of masterful domination. As long as insults are presented offstage or are disguised in such a way that they may be ignored, then no action is necessary. But clear, overt insubordination is "a dare" that calls into question the carefully constructed relationship between dominator and dominated.[30] Power is sometimes illusory, and the "smooth surface" of the German display of control and the apparent consent of the governed could be readily challenged by public acts that erupted into view at odd moments.[31]

Some Guernseymen and women kept their performances right below the surface successfully, a mimetic display of apparent compliance but shadowed by an insubordination that was readily apparent only to those with the eyes to see it. Obviously, Miss Gaudin specialized in burlesque with double meaning, using the small stage of her bookshop to entertain her fellow Islanders with challenges to German dignity. In November 1940, a German officer came in to find an English storybook, a gift for his daughter who was taking English lessons. Did Miss

Gaudin have a good book that she would recommend? Instantly, Miss Gaudin pulled out a copy of the political parody "Adolf in Blunderland." "Ah yes!" the officer said, looking it over. "I have heard it is a classic, but I do not read English well myself."[32] Such publicly performed humor is a type of verbal jiujitsu, using the weight of an opponent's dignity as an effective weapon and a means to neutralize power.[33] The story of such an encounter would be told and retold, multiplying the effect as it passed from person to person.

This enlargement through retelling made stories of "back talk" into an important aspect of Islander understanding of their own resistance. In February 1944, Colonel Knackfuss attempted to crack down on increasingly offhand treatment of their German patrons by shop owners and assistants. These very public places were ideal venues to display a subtle contempt toward the occupier, and tensions were natural when the Germans were not treated with the respect, or the subservience, they expected. Thus, Knackfuss sent a letter on February 12, 1944, to the Bailiffs of Guernsey and Jersey stating that proprietors of retail shops, public houses, cinemas, hairdressers, etc., must attend and serve members of the German army "in preference."

An incident in a Guernsey hair salon at this time pointed up the reason for the Knackfuss letter. A Guernseyman had entered the hairdresser's for a shave and haircut and was asked to have a seat. He was followed closely by a German naval officer, who fully expected to be attended to first. Adele Lainé recorded the exchange in her diary:

> ASSISTANT TO GERMAN OFFICER: Excuse me sir but this gentleman was in first so I must attend to him first.
> GERMAN OFFICER: If Mr. Anthony Eden came in would you ask him to wait?
> ASSISTANT: It would not be necessary. He is too much of a gentleman to want to take anybody else's turn.

The assistant was fined 20 reichsmarks for his clever comeback, and shortly following this incident, on February 21, an order appeared in the paper detailing the new requirement for preferential treatment. According to Adele Lainé, the assistant became "quite a hero in the eyes of his compatriots."[34] Average people saw in his response the expression of a "communal identity,"[35] a vital part of the flexing of a collective muscle.

Spontaneous outbursts that are simply an overflow of high spirits may have the same effect as humor that is more deftly wielded, or the simple belligerence of talking back. When word spread across Guernsey of the resignation of Mussolini in July 1943, the civilians in St. Peter Port were "full of unconcealed joy" that burst out in "jokes about macaroni, spaghetti and ice-cream." When Rev. Ord reached the crowded Arcade, Rex Priaulx, a noted local vocalist, caught his eye. Priaulx swung up onto his bicycle, while singing loudly, "O. . . . h! WHAT a surprise for the Duce, the Duce! We've had no spaghetti for weeks."[36]

The unexpected or comical verbal outburst is one that is effective in the weakest of hands, even those of children, drunks, and the mentally challenged. Gertie Corbin and some of her friends were kept laughing by the sight of Jean des Mares ("quite drunk") in the Coudre, who was shouting, "Good old England" and "Buy British." It seems that des Mares managed to avoid punishment for this boozy patriotism, leaving Gertie to ponder, "It's a wonder the Germans don't put him in prison."[37] When a civilian manages to pull off such blatant tweaking of the nose of the powerful, it only emboldens others among the dominated. Those in power must make constant decisions between coming down hard on such instances, expending resources, straining whatever goodwill exists, and dissolving the illusion of complete control, or selectively ignoring them, gambling that such little sparks do not presage a wider conflagration.

Under the right circumstances, the smart remark or confrontational speech may be potent enough to trigger violence. In May 1943, Bill Warry watched out of the open windows of his club as an RAF raid attacked German vessels in the harbor. One of Bill's friends, Harley Guiton, was also busy looking out the club windows at the troops filling the streets, particularly at two German NCOs, and "said something rather loud." Although Bill does not record what that "something" was, it had a galvanizing effect on the officers, one of whom instantly took out his revolver. Bill and his friend "quickly withdrew from the windows, till he cooled down." Bill was fully expecting a shot through the window; "it never came, but it might have done so." He was, of course, right that the heightened tensions of open warfare would make the Germans more sensitive and trigger-happy. This threat did not seem to stop the locals, who despite how "the Germans glared at them" milled around in groups, discussed the attack, and "had their say & laugh."[38]

It is in such incidents that we see the cumulative effect of small acts of verbal insubordination and their ability to blossom into more widespread challenges to authority, even under threat of violence. The Germans had a particular stake in controlling who spoke to whom, and a significant portion of their surveillance was directed at preventing unauthorized conversations. If contemporaneous accounts are to be believed, this was particularly true when it came to conversations with prisoners. Stories and rumors swept through Guernsey of captured Allied forces and attempts made by the Islanders to talk to them. Many of these stories, as they made their way into private diaries, were quite fantastic, although they followed a common pattern: a battle over or near the Island, a downed Allied parachutist or captured sailors, successful attempts by Islanders to speak to them (before or after they were taken into custody), hopeful words from the men about the war—usually to the effect that Allied victory would not be long in coming—and steps by the Germans to prevent or punish such conversations.[39] The story would come to the satisfying conclusion that the Germans did not want Islanders to "know the truth" of the coming end of the war. The past history of small verbal defiances made such stories, some undoubtedly more fiction than fact, believable and bolstered the Islanders' morale. One woman told Rev. Ord that she passed an RAF pilot, forced to bail out over the Island, as he was under guard and on his way to custody. He returned her cheerful "Good morning," and the little exchange "did her a world of good," despite her concerns for the young man's future.[40]

The simple act of breaking silence, to speak when forbidden or to reach out to those held incommunicado, is a distinct gesture of defiance. Rev. Ord also found his moments to make such moves, seeing them as part of his ministry to provide comfort. One May morning as he cycled back from a funeral at the cemetery in St. Martin, he happened upon a group of Russian prisoners waiting to be taken from their work detail back to their billet. The men were clustered in a semicircle around a giant of a man, but there did not appear to be any guards present for the moment. Ord stopped and gave them some encouraging words in his relatively "rusty" Russian, describing the response: "For a moment they were taken aback, then their faces lit up with delight, and the giant let out a mighty yell in which they all joined." Then Ord heard the sound of heavy boots around the corner and swiftly pedaled around an opposite corner, darting into one of the narrow lanes in that area to avoid being followed. "But," he concluded, "the joy of the Russians was worth seeing."[41]

Some verbal defiance was sung rather than spoken, as we saw with Rex Priaulx's spontaneous operatic take on Mussolini's resignation. Most acts were not as overt as that of a Mrs. Garland, who was sentenced to two years and three months in prison for composing a song considered "deprecatory to the Reich."[42] Islanders had an attachment to patriotic songs, and once the wireless sets were confiscated, they sorely missed the Sunday playing of the National Anthem on the BBC broadcast. Thus, there were little private means of patriotic display, as during the first calling in of wireless sets in 1940. Each Sunday night at 10 P.M., when Big Ben struck in England, Guernsey being one hour ahead, Winifred Harvey would play "God Save the King" on the piano, while the elderly Mrs. Clayton stood. At first, Winnie admitted, her playing was "very piano and timid," but soon she was ringing it out "as bold as brass."[43]

What were small private acts took on an aspect of unifying patriotism when they were performed at some of the dances and social evenings allowed in the Island. Bert Williams's band played often at these gatherings, and he served as a witness to music as a resistant act. For example, there was a New Year's Eve social evening at the town asylum, with Bert's band playing from 8:00 to 12:15. And Bert casually records, "We sang the 'King' at the end of the evening." Because Hitler was speaking at 12:15, the electricity was still on, and many Germans were likely about, staying up to hear Hitler's address.[44] It may have been the sense of the change in the war that encouraged such defiance, because there was plenty of shared history that singing patriotic songs could bring down strict punishment.

On September 30, 1943, a dance party was held at Stroobant's Café as a farewell gesture to Roy Machon, a young man being deported to Laufen in Germany for resistant acts. All was going quite well until the small band swung into "Pack Up Your Troubles in Your Old Kit Bag." The dancers took this to be a defiant rendition of "We're Going to Hang Up the Washing on the Siegfried Line," and they entered into the spirit of the moment, singing with gusto. Here, different versions of the event enter in. Bert Williams described the German police intervening to stop the dance and check everyone's identity cards. Ken Lewis, hearing the story by way of Vera Lloyd, who was present at the dance with her sister Jane, claimed that no one thought much of the song until they prepared to leave. At that point, they found the doors barred by sailors, and the Feldgendarmerie appeared to demand identity cards from all present. Eight people were without their cards, Jane Lloyd being one of them, and they were kept in prison overnight. The others had their cards confiscated and had to report to the Field Police at Hauteville to get their cards back. For a while, dancing in general was forbidden and Stroobant's Café was barred from holding further entertainment. This incident became instructive of the slippery boundary between the acceptable and the punishable. More to the point, it reveals the contagious nature of verbal defiance, and the stake the Germans maintained in its control.[45]

MESSAGES IN DISGUISE

It became clear to Islanders from the onset of the Occupation that their group politics would have to come in "disguise and anonymity."[46] And, because of the heavy censorship of Red Cross messages, that disguise extended to written contacts off the Island. As Kitty Bachmann put it, "We live in an age of 'cloaking and dissembling' as the Book of Common Prayer would have it," and she was quite proud of Peter's ability to share local news in carefully worded messages to friends in the outside world.[47] Many families had simple code words, presumably established before the initial evacuation or the mass deportations to Biberach, that they could drop into messages as a blanket indication that all was well. Although such phrases were frustratingly short on detail, they served the general purpose quite handily.[48]

Sometimes the more specific messages that were sent could slide past the German censors simply because they were based in British terminology. Local knowledge was the basis for Kitty's message to the family that they had been evicted from the family home: "Left La Guelle. Crampen ordered us, take Basil & Dudley with us. Knew you'd appreciate the effort." By using her father's favorite term for the Germans ("Crampen") rather than "Jerry," which was recognizable and resented in German eyes, and combining it with the names of their home furnishers, Kitty believed that this message that they protected the family household goods would if "properly deciphered . . . speak volumes."[49]

There was a certain enjoyment in concocting the Red Cross messages, because it called to mind family jargon, with its attendant good memories, and it allowed an exercising of imagination. Dorothy Higgs and her family exchanged messages discussing whether the "onions" were decent—not as an agricultural reference, but using the name for Hitler and the Nazis coined by Dorothy and Phyll during a 1936 visit to Germany.[50] One notable pattern in these codes to escape the censor was the use of supposedly proper names. Thus, Rev. Ord and Grae sent home to England a Red Cross message after the confiscation of the wireless sets: "You'll be sorry Uncle Bebecey passed away quite unexpectedly this week. His cheerful company sorely missed."[51] These were sometimes a bit of a stretch, and Dorothy Higgs wondered if her news that "W. Machin, Friggie, and Vac" were still working for her was understandable to her family or perhaps too transparent to escape the censor.[52] Jack Sauvary got a kick out of various similar messages: "My Cossar gone, Nothing from Lydell or Belfrage lately. We miss Pye, not apple"—all of these names of newscasters or makes of wireless sets.[53]

Although many of the proper names appearing in Red Cross messages might have been obvious to the German censors, such as the ubiquitous "Winnie" to refer to Churchill, these messages might go through easily because they could also refer to the numerous Winifreds in the Island. It seems that simplicity worked well for these coded messages, but so did more complicated efforts. Thus, Dorothy Higgs wrote to her mother, "Little Mary sends love to Anna Gram. Dr. Santiro's prescription was inadequate but she's thriving on home produce." Later, she learned that the reference to anagram helped the family sort out that the imaginary Dr. Santiro meant rations. The family sent the message around, so Dorothy received several return messages addressed to "Anna."[54]

It did not take long for families at a distance to adopt caution in their wording, probably sensing the need from the cryptic messages they were receiving from Guernsey. These messages, too, were based on a blend of past history shared with the recipient and some facility with language. Ken Lewis's Auntie Ede received a message from Roy after fourteen months of silence that read, "Received news of all. Doing what I wanted—happy and well—glad you are too. Don't worry—I'm not. Love Roy." They took "doing what I wanted" to mean that Roy had joined the RAF, an ambition that he apparently shared with many family members. It might also be speculated that his admonition for them not to worry and his bluff "I'm not" contained a hint that he would soon be seeing combat.[55]

Some were exceedingly clever at getting around the censor with a message that would be readable to Islanders and invisible to the Germans. The names and addresses of people who were to come to the Red Cross bureau to claim the messages awaiting them were published regularly in the local papers. So, one ingenious person sent a message to the following address:

Jean Tendras
Vos Araines
Par Tchieu

As was usual, this "address" of the recipient subsequently appeared in the local press. But in Guernsey patois, this address roughly translated to "we hear your news over here."[56]

Red Cross messages were occasionally published in their entirety in the *Press* or *Star.* It was probably at the urging of the Guernseymen on the staff that a message from Frank Le Poidevin, the headmaster at Torteval, was published in the *Star.* It spoke of the progress of evacuated children at school, so it would be of general interest and what could be the harm? The message read, in part, "Children progressing very well, especially Tommy. Jack showing good initiative, should improve rapidly from now on." Of course, the reference to Tommy as the army and Jack as the navy made this a clever way to deliver general war news around the censor.[57] A similar message from the headmaster was published two months later: "All children very fit. Tommy, Joe and Sam's boys working hard. Doing very good work. Should graduate with honours, near future. Delighting parents."[58]

Ken Lewis was often amazed at the messages that managed to make it past the censor. He was shown a message by Mr. Hollard at the office that read, "All well. Be of good cheer your day of deliverance is near . . . -" The three dots and the dash that closed out the message provided a common form of the "V" sign.[59] Other messages that slid past the censor were so coded as to be worthless to the recipient. Ken was rather miffed at a message his Mum had received that "contained all foolish statements . . . and gave no news whatsoever." Instead, the message was filled with oblique questions, such as "Have you got patches on your feet?" and "Have you any pretty biscuits in your tin?" Whether these were intended to be read as codes, or simply references to shared events from the past, they were thoroughly lost on the Lewis family.[60]

If there was a master of the coded message, it had to be Rev. Ord. It was not simply his intellect but his intimate knowledge of the Bible that made his coding so fascinating to read. Ord includes full transcripts of some of his coded letters to Biberach and seemed to enjoy the creative game of devising means of discussing the war when only limited to news of the family. Some of the more entertaining of these offerings contained a detailed description of the passing of Uncle Ron (Rommel's army in North Africa) and gave hymns with specific verses, as they were "long hymns," and Bible verses that were delivered at the funeral. Naturally, all of these verses and hymns contained specific messages and exhortations, at least when read between the lines.[61]

Not surprisingly, Ord found the Bible to be a fertile hunting ground for sources of coding. Early in the summer of 1942, he tucked into a Red Cross message a reference to "Last two verses, Acts, Moffatt's version," which reads, "For two full years he remained in his private lodging welcoming any who came to visit him. He preached the Reign of God and taught about the Lord Jesus Christ, quite openly and unmolested." There could have been few better descriptors of his position or more effective means to convey the news that he was still in his home and able to perform his duties as minister. Ord marveled that "Some of these passages seem designed for the conveyance of messages, IF ONLY they are not censored!"[62]

In August 1942, the Germans cracked down on all the "cryptic messages" that were being sent,[63] and the use of biblical texts.[64] As a minister, Rev. Ord could get away with the use of Bible verses to send external messages longer than could the average Islander. Yet, it was in messages aimed at the support and encouragement of his own congregation where Ord was the cleverest and boldest. Some references tucked within his sermons were directly tied to war news. On September 14, 1942, a woman stopped Ord in the Arcade with "Shepherd's Hotel—you naughty man!" The night before, Ord was preaching on Isaiah and the attempt by Sennacherib to take Egypt (war references in the Bible being one way to broach the topic of the current war) and had dropped into his description of Napoleon's retreat from Egypt in 1799 a mention that it was so sudden, "he never got to stay at Shepherd's Hotel." The BBC had been reporting that Rommel expected to take Cairo and make Shepherd's Hotel his headquarters. Ord could tell that the congregation "took up the significance directly."[65] It is also little wonder why Ambrose Robin, describing some "startling remarks" made by Ord in one sermon, could only write in admiration, "He's got pluck."[66]

And it is Ord whose coded message through the Red Cross early in the Occupation beautifully captured the developing communal identity that would sustain the Islanders through the years to come. He replied to a message by asking, "Do you know closing sextet Tennyson's Ulysses?" He believed that Tennyson's words would convey much that they were not allowed to detail in a message:

> Though much is taken, much abides; and tho'
> We are not now that strength which in old days
> Moved earth and heaven; that which we are, we are;
> One equal temper of heroic hearts,
> Made weak by time and fate, but strong in will
> To strive, to seek, to find, AND NOT TO YIELD.[67]

Just as Tennyson's words embodied the evolving self-understanding of Islanders in their new subjugated position, Ord's construction of a coded message enacted the rhetorical resistance of Islanders to that subjugation.

BODY RHETORIC

In the 1960s, Leland Griffin coined the term "body rhetoric" to describe the use of physical acts of dissent developed by the New Left in the social protests of the day.[68] This concept has evolved over time to encompass the many ways that the physical body may be used as a "mode of argument" and a means of defiance.[69] In considering the means of rhetorical resistance utilized by the Guernsey Islanders to counter the domination of their captors, some fall into more overt physical actions. Some of these deeds were of a type considered to be classic resistance, such as took place in a more organized effort during the same period on the Continent. Yet, other forms of body rhetoric are still more interesting to us in that they align with the general subtlety of resistance efforts during the Occupation. Being in continuous close contact with the occupier under conditions of domination could not help but spark spontaneous instances not just of verbal explosions but also of physical violence. Thus, throughout the contemporaneous accounts, we see mention of arrests and imprisonments for striking a German soldier or officer.

It is obvious that Islanders were lucky the Germans chose not to treat low-level physical violence with the mass hangings and shootings of randomly selected civilians that were then taking place in Pancevo, Vinkt, and so many other locations in Europe. It is impossible to know whether the work of the Controlling Committee and the "model occupation" meme established early on had an effect on this restraint, or whether it was based on the demilitarized nature of Guernsey and continued German belief that Islanders were potential allies that they had "liberated" from British tyranny. Of course, there also was not an armed resistance, and had there been, any deaths of Germans would likely have been followed by the hostage executions that were already being threatened behind the scenes.

Still, spontaneous acts of violence were bound to happen. The type of deference necessary for constructing an opaque "veil" of willing subordination,[70] behind which rhetorical acts of subversion may be refined and enacted, is not natural to a free people. It requires "controlling what would be a natural impulse to rage, insult, anger, and the violence that such feelings prompt."[71] Sitting on such feelings was particularly challenging for Guernseymen and women, noted for their stubborn independence, and now forced to deal with sometimes belligerent German soldiers. Even self-defense was not a viable excuse for returned aggression. In 1942, Bill Warry described yet "another" young Guernseyman sentenced to two years in prison for having struck a German soldier. Rumor was rife that the act was one of self-defense after the German struck the young man first and was continuing to hit him with his belt. "*But*," Bill emphasized, "you are not allowed to strike a German soldier, even under any conditions."[72]

Bill Warry was able to observe for himself a "nasty incident" that occurred right outside his shop, coincidentally on Hitler's birthday in April 1944. That morning a German officer came riding a pedal cycle through the Arcade, and the policeman on duty, Officer Smith, held up his hand to signal that cycling was not allowed. The German dismounted and "let out full tilt with his fist on the policeman's jaw," stood yelling in rage over the felled policeman, took down the policeman's badge number, and left. Bill worried about what would happen in days to come, but noted, "The constable took the blow & said nothing. It's fatal to retaliate." It is obvious that Bill considered Constable Smith wise in his restraint, although it was "damned hard to get your face punched in a main thoroughfare when simply carrying out your & their orders."[73] Being involuntarily intermingled with German soldiers—surrounded by them at work, in town, even in their own homes—Islanders would have ample practice over five years learning to swallow feelings of rage and humiliation.

In addition to individual and spontaneous aggression, the Germans seem to have made plans to counter a second form of physical resistance. From the beginning, it is clear that they anticipated small acts of sabotage as one of the few overt activities that Islanders could take to impede the German war effort. Under conditions of clear domination, such as existed with the unarmed population in Guernsey, any efforts by individuals or small bands of activists to attack property would be "anonymous and usually nocturnal." In some situations, small acts of property destruction could remain disguised, chalked up to natural causes or incompetence by those in power. In those cases, the secret hand at work remains entirely invisible. The advantage of such acts, if accomplished with the necessary "prudence and secrecy,"[74] is that they deny the dominant the smooth running of the machinery of control without ruffling the placid surface of power and triggering reprisals. Carefully conducted, sabotage and tampering are effective means for the dominated to assert some measure of their identity, signaling to peers that their forced compliance with power does not reflect a true self.[75]

More often, however, the sabotage is detected but the saboteur is not caught. For the Islanders, the danger was that a momentary sense of empowerment came at the cost of the Germans reinforcing their power base through discipline. Reprisals against the population at large would then further establish the Germans' ownership mentality and the right to control inherent in the Occupation situation. Small acts of sabotage are unlikely to "destabilize" a system overall, but they provide a legitimate excuse for the dominant to exercise their power.[76] It was, in other words, a dangerous game to play, and the Islanders knew it. Detectable acts of sabotage also serve as generally ineffective means of resistance because they are, in Jordan's words, "*expected* rather than *confounding* behaviors."[77]

Small acts of sabotage seemed to come in waves, another indication of the contagious nature of resistance. Ambrose Robin quietly heralded the advent of one major spate of sabotage in January 1941 when he described a young workman, believed to be about twenty-five years of age, who had been detained for cutting German telephone wires.[78] It is difficult to know whether this small incident inspired the person who cut German field telephone cable near the airport in March of that year, but this second act would be commented on by almost all of the diarists. On March 18, 1941, close to half of the front page was taken up with a special *Bekanntmachung* from the Feldkommandant in the largest type used to that point. It informed the Island that due to the severing of a telephone cable in the St. Martin area of Guernsey, the curfew would be fixed from 9 P.M. to 7 A.M. (moved back from 10 P.M.). The second part of the order was ominous: starting the next night, sixty Guernseymen from eighteen to forty-five years of age would be designated to perform guard duty during the night hours.[79]

Ken Lewis learned of this order when he reached work that day, and described himself as "dismayed to hear that some stupied [*sic*] person" had committed this useless act of sabotage. Partly, his concern was that the new curfew hours meant they had to be home before darkness fell. He quickly realized that since the civilian guards would be comprised of men of every class, chosen from the parishes of St. Martin, St. Andrew, St. Peter, St. Saviour, and Forest, he would be among this group that was set to guard the telephone wires at the water tower and the airport. He reported for duty on the Forest Road on a terrible night of wind and pelting rain, but fortunately he was considered a reserve man and allowed to go home.[80]

Dorothy Higgs saw this guard duty in a darker light than did Ken. One concern was that the men were on guard without arms (or, Dorothy believed, "even a torch"), which seemed to indicate that they were not seriously intended to stand guard. Rather, what made this a "pretty rotten job" in Dorothy's estimation was that "it actually means they are hostages and if any more damage is done they will be for it."[81] There is an excellent chance that Dorothy was correct, and that these men would have stood proxy for the entire Island and faced the same treatment meted out to hostages on the Continent had further acts of sabotage occurred during their time on duty. The States seemed very aware that these men were hostages more than guards, and an emergency meeting was held, with Jurat Leale to address the situation.[82]

Whether most Islanders grasped the full implications of the situation or not, the condemnation for the anonymous saboteur was fairly universal. Winifred Harvey considered the whole thing "very foolish," because it was ineffective in accomplishing anything concrete, and everyone was punished for the act of a single person.[83] Elizabeth Doig was still more condemning of the act, although her sole focus seemed to be on the disruption of the 10 P.M.

curfew, which had only been in force for four nights when set back as punishment for the act of sabotage. Elizabeth described the act more in terms of a prank, and its result as "most disappointing & we feel very sore about it & trust the delinquents will be caught & punished."[84]

In fact, the act seemed so heedless of consequences that many doubted it to be a case of determined sabotage at all. Jack Sauvary considered the perpetrators could be not necessarily resistance activists, but "probably irresponsible boys."[85] Reverend Ord went one further and floated the concept that it might have been "a disgruntled German who did it for a malicious prank." He then hypothetically removed the act not only from the hands of Islanders but also from human hands entirely: "The Island is enmeshed in telephone cables now, many of which are carelessly slung from branch to branch of trees OR SHRUBS AND HEDGES. Those from trees could almost touch the heads of passers-by, while those on hedges etc. could be dislodged very easily by accident."[86]

In these accounts, we are able to see the developing community attitude toward resistance as it was being constructed. In general, Islanders held instrumental acts of resistance, those that were not predominantly symbolic but intended to have an actual impact on the functioning of the German war machine, to a higher standard before granting their support. The underlying attitude was very practical. If these acts had been large enough to have a real impact on the Germans and had constituted a coordinated uprising against the Occupation, approbation for the acts most likely would have been widespread among the braver of the civilians. Dorothy Higgs revealed Islanders' willingness to revolt in her response to an August 1944 rumor that British leaflets would soon detail the precise resistance desired by the British government. Dorothy was more than eager for these marching orders "telling us what to do. And we'll do it!"[87] But small actions that had no particular goal and yet could bring down such mass reprisals as hostage executions were viewed as stupid, irresponsible, or even childish acting out.

What *did* pass muster with Islanders was the clever, invisible sabotage undetected by the Germans as deliberate yet lauded quietly in civilian circles. Some of these *sotto voce* acts were minor but delightful in the telling. One classic example, related by Rev. Ord, involved a tomato grower who had been ill-treated continuously by the Germans and determined to pay them back in kind. His tomatoes were designated to be shipped to Germany. Knowing this, he told his packers as they were busy at their task, "Give the lower layers a bit of a press down before you put in the top layer."[88] This is the type of performed compliance, masking personal acts of small subversions, that constitutes effective resistance among the powerless. As far as the Germans would ever know, the grower had complied with their demands, and any damage to the tomatoes would be read as accidental. The hidden transcript, passed orally from person to person, revealed the truth to those privy to it, providing a point of commonality and counter-reading of apparently compliant acts.

Certain individual acts of serious sabotage came to light, and in those cases, the person responsible for them took the punishment and received the admiration of Islanders. Ambrose Robin was concerned for a man named Ferbrache, compulsorily employed in the cleaning of ammunition, who did "something to the fuses of shells to make them immune and damaged clips of machine gun cartridge belts to cause gamming [*sic*] in the guns."[89] Other secret sabotage was conducted so subtly that its impact never came to light until long after the Occupation. When I talked with the resister Alf Williams in 2003 and 2004, he casually mentioned that one job he had at the airport afforded him a chance to work around and on the airport runway. Alf used the opportunity to surreptitiously dig on the runway, hoping to put enough small holes, pits, and ruts in the runway surface to cause German airplanes to crash upon landing. Telling me of one German plane that touched down, could not get a sure footing on the runway, and skidded off in a resounding crash, Alf's eyes sparkled; he laughed loudly and said, "I knew that one was mine!"[90]

One of the physical means of resistance for the otherwise powerless is simply flight. Leaving the onerous situation is a practical way to exempt oneself from the daily tyrannies and dangers, large and small, that constitute domination. Flight is also a rhetorical form of resistance because it speaks loudly to the truth of conditions under the power structure. In more mundane situations—office staff, fast-food workers, graduate students trapped in the petty dictatorship of a harshly enforced pecking order—leaving exists as the difficult final option. When a company or university begins to hemorrhage its people, it will be taken as an unmistakable sign that complaints about conditions were accurate. Yet escape to freedom, fleeing a situation of armed control despite the dangers of the passage, has still more to say to an external audience. The number of slaves willing to take their chances on the Underground Railroad, sometimes leaving family behind in a bid for freedom, belied the Southern rhetoric of contented slaves under the benign care of paternal owners. The missing person is a lacuna in the community landscape, whose very absence is read by the dominant, the dominated, and those external to the power situation.

For a fishing community adept at navigating the sea surrounding their Island home, Guernseymen could not help but be tempted to flee to a freedom that was so tantalizingly near. It would be a daunting passage. Managing to get past the mined beaches, eluding the armed guards watching those beaches, and navigating the treacherous tides and rocks was only part of the journey. The English Channel could be unforgiving of small craft, so it took an adept sailor and a good quantity of luck to make it all the way to England from Guernsey. Joe Mière conducted research on the number of escapees from the Channel Islands during Occupation. There were 225 total efforts to escape, with 156 of those making the attempt from Jersey. The higher number of escapees from Jersey makes considerable sense, not simply because of the larger population of that Island. During the final year following D-day, as food and fuel conditions worsened, Jersey Islanders had a great desire to reach the free coast of France, only 22 kilometers (or 12 nautical miles) away, and bring information about the dire conditions in the Channel Islands.[91]

The earliest escapes came in July 1940 immediately after the Occupation commenced in both Guernsey and Jersey, when events were still highly confused and before the Germans were fully in control of the beaches and waterways. Louise Willmot states that over half of the escapees from Guernsey slipped off the Island in the first two days. These were primarily family groups that included far more women than would be typical of later escapes. Although Willmot mentions that the Controlling Committee officially condemned these escapes,[92] they were treated for the most part like post hoc evacuations, not meriting comment from the diarists or retaliation from the German officials. It took until early September of that year before an escape occurred that set the pattern for German response. This was the escape of eight men, described in the last chapter, whose success was detailed in British leaflets dropped by the RAF.[93]

The Germans immediately retaliated, forbidding fishing and publishing an edict that all boat owners had to take their boats to the St. Peter Port harbor within the next two days. Because boating was banned, the fishermen had to wheel, haul, or otherwise transport their boats over land through the narrow roads and the hilly terrain. Winnie described boats coming from the north, the west, and from Torteval, the far southern tip of Guernsey, and wrote of the lorries and horse vans being used to help transport the very big boats. "Poor men," Winnie sympathized, "their living is gone, also our fish."[94] The shortfall of food was problematic, but the follow-up edict by the Germans was potentially devastating. In the *Star* on September 28, a warning appeared from the Germans that a further escape might well result in all of the male population of Guernsey being deported to France.

The response to this escape and the resulting reprisals varied, but was generally negative. Kitty considered the loss of fish (and, for the fishermen, the loss of a livelihood) to be a "blot on the name" of the escapees. She understood that they had received quite the reception in England, but anticipated that their reception in the Island following the war might be another matter. In light of the potential impact to her Island home, Kitty only hoped that no one else was "contemplating such an unpatriotic move." Patriotism was thus characterized as choosing loyalty to the States and the Island population over a grandiose move that might seem patriotic and resistant to some, but achieved little past the self-interest of the men who escaped.[95]

Commentary on this first major escape was overwhelmingly negative, most agreeing with a letter from Sherwill in the paper that it was a "crime against Guernsey."[96] Elizabeth Doig wrote in her prim way that "It seems such a pity when so far we have had the reputation of behaving well."[97] Jack Sauvary took a more light-hearted approach to the disturbing possibility that all men would be deported if there was a repeat occurrence: "The women would get a grand time looking after things here!"[98] For all of Jack's whistling past the graveyard, the situation was hardly humorous now that there was a threat of mass deportation as retaliation for future escapes. The Islanders held their collective breath whenever it appeared that someone had slipped off the Island for England. Rumor went around in June 1942 that some men had left in a fishing boat. Simply the rumor was enough to shut down fishing while the Germans investigated. "Happily for us," Bert Williams reported, "there was only a punt missing."[99]

Guernseymen and women still faced retaliation during this same time for the young men who had attempted an escape from Jersey with photographs of some military interest. One boy drowned in the attempt and the other two were arrested.[100] At this point, all cameras and photographic equipment were called in for all of the Islands, although Ken Lewis bluntly wrote, "However I have resolved that my camera will not be given in on any account."[101] Bert Williams was tart about the need for everyone to suffer for "some silly fools."[102] But if Guernsey Islanders were not happy about the subsequent punishment, it does not mean that they would cooperate with the authorities to prevent escapes. Gertie Corbin mentions that George Le Couteur had been ordered to take a boat and pursue the men who had supposedly sailed from Guernsey at this time. To which news, she appended a telling "No fear."[103]

The escapees also were dangerous to the Islanders left behind because they became a source of "leaks" of the hidden transcript. As a former part of the general populace, they were privy to all of the tricks and methods used to circumvent and undercut authority. This unveiling of disguised resistance occurred with two Guernseymen, named Lawrence and Bichard, who escaped in fall of 1942, picking up two French girls standing in wait for them on the rocks at the north shore of the Island. They only had a 17-foot boat, so it was assumed for some time that they had drowned. However, after drifting for fifteen hours, they were sighted by an RAF aircraft and picked up. Guernsey learned of their safety when the BBC broadcast an interview with the four escapees. Some of the material divulged in this interview was benign enough. One girl told of the lack of food and secondhand nature of the clothing, of her opinion that German morale was low, and that wireless sets were confiscated, adding—with some drama—that the death penalty was imposed for listening to English news.[104] Then, one girl heedlessly gave an important game away by mentioning that billeted Germans were allowing their civilian hosts to listen to London. Rev. Ord described this as a "wretched blunder on the part of the B.B.C.," because Müller would now be eager to end this particular leak of outside information. Ord could not understand why news of the escape was broadcast at all, because the Germans might well have considered those involved to have perished in transit. Knowing of their success at reaching England could only bring reprisals to prevent similar attempts. But it was far worse to have news of secret listening ploys broadcast for the Germans to hear. Ten days later, Ord found out just how devastating such revelations could be when he rang up the Chilcotts asking to hear a Churchill speech on the set belonging to Eduard, the friendly German boy billeted with them. Trixie Chilcott replied with the news, "It's DEAD!" Eduard had been forced to remove the wireless from his billet now that the Germans knew that such sets were potential sources of information for civilians. "So much," wrote Ord, "for the pundits of the B.B.C. who divulged the remarks of that fool of a French girl."[105]

Perhaps the BBC was given some feedback as to the effect they were having by their broadcasts, because one year later, when two men and three women escaped from Guernsey, Dorothy Higgs did not expect to hear of their safe arrival through the wireless. This escape was conducted by two fishermen, Courbet and Le Page, who picked up their wives and a male friend from the rocks at Bordeaux and took advantage of thick fog and a favorable tide to make a run for it. Winifred Harvey said that little was discussed in the Island except this escape for several days, with two highly divided opinions emerging. Some felt that this was a "brave and courageous act," and that it was the duty of those imprisoned in Guernsey to take whatever important information they might have to the government. On the other hand, many believed it to be "disgracefully selfish" for those with an opportunity to flee and "save their own skins" to do so at the cost of greater peril for the 23,000-plus Islanders left behind. Winnie counted herself in the second category, especially after learning that all the relatives of the escapees, including elderly parents, had been thrown in jail. Stanley Noel, the manager of Bougourd's Garage, had also been seized for aiding and abetting the escape. Of course, the usual curtailment of fishing occurred, and the beaches were closed off.[106]

Most people seem to have agreed with Winnie's reluctant condemnation of the escapees. Bert Williams was quite simply livid. The escapees "should be shot for doing it." The closing of the beaches would be a blow for the children, but the loss of fish for a community with only a fortnightly meat ration was serious business. Bert declared that the Islanders were all afraid to look in the papers for fear of the next order of retaliation, and "those people [the escapees] are no heros [*sic*] anyway, they have done nothing to be proud of."[107] For Peter and Kitty Bachmann, who spent a sad evening with Stan Noel before he was sent for internment in a German camp—the authorities not accepting his denials that he overhauled the engine of the boat—the personal consequences of escape were very real. Stan was weak and demoralized, having already been severely treated during inquisition, and it was with deep concern that the Bachmanns parted with him in the morning. Little wonder, then, that Kitty viewed the "escapade" of the five escapees to be "daring but thoughtless."[108]

The value of the escapees' information seems to have been the major determinant of Islander support, or lack thereof, for escapes.[109] Ken Lewis applied this same standard in assessing the escape, believing it to be "a selfish act" of little importance, and noting that the Secret Service "were probably as much aware of the fortifications as the ones that got away." Thus, it was with some satisfaction that Ken reported news from England that this particular group received a "cold reception" when they landed, that they regretted their actions, and "would return tomorrow if at all possible." Ken is not clear about his source of information, and this ending to the story of escape resembles the type of rumor meant to warn others and influence their actions. Quite likely, this tale of the regretful escapees grew as it provided a norming device, designed to discourage acts that endangered the community.[110]

Escapes are active and dramatic, falling in more decidedly with notions of what constitutes resistance.[111] Most Islanders were willing to suffer the consequences if the escape served a good enough purpose. And we can see a distinct shift in attitudes toward escape during the final year, when conditions had deteriorated and it was unclear whether England knew the full extent of Guernsey's plight. In November 1944, pilot Fred Noyon and a younger man named Endicott had a permit to go ormering and they simply did not return. Pilot Noyon lived in St. Sampson and had spent the war years as a fisherman. He was also one of the oldest and most adept of the Guernsey pilots and for many years had ferried the *Island Queen*, trading to London twice a week from Guernsey. Winnie Harvey described him as knowing "every tide, rock, and passage of these waters." This knowledge meant, of course, that Noyon had every opportunity to leave whenever it suited him, but he resisted the impulse. He made clear over the course of the Occupation that he would only leave when the situation was desperate and his escape could do some good. As food and fuel were dangerously low and winter approaching, now was the time to take the information about conditions to London.[112]

After attending an urgent States meeting where the food shortages were made clear, as were the demands by the Germans for more tons of potatoes than the States even had, Noyon decided to act. "This time," as Kitty Bachmann put it, it was "with our blessing."[113] Ken Lewis called it "the best thing that could have happened," and Bert Williams asserted, "They will be able to tell a tale when they reach the mainland." Winnie Harvey simply stated, "Our hopes are fixed upon their mission." Noyon and Endicott were picked up by an American patrol boat, taken to Cherbourg, and from there to London. The decision to send aid may already have been made, but the evidence of Noyon and Endicott combined with that of some intrepid Jersey escapees would have reinforced it.[114] This Islanders' approbation extended to other escapees during the final desperate year, and when word of escapes came, many echoed Bert Williams's words, "Good luck to them."[115]

Another aspect of the body in absence is the hiding of those sought by the authorities. We have already seen the efforts made by family and friends to shelter British commandos during the early period of Occupation, and the acknowledgment that such efforts could not be sustained indefinitely in an island the size of Guernsey. This difficulty was particularly true with the widespread billeting that interwove a German presence into the parishes and homes of the Island. However, we have indications that such efforts took place despite the dangers. Rev. Ord described in July 1943 that a friend had a set of buildings on his property pulled down by the Germans. In the ruins, the Germans found a young French boy who had managed to slip away from the Organization Todt. Of course, the farmer was immediately suspected of sheltering and feeding the boy. Ord followed this account with a story of another friend with a "similar experience." In this case, the friend was approached by a Frenchman who had been brought to the Island by force but who was refusing to work for the Germans. For a considerable period of time, the Guernseyman fed and sheltered the Frenchman. Then an acquaintance, "whether deliberately or by lack of caution," gave the game away, and at the time of Ord's writing, the benefactor was awaiting space to serve his time in prison. As Ord put it, "One is not allowed to be a Good Samaritan."[116]

Another instance of hiding occurred in July 1944 and was publicly heralded by an order in the papers. Beside the photograph of Graham Buckingham, a well-known Guernseyman of St. Peter Port, was the news that Buckingham had escaped his guards at the harbor while on his way to serve a period of imprisonment on the Continent for theft. Reportedly, the word "theft" was really the pilfering of German supplies as an act of resistance. The order further stated that Buckingham was, in the quaint construction of German-written English, "holding himself in concealment," and the public was admonished that giving him food and shelter would result in "the severest penalty."

Of course, the entire Island already knew of this daring escape and how the authorities had already searched the house of Miss Cherry of Elm Grove, "his young lady," and bullied even distant relatives of the man. Rev. Ord expressed the Island viewpoint: "We all wish him a successful hiding till we are released." Despite the odds against him, Buckingham managed to remain concealed until January 1945 when, while staying with relatives, he was cut badly trying to uncork a bottle. Imprisonment on the Continent was not then an option, and after four weeks in the Emergency Hospital, he served his time in the Guernsey prison until Liberation. The Buckingham case was a rare exception to the near impossibility of secreting individuals in Guernsey for an extended period of time. With the food shortages and an Occupation that stretched on for years, it was a form of resistance that few could even attempt.[117]

The Germans were exquisitely sensitive not simply to physical absence, but to the dangers of mass physical presence. Many of their orders reveal a fear of possible group actions, combined with a need to keep the Islanders individuated and thus easier to surveil and control. These concerns are seen in the ban on organizations and meetings, and even in the regulations guiding response in the movie theaters. From the fall of 1940, notices were posted outside the Gaumont and other Island theaters that read, "Demonstrations of displeasure or applause will lead to the closure of this place of entertainment."[118] This German awareness that bodies en masse are less easily controlled makes the incident of the *Charybdis* funeral more surprising. On October 23, 1943, HMS *Charybdis* was sunk off the coast of Guernsey, resulting in the death of 464 men, the largest loss of life in the Channel during the entire war.[119] The 107 survivors were rescued by other boats, but soon bodies of the sailors started to wash up on the Guernsey beaches.[120]

For whatever reason, the Germans decided to accord full military honors, with Union Jack–draped coffins and a firing squad, to these members of the Royal Navy and Royal Marines. Guernsey turned out in vast numbers to Foulon Cemetery for this rare opportunity to pay respect to their dead sailors, with Islander attendance estimated in excess of 5,000. The over nine hundred wreaths brought by the Guernsey populace were so remarkable that Islanders spent the next week going back to the cemetery to see them piled on the sailors' graves.[121] Yet the most amazing scene was at the funeral itself. Bill Warry found it "strange to see the enemy there, and also the civilians, some of our retired Generals, etc., also to hear the German artillery firing away in the distance, a thrilling scene."[122]

Ken Lewis, who attended with some other clerks from the office, could not see much because of the crowd. He did note that the German commander of the firing party said "Furs Vaterland gefallen" (For the fallen for the Fatherland) before giving the order to fire the three volleys in honor of the dead. Ken was disappointed in the attitude of the crowd, believing that "many treated it as a football match rather than as paying tribute to the dead."[123] What Ken sensed as the "us versus them" nature of a football match was the patriotic fervor that was being engendered in the crowd and that swirled on the edge of physical demonstration.

Restraint in making resistance public is often determined by "tactical prudence." This discretion, however, may easily be lost when the subjugated are granted the sheltering anonymity of a crowd.[124] It was a potentially dangerous moment to combine a crowd of that size, grief over the loss of the young men, bottled-up patriotism, and the enemy responsible for the deaths of the sailors within reach. If the Germans wanted to display their higher culture and receive respect from the civilian populace, they miscalculated the likely Islander response. It is notable that they subsequently banned the civilian populace from funerals for the twenty-nine sailors whose bodies later washed up on the Guernsey beaches.[125]

Finally, and perhaps oddly, the resistance of body rhetoric is not just the absence of the body in flight and in hiding, or the potential for bodily action en masse, but also the refusal of the body in compliance. Although the primary survival technique among the Island's subjugated population may have been the kind of overt compliance sheltering covert subversion described thus far, there was also a place for noncompliance in their repertoire of resistance. Just as silence may serve at times as a form of verbal criticism,[126] both noncompliance and hypercompliance provide an unstated commentary on the actions demanded by the powerful. To decline to act in the face of an order to do so is as challenging to the structure of power as a refusal to speak when information is demanded. And it is just as dangerous.

Some of the scofflaw mentality in Guernsey concerned minor infractions and served more as an assertion of will than as anything effecting a physical change. Still, small refusals were vital to communal identity among the Islanders, a fact that the Germans acknowledged in their desire to crack down on even minor flouting of their orders. Some infringements allowed the Islanders to see themselves as superior to their masters and were designed to confound the Germans' understanding of their civilian possessions. For example, when the sirens went off one morning in November 1941, the civilians on the street in St. Peter Port simply went about their business unheeding. The Germans had ordered that whenever an alarm went off, the population was to take shelter immediately. The Islanders intuited that it was merely a drill, a "sham invasion" that the Germans were practicing, and refused en masse to play their role. In one sense, it disrupted the reality of the drill, and the presence of civilians in the streets of St. Peter Port and at the harbor could not help but impede the smooth running of the German rehearsal. On the other hand, it allowed the civilians to assert their lack of fear and willingness to take the consequences if the invasion had been real.

As with many of these small infractions, the symbolic value was greater than the practical outcome. The Germans were highly irritated by this lack of compliance and stopped people in St. Peter Port and on the Front up to St. Sampson to hand out fines of 2s. and 4s. 2d., to be paid on the spot. Those without money on them had their names taken down for later court action.[127] This instant retaliation actually encouraged the Islanders to believe that they were having an effect. A year later, Ken Lewis described the sounding of the raid sirens, a replication of nonresponse by the civilian populace, and the satisfying common understanding that "the German authorities were annoyed."[128]

This casual scofflaw mentality comes out in various accounts of public as well as private infractions. Young people had "cycle parties," sometimes with as many as fifty in a group, casually violating the injunction forbidding riding two abreast, and simply taking the fines and court appearances in stride.[129] "Defeating" the curfew was a common game. But being caught out after curfew was not a relatively benign affair. The lovely fictional account *The Guernsey Literary and Potato Peel Pie Society* uses as a plot device the quick-witted establishment of a literary society as an excuse by a group of people stopped by the Germans after curfew. In the book, the group paid a small fine and listed their society membership at the commandant's office; with the commandant declaring himself "a lover of literature—might he, with a few like-minded officers, sometimes attend meetings?"[130] What is perfectly acceptable to establish the plot in fiction may give a false concept of the seriousness of violating curfew, especially by a group of people during a time when societies were banned and nocturnal sabotage was a potential problem for the Germans.

The seriousness with which the Germans treated curfew violations did not prevent their occurrence when conditions permitted, particularly by young people. Following D-day, the Germans were kept very busy manning the gun positions on the coast of the Island, because they anticipated an invasion as the next step in the Allied plans. For the first time since the Occupation, the roads were relatively free of a German presence, and young people were quick to take advantage by walking or riding their bicycles to their homes after curfew, singing or laughing as if to court arrest.[131] It was an enactment of a change in fortune, a short-lived but defiant expression of popular belief that the war had turned decisively in favor of the Allies, and their imprisonment must soon come to an end.

Individuals would test in more serious ways the power of refusal. In complying with an attic-cleaning order in 1941, Dr. Dick Gibson found a revolver and 150 rounds of ammunition, which he subsequently reported. As his reward for compliance, he was immediately arrested and questioned by the Germans, apparently miffed that such a stash of arms had evaded earlier detection: "You English have no discipline. You do not understand how to obey orders." Before signing his statement detailing the discovery, Dr. Gibson noticed that there was a paragraph at the bottom stating that in the future he would be loyal to the Third Reich. Gibson flatly refused to sign. After considerable argument back and forth, the Germans relented and removed the paragraph, allowing Gibson to simply sign his account of finding the revolver and ammunition. Such refusal to sign the full statement by the average Islander would have brought down harsh punishment, but Winifred Harvey believed Gibson to be "too useful and clever a surgeon" for the Germans to incarcerate.[132]

Hypercompliance with the Germans' own orders was a form of resistance that is more impervious to punishment. It is difficult for those in power to publicly bring to task those who are complying with rules and regulations, even if that scrupulous compliance with the letter of the law rebounds against those who made the law in the first place.

Rev. Ord was good at such games in his gentle way. Hypercompliance provided a means of comical reprisal, as when Ord was fined a mark by a passing pair of German police for his home not being sufficiently blacked out. At the close of the interview, Ord sweetly told them that he would now be in complete compliance, turned out all the lights, shut the door, and allowed the pair "to stumble their way to the gates." "Perhaps," he mused, "they might get tangled up in the bed of roses that lined the pathway."[133] The greater satisfaction was in the subsequent relating of this story to others.

Pure stubborn refusal to comply was sometimes much admired and fit with the Guernsey Islanders' view of themselves as "Donkeys." Elizabeth Doig, very afraid and condemning of most resistance early on, became gradually more radicalized over the course of the Occupation. When the Germans called in bicycles, the necessary form of transportation for Islanders, many complied, but others took no notice of the demand. One of Elizabeth's friends ignored the notice and was sent a letter asking the reason for her lack of compliance. She replied, "My reason is that I will do nothing to help my King's enemies." Elizabeth wrote, "I admire her spirit."[134]

The experiences of two women will serve as examples of overt and covert refusal to obey German orders. One woman has been recognized in subsequent years as a resister, her bravery and the consequences of her resistance honored. The second woman, although the hidden purpose of her actions has been acknowledged, is not generally considered as a resister. Her actions, however, are more in line with the special nature of resistance in the Island during Occupation. Marie Ozanne, a native Guernseywoman, was a major in the Salvation Army who had spent fifteen years with the organization's work in England, Belgium, and France. She had returned to the Island in March 1940 for what could be considered a working holiday and a visit to her parents, planning to return to the Continent in September. Events of the Occupation overtook her and forced her to remain in Guernsey. The Salvation Army was one of the first organizations singled out by the Germans, although it is difficult to know why they drew special attention. Coupled with their polemical nature, their church militant style may well have been the reason that the Germans immediately banned their wearing of uniforms and holding of open-air meetings. By January 1941, the Salvation Army was ordered to permanently suspend all meetings and to close their buildings: Clifton Hall, perched high and visibly over St. Peter Port; Nocq Road at St. Sampson; and L'Islet in Vale.

Marie Ozanne was devastated by this suppression and protested immediately in dramatic fashion. On the Sunday following the closing of the buildings, she stood outside against the door of one building as a silent protest. She also was seen often in town carrying around her Salvation Army bonnet in her hand in protest, and even appeared at Grange Lodge in full uniform with badges. At that point, Inspector Sculpher was ordered to confiscate her uniform and other articles symbolic of her Salvation Army work. Marie wrote several letters to the Feldkommandant in protest of the closure of the halls, threatening to open a new building in St. Sampson. Other letters followed in August 1942 protesting the mistreatment of Organization Todt workers near her home. These letters and Marie's continued efforts to preach in the streets were the tipping point for the German officials. Marie was arrested, and the Germans ordered that she be medically examined as to her sanity. While pronouncing her as "fully responsible," they described her as a "religious maniac" seeking martyrdom.

In October, the proceedings against her were halted and she was released from prison. The ostensible reason was that she was delusional and in the thrall of "religious fantasies," and the Germans were planning simply to ignore her in the future. This excuse for her early release is quite transparent. Marie's health had broken down under mistreatment in prison, and the Germans wanted neither the trouble to care for her nor to have a Christian martyr on their hands. She never regained her health and died in February 1943.[135] Perhaps the only way for the Germans to understand Marie Ozanne's Christian efforts for others was through a frame of mental illness, or perhaps this was purely an attempt to nullify her resistant actions. Marie would be posthumously awarded the Salvation Army's Order of the Founder in 1947, and she provides a clear example of determined public resistance in Guernsey.

Now let us compare this overt resistance that called down immediate punishment by the Germans to a piece of covert action more in line with the overall nature of Channel Island resistance. The woman in question is, by now, very familiar to us in her attitude and actions. Winifred Harvey was an ardent leader of the Girl Guides (the British equivalent of the Girl Scouts), which was established in 1910. Rosemary Booth describes a photograph of Winnie taken in 1921, in which she is attired in the uniform of senior guiders, complete with its gauntlet gloves and the slouch hat of the day, accompanying a group of St. Martin's Brownies to an Island visit by Princess Mary. In the 1930s, she became camp advisor to the Island

Guides, and in 1939 became Island commissioner.[136] Winnie believed in the Guides, devoted herself to the cause, and in the first fall of Occupation would have an opportunity to prove that devotion.

Winnie learned in late November that the main Guide room had been pillaged. She was primarily concerned for the colors of her troop and that of the Câtel company that were stored there. Winnie headed out on her bicycle to rescue the colors, but realized that she could not take the most direct route home with them. The order was out banning meetings, and specifically forbidding flags and badges. If she went past Government House with the sets of flags, and particularly the poles, she would likely be stopped and commanded to unfurl the Union Jacks right there in the road. She opted to go by King's Road, but almost ran straight into an armed guard at the end of Brock Road who was stopping cars and quizzing passersby. Like an escaping felon, she turned her bike around and mimed a casual walk away from him, seeking another route home and successfully completing her rescue mission.[137] This emergency action was the one explicit move by this cagey woman who, from this point, led an underground effort to maintain the Guides leadership structure through the long years of Occupation.

During the same time as the colors rescue, Winnie held her first Guide "tea party." This tea party and subsequent "socials" were actually Guide meetings, carefully designed to circumvent the order against meetings. Unlike other clubs and societies that tried to challenge the ban on meeting, the Guides adopted from the start a public pose of having totally dissolved. In January 1941, an order appeared demanding that all associations and clubs, particularly ones with their headquarters in England, send in a full listing of their membership and property along with three copies of their rules. Winnie was "perturbed about this as the guides have kept very quiet," and despite friends' advice that she must comply, she took another tack. Going to the constables, Winnie claimed that the Guides were not meeting and had no desire to do so. The constables replied that since the Guides had not applied to meet originally, they were officially considered "washed out" and were not allowed to register now. This, Winnie wrote in her diary, "was exactly what we wanted." Other groups who tried a more direct tactic failed to survive. For example, the British Legion had continued to meet in their hall as a social club and now wanted to petition for permission to carry on in this manner. The Bailiff refused to put forward what was so transparent an evasion, fearing the grimmest of consequences were it discovered. So, the British Legion was forced to close.[138]

Thus, while other clubs and organizations were forced to close, and the direct resistance of Marie Ozanne could not rescue the Salvation Army, Winifred Harvey and the Guides leadership simply carried on meeting under a guise of socials and tea parties. Because they were clever enough to have publicly disbanded and never sought permission to continue, the Guides flew under the radar of German surveillance. Guide members would show up at a "party/social" in discreet groupings of one and two, with their Guide badges pinned under their collars. Winnie did not give details of what went on in these meetings past playing "progressive games" and singing, but she described one such party: "It went with a swing."[139] More important, it kept the Guide structure alive and allowed the Guides to discuss the young girls in the Island who would normally be in their troops during these years.

These meetings were much like Winnie's musical parties, conducted with "one eye on the gate all the time," but designed to skirt German restrictions without ever confronting them directly. As Winnie's friend Marie Louise said of one musical party, held despite mass evictions and the deportations to Germany, "It was a slap in the face of Hitler."[140] Winnie's efforts did not escape the Island Guides, who, toward the end of the Occupation, presented her with a plaque in gratitude for her work. The Guide Movement would later honor Winnie with a Gold Cross.[141] However, the subtlety, and indeed the very success, of her efforts kept Winifred Harvey from joining the pantheon of Occupation resisters. This lack of widespread acknowledgment has been the fate of much resistance in the Island because of its low-key and sheltered nature, but such covert strategies under domination make up in effectiveness what they lack in notoriety.

In the efforts of Winifred Harvey and other Guernsey Islanders, it is possible to see how simple normality becomes a dissident act. The ability to carry on with life, as unhampered as possible by the demands of those in power, is also a means of "foiling the dominant other's game in singular instances."[142] These individual acts are generally uncoordinated with others and only rarely surface into the public transcript as acknowledged resistance. Even for those who plan and carry out efforts to avoid compliance with an authoritarian regime, the very improvisational nature of their acts gives them a prank-like quality. Although the penalties for being caught might be harsh, few conducting these scofflaw moves would accord them the grand accolade of "resistance." But these dissidents were involved in a process of gradually regaining proprietorship over their own lives and slowly wresting back control from the dominant. It is not the drama of a flood, but simply the drip-by-drip wearing away of power, the most effective means to erode the control of the dominant over time. Such small acts of rebellion helped to structure the communal identity necessary for a heightened and overt opposition to power. Soon, however, resistance took on a more coordinated and semi-coordinated form, fashioned around the ethereal promptings of voices from out of the air.

RADIO GOES TO RESISTANCE

It was late November in 1943, and Ken Lewis came home from chapel to settle down by the fireside and read until nearly 9:00 P.M. Rousing himself from his cozy roost before curfew began at 9:00, Ken went with his dad by way of the main roads to Uncle Ed's house. The point of the journey was not a familial visit, but to listen on a now-illegal wireless set to a speech by Churchill. Ken's Uncle Alf and Aunt Glad were already there for the same purpose, having planned to spend the night so as not to be caught violating curfew on their long way home. They were the only other people let in on the dangerous secret that Uncle Ed had retained his wireless.

Ken and his dad stayed long enough to listen to the evening news after the speech. Then, slipping out the back door, they made their way in the dark night through Ed's back garden, over three fields, and into their own garden in order to dodge the German patrols that walked up and down the roads all night long. Ken delighted in the fact that they could use this alternate route home any time that they wanted to listen to the wireless after curfew.[143] But Uncle Ed was not the only source for illegal listening. Just over a month later, Ken went to hear the news at Herbie Taylor's house. On his way there, German patrols shone their lights on him twice, but never stopped him to ask where he was going. Ken considered it "quite a thrill" to sit with Mr. Taylor listening to the wireless "knowing full well the penalty for doing so, that is imprisonment and in some cases the death penalty."[144]

C. J. Rolo's 1943 book, *Radio Goes to War*, claimed that radio had added "the ether" as a fourth front to the land, sea, and air fronts of the previous war.[145] If the Nazis had pioneered the concept that radio could be an effective form of aggression, an additional "instrument of conquest" in the war, then it behooved the Allied nations to develop similar weapons.[146] In Rolo's view, the psychological battleground was finally entered on the evening of September 1, 1939, when the following words came over the airwaves, "This is the B.B.C. Home Service"—words that meant, Rolo dramatically continued, "that the B.B.C. had gone to war."[147] Radio became a vital instrument of rhetorical resistance during the Guernsey Occupation. Not only did broadcasts from the BBC inspire and coordinate individual acts of Island resistance, but secret retaining of wireless sets, listening to forbidden information, and the circulation of war news through newssheets passed hand to hand also became important resistant acts in themselves.

It is not overstating the case to claim that Guernsey resistance crystallized around the crystal sets that Islanders learned to build, and that the exchange of forbidden information established a permanent link between communication and resistance. In this section, I will first examine the V-campaign, the symbolic offensive inspired by British broadcasting, and the special twist two young Guernseymen gave to this campaign. Second, I will turn to the importance of wireless information itself, and the perilous steps that the Islanders would take to maintain their connection to the outside world. The stories of tricks to retain the wireless, and close calls in their detection; organized resistance groups that spread information from illegal sets; and anonymous letters exposing these sets to the Germans form the legacy of a micro-war waged behind the quiet façade of daily life.

As may already be clear, the Guernsey Islanders were very sensitive to symbols and symbolic display, so much so that efforts by the BBC to stimulate a symbolic resistance were likely to fall on fertile ground. Whenever opportunity presented itself, Islanders would make small personal displays to assuage their feelings of distance from Britain. Christmas, that most symbolic of seasons, filled with nostalgia and heightened longing for families on the mainland, brought forth particular efforts. Ambrose Robin could write on Christmas Day, 1941, about having dinner with relatives who "hoisted a Union Jack across the dining room; we therefore had our Xmas Dinner under the good old flag." They listened to the still-legal wireless while eating and heard a special Channel Islands broadcast, disappointing for its lack of a special message for those under Occupation. Then home for the King's speech and a special cobbled-together Christmas cake, decorated with a small Union Jack. This little cake was placed in the middle of the front-room window and, according to Robin, "attracted the attention of passing German soldiers."[148]

Reports of such relatively inconsequential private displays reveal a hunger for symbolic patriotism and participation from afar in the war effort. Sometimes these displays took on a more daring quality as they were made public in varying ways. Winnie described a window in town decked out in midsummer in bathing suits with red tops, blue trunks, and white belts, the display of patriotic colors filling the entire window. The genius of such an exhibition hinged on its deniability as having any real meaning should it be challenged by the Germans.[149] Equally daring was a display described by Rev. Ord in July 1943 as "in direct defiance of the Gestapo." It seems that the woman managing Roger's jewelry business in the Arcade took it upon herself, during the owner's absence, to construct a lovely window of a red cloth base, a blue vase, and ivory elephants. Ord lauded the courage it took to construct what was so plainly a patriotic display, and one speaking "a silent message to all who pass by." He continued, "Nor, has it been ignored," although it is unclear whether he meant by the Islanders or the German Field Police.[150]

It was into this heady mix of repressed patriotism and sensitivity to symbols that the BBC dropped the exhortations of Colonel Britton in 1941. Britain's aim was to establish a presence in the occupied countries, a means to offset the influence Germany had on the civilian population. The problem of how to do this effectively was of particular interest to Victor de Laveleye, the Belgian program organizer for the BBC. De Laveleye initially wanted to find a symbol that transcended language barriers in the bilingual country of Belgium that would lend itself to rapid writing on a wall at night, and that had an unmistakable meaning for the occupied nations. On January 14, 1941, de Laveleye broadcast the result of his deliberations:

> I am proposing to you as a rallying emblem the letter V, because V is the first letter of the words 'Victoire' in French, and 'Vrijheid' in Flemish . . . the victory which will give us back our freedom, the victory of our good friends the English. Their word for Victory also begins with V. As you see, things 'fit' all round. The letter V is the perfect symbol of Anglo-Belgian understanding.[151]

Thus, the V-campaign was born and "V's" sprouted overnight, chalked on walls and roads and practically any stationary object in the occupied countries of the Continent. One French listener to the BBC described them as "growing like mushrooms on the best sites."[152]

It would not be long before "Colonel Britton," a fictional entity actually voiced by Douglas Ritchie, a BBC news editor, gave further ideas for the V-campaign to English speakers in the occupied countries. He described how the Morse code for "V" of three dots and a dash could be used to knock on doors, to call for waiters in a village café, and to provide the rhythm for blacksmiths at work. He recommended Beethoven's Fifth Symphony with its "Fate Knocking at the Door" opening motif, and the BBC incorporated the Morse signal into their British broadcasts beginning on June 27, 1941.[153] A *Time* magazine article from July of that year rapturously recounted further ideas from the BBC campaign, such as sitting in cafés with legs stretched out in a V and leaving the knife and fork to form a V on the plate when the meal was done. Stopped clocks could be left at various locations with the hands set at five after eleven. The variations were quite endless, with the RAF reportedly getting into the act by flying over Europe in a V formation (a symbolic visual that would later form the end shot for the popular 1942 movie *Mrs. Miniver*).[154]

Although the V-campaign was seemingly intended for the Continent, 1941 became the summer of V's in Guernsey. Ken Lewis described the V-campaign as "in full swing" by early July, with everyone involved in giving a V knock of three soft and one hard raps, and with V's chalked and painted all over the Island. Because the Islanders still possessed their wireless sets, they heard the instructions from Colonel Britton directly and also the BBC's assessment that the campaign was working well in France. In de Laveleye's initial broadcast, he described the psychological impact the V-sign was intended to have on the occupier. When confronted with V's on every building and signpost and hearing the V sound constantly repeated around him, he was to "understand that he is surrounded, encircled, by an immense crowd of citizens eagerly awaiting his first moment of weakness, watching for his first failure."[155] This intended impact was not lost on Ken, who described the success of the French V-campaign "as it put the German soldiers on their nerves to be confronted with the Victory sign everywhere."[156]

The Guernsey populace was soon to find out just how nervous this small psychological war made the Germans. Despite understanding the purpose of the campaign, Islanders seemed surprised when the Germans reacted with swiftness and vehemence. Almost immediately after the first V's appeared on walls, signposts, and roads, the warning appeared in the paper over

Victor Carey's signature declaring that the letter "V" was considered a form of sabotage by the Germans, and the culprits needed to be discovered within 72 hours. If anything, this proof of impact encouraged the nocturnal graffiti artists, and three days later the infamous reward of £25 for information about perpetrators, discussed previously, appeared in the papers. To the average person, this appeared to be a massive overreaction. After all, the V-campaign was simply a more visible version of all the little symbols quietly exchanged between Islanders to keep their spirits up.

Because resistance in the Island favored the covert rather than the overt, there was also a sense that many of the V-campaigners were schoolboys enjoying the prank of quickly chalking or painting a V. This possibility dawned on the Germans as well. The German police descended upon the Castel School one day and carted off a dozen little boys around ten or eleven years of age to stand before the commandant. Their concerned parents gathered at the school in anxiety over their children, only to have the boys return in high style with their pockets laden with chocolates and even a cigarette or two for the parents. Some of the V-army were certainly children, for one young miscreant, Edmund Corbin, was caught in the act (literally "red-handed") by German soldiers. He had been hanging around watching some German sign-writers who had been busy that summer adding arrows, letters, and numbers to the many crossroads of Guernsey. In the inspiration of the moment, Edmund slipped up, picked up a paint brush, dipped it in red paint, and put up a quick V right beside a kneeling soldier. Of course the boy "bunked" before the soldier could rise, although he was caught by another soldier.[157]

Yet, the Germans were right that this was more than children's work, for some of the V's were chalked or painted above the reach of a child. When a Frenchman, de Guillebon, a grower in Grande Rocques near Cobo Bay, was caught chalking V's on military cars, he was given twelve months' hard labor.[158] The sixty-year-old de Guillebon had lived in Guernsey for so long that he was considered a Guernseyman, and he certainly seemed unusual in his audacity and sense of humor. Although he only had one leg, he got around quite handily, scrawling V's on various roadways. Most famously, he chalked V's on the cycle seats of a group of Germans who were taking some liquid refreshment in the hotel bars. The prank was successful, with the soldiers unaware of the new addition to their pants until pointed out by others.[159] De Guillebon's punishment, so out of sync with the seriousness of the offense, clearly sought to make an example out of him.

Most of the reactions by the Germans to the V-campaign were familiar parts of their repertoire, but then they took a tack that was truly a surprise. Rev. Ord wrote of the Islanders' "utter astonishment" to find the Germans, after their heavy-handed efforts to suppress the V-sign, suddenly painting V-signs on their billets and vehicles.[160] Many of the V's were further decorated with laurel wreaths, particularly the ones on official buildings such as the Inselkommandantur in Mount Row and one on the Grange Lodge. The extra artistic touch was presumably to improve the German efforts over the V's that continued to appear overnight around the Island.[161]

Quite soon, the papers produced an explanation that came straight from Goebbels's Propaganda Ministerium in Berlin with an article titled "'V'—GERMAN VICTORIES ON ALL FRONTS." This amazing little screed claimed that the V was actually the first letter of "Viktoria," which stood for victory: "Great Germany's Victory in the war is the victory of Europe in peace." Warming to its argument, the article described how V's were appearing everywhere as a sign of support for the Germans. Rev. Ord found particularly charming this sentence: "In Holland, thousands of people are walking about with the little "V"-brooch in orange colors." According to the article, a gigantic V-sign had been put up in Prague, and the main thoroughfare had changed its name from "Volkstrasse" to "Viktoria Street." Example after example was given of cities on the Continent choosing the V-sign to be "worn and displayed with the certain confidence of a German victory on all fronts."[162] The response of the Guernseymen, always a bit cynical and quick to enjoy irony, can be imagined. Ken Lewis snorted that the Germans taking V to mean Victory for them "was, of course, hopeless as in German the word victory is 'Sieg'" and was obviously adopted in sheer frustration over their helplessness to stop the V-campaign. If anything, it was proof that "the 'V' campaign must have been a great success."[163]

Rev. Ord found the entire attempt to co-opt the V fairly ludicrous, and puckishly observed, "We thus presume that, in future, those who must greet the Führer must now say: 'Viktoria Heil'!" Coming so close on the heels of a serious offer of reward money for anyone caught in such "sabotage," it was a source of "real entertainment"—unconscious on the part of the Germans—to see the soldiers busy with paint brushes in broad daylight, "hard at work everywhere" slapping V's on billets and vehicles. "Why sir," Ord's parishioners exclaimed to him, "they're sabotaging their own things!" Ord had the added pleasure of overhearing two girls as they rode their bicycles past him in front of the Government House gates: "'Look!' cried one, 'they've put a 'V' on the Governor's gatepost!' 'Well,' said her companion in a voice all could hear, 'The blooming babies!'" Ord further enjoyed the joke supplied by a friend of his who served as a telephone engineer for the States. All of the cars commandeered from Guernsey citizens for the use of the Germans had been stamped with "WH," meaning Wehrmacht Heeres, a reference to the army portion of the German forces. Now the rear mudguards bearing the "WH" also had a prominent "V" added to the letters. In a playful mood, Ord's friend asked one of the Germans with whom he dealt regularly concerning technical matters exactly what the letters stood for. The German replied, "Don't you know? It means Victory, Wehrmacht Heeres." "Oh," Ord's friend replied, I thought it meant 'Victory, What Hopes'!" Perhaps fortunately for Ord's friend, the German completely missed the irony.[164]

If Rev. Ord thought that the initial V-campaign had "surely turned the German's brain," there would be further evidence of this to come.[165] As might be imagined, those now feeling themselves to be part of a V-army were not easily dissuaded by a little poaching of the concept by the Germans. One morning, in front of the German V-signs in some locations, there appeared a large E, daubed in tar, turning the supposed victory symbol for the Reich into E V (English Victory). Notably one of these new versions appeared on a signpost near the Hotel Beaulieu, and on the hotel itself. At this point, the Germans seemed to lose track of their theme that V's equaled support for the Nazi cause and issued a new *Bekanntmachung* describing the "V-propaganda carried on by certain culprits of the civil population" as being "anti-German manifestations."[166]

Those living within 1,000 meters of the Hotel Beaulieu would have their wireless sets confiscated, and two men from the area were to stand sentry by three of the local German signposts. Ken Lewis's family was among those affected, and he was tapped both to supervise the collection of wireless sets and to stand as one of the sentries. Although it was irritating not to have the wireless in the house in this period when they were still legal, he had plenty of offers of places to listen. And, quite naturally, he found the sentry duty to be more interesting than anything else. His stint began at 1:00 A.M., and most of the time was spent sitting on a wall and chatting with his sentry partner, Owen Lucas. They only saw Germans, some on bicycles, some in cars, and two quite drunk who asked directions to the hotel. Because his replacement was a bit late, Ken was given a cigar to make up for the delay. Not a bad evening all around.[167]

As quickly as it appeared, the V-campaign apparently died away. Some maintain that the Germans were successful in draining the V of meaning, but that seems not to have been the case. Other clever V-campaign versions persisted, such as the notice in a St. Martin's window: "VVanted **R**abbits **A**nd **F**owls."[168] "V" and "RAF" were written on the car of a German doctor near the Victoria Hospital.[169] Ken Lewis heard of drawings that were pinned up overnight at one signpost showing a British Tommy holding a flag with a plain V on it. Underneath it read, "We don't want laurel leaves." A second drawing showed a Spitfire chasing a Messerschmitt. In the background was another Messerschmitt going down in flames, with the pilot of the plane saying, "Mein Gott, another VIKTORIA for the German Luftwasse!"[170] Undoubtedly, the Islanders did not lack for comebacks or the wherewithal to make the V-campaign their own. However, the impetus for the campaign came from the outside and was not their own creation; thus, it was easy to lose interest.[171] In a sense, Guernseymen and women were a step ahead of Saul Alinsky, anticipating his Rule Seven in *Rules for Radicals*: "A tactic that drags on too long becomes a drag."[172] By the time Colonel Britton was calling for a "flood of V's," Jack Sauvary had proclaimed the V-sign "so silly,"[173] and Winifred Harvey found it "no longer funny or amusing."[174]

One version of the V-campaign was truly the work of Guernseymen and persisted for many years. In a 2003 interview, Alf Williams told me of the day in 1942 when he was walking up the street with his friend Roy Machon. Just outside the La Quinta Hotel, they came across a "little Belgian fellow" (Guy Guillard)[175] who had been sent to Guernsey to do some work. The men stopped and chatted, and in the midst of the conversation, Guillard showed Alf and Roy an English penny crudely cut out in a V. "So, we said we can do better than that," Alf told me. "So we went home and we done better." Alf and Roy decided to do a finer version of the design, cutting out the King's head over a V and making a brooch or badge (by attaching a safety pin to the back) that could be worn. Roy, it seems, was the better craftsman, and as the projectionist of the Regal Cinema, he often made his V-badges during the running of the films, with the Germans seated in the theater below him. Alf worked on his badges in the dairy of his family's farm and initially had some trouble with getting the King's head cut out properly. "You've got to be careful," he explained. "The King always had a quiff on top of his head. And you cut that off and the whole thing is ruined." It may have taken some time to master the use of tin snips and files, but the badges that are still in existence are nicely done, with the profile of George VI seeming to rise triumphantly from the cut-out V in which he is centered.[176]

The residents of Guernsey became aware of these badges very quickly, and they were soon in demand—for some as a patriotic keepsake, and for many as a means of expressing defiance on the town streets. They were generally worn under the lapel and could be flashed quickly to a friend in passing. Roy and Alf charged an Occupation reichsmark for the work (not to mention the danger) of producing the badge, and the purchaser needed to provide the English coin from which the badge would be cut. These details were widely known, and the badges were very popular. Rev. Ord knew that "brooches are being sold for a mark" and that the German police were on the watch for the wearers and those who were making them. If they could catch a civilian with a badge, they could "use third degree methods to track down the maker."[177] The danger of this symbolic campaign to Roy and Alf seems apparent and may be sensed in Violet Carey's diary entry. She wrote:

> I met Mabel Kinnersly who gave me my 'Kings Head.' She knows a mysterious boy who cuts out the King's head in an English shilling and also cuts out a beautiful "V" under the King's head and mounts a pin on it. He does it with a fretsaw. It is lovely; I wear my marquisite crown and G.R. on top of it. We have to provide the shilling and pay him a mark. We all wear them under our coats. Mabel wears hers openly, but it is rather silly because if the Gestapo spot it they will take it from her.[178]

It sounds from this description of the fretsaw that Violet's badge may have been produced by Alf Williams. The naiveté of the entry is notable, because Mabel's wearing of her badge openly was more than "silly," it was extremely dangerous, not just for herself but for the maker. The Field Police would not be content to merely take the offending brooch away from her, as a number of wearers discovered.

By June of the next year, Rev. Ord was aware that people were being arrested for "wearing patriotic insignia particularly the "V"-sign brooches, the wearing of red, white and blue colours—even in dress."[179] At the same time, Ambrose Robin noted that several people had "been locked up for wearing Victory brooches and badges made out of 1/-s and 6ds."[180] It was not merely that the Germans had arrested those wearing the brooches, but they had also managed to snag one of the makers. Alf recounted how Roy was caught: "Two of our mates [Roy Machon and Jack Perrot][181] were walking up the Town and they were showing the V sign on their lapel and down comes the German police and 'What have you got there, let's have a look at that,' saw what it was, put him in prison and bashed him up a bit."[182] Roy was given six months in Germany and served the rest of the war in a civilian prisoner-of-war camp. Notably, despite the third degree, he did not give Alf away, who carried on making hundreds of V-badges throughout the Occupation.

How Alf was not caught out is quite remarkable because he had the heedless bravery of a young man. For example, he made one for a German that he met only a half mile from Alf's home. Alf showed him one of the V-badges, and the German asked him to make one, which Alf did out of an English penny. Just like the Islanders, this German wore the V-badge under his lapel. I asked Alf how he could trust this German not to betray him, and he replied, "How could you trust anybody?" Alf seemed to have come to the same policy of differentiation that Rev. Ord practiced, separating the ardent Nazis ("They were 'nice' people," Alf said sardonically) from the common German soldier, many of whom were apolitical or even anti-Nazi ("They didn't want to go to war. It was only these fanatical Nazis and I met quite a few of them").[183] This local version of the V-campaign fit far better with the nature of resistance in the Channel Islands than did the showy, but externally inspired chalking of V's on buildings and signposts. It fulfilled the need for symbolic patriotism and communal identity, while passing for as long as possible beneath the radar of German surveillance.

NEWS VIA THE UNDERGROUND

The importance of their wireless sets to the Guernsey civilians can be gauged by Bill Warry's response when the sets were permanently confiscated in June 1942. In an entry scrawled with many underlinings on the side of the news articles in his scrapbook, he wrote, "Today, we had a shock. Our wireless sets are *all to be taken away*, German orders . . . It's a terrible affair not to know how the war is going on at all or what is happening to our & other people." As if addressing readers from another, later era, Bill sought understanding of the magnitude of the blow: "Just figure it out for yourselves, to be cut off in these times." That day, a German who spoke French entered their shop and Mrs. Warry had "tackled him" about the reasoning behind the taking of all wireless sets. This particular German believed that it was to prevent England sending out news to those in occupied countries that might coordinate acts of sabotage. That reason seemed logical to Bill, although he also thought that it might be retaliation for the recent massive bombing of Cologne.[184] Others believed that the war must be turning in the Allies' favor and the Germans simply did not wish this information to be widely known.

Whatever the reason for the confiscation, which seemed to come from out of the blue as far as the Islanders were concerned, it was truly like the loss of a family member. Bill Warry treated it as saying goodbye to a buddy, writing mournfully of his "last day with our good old Radio 'Murphy,'" and describing how he planned to put a label with "a bit of poetry" on the set in protest.[185] Ord treated this second confiscation much as he had the first loss of wireless in 1940, returning to a metaphor he had used at that time. In 1940, he wrote of how his source for the BBC news had "dried up," but that he expected that "the stream will burst forth in another place," because so many had retained their wireless sets.[186] Now that the sets were gone, apparently for the duration, Ord returned to this watery concept with his assurance that "news will leak out somehow."[187]

Little could Rev. Ord have anticipated just how quickly the British news would make the rounds despite the wireless ban. By August 1943, he was forced to switch metaphors, as news continued to circulate "hot from secret sets, and spreads like a prairie fire" across Guernsey.[188] It is clear that the very act of the Germans denying news access to civilians turned information into a scarce and valuable commodity. Ord was aware of the same effect occurring among the German forces. When Bödeker brought Reinhold Zachmann to visit Ord for the first time, before the civilian wireless sets were taken, both men had begged to listen to the German transmission from London to hear an accurate account of the raid on Rostock. Knowing personally this hunger for accurate war news among anti-Party Germans, Ord gave credence to a story making the rounds now that wireless sets were confiscated. According to this tale, a German officer called requesting to see Madame and asked to see her wireless set. Taken aback, she quickly replied that all the wireless sets had been called in several months before. He replied, "Madame, I know you kept yours, and I can tell you where you keep it—it is in that coal box. But I shall not give you away. All I wish for is an opportunity to listen to London myself. I MUST HAVE THE TRUTH!"[189] Whether or not this story was based in fact, it bolstered the concept that truth resided with British transmissions, and that the taking of the wireless sets was designed by Germans to keep Islanders from that truth. With such a view, circumventing the German ban became an important aspect of resistance to German control.

Ord had proof very quickly that the ban on wireless would fail to result in a dearth of news transmission. In early January 1943, barely six months into the ban, Ord had some workmen installing a new fireplace in his lounge (one of the last of the new fireplaces available in Guernsey) when one of the workmen gave him the latest news in his own style: "They 'aven't 'arf given 'Itler a wipe in Russia—twenty more places was took yesterday!" Whatever Ord could make of this somewhat garbled version of the BBC news, he could add that "It is fine to meditate on the banning of the wireless and at the same time on the free circulation of news!"[190]

The more exciting the news, the more energy and meaning seemed to be attached to its transmission. The capitulation of Italy in September 1943 was one event, for example, that fired up the underground information exchange. Bert Williams declared it "wonderful" how the news traveled across the Island "in record time."[191] Ken Lewis heard the news of Italy at Mr. Taylor's, and believed that this event would spur the liberation of the Channel Islands. In all eagerness he headed for home, wanting to be the first to share the news with his father. Yet, Uncle Wils, who had heard the same news at Mr. Le Caer's, beat him to the punch and had the pleasure of making the announcement to the family. Despite Ken's disappointment, he "did not grumble as it was such good news."[192] To Ken and to many others, news from the outside world (especially war news) was treated as a gift, inherently valuable in itself and purchased through the willingness of Islanders to risk severe penalties for listening to illegal sets.

Guernsey may have been efficient in the rapid dissemination of news, but speed often came at the cost of clarity. As in the game "Telephone," where a phrase whispered around a circle becomes increasingly mangled as it travels, the wireless news that passed orally from Islander to Islander was prone to unavoidable distortion.[193] Ord found this process rather comical, as when a Guernseyman provided quotes to him from the speech made by Churchill the previous evening. Supposedly, the prime minister had described Britain as on the eve of "the biggest *ambiguous* ventures in history."[194] Equally amusing was his milkman's report at the time of the new "doodle-bug" weapon: "Gerry's got a second secret weapon. It's a sort of box affair. It goes up BUT IT DON'T DO NOTHING!" Ord considered this report and pondered, "What can he have heard?"[195] The need for direct information and the desire to hear the BBC for oneself made resisters of even the most upright civilians. Ord spent considerable time "tucking away" his set in August 1944 until he felt that "sheer hard luck" would be the only way for it to be detected. He had actually had the set for some time, having bought it with a check made out to the fourth man removed from the maker.[196] By 1944, many people had the small crystal sets that were being secretly made and distributed widely. Ken Lewis, who had previously gone to a variety of relatives' houses to hear the news, now lavished great care on his own crystal set. Uncle Ed came over to adjust the set and put in a new holder for the Cat's Whisker, the thin vertical wire that made contact with the crystal and allowed reception of the radio signal. The Cat's Whisker was notoriously sensitive to vibration, and Ken had difficulty getting more than a faint signal. With a little fiddling with aerials, Ken finally achieved a clear signal and even had an extra pair of headphones attached for shared listening.[197]

The danger inherent in owning and listening to illegal wireless may be gauged by the hesitancy to acknowledge owning a set even in private diaries. Ownership may be read between the lines of Gertie Corbin's brief entry, "People are in prison, because they have radios, I tremble."[198] Many of the diarists wrote in code. Winifred Harvey would be invited by her dressmaker for "fittings" if an important speech or news was expected.[199] Dorothy Higgs described how they were busy "counting the beans."[200] These were the same types of codes used in everyday life to invite friends and family for a listening session. Kitty Bachmann would phone a friend whose husband was serving with the British forces and say, "We have a nice bowl of 'fruit' if you'd care to collect it" (or, to fit the season, "cake") to invite her over to hear the news.[201]

It is telling of the sense of changed fortunes that the diarists became more overt in acknowledging their wireless sets after D-day, and particularly during the spring of 1945 as the war headed toward its conclusion. Before Christmas 1944, when electricity appeared to be ending,

Winnie received a crystal set through a friend of a friend, describing it as "the joy of our lives." In the mornings, when the cleaning woman was about, the crystal set was hidden away under slats in a rabbit hutch at the lower part of the garden. It was restored to the house in time for the one o'clock news, then put back in the hutch until Winnie took it up to her bedroom in the evening. Winnie was thrilled with the little device fitted inside an electric light switch and easily hidden in the palm of a hand. It was, in her eyes, the "neatest little thing" and a source of "enormous pleasure," although she had to keep one ear cocked for a knock at the front door." There were times when houses in the general area were being searched for wireless sets, and Winnie would tuck away her little set in the bottom of the pram that she regularly used going back and forth to Newlands. She would leave the pram there, with the wireless hidden "under the Germans' noses."[202]

Most of the Islanders who listened to secret wireless shared Winnie's concerns over being detected and arrested. But they worried as much about harming their source of information. There grew up an etiquette about news sharing that was designed to protect friendly sources from those who might inadvertently give the game away. The milkman was very upbeat one May morning in 1943, telling Rev. Ord, "The war is over in Africa! Mr. Churchill is in Washington and the BBC says our hopes are soaring." The reverend thanked him profusely for the news, which was anything but "new" to Ord, but "it would never do to reveal other sources of information."[203] This same little charade went on whenever Ord ran into Mr. Lihou, the postmaster. The two men would spend some time discussing the latest news without ever revealing their sources. "He clearly believes I have kept my set," Ord wrote, "and I am sure he still has his, but we are elaborately innocent in our references to sources of information. There are laughs even in Occupations!"[204]

This was not some idle paranoia, but a reasonable caution. A tradesman named Arrowsmith, a dyer on Victoria Road, was arrested for possessing a wireless set and listening to the news from London. His case became an object lesson for Guernsey, although there were several versions of what actually happened. The most detailed report had Arrowsmith in a bar that was frequented by Wolff, a plainclothes member of the Feldgendarmerie, tasked with hanging about the bar listening in on conversations. In one version of the story, Arrowsmith was very much in his cups and bragging about the British news; in another version, it was not Arrowsmith who was in the bar, but someone quoting what he had been told by Arrowsmith about the news.[205]

Both renderings of this incident pointed to very real fears on the part of the Guernsey population and made caution a necessary element of interpersonal discourse. One day, Kitty Bachmann was talking to her friend Stan, who happened to mention that Winston Churchill would broadcast that night. Stan continued in exasperation, "It will be on the Overseas Service and we can't get that station on our set!!" Kitty looked up with an innocent expression, a little smile, and raised eyebrows: "Can't you, Stan?" Stan caught himself and then came out loudly with, "Hell! You could have been—just anyone!" It was funny between friends, but Kitty admitted that she still did not reveal her own hidden set to Stan. It was just too easy to let the wrong information leak out accidentally.[206]

Rev. Ord found out just how easy it was to be caught out as a source of British news. He was part of a small crowd waiting for the road to clear after General Müller passed on a troop inspection. Old Dr. Foote, a nonagenarian veterinary surgeon, came up to Ord to ask why the road was blocked. Ord was trying to explain, talking loudly because Dr. Foote was extremely deaf, when Dr. Foote bellowed out, "Well, what's the latest news you have to tell me?" This brought forth a knowing laugh from the little crowd, but with the armed sentry standing by, it was an uncomfortable situation for Ord, who found it "quite hard to put the old man off."[207]

Ken Lewis was remarkably sensitive to the problem of inadvertently revealing that a friend or family member had a secret wireless set.[208] Ken was over at his Uncle Wils and Auntie Ede's house and saw a wireless mains set in the dining room. He simply pretended not to see it.[209] This delicacy seems an overabundance of caution, but the possession of an illegal wireless was generally treated as very private business. It was, therefore, an act of trust when, in 1944, Ken invited Ralph over to listen to his crystal set. Ralph had not heard the news headlines since the wireless sets were called in during 1942, so he was obviously excited to have the opportunity. This was a gift that Ken could extend to his best friend, but it was also a sign that he could trust in Ralph's discretion.[210]

The underlying reason for this caution became apparent as arrests followed arrests and the prison was filled with those caught for wireless offenses. It quickly reached the point where offenders had to wait until there was an "opening" before they could serve their time. These arrests were facilitated by a true scandal in the eyes of the Islanders and the one real break in the solidarity of the Guernsey populace. It quickly became apparent that the German police were not catching so many people by chance or through general sweeps, because they often knew precisely where wireless sets were hidden in the houses that they searched.[211] The Germans were more than happy to show some of those arrested the anonymous letters by which they had been betrayed.

The Islanders already knew that there were some collaborators in Guernsey, most of them known and treated with contempt. But these anonymous letters were something entirely different. They could have been sent by anyone—neighbor, relative, supposed friend—and often they related such specific information that they seemed likely to have come from someone close to the person arrested. Islanders recoiled in horror at this chink in the wall of solidarity. "What demons some people are to round on their own countrymen," wrote Bill Warry.[212] Bert Williams shared this assessment and only hoped that the names of the people who had "'sold' their own countrymen to the enemy" would be uncovered, so that they could be dealt with after the war.[213] Even mild-mannered Ken Lewis described how these letters were viewed as "treachery by the local population and would not be forgotten after the war."[214] Little could be done about this form of betrayal, although H. C. Chapell, the head postmaster, was adept at steaming open letters when they were addressed to the Feldkommandant at Grange Lodge. Somehow, many letters revealing the location of a secret wireless disappeared at that point in their journey.[215]

Even now, these anonymous letters seem inexplicable, based on all we know about the Islanders and their response to the Occupation. At the time, Rev. Ord tried hard to account for them, at one point categorizing them as a "token of the degeneration of morals in a hitherto very upright community."[216] This was not a satisfying explanation, because the general morality of the Islanders had held up quite well under the intense strain of Occupation. He returned to contemplating these anonymous letters later when describing the overall dangers of owning a wireless and passing news items along to others:

> Worse still, a local Quisling—for to our shame there are some among us—moved by some grudge or spite or jealous envy, may write the anonymous letter which will prove your undoing.
>
> "They took my set. Why should you keep yours?" The Occupation makes many appeals to the baser instincts of the meaner sort.[217]

Ord was most likely correct in his assessment that some anonymous letters were a means of settling old scores, an opportunity for payback to a disliked relative, or an effective weapon in the war between feuding neighbors. The very anonymity of the letters meant that the sender would be unlikely to receive any reward from the Germans, thus bolstering the probability that personal motives were involved.

The damage to personal relations and the trust between neighbors was obvious. As the result of an anonymous letter, the Feldgendarmerie searched Mrs. Terrell's house,[218] one of Ken's neighbors, for a wireless set. She had actually never owned a wireless in her life, so it was not that she was in any danger of arrest. However, the sense of betrayal was very upsetting, and the nearness to Ken's house sparked a flurry of securing his diary, news notebooks, wireless, and camera from detection. The German police actually apologized to Mrs. Terrell and asked if she had any enemies, perhaps hoping for names that would allow them further searches. She suspected that it might have been two specific women, one of them a woman for whom she used to work, but she did not reveal their names. Yet this suspicion, never to be proven or disproven, would surely have changed her relationship with both women.[219] The anonymous letters produced a worm of doubt in more than one interpersonal relationship, likely never to be resolved.

Stories of the near detection of wireless sets and tricks used to retain them became a narrative resource in the transcript of Guernsey resistance. Some accounts were simple reports of good hiding places, such as that used by the Blampieds, who kept their wireless in a bucket on the roof of an outhouse.[220] Most of these stories are more detailed and lauded cleverness and quick thinking, providing heroes of a domestic type pulled from tales of average Islanders. Such narratives absolutely pepper the contemporaneous accounts and seem to fall into some common categories. Many are of the purloined-letter variety, where a set is in a readily apparent place that is not then searched by the Germans. When the Germans searched one home, prompted by anonymous letters, the maid showed police to the lounge where the lady of the house was seated on a little stool close to the fire. She excused herself for not rising, because she was not feeling well, but invited them to "Search the house by all means." The maid showed them around; they searched thoroughly and returned to apologize for disturbing her, leaving Madame comfortably seated on the stool containing the wireless inside it.[221]

A similar story involved a man hurriedly putting his all-mains set on the settee as Germans approached the house and tossing his wife's coat haphazardly on top of it. The Germans never searched beneath, leaving Ord to theorize that "The best 'blind' is perfect openness."[222] This first type of narrative reveals the importance of "the ruse" as a theme in many Occupation stories and anecdotes. The goal of the ruse is to outsmart rather than overpower those in control, to provide "an exhibition of intelligence, wit, and taking a bit of power." Although the activities described in the stories are improvisational, once they enter the realm of repeated tellings, they have the opportunity to replicate themselves by inspiring others to similar acts.[223]

Individual Islanders' ability to bluff and bull their way through trouble was a characteristic highly prized in a second type of wireless narrative. Typical was the tale of Miquet Kinnersley, who happened to be cooking a rabbit, caught in the rough area of her property, as a treat for guests when the Germans arrived looking for her wireless set. The reported exchange went, "You are under arrest, Madame!" "Oh, that's all right! But I can't possibly come now as I've got guests coming any minute and I'm in the midst of cooking. Won't you come in?" Keeping up a tone of "gay raillery" and unperturbed courtesy, she denied having either wireless or the typewriter needed to produce BBC newssheets, as she excused herself often to check on her cooking. Soon, her charm seemed to distract the police enough that they took themselves away without a search, complimenting her on the delightful smells issuing from the kitchen. "And, do you know," Miquet later reported, "I verily believe they would gladly have stayed to dinner if there had been any chance of my inviting them!"[224] Such stories made the feared German police into bumbling incompetents, all too human and easily gulled by feminine wiles.

Of a similar nature was the story of the young Pearl Luff, who relied not on charm but on spirited refusal in her dealings with the German police. When ordered to empty her pockets during a house search, Pearl flung her tiny crystal set into the corner. Told to look for it, she replied, "That's what you were sent here to do. You'd better make sure what it was if you want to!" Threatened with prison, she said, "Very well, I accept responsibility. Take me now!" Such frankness seemed to startle the police, and they left the house without her. She was clearly the winner of this test of wills in Rev. Ord's eyes: "For sheer courage it would be hard to beat."[225] It is here that we can glimpse the protection of the private home as an "offstage social site" where resistance would find a place to flourish. Small battles over the right to receive information and to communicate this information to others seized the ground of an autonomous "social space," as valuable to the Islanders as the battleground of a physical war. As Scott maintains, the maintenance of such spaces is "an achievement of resistance; they are won and defended in the teeth of power."[226]

If such one-up tales could be expected, the third form of wireless narrative is more of a surprise. They tended to be comical or ironic stories of Islander misadventures in attempting to retain or hide a set. In one highly circulated story, a man was listening in to the news one evening when Germans pounded on his door. He quickly returned his set to its hiding place, opened his door, and was greeted with "You have a Vireless set!" "No," the man returned, "I have no set." "Then," bellowed the German, "Vy are you vearing a headphone?" And off went the man to his date with prison. Kitty Bachmann followed the relating of this little story with the supposedly true incident of a mother and daughter visited by the Germans in a similar way one evening. While the daughter answered the door, the mother desperately tossed their crystal set into a pot of "pseudo soup" on the fire. As the search was going on, the daughter lifted the pot lid and stirred the soup. "What have you put in the soup?" the daughter asked. "Bones!" said the mother under her breath. "Bones?" asked the daughter. "Bones, you idiot!" hissed the mother. Luckily for the pair, the Germans did not pick up on the meaning behind their exchange.[227]

Although both of these stories have the feel of fiction, they would be the type of apocryphal tales told broadly to find the comedy in intimidating circumstances. They also capture the sense of gentle self-mockery that bolstered a communal identity more effectively than heroic posturing. In them is an acknowledgment that resistance in Guernsey would be private, improvisational, and attenuated rather than steeped in the sudden drama of arms and sabotage. As Jack Sauvary said to bolster the spirits of Eddie, the parish cross-bearer, facing three months in prison for possessing a wireless, "I tell people here that unless we can say that we went to prison we won't be heroes!"[228] Islanders knew intimately the risks that they ran and the level of resistance that made sense in their very particular circumstances. Heroism lay in private actions that did not endanger the larger community but thwarted in some small way the goals of the German occupiers.

GUNS AND GASP

Resistance by way of the wireless took on an organized form with the advent of GUNS (Guernsey Underground News Service) and GASP (Guernsey Active Secret Press). GUNS was the better-known of the two, and the story of the brave men who operated this service for their fellow Islanders is one of the generally acknowledged aspects of Guernsey resistance. It was Charlie Machon, a linotype operator for the *Star*, who developed the concept of operating a daily newssheet for Guernsey now that wireless sets were banned. Five men formed the core organization, including newspaperman Frank Falla, who came up with their acronymic name, plus Cecil Duquemin, Ernest Legg, and Joe Gillingham. The basic operation of GUNS involved listening to the 9 P.M. BBC news broadcast and the 8 A.M. news the following morning. The highlights would be typed on very thin 13½" x 8" tomato packing paper under a heading of a large V made up of smaller V's. Occasionally, the shorthand skills of Bill Taylor would be used to record verbatim an important speech by Churchill. Originally, there was a directive at the top, "Burn after reading," but it was soon assumed that readers knew this and the typists could dispense with this admonition.

Every morning except Sundays, three sets of eight typings would be prepared and then sent out for retyping and distribution. GUNS was a highly popular and well-read newssheet, with a copy read by a number of the States officials, including the Bailiff. It operated from May 1942 to February 1944, but its demise may have been inevitable. Reading Frank Falla's account in his excellent little book *The Silent War* makes clear that there were continuous near misses, and some risks that were inherent in trusting the discretion of the many distributors and readers.[229]

On February 11, two Guernsey police constables came upon an Irishman named Peter "Paddy" Doyle in the company of a small group of Germans near Trinity Square. Because it was after curfew, the constables approached Doyle, who then hastened up the Bouillon Steps with the Germans while two more armed Germans blocked the constables' way. Because this was the evening when Cecil Duquemin and Charles Machon were arrested in their homes in Victoria Road, it was clear that Doyle was on his way to finger them for the police. Later would come the arrest of Frank Falla, Joe Gillingham, and Ernest Legg. But for the chance observance of the constables, Doyle's role in this betrayal might have never been more than speculation.[230] He had been considered a close friend by Charles Machon, who supplied him with GUNS newssheets, copies that would later be used against the five Guernseymen in court. The sentences to be served in German prisons were stiff: Charles Machon, 2 years and 4 months; Cecil Duquemin, 1 year and 11 months; Ernest Legg, 1 year and 10 months; Frank Falla, 1 year and 4 months; and Joe Gillingham, 10 months.[231]

There would be a ripple effect, as many Islanders were pulled in and given two- to three-month sentences for reading the GUNS newssheets.[232] Yet, it would be the five Guernseymen responsible for GUNS who suffered the most in their imprisonment in Germany, a tale of brutality at the hands of the Germans that is well documented by Frank Falla. Charles Machon, whose health was tenuous at best from an ulcerated stomach, died after five months of mistreatment and is buried in Wehl Cemetery in Hameln. Full details of the German experiences of the four remaining GUNS operators and that of the other Islanders removed to the Continent for resistant activities have only recently come to light. In the summer of 2010, Frank Falla's daughter gave to Cambridge University a file that had languished in the back of a wardrobe in her home since the 1960s. Roughly two hundred pages in length, this compilation of testimony put together by Frank Falla contains first-person accounts of Islanders who served time in Germany for resistance activities.

Falla's desire was to guarantee that Islanders would receive compensation from the German government for the unspeakable treatment to which they had been subjected while in custody. Some of this material enlarges on Falla's own recollections in his book, but most is testimony unknown up to this point. Cecil Duquemin described, for example, how he was one of four hundred prisoners transferred in cattle trucks to another location when their prison was bombed near the close of the war: "We had no sanitation and though suffering from starvation and malnutrition, we were forced to bury the many prisoners who died in the trucks. This was a daily occurrence and we hardly had any strength left in us to dig the men's graves." This file also contains testimony by Joe Gillingham's widow. She knew that he was "ill-treated, starved, and denied all the rights one would expect even from an enemy." What she never learned was how her husband died or where he was buried. He was last seen February 2, 1945, after being released from Salle Prison, Nuremberg, and it was presumed that he was sent to a concentration camp or taken with the Germans as they moved ahead of the Allied advance.[233]

The GUNS compatriots were not the only ones to produce a newssheet to meet the demand for information from the BBC. A lesser-known but quite successful effort revolved around T. Moullin's cycle shop as its base of operations, allowing readers to pick up a newssheet by using the pretext of cycle repair. Edited by Ludovic E. Bertrand, the GASP newssheet also consisted of BBC news gleaned from hidden wireless sets to be summarized and typed out on tomato packing paper. Then, a number of "agents" served as distributors, including Madeleine Sims, who worked in the Bailiff's office, and Matron Finch, who supplied her patients at the Emergency Hospital with the sheets in order to raise their spirits. Despite some feeling that the cycle shop was a little too well known for safety, GASP continued to operate right up until Liberation.[234]

Individuals and small groups of friends also took on the duty to spread what they had heard on the news, though in a more casual or spotty way. On August 31, 1943, Rev. Ord participated with a group to record Churchill's speech to the Canadians. This obviously was not the first time that Ord took part in such an activity, because he described it as "more and more of a strain" due to the need to have the volume set so low and always with the consciousness that they could be "caught red-handed" at any moment. He could "confess to a sense of relief when I have got everything taken down and the little party breaks up." On this particular occasion, Ord only reached his home five minutes before curfew, to find Grae in an anxious state. She had watched the German police walking down the road in the direction of the house where Ord and the others were listening, and feared that they would be surprised in the act. "The next thing," Ord wrote, "is to type out copies, and to see that the news gets out."[235]

The most exciting aspect of the recently found Falla file is its recognition by name of the many civilians who resisted during the Occupation and suffered for their acts against the Nazi occupier. The Channel Islanders have often been treated as if they were exempt in some way from Nazi brutality, even when imprisoned in Germany. The stories in this file of beatings, starvation, and other mistreatment, including the deaths of some of the brave Guernseymen who served as resisters, will do much to set the public record straight. Because some fifty of the Islanders whose stories are contained within its pages received compensation, it authenticates their suffering for those requiring some form of official confirmation. When all of the information in the file is publicly released, there will be some surprises, too, for individual families about their relatives' participation in resistance. The material in the file will not, however, come as news to those Guernsey Islanders who have been privy to the echoes of the hidden transcript of the Occupation years, and who are sensitive to the nature of Islander resistance. This new information comes as confirmation of the narratives of Occupation—the stories, jokes, and contemporaneous accounts that form such a rich legacy of those years.

The genius of the three forms of rhetorical resistance detailed in this study lies in their ability to "nibble away"[236] at the resources and power of the dominant. I believe that Scott is correct when he admonishes us not to "overly romanticize the 'weapons of the weak,'" for such actions are likely to be subtle, and the outcome of their use incapable of effecting the overthrow of an oppressive power structure.[237] Still, the practical aspects of this choice of resistance, as opposed to more dramatic forms of violence and sabotage, may be appreciated in two ways. Small and hidden acts designed around information flow, narrative, and the manipulation of symbols are perfectly designed to evade the surveillance that is the key component of systems based on panoptical power. The fact that such resistance is difficult to detect and sometimes even masquerades as cooperation means that its true significance becomes accessible to the powerless even as it is rendered invisible to the dominant.

Second, and perhaps most important, "everyday resistance is tenacious,"[238] and designed for the long haul. Thus, the acts of rhetorical resistance by the Guernsey Islanders, clustered as they were around symbolic communication and the flow of information, were sustainable during an Occupation lasting five years, and ideal for a situation where, in case the war was lost, current conditions could become permanent. Had the worst happened, resistance forms would have already been in place to maintain an ongoing culture of subversion. Liberation would come to the Channel Islands, but only after a final year that would sorely test the Islanders' physical and psychological resources. In the concluding chapter, I will discuss the end of Occupation, the complications when Liberation finally occurred, and the public memory of those years as Islanders have been embroiled in a second war to set the Occupation record straight and regain control of their own story.

Conclusion

Reverend Ord and Grae were in the habit of being in bed no later than 9 p.m. on these June evenings. They found that their restricted diet made them tired enough, and despite the summer date, they were both feeling the cold more than in the past. On this night, they settled in to rest and read by the single small light at the head of the bed, turning if off at 11:00 to call it a night. But there would be precious little sleep on this June 5th/6th. Almost immediately, they heard planes flying over, unusual only because there was no echo of flak from German installations in the Island. Ord and Grae played the usual guessing game of where the planes were headed, and settled on the Loire Valley as the likely target for the raid. Yet this time the planes did not stop coming, and by 11:30, they filled the skies in increasing numbers. Soon, Grae said, "This is IT!" and the two of them threw on dressing gowns and went out on the balcony, which allowed a clear, wide view from Cobo Bay to Herm Island. Soon, flak came up from Alderney and from the French coast near Cherbourg, as bright flashes lit up the sky behind the thick white clouds that obscured the Ords' view of the passing planes.[1]

This, then, was the long anticipated invasion that the Channel Islanders felt sure would liberate them from German control. The Ords could not know as they stood on their balcony on that chilly June night, more excited than at any time in their lives, that the roar and lights did not herald the end of Occupation, but rather the advent of the most difficult year of all. This concluding chapter will begin with a consideration of that final year, one that unfolded in a manner that none could have anticipated. The effects of having France liberated while the Channel Islands remained under German control were both physical and psychological. The line that separated occupier and occupied became more indistinct, as both the Germans and their Island possessions appeared to be caught in the same isolated trap. As easy access to Continental supplies ended, food rations were reduced to starvation levels, and fuel was cut off during one of the coldest winters Islanders could remember. Worse still, the Islanders were effectively locked in their prison without bars with armed and increasingly desperate men.

This year would give the Guernsey civilians new revelations about their German captors and provide a unique perspective on the entire Occupation experience. This viewpoint, honed through many years of Occupation and sharpened by the difficulties of this final year, would color Guernsey's response immediately post-Liberation. More importantly, it would become a source of misunderstanding and contention in the public memory of the Occupation.

I then conduct a close reading of two forms of vernacular public memory, those structured "from below" by the Islanders themselves. Attention to these forms of memory is key to a recovery of the story of the Occupation as actually experienced. Finally, this study ends with conclusions about the nature and structure of rhetorical resistance as practiced during the Guernsey Occupation, and implications for this form of resistance in other situations of domination.

LEFT IN THE LURCH

Oddly, not everyone in Guernsey was treated to the same show as the Ords during the morning hours of June 6. It appears that those living on or near the coast were more likely to have heard the raid in progress, and some in other parts of Guernsey slept through the entire event.[2] What could not be missed were the changes on the streets and roads of Guernsey the next day. Peter Bachmann was stopped by a soldier on guard at the end of their lane, only to be told that he could not go any further and that the town was off limits for the immediate term.[3] Unlike the experience of the Bachmanns, there seemed to be little to no restriction on most Islander movements. Winnie Harvey went into St. Peter Port and saw few Germans about.[4] The dearth of off-duty Germans wandering about the streets combined with other equally tangible signs that something major was afoot. The telephones had all been cut off and the post office was closed, with guards posted outside. Finally, when the *Star* came out that night, the Germans confirmed in large letters the start of the invasion, although with their usual spin on the news.[5]

As the Germans disappeared from the streets and shops and were called to duty in response to the new military situation, the few Islanders about St. Peter Port were "beaming" in undisguised excitement. Winnie ran into Major Scott, a prominent Guernseyman who had been looking "dreadful" in recent weeks but now hailed Winnie with a thumbs-up signal. Winnie responded, "Are you feeling happier now?"—to which the major replied, "Very much so. Both thumbs and big toes, too!"[6] But mingled with the joy and anticipation was an equal concern about what it meant to be "in the front line of war."[7] These concerns were not unreasonable and were borne out by events of the invasion and the weeks immediately following.

Islanders already knew on June 6 that at 7 A.M., a German shell fired at one of the planes passing over the Island had fallen short into St. Sampson.[8] It was reportedly the nose cap of the shell that killed a man who had the misfortune to step at that moment from his outdoor lavatory.[9] More violence and likely more deaths could be anticipated, and the raids were quick to follow, particularly in the harbor area of St. Peter Port. Bill Warry reported four RAF raids on June 7 that dropped bombs on the harbor and Castle Cornet, causing his house in the heart of town at 14 Arcade to shake ("but we are still standing") and catching him twice outside by surprise and without shelter. Bill's response was echoed by many Islanders eager for liberation and willing to face any peril to achieve it: "We are in the war zone properly, but let them (ours) come as often as they like. We welcome them."[10]

And come they did, although not with the liberating effect that the Islanders desired. One of the major raids that passed into Island lore occurred on June 19 at 8:30 in the morning when American Lightnings passed high over the Island and bombed the Harbor, targeting the spot where a German submarine had only hours before been positioned. What Bill Warry called a "big 'un" was dropped at that point, later to be estimated as a 500 lb. bomb that took out most of the glass in the town center. The Anglican Town Church, so prominently tucked in the corner where the streets intersect by the Harbor, lost many of its historic stained-glass windows. In the Arcade, only the Warrys' shop and Mackay's Wine Merchant escaped damage to their shop windows. Bill had experienced a small stroke in early June and was on bed rest at Blanc Bois (where his wife had been located since early May as she recovered from a possible heart attack and a failing gallbladder). He was so determined to assess the damage to their shop that he went into town, against doctor's orders, to see for himself.

It must have been a stunning sight as bank clerks and shop owners swept up what Peter Bachmann estimated at the time to be £100,000 worth of glass, and the High Street was shut to pedestrian traffic until the "sea of broken glass" was cleared. Islanders knew that they were lucky, for despite the number of ceilings that collapsed in buildings at the same time, there were no casualties. Opinions varied about whether this was a matter of dumb luck and whether the raid was worth the damage. Winifred Harvey was aware that had it been an hour later, shop assistants and bank clerks would definitely have been at work, and the outcome far more tragic. She was a bit tart in noting that "No damage whatsoever was done to the Germans or to the shipping." Rev. Ord, on the other hand, took a positive slant on the entire event, describing how "The aim of the bomb was excellent. So was the timing of the raid—just before people began to open shops and offices."[11]

Competing theories for the future seemed split between the Islanders starving or undergoing a full-out attack by the Allied forces, with the harbor bombing as merely a taste of things to come. Neither was an appealing scenario, although most seemed ready to face any future in order to rid the Island of German control. Optimists believed the Germans would be gone by the end of June, timed pleasingly by fate to coincide with the anniversary of Occupation. It was only the most pessimistic who maintained that they would be trapped with the Germans in the Island until the war's end, and this estimation came with the further grim assumption that all civilians would be starved to death by that time.[12] It was with no lack of courage that the Islanders faced an uncertain future now that the war threatened to come directly to their homes. They may have been just "flotsam in the path of the current," only able to "await the outcome of the gathering storm," but most did so with hopeful anticipation.[13] News of Operation Valkyrie, the July 20, 1944, attempt on Hitler's life, was encouraging, but frustrating at the same time. Elizabeth Doig heard of this failed plot and applied the proverb "Hope deferred maketh the heart sick" to Guernsey attitudes, for "we had so hoped our release would have come 'ere now."[14]

One of the worst aspects of being cut off was the silence from evacuated family in England and deported family in Germany. With no Red Cross messages available now, and no German boats to bring messages from Biberach, the sense of isolation was quite complete.[15] So, here they were, cut off entirely from those they loved and saddled with the Germans in that strange position where, in Ord's words, "our captors are our prisoners now until they are taken off our hands."[16] It simply seemed unbelievable that there could be so many victories in France, and the Channel Islands—a part of Britain, after all—bypassed. Everything was frozen in place, "at a standstill waiting for the Germans to give up and release us from this stupid bondage."[17] All the talk was of the irony of being bypassed, a line of talk that held some humor for Dorothy Higgs when her gardener/stableman, "who is definitely simple," told her quite seriously that Churchill had passed over the Channel Islands while flying on the way to Italy. Churchill asked the pilot what that land was down below them, and the pilot responded that it was the Channel Islands. "Oh," Churchill supposedly responded, "I'd forgotten all about them. We'll send them a message." Of course, the gardener was trying in his own manner to filter all the talk that Churchill had "passed over" the Island.[18]

It was all too apparent that if the Germans were cut off from supplies and food, the civilians were similarly severed from outside food, fuel, and medical supplies. The food situation, always tenuous, now seemed likely to end in starvation for captors and captives alike. Soon after the invasion, rumors of white flags in various places cropped up,[19] none particularly reliable, and life under increasingly arduous conditions settled into routine. In late September, as the new reality of a food and fuel crisis loomed on the horizon, word came of a white-flag sighting that was not a mirage. Ken Lewis and his fellow clerks raced up to the highest window at work to try and distinguish details of the approaching vessel through a telescope. They could clearly see the white flag, and they watched as a German launch went out, returning about an hour later.

Ken did not have solid information about this meeting until a convocation the following day held at Mount Durand, involving Jurat Leale, J. E. L. Martel (the acting attorney general), Col. von Heldorff, and L. A. Guillemette. Ken attached the memorandum of this meeting in his diary, during which Leale made clear to the colonel that all in Guernsey were well aware of the ship. They requested any information that resulted from the meeting and might impact the local population. The colonel claimed that nothing had resulted from the meeting, except that the Americans "asked some silly questions" that "had nothing at all to do with the civilian population." He said that the Germans would not discuss the situation in the Islands with the Americans; however, the issue of dwindling food supplies was being discussed with the British through a neutral country. The Germans gave the date of the end of essential supplies as October 15 and believed that a ship would arrive with relief by then.[20]

They were overly optimistic with their estimation. October 15th came and went, with no relief ship from a neutral country appearing. In November the truth of the Islanders' predicament became apparent to all. Official estimations at the meeting were that the bread would be depleted after December 15, that the potato ration was vanishing quickly, and that gas and electricity would be at an end in about five weeks (with no wood fuel available). Many were now turned away from the Market without even the small amount of vegetables that had been previously available. Miss Ellis, at the corner shop near to Jack, had only 2 cwt of carrots (an imperial cwt being about 112 pounds), 1 cwt of swedes, and just a few parsnips, all to be shared among one hundred customers. Jack "did not envy her the job."[21]

Quickly, things became even worse. Winnie started her diary entry on November 19 with the simple word "Potatoes." The States now had no potatoes to give in a ration, for the Germans had taken all of the potatoes (500 tons) stored in the depots for themselves. Then, they demanded all of the potatoes in private hands, leaving only 90 pounds per person to last for the entire winter. Immediately, a small game of hide-and-seek sprang up as Guernseymen and women sought ways to hide any potatoes they had above the allowed amount and prevent them from falling into German hands. Winnie herself was determined to thwart this German theft, and she set to work to arrange for the gardeners to come with a hand truck to carry her store of potatoes into hiding. Despite gale-force winds and a continuous downpour of rain, the potatoes were loaded, covered up carefully, and hauled toward Newlands, with Winnie following on her bicycle. As they passed one corner, a Guernsey policeman on duty said to them, with a grin, "What's that? Potatoes?" Once at Newlands, after ascertaining that no Germans were in sight, the potatoes were stowed away in boxes at the back of the stable. Each week, Winnie would go and bring her ration of potatoes back to Grange Terrace, neatly tucked away in a pram.[22]

The Bailiff made an appeal to Guernsey citizens to relinquish their potatoes willingly, which was widely read as his desire to prevent the Germans from searching each home and finding hidden wireless sets. He was unlikely to meet with cooperation from a hungry populace, for that same week, it was announced that the bread ration was being cut to 3 lbs. per week.[23] The apparent determination of the Germans to survive at whatever cost there might be to the civilian population was borne out as November continued and turned the corner to December. Five hundred head of cattle were confiscated from the farms, and then began a sad parade of Islander cows taken to the Grange to be slaughtered for the Germans.

This meant even less of the ration of milk, already at only a quarter of a pint of skim a day per head. Soon it was the vegetables, the one thing remaining to the average person, that began to disappear. All green vegetables now had to be sold to the States depots, and the Germans took half of them.

On Tuesday, December 5, Winnie reported that there was nothing on the Market stalls but sacking, and she left to push her empty pram up the hill to home "feeling rather frightened." As her friend Marie Louise said of the Germans, "We are at the mercy of their stomachs," and it seemed likely that slow starvation would be the end result. This grim future could not help but affect the usual stoic positivism so notable throughout the Occupation. There had been times of depression before, but now women could be seen standing in the Market, with their empty baskets and prams, simply crying.[24]

The black market appears to have dried up for the most part, and Elizabeth Doig, who made no excuses about her need to rely on this underground trade at times, worried that for those like herself, it would be hard to "eke out our supplies."[25] But if the black market was moribund, other bad players in Guernsey carried on undeterred by the obvious state of emergency, much to the anger of the average person. Rumor went around that some of the local women standing in endless queues for the few vegetables available were actually shopping for German soldiers.[26] This belief was probably based on recognizing women in the lines who were known fraternizers. There were similar beliefs, also likely tied to known collaborators, that some people in Guernsey were cooking meals for the Germans even under this starvation situation.[27]

A notice from the Bailiff appeared in the newspaper on November 11 stating that the Germans had allowed him to read a radio message to the International Red Cross in Geneva, and that the message, according to the Germans, had been dispatched.[28] But could anyone trust that this was actually so? It was not until an announcement was made through the BBC that Guernsey believed that help was truly coming their way and the wait for the supply ship began in earnest. Because many anticipated that the ship would arrive by Christmas, the rumors started to fly at mid-December: the ship had left Portugal, she would dock in three days, she had been spotted off the Casquets, she was close to St. Martin's Point, she was near Les Hanois Lighthouse.

And right in the middle of all these various sightings of "a fleet of ghost ships" came news from the BBC that the ship was due to leave for the Channel Islands next week. "Alas!" Kitty commented, "those taunting mirages have besotted their starving and gullible victims."[29] Christmas passed, a hungry holiday for most. Many now believed the ship to have been recalled, if she had existed in the first place. Then, as Dorothy Higgs was walking down the road on the 27th she came across an old Guernseywoman who said, "Don't get excited! But I have *seen* her—*seen* her with my own eyes!" It was all Dorothy could do to resist crying, simply to see this woman's relief and to think how much it would mean to all in the Islands. And this time it was no illusion, but the SS *Vega* that steamed into harbor at 6:15 in the morning.[30]

Men and women cycled and walked from all across the Island simply to see the ship in her harbor berth, cheering at the least provocation as they watched from their barricaded position at some distance.[31] Distributing the parcels was not an instantaneous task. On Saturday, December 30, many lorries could be seen going by, filled with packing cases containing the Canadian and New Zealand parcels as they were being taken to retailers. Registered customers were then to pick up their parcels the next day, meanwhile tantalized by the lists of their contents that were being circulated.

Rev. Ord actually expected a modest turnout at church services on Sunday, believing that the temptation to fetch the parcels would be too much for almost everyone. He found instead that his congregation came "with more thankful hearts to worship than ever they had done," having gone already to secure their parcel, or planning to do so straight from church. As he came home later with his own parcel, slowly pushing his bicycle up the steep incline of Victoria Road, he came upon an old man he knew, a "mere skeleton," carrying his own parcel with tears coursing down his cheeks: "Oh Reverend Ord, Oh Sir! THIS is the most wonderfully generous gift. How can we be thankful enough?"[32]

Any reader of the contemporaneous accounts cannot help but be struck by all the loving recitations describing the contents of the parcels by their enraptured recipients. The Ords received the Canadian version, and there appear to have been some differences between the contents of the parcels, such as coffee instead of tea in some, or extra cheese in others. There was protein in the form of tins of sardines, salmon, corned beef, and beef or pork sausage. There were dried raisins and prunes and much-desired marmalade or apple and peach jam (Dorothy claimed that "nothing will ever be so perfect as that first taste" of marmalade). Some needed fats came in the form of butter, cheese, and 5 oz. of chocolate. A large packet of hard biscuits ("something hard to get our teeth into after all the vegetable mush," enthused Ord), and staples such as sugar, salt, pepper, tea, and coffee rounded out the parcels. Dorothy wanted to carry her parcel with her around the house, like a child with a favorite toy. And Peter-John Bachmann was told that Diana sent him the parcel, allowing her to play the role of Santa Claus. And this was the universal reaction: a Christmas miracle had occurred a few days late, but for the Guernsey people only just in time.[33]

The coming of the *Vega* and the Red Cross parcels is always told as a beautiful story of rescue, which it is at its heart. However it is important not to view the arrival of these desperately needed supplies as ending the food crisis in Guernsey. It was during this time following the arrival of the parcels that Dorothy Higgs's "little gnome of a gardener" died of malnutrition.[34] Ord, in his wry way, also confirmed such deaths in January when he described an old woman who stopped him on the street: "There's a fine young man I knows of, Sir, as used to sweep the roads 'ereabouts. 'E's just gone an' died of starvation . . . 'E was goin' to be married very soon—nice young man, only 65—but they've took 'is life through starvin' of 'im."[35] The *Vega* would come seven times to the Island, and it is difficult to know how many would have died of malnutrition without the parcels—or from other causes, since she also brought medical supplies.

But what the *Vega* brought on the one hand was often matched by denials of food by the Germans. When the ship came on February 1, there were double parcels but no flour, and bread gave out February 13, the Germans reneging on promises to provide a 2 lb. loaf a week. Winnie described how she would "eke out" her supply of Canadian biscuits by soaking them in water so that they swelled, and allotting herself one a day for breakfast. By evening, Winnie was exhausted simply from lack of food and found that she could not sleep at night. Most people could only manage to find food for one meal a day, far too little sustenance for a working man. At this point, the butter ration stopped and the milk was cut back severely, even for the children, who Winnie described as "so thin and white-faced."[36]

As late as May 4, with Liberation on the horizon, the *Vega* arrived for the seventh and final time and was a welcome sight, for there were no green vegetables in the Market. Winnie would go out and gather stinging nettles from the fields and boil them as spinach or to use as a soup.[37] So, the parcels definitely saved lives and provided not just a dietary but an emotional lift, as when white flour in March provided loaves of bread unlike any the Islanders had seen in years. Still, the threat of starvation did not magically end with the first arrival of the *Vega*, and during the winter months, the gnawing hunger was aggravated by the terrible cold. It was a notably brutal winter, and Bill Warry described weeks of snow, sleet, and frost.[38] His entry for January 11 was telling: "Snowstorm today, & half gale easterly winds, little, or no fires, and hungry as hunters, and the cubboards [*sic*] empty, or nearly so & nearly everyone suffering from chilblains."[39]

Gas ended before Christmas, followed by limited hours of electricity until that, too, was at an end. There was no coal and no wood fuel provided, so fires were a matter of whatever one could scrounge.[40] And scrounge was the proper word. The Warrys burned their daughter's old books to keep warm, much as their friends were burning furniture for the same purpose.[41] Those who had wooden gates on their land or in front of their houses had to lift them from their hinges and store them overnight in the house. If they didn't, they ran the distinct risk that they would awaken to find them stolen in the night.[42] Many people were driven to bed by the numbing cold.[43] Bert and Dell Williams seemed to spend the majority of the winter sick, and they turned in early each night, since with the fire out, "bed is the only place."[44] Both of them suffered ongoing stomach pains from the diet, and it must have been particularly wearing for the newly pregnant Dell. Even when Bert stayed home with a cold at one point in February, he spent the time outside cutting up a stump in the garden for wood to keep the fire going.[45] And, of course, without heat how could the Islanders' rations be cooked?

This problem led to the solution of bakehouses to prepare the rations brought to that location, a plan that worked well for some Islanders and not so well for others. Many seem to have memories of taking the bean jar—a traditional Guernsey recipe, but obviously with lesser ingredients during the Occupation—to the bakehouses. The jar was tied with a label bearing the owner's name, covered up with brown paper, and then carried in a bucket to the bakery for cooking overnight.[46] Winifred Harvey and Annette tried the solution offered by the communal stew. They had to give up seven pounds of potatoes, any meat or macaroni ration (if such existed), and half of their vegetable ration. At first, they found the stew quite tasty, especially the broth, and it had potatoes and bones in it along with macaroni. By the time the communal kitchens closed due to a lack of potatoes and roots, Winnie and Annette had already quit theirs. It had not been long before the stew was "nothing but water with a tablespoonful of minced swede at the bottom."[47]

Although not the perfect solution for everyone, the bakehouses are emblematic of the many improvised adjustments and solutions designed to meet the deteriorating conditions of the final year. Like one of the old horse-drawn wagons that filled in for cars and buses during the Occupation, the Guernsey population lurched unsteadily through the winter and spring of 1945. Depleted physically by hunger and cold, but buoyed by the encouraging war news that they heard through their illegal wireless sets, the Islanders waited for the liberation that seemed so slow in coming.

PRISONERS TOGETHER

In this final year, Guernseymen and women had a last opportunity to read the Germans in their midst, and a greatly increased need to do so. Soon after the D-Day invasion, that astute observer of human nature Rev. Ord found much that was amusing in the German attitude. He had reports from those forced to work with the Germans on a daily basis that their tendency toward autocratic display was draining away, to the point that one particularly "hectoring" minor officer now "almost grovelled to the civilians." Even among the common soldiers in the garrison, there seemed fewer who were "boastfully self-confident, a few sleep-walkers excepted." Particularly those who had to deal with civilians on a daily basis seemed to be more careful with their attitude, sometimes turning a "blind eye" to certain violations of regulations in an attempt at ingratiation. It was often the ones most likely to "lord it over" the average citizen that were more inclined to "sidle up obsequiously" to them now. This was satisfying to the common person, but also provided a new source of information at times. Some Germans were even willing to share what news they had about the war, confirming the damage of the bombings in Berlin and Frankfurt.[48]

It was a matter of the Germans slowly feeling their own isolation and realizing that they too were prisoners in the Island, although ostensibly still the captors of the civilian population.[49] Always adept readers of the occupiers in their midst, Islanders now watched the Germans' so-called higher culture and discipline slowly implode in various ways. In July, after the failed attempt on Hitler's life in Operation Valkyrie, all the Wehrmacht were forced to take a loyalty oath to Hitler, and the Nazi "stretch" was demanded universally, much to the delight of Islanders when they watched it performed in the streets. At times, some of the troops were not good at hiding their contempt for this "gymnastic feat," and some had difficulty keeping a straight face, even to the point that some laughed or try to "dodge out of the way" and avoid it entirely. This appeared to some observers as a "notable revelation of mentality" and made clear that no ceremony could increase a sense of loyalty.[50]

There were other signs of dissension in the ranks, at least if a combination of inside knowledge and widespread rumor were to be believed. Ambrose Robin heard in November that the troops were becoming difficult to handle as supplies grew smaller, and around three hundred "discontents over food" were now cooling their heels in prison. More solidly in the rumor line, he reported that a general or admiral (the uncertainty evidently marking this as rumor) was shot and wounded by one of the men under him, who then shot himself.[51] Jack Sauvary partially confirmed this latter rumor when the gravedigger came to visit him the same week that Robin reported this shooting. According to Jack's visitor, he had been busy digging a grave for a German who shot himself after trying to shoot the chief of naval staff. "Maybe true," mused Jack.[52]

More objective proof that discipline was breaking down among the occupiers was provided by the advertisements in the papers seeking deserters from the German forces. Notably, Ernst Lickfeld, condemned to death and imprisoned in the Wehrmacht Prison, escaped during the night of February 25, 1945, and went into hiding. His photograph and description appeared in the newspaper under an "Attention-Wanted" heading—a handsome man in his thirties, described as tall and slender with blue eyes and dark blond hair. Warry included this clipping in his scrapbook with the notation "Since fusilated, and a few others."[53] Lickfeld was not the only German to attempt hiding in the Island, for Rev. Ord estimated at the time that roughly seventeen German deserters were hiding out, "even in so small a place as Guernsey."[54]

Islanders were torn between a certain amount of satisfaction in the difficulties of the Germans, and fear over the breakdown of discipline in the armed forces in their midst. There was hope that the Germans would pack it in if they were starved out and perceived their position as untenable. By the winter and spring of 1945, the Germans were "looking ghastly with hunger,"[55] a turn of events celebrated in many quarters. Others were not so sure that there would be such a positive outcome.[56] Not only did the Germans seem unlikely to surrender based on the hunger of the troops, it became clear that only German discipline stood between the Islanders and disaster. By international law, the Germans could not touch the parcels that were provided to civilians, but how long could this keep up, and when would hunger overrule the officers' ability to control their men?

Bert Williams, generally upbeat about indications of hunger in the German forces, knew that "a starving man is dangerous."[57] There could be no mistake about the depth of German hunger, for it was confirmed not only by their appearance but even more obviously by their actions. In late November, word went around Guernsey that seven Germans had died from digging up crocus bulbs, cooking and eating them (or, in another version, eleven Georgians—Russians in the German army—died from eating wild garlic).[58] A doctor at Vauquiedor heard of Bill Warry's skills as a botanist and sent a messenger down with a plant. When the Germans called on Bill's expertise, several Russians had already died and others were seriously ill. Bill had little difficulty identifying the tap-rooted plant as "hemlock" (*Conium maculatum*), an extremely powerful vegetable poison. This plant looks enough like celery that when the men came upon it, they cooked it and "partook of same with usual results." Ultimately, eleven Georgians and one German would succumb from their impromptu meal.[59]

Such desperate hunger led to one of the more psychologically disturbing situations of the Occupation for the Islanders. Pets were disappearing all across Guernsey, and it was no secret that they were ending up as dinner for German soldiers. This was known to go on earlier in the Occupation, but now dogs and cats were being sought by the soldiers not just at night but in broad daylight. Any stray would be scooped up immediately, stuffed in a haversack, and carted away to be prepared for the stewpot.[60] Little could be done, even when the perpetrators were known. One woman told Rev. Ord that her cat was killed and eaten by the men billeted next door. In the same neighborhood, there were four dogs missing, and another person reported seeing the severed heads of five cats all lined up in a row.[61] There are photographs of smiling Germans posing with the severed head of a cat, but dogs (though also eaten) did not seem to be treated in such a cavalier fashion.[62] Yet, dogs too met the same fate, and it was difficult for some Islanders to change ingrained habits and protect their pets. Rev. Ord warned one lady not to let her spaniel run loose, to which advice she replied, "You needn't worry over him. He hates the Huns!!"[63]

Once a family pet turned up missing, the realization of their probable fate and the pain that it caused are clear in the diarists' accounts. Bert Williams mentioned on January 4, 1945, "Jack our Dog is missing." By the next day, when there was no news of Jack, he wrote, "I am afraid he has been taken by the Germans for food." And by January 6th, although there was still no news, his pet was now "poor Jack the dog." And Bert records each day the lack of news about Jack until the 11th: "No news of the dog, I have given up hopes of ever seeing him again."[64]

And Winifred Harvey actually found a measure of peace from all of this pain. Her friend Maude lost her cat, and Marie Randall's dog also seemed to be "among the victims of the stewpot." Winnie felt the most grief over General de Lisle's "dear little Scotch terrier, so like my Rolf," who also turned up missing. So finally there came a time when Winnie was not just trying to convince herself that Rolf's death had some saving grace rather than being a horrible mistake made under pressure. She could honestly compare Rolf's end, quick and without suffering, to friends' pets now missing and likely to have suffered a terrible end. "I am thankful," wrote Winnie, "that has not been my Rolfie's fate and would not now have a cat or dog for anything."[65] And she seemed finally able to consign Rolf to the past and absolve herself of the burden of guilt and regret that she had carried for nearly five years.

Pets were not the only items stolen, as "robberies organized and unorganized"[66] became increasingly widespread. Some were fairly large-scale or at least preplanned operations, as when Symon's Butcher Shop was raided and sides of pork stolen. Other thefts were smaller or less coordinated, such as snatch-and-grab break-ins of shops, or missing rabbits or swedes taken from a garden in the night.[67] Kitty and Peter's friend George was treated to the sight of the few hens he had left reduced to a series of heads left behind on the ground.[68] Occasionally, these smaller thieves were caught, as when one German soldier was shot and killed, and another wounded, in the act of stealing from a broccoli patch. Robin believed that this would be a warning for certain civilians, some of whom he thought were also "rogues" who "prowl after curfew hours."[69]

Germans were going door-to-door begging for food, which was troubling and frightening not only to women living alone, but really to all of the Islanders, who were, of course, unarmed.[70] These Germans would ask for potatoes, but when turned down would simply come back in the night and steal them.[71] Incidents abounded of soldiers simply walking into civilian homes, grabbing whatever food was on the table, and bolting away. Rev. Ord was told of one woman who was robbed "in grand style," for she found a German sitting at her kitchen table tucking into her "ersatz pudding" with a will. He looked up at her and, cool as could be, complimented her on her cooking.[72]

Islanders were aware that they were often being "cased" by the Germans in these final months—to see what food they might have, and to gauge how easy it would be to carry that food away. The Germans started large-scale house searches under the guise of uncovering caches of food held by hoarders.[73] What became clear was that such searches were means for the German soldiers to plan a nighttime robbery.[74] Most Islanders took simple steps to secure the small amounts of food that they had. Locked doors, barred windows, and casual forms of what would now be called neighborhood watches were the first lines of defense. Many took the contents of their precious parcels upstairs to bed with them at night, and the Ords not merely took theirs upstairs but also stashed them in the piano.[75] Others went to more elaborate means of protection. Bill Warry put tripwires in his garden to try to foil thieves, and was pleased to see signs that someone had a "nasty fall" and left marks to that effect on the ground.[76] Frank Higgs set up clatter traps to fall and wake the dog if anyone tried to break in. All of these efforts worked well for a while, though on Easter Monday, Dorothy woke to find that her youngest milker, Chloe, had been killed and carried off. At that point, they built stalls actually in the back scullery of the house and went to sleep each night to the sound of goat noises.[77]

There was always the chance that Islanders would fall into the trap they had set for another. One of the most amusing stories of someone hoist with his own petard was told to me by Alf Williams. Someone had been "pinching" their milk, so Alf said to his father, "I'll have him," and he set up an elaborate trap using a series of ropes to rig up a bath of cattle liquid over a door. In the old farmhouses there was a second door to go into the barn, and the plan was that anyone opening that door would pull the rope and all of the liquid would come down on him. This type of cattle insecticide has an absolutely vile smell that would last a week or more and would be fitting justice to anyone attempting a break-in and theft. All seemed well until Alf's father was listening to the crystal set at 6:30 in the morning on March 24, hearing the news that Montgomery had crossed the Rhine. All excited and shouting with glee at the news, he grabbed his milk cans, jerked open the door, and Whoomp! received the full bath all over him. He had simply forgotten that the trap was there. Of course, his clothes were worthless and had to be burned, and this when replacements were hard to come by. Alf said, "I went to work very, very early that morning." But if Alf anticipated that his father would blame him for the incident, he was in for a surprise, for he "never heard another word" about it.[78]

Burglary was one thing, but the final year saw mounting fear as thefts took a violent turn. As early as August 1944, the Island was deeply disturbed by the shooting of a St. Saviour's farmer named Jehan and his son. Hearing a soldier in their potato patch in the night, the thirty-nine-year-old farmer ran out with his son to chase the man off their property. But the soldier turned and fired, striking Jehan in the stomach and his son in the heel. The next day, Jehan died. Bert Williams later reported on the inquest, describing the verdict as "the funniest one imaginable." According to Bert, the magistrate appeared frightened of what the Germans would say to a verdict of murder, so he rendered the odd decision of "murder or manslaughter."[79] Islanders were not at all conflicted about whether or not this was murder.

The other open question was whether the soldier involved was a German or Georgian (Russian). There were Russian units in the Island, composed of a blend of volunteers willing to fight against the Soviets and men who had donned the German uniform rather than starve in concentration camps. The latter were truly men without a country—having turned traitor to Russia, but without the discipline of the German soldiers, or any ideological stake in the war. Their game was personal survival, and they seemed willing to play it in any way necessary. In the Jehan case, Colonel von Heldorff, the German supply chief, met with the Bailiff to assure him that guns had been taken away from the Russian units, and that any Germans who had threatened civilians had been punished.[80] A German official attended Jehan's funeral—perhaps as a show of solidarity with the civilians, but a presence that Bert Williams read as an indicator of German guilt.[81]

As desperation mounted over food in the forces, violence also increased. Then, on February 22, a neighbor of Mr. Sigwart, a watchmaker in Hauteville, became concerned when neither Sigwart nor his wife were up and about their daily errands. She noticed that the blackout was still in place and tried banging on their back door with a hammer to rouse them. Failing to get a reply, she called the police, who found the couple's bodies in their house—she strangled, and he drowned in the bath. Testimony was given by neighbors of heavy footsteps going up the Sigwarts' stairs, and a bicycle inside the gate during the evening before the bodies were found. Also, the police reports described seventy-four-year-old Mrs. Sigwart lying in the dining room, strangled by a piece of material tied tightly around her neck. Mr. Sigwart, seventy-seven years old, was found in the upstairs bath, in a tub that was only a quarter filled. His left foot was dry, although his body was wet and in the tub. Two handkerchiefs were tied around his neck, one tightly and the other loosely. This scenario seems to speak more to someone pushed backward into a tub (with one foot left outside of it) rather than climbing in to commit suicide by drowning. It seems unlikely that a suicide would bother with strangling himself with a handkerchief. The inquest, which lasted a long time and was twice adjourned, brought in a verdict of murder/suicide, a conclusion that was not shared by most Islanders. As Winifred Harvey put it, "Many think they were the first victims." She did not need to elaborate.[82]

On March 31, at the De Garis farm, men going in to milk the cows came upon some Germans who were "there for the same purpose." The German police were called in, and one

German policeman, going in to arrest the Germans, was shot and killed. De Garis's throat was cut and he was rushed to the hospital.[83] This was the increasing danger: that civilians might surprise armed thieves in the night in their own homes and yards. At this same time came news of the most shocking murder of the Occupation, when an elderly couple, the Robins of St. Martin, were savagely butchered in their own home, their poultry taken, and the contents of their Red Cross parcel stolen.[84] The violence of the attack (their heads bashed in and their throats cut—Mr. Robins with twelve bayonet wounds to the head) led most to suspect the Russians. It seems that the Robins traded with both the Germans and the Russians, and whoever killed them was known to the couple, as there was no indication of forced entry.[85] Islanders could hear on their hidden wireless sets that the war was coming to a close and liberation was close at hand. Murders like that of the Robins raised one question in their minds: Would liberation come in time?

AND BRITISH AGAIN

Despite the positive information coming through their crystal sets signaling that the war with Germany was moving toward its close, particularly the welcome news of Hitler's death, worries still existed over how the end would play out. Part of the concern was that the Channel Islands were now under the charge of Vice Admiral Hüffmeier, described by Jurat Leale as a "red-hot Nazi."[86] Stories abounded that the new admiral was a "perfect terror" and that more than one attempt had been made on his life, necessitating a double guard of soldiers around him at all times.[87] Rumors started as early as February that it was only the vice admiral who was holding up a raising of the white flag, and that the troops under his command were eager for the end.[88] Right down to the bitter end, it was believed that Hüffmeier might hold out and was laying down mines in the harbor in preparation to defend against a final siege.[89]

It was the women of the Island in particular who predicted a "gory ending" to the Occupation and believed that open conflict would ultimately come to their shores.[90] It was often the women who kept their eyes open in the Market and on the streets, and they were able to read some disturbing differences among the Germans in their midst. One concern was the obvious dichotomy between officers and average soldiers, the officers appearing well-fed while the troops were so noticeably starving. Only some of the officers retained their accustomed swagger, still peering down their noses at the Islanders and treating them as the vanquished spoils of war for the superior German forces. Such arrogance, seemingly oblivious to the true state of the war, was amusing to many Islanders, who had to suppress smiles as some officers, determined to maintain their image of superiority, pranced and strutted by. What was not amusing was the widespread belief that the officers might hold out longer against surrender because they did not feel the compelling force of hunger as experienced by the common soldier.[91]

Rev. Ord, who from his Christian perspective retained hope that Islanders could differentiate the good individual from the detested Nazi culture, knew that the final year was challenging in that regard. His hope was always for the souls of his parishioners and that they would not be "warped and embittered" in the day of liberation. It was the coming victory that would provide the "supreme spiritual test."[92] The pressure of Christian obligations became important as parcels relieved some of the civilian hunger and the common soldiers increasingly took on the appearance of gray-green ghosts. In January, Mülle, the Germans' clerk at

Newlands, came up to Moullin, Winifred Harvey's gardener, and tearfully begged for food. He was an Austrian, he said, and he did not want to fight—and look at his clothes, they were paper-thin and in this cold . . . Moullin conveyed this message to Winnie, who at first said she could not help him. And then she thought, "if thine enemy hunger, feed him," and after all, she reasoned, Mülle was not an enemy but a "decent fellow," whom they all liked. So, she told Moullin to give him some artichokes that she could ill afford to give away. Mülle knew this to be a personal sacrifice, and greeted this gift with tears and an assurance that he prayed "every night for this beastly war to be over."[93]

But fellow feeling and Christian impulses were not applied simply to those known personally to the Islanders. Winnie was obviously touched by a German soldier who came up behind her while she waited in line at the Market hoping for two small pieces of broccoli. The soldier asked, "Bitte, madam, wollen Die für mich Bluhmenkohl kaufen?" (Please, madam, would you buy some broccoli for me?). That she was torn can be seen in Winnie's description: "He was young, ghastly white, tears in his eyes." He pleaded, stroking her arm, but in this case, she had to harden her heart and replied, "No. I shall only get two small ones myself. It is against the law. I cannot do it." She watched him move to the next stall, knowing he would have no better luck there.[94]

Despite maintaining their unalloyed hatred for the German system and for most of the officers who represented that system, some Islanders could not help but feel sorry for the common soldier. Kitty Bachmann believed that these starving men saw themselves as allied now with the Islanders as "co-exiles and 'brothers' in adversity." Kitty, for one, could "derive no satisfaction from their pathetic state."[95] Dorothy Higgs could not feel sympathy for these men "dragging about with hunched shoulders and arms hanging loose" as long as civilians were hungry as well. But, she wondered, what if in the future the Red Cross could feed civilians to the point where they were not hungry at all? Could they watch the soldiers die when it already "tears one's heart" to see them suffer? It was an interesting hypothetical that pitted the need for the British to starve the Germans out—an outcome that Dorothy supported—against the fact that the Islanders would be compelled to watch these young men of the enemy forces slowly starve to death before their eyes. Already by the spring of 1945 there were many cases of death by malnutrition and hospital cases of collapse in the occupying forces, but as the civilians continued to be driven to stinging nettles and moss for food, this hypothetical was never tested.[96]

Then, into these small stirrings of sympathy for the weakest among the enemy troops came the news of the liberation of the concentration camps in Germany, and Islanders recoiled with horror. They knew of German cruelty firsthand and could see it in the treatment of the Organization Todt workers. But the extent, the organized cruelty, and the horror of the Holocaust now being uncovered staggered them. Their response was even stronger than most, because they realized that they could have all shared a similar fate had the Germans wished to rid themselves of the local population and keep the Channel Islands as a physical asset. And what could have been the fate of their family and friends, the deportees to Germany, had the Germans made different choices? Perhaps at this point, too, the likely end of the Jewish deportees became apparent to those who had known them. It was terrible and disturbing news on multiple levels, and changed utterly any inklings of fellow feeling Islanders had begun to have toward the starving troops.

These revelations made Kitty question whether the Russians really were the perpetrators of much of the recent violence in Guernsey, or simply convenient scapegoats for the Germans to blame for their own actions. "Many generations must pass," she wrote, "before the soul of Germany can feel purged of the guilt and degradation of this real-life version of Dante's Inferno." And learning of the "dreadful martyrdom of those pitiful, innocent victims" put the five years of Occupation into an entirely new frame: "They make our little Calvaries look very mean indeed."[97] Elizabeth Doig was relieved that pictures were being taken of the atrocities, so that the "German nation" and the entire world could see "what they (these criminals) have done to their fellow creatures." With this, Elizabeth seemed to separate the German nation from the actions of the Nazi leadership. But then she went on to write, "One can not believe it of a whole people. They can never be trusted or forgiven"—a foretaste of the same questions of collective German guilt that have been explored in recent decades.[98]

The liberation of the German death camps caused Rev. Ord to think deeply again about his theory of differentiation, his "formula" that each man should be allowed to reveal his true nature and then be treated accordingly. He concluded that, while Christ hated the evil done by men, he could not "find that Christ hated PERSONS." It meant that the innocent would need to share with the guilty in history's "terrific judgment of a nation" that had allowed its liberties to be drained away, and that had put in place men capable of such evil as the concentration camps now revealed. Still, he believed, thinking obviously of those anti-Nazi Germans that he had come to know during the Occupation, that "such things are not the work of those whom we know to be decent-minded."[99]

Ord also knew through Reinhold in mid-April that revolt in some parts of the German forces was a distinct possibility. Reinhold was speaking quietly to his closest friends and had come to agree that with the fall of Berlin, they would no longer feel honor-bound to any oath of allegiance and would refuse at that point to serve as soldiers.[100] Some others of the common soldiers were more definitely self-serving and tried to escape retaliation they believed would come at the end, saying, "Me nix German; me Polony!"[101] And stories went around that the Germans were offering to give their revolvers to the locals and showing them the white flags they had all ready for "when the British land."[102]

The true end of the Occupation had a stutter-start feel to it. First came the announcement through the BBC that news of total German surrender could come at any time, and that Churchill would make a speech as to the freeing of the Channel Islands. This news was galvanizing, and Winifred Harvey went first to tell Mrs. Clayton, and then to her friend Maude to share the wonderful news. Winnie and Maude felt there was only one way to react to news of their coming freedom, and they knelt to thank God and seek strength for the days to come.[103] What both women sensed was that the war for Guernsey would not be over until Admiral Hüffmeier surrendered. Rumor was increasingly strong that he planned to hold out, and that the airport was being reinforced and mines being laid to withstand a British siege.[104]

During this uncertain period, Islanders could not be restrained from symbolic displays. After Roosevelt's death, a red, white, and blue wreath appeared on the War Memorial and had remained there untouched. Now someone put a rosette collar of red, white, and blue around the neck of the statue of Prince Albert down at the St. Peter Port harbor.[105] Small shops were selling these red, white, and blue rosettes, and children were wearing them openly. One woman was seen walking happily about St. Peter Port with a Union Jack folded over her arm, with all of these patriotic displays ignored by the Germans walking about the same streets.[106] As May 7th came with no definitive word, red, white, and blue began to appear everywhere, a display that Ord comically likened to "cutting the cake before the bride had signed the register."[107]

Whatever the hardship and challenging decisions of the Occupation, whatever the doubts and difficulties of the postwar period, Guernsey had its moment of untarnished joy at Liberation. Worry that the Germans would hold out changed to wild excitement when the *Star* issued a broadsheet at 10:00 A.M. on May 8th stating that "The War Is Over for Guernsey: German Officers Inform the Bailiff of Surrender." A proclamation was to be read at the Royal Court House at noon that day, Churchill would make a speech at 3:00 P.M., and flags could be flown after that time.[108] And the people took full advantage of the opportunity for display: flags came out of hiding and were flaunted everywhere, houses were bedecked in colors and patriotic symbols.[109] At the Court House at noon, Winifred Harvey found the proclamation to be touching; "our worn, strained Jurats and the old Bailiff who had such a weary anxious term of office" were nonetheless impressive and the scene was pronounced "historic."[110]

While joy and thankfulness were on every hand, there were no angry demonstrations and no attacks on the Germans still in their midst. Ord was pleased at these signs of restraint as the Islanders awaited the arrival of the British troops that would signal the transfer of military authority. Germans walked "gravely" through the streets, unmolested by the swarms of excited civilians; one German even wore a red, white, and blue rosette, perhaps a sign of his own happiness that the war was over.[111] Both Bert Williams and Bill Warry mentioned that it was a good thing that pubs were not open and no liquor was available, for one thing because an unaccustomed drink would "knock most people over" due to their frail condition. Also there was the possibility that the young people might "go mad & start trouble with the Germans."[112]

Yet, despite the proclamations and speeches, Guernsey could not be truly free until the surrender papers were signed and the British troops came ashore. We now know that Hüffmeier was disinclined to surrender, even following orders from the remnants of the German High Command to do so. On May 8 at 2:00 p.m., Hüffmeier sent his envoy, on board a heavily armed minesweeper, to meet with the HMS *Bulldog*, which had been dispatched to effect the surrender of the Channel Islands. This envoy, Kapitanleutnant Armin Zimmermann, was a comic-opera expression of the strutting Nazi prig, and film of his boarding shows him making an exaggerated Nazi salute. Zimmermann had no authorization to sign the surrender and came to arrange terms of an armistice. Told bluntly that there would only be an unconditional surrender, Zimmermann returned to the minesweeper after haughtily suggesting that the *Bulldog* could be taken as hostile and fired upon. It is rather satisfying to note that Zimmermann ended up getting his backside dunked as he sat in the dinghy on the return trip to the minesweeper. Ultimately, the minesweeper returned at midnight—its guns now unmanned—with Generalmajor Heine, who had Hüffmeier's written authorization to sign the unconditional surrender. The signing took place at 7:15 A.M., on May 9, and after four years and ten months the Occupation was over.[113]

Thus, on May 9, 1945, the day to be celebrated each year in the Islands as Liberation Day, the British troops arrived. Winnie went with the crowds through the festooned streets to see the British troops, the crowd bursting forth with "God Save the King" as the flag was unfurled. Winnie was struck by the ruddy faces and solid frames of the soldiers, in such stark contrast to the "grey and yellow" faces and skeletal physique of the Islanders: "I had forgotten that people could look like that." It was joy unmarred by any concerns but the appreciation for being free, and many had tears in their eyes while watching the scene unfold.[114] It was best summed up by Dorothy Higgs's small display of the triumph of survival when she wrote, "We are alive and well and BRITISH again!!!"[115]

AND THE VAGARIES OF TIME AND MEMORY

There have been many years to try and sort out the Occupation experience since the heady days of Liberation, but certain factors seem to intervene and make understanding difficult. In reading some of the most recent accounts, including those from British journalism, one sticking point has been the lack of Guernsey civilian retaliation against the German forces or known collaborators, fraternizers, or profiteers. One issue concerns our sense of what constitutes retaliation. Where were the photographs of women with shaved heads clutching their German-fathered babies and fleeing from angry, taunting mobs? Where were signs of overt retaliation, such as swastikas painted on buildings, pointing out businesses and individuals known to have collaborated or fraternized? Did this mean, as some imply, that the Guernsey Islanders were all collaborators/fraternizers or perfectly comfortable with those who were? Does it mean, as others imply, that John Leale's speech on May 23 lulled a sheeplike populace into acceptance that all decisions made by their leaders during the Occupation were uniformly sound?

It is clear from the diaries that prior to Liberation, many had fantasies of extracting some measure of satisfaction from punishing the Germans and those who collaborated. These vary in intensity based on the personality of the writer, but there were signs that things could get ugly in some quarters. It was deprivation that sparked much of the desire for revenge. Rev. Ord reported the great excitement caused by the notice found affixed to Admiral Hüffmeier's door in February 1945:

Who stole our BREAD?
Who stole our MEAT?
Who stole our BUTTER?
Who is drinking our CHILDREN'S MILK?
YOU!!
WE WILL REMEMBER![116]

Kitty Bachmann heard this same account and believed that the notice was contrived by some enterprising "outraged parents." The Germans apparently took the threat seriously and doubled the guard at the Grange Lodge.[117]

Bert Williams had plenty of ideas for the appropriate postwar penalties to be assessed against profiteers and others who shirked their patriotic duty in various ways. In March, he was hoping that some type of "super tax" would be affixed to the "local bloodsuckers which will leave them penniless after the war."[118] His ire was particularly raised by those charging exorbitant amounts for the cigarettes he still craved but could not get. His anger was aimed at a shop owner who, just days before Liberation, was selling cigarettes at 7 marks each. "He should be shot at sight. He is a real blood sucker & no mistake," fumed Bert, who was completely out of "smokes" and "dreading tomorrow with nothing to smoke. Good thing when this damn war is over."[119]

There is something comical about this anger expended specifically on those standing between Bert and his smokes, particularly considering how much real deprivation he had suffered during the past year from hunger and cold. But his deeper wrath and desire for retaliation extended to any growers or other Guernseymen who sold to or fraternized with the Germans in any way. And he shared a common desire with other Islanders when he maintained, "I hope all the Guernsey quislings will be rounded up after the war & either deported or branded."[120] With such indications of a desire for retaliation after the Occupation ended, why were there no ugly scenes or violent attacks when Guernsey had the opportunity at Liberation?

Multiple factors seemed to dampen this need in the Island. The first factors, of course, were simply the personalities and moral values of individuals. After Liberation, reports reached the Island that Jersey girls had been tarred and feathered. Further accounts said that they were tied to railings and their names written on walls with swastikas painted over them. Ken was aghast at such "hooligan like actions" and prayed that Vera, whom he knew to have "perhaps fraternised too freely with the troops," would not suffer such a fate. He did not believe that Guernsey Islanders would take part in such actions, particularly against girls that they knew, despite strong feelings about such fraternization.[121] It may be that such rumors from Jersey, many highly exaggerated in the telling, cooled the ardor of those who might lead such retaliation. Violent actions, so satisfying in imagination, seem simply ugly and mob-like when actually carried out. As to attacking the Germans, Rev. Ord held fast to his belief that it was counter to British nature "to hate for long" regardless of the extent of the provocation.[122]

Then again, the change from being captives to being free was so sudden that it was enervating mentally and physically. The most common metaphor for feelings right after Liberation was that of waking from a "nightmare of fear." Ord described the streets of St. Peter Port as filled with "citizens whose expression was that of people awaking from a long nightmare sleep to find themselves in a world of reality unbeset by evil dreams."[123] This concept was echoed by Dorothy Higgs, who described the "five years of dreadful isolation" as the nightmare that now seemed to disappear into unreality "now that we are alive and awake again."[124]

A somewhat different idea of the end of the nightmare and the beautiful dream that took its place appears in many of the accounts. Bert Williams described it as "We are all going about in a dream as yet but it is a fine dream." He returned to the dream concept repeatedly as he described each new taste of unaccustomed food: a particularly fine trifle with prunes and cream, the first taste of an orange after five years.[125] Repeatedly for many days after May 9th, similar words were evoked by Bert and by Bill Warry to capture the feeling: "We still can't realize that we are free"; "We haven't realized that we are free as yet."[126] And universally, the Islanders found that they had lost their appetites. Some assumed this effect was caused by all of the excitement, and others that it was the sight of all the unaccustomed food, or the fact that their stomachs had "shrunk to pygmy proportions."[127]

With all of these mental and physical dislocations, it is not surprising that retaliation was not foremost in Islanders' minds. But I believe these are minor factors in Guernsey's response to the end of Occupation. More important was their orientation towards the future and their understanding of appropriate ways to settle old scores. This sense of the excitement of a new and fresh future started before the war ended. During the final spring, even as Bill Warry was contemplating just how hungry he was and how much he would spend for even a mouthful of food, he added, "but we know the war will soon be over, then we will be living in a new world."[128] This feeling grew stronger after Liberation. Ken found that reading about their liberation in the English newspapers and listening to wireless accounts of the events "seemed to galvanise one into a new life instead of the dull monotony of the past years."[129]

And before the final prayer that closes his diary, Rev. Ord turned to this same theme:

> And so, with the khaki tide welling ever stronger across our beaches; with the dark night of restriction and repression behind us; and with emotions we know not how to control, we look forward with confidence to the future.[130]

This image of a dark night behind them and the beckoning of a beautiful new day of freedom ahead captures well the general feeling of Guernsey at Liberation.

Others were concentrated on the work ahead to reclaim the physical Island, now with mined beaches and barbed wire, and to restore their reputation as suppliers of fresh produce for Britain. This last concern was enough to inspire Frank Higgs, silent throughout Dorothy's account, to weigh in. He described the difficulties of the "poor old growers" and the greenhouses now "riddled with falling shrapnel, unpainted and unrepaired." But despite losing their livelihood, "we've helped to feed our people," and that would have to do as compensation. With this nod to the past, all of Frank's thoughts were to the immediate future: "However, we are still alive and kicking, and it's off hats to the Tommies, and off coats to the work of reconstruction."[131]

Of course, all was not sweet forgiveness of the misdeeds of collaborators and fraternizers; the Islanders simply found ways to get their own back more in keeping with the subtlety they had displayed throughout the Occupation. It is Bert Williams who provides some insight into these methods. One pleasure was in seeing the change in fortune of the Germans, forced to stay and clean up the Island before being sent to POW camps. Bert described them in the common phrase of the time as "working like blacks packing up . . . also taking down the barbed wire along the coal quay and White Rock." He fairly crows when watching the officers taken away, writing in all caps, "THE GERMAN ADMIRAL WAS MARCHED FROM THE CROWN HOTEL TO THE WHITE ROCK UNDER ESCORT."[132] It was highly enjoyable to watch the German officers and soldiers down at the harbor being searched by the British Tommies, who served in the Islanders' minds as their surrogates. "What a come down," wrote Bill Warry with deep satisfaction.[133]

The moves against civilian fraternizers were largely a matter of lateral surveillance and public shaming. Bert described how, at the big celebration at Candie Garden on May 19, with 2,500 in attendance and British soldiers sitting in on the piano and drums, "all the girls who have run after the Germans were there." It was intensely irritating to see those civilians who had cozied up to the Germans now trying to do the same with the British Tommies. Bert was clear about the Islander response: "A lot of Guernsey people are being told where they get off owing to their dealings with the Germans and the girls who have had babies for Germans are being pointed out to the British Tommies. These people are in for a hot time well they deserve it."[134]

Some official moves were made to lessen the profiteering of those running the black market or selling voluntarily to the Germans. Near the end of May, the banks were crowded with people trying to change their old £1 Guernsey notes, which they had to accomplish by June 2. Just as with an early exchange of German marks, it was a move to strip the black-marketeers of at least some of their "ill-gotten wealth."[135] But it would be the court of public opinion, rather than an actual court of law, where common fraternizers and low-level collaborators would be tried. Their sentence would be in changed interpersonal relationships, subtle retaliations, and in the perfect knowledge of their neighbors, and themselves, of how poorly they had acquitted themselves during the time of testing.

There would be ample time for backlash during the immediate postwar period. The Guernsey Islanders, like the rest of the British nation, would be catapulted from wartime deprivation to the difficulties of what has been called "Austerity Britain."[136] There would not be the plenty and rosy days anticipated, but years of struggle. Although this story of the postwar years is beyond the frame of this study and really deserves a complete examination in itself, some aspects are worth noting. England sought a change in government more in keeping with the new decisions that now were needed. In July 1945, a general election defeated Winston Churchill, to whom they owed so much and who was stunned by this massive swing in public confidence, and put in place the Labour Party under Clement Attlee. The Channel Islands also were eager to shift to a different form of government, and the Controlling Committee came in for close scrutiny. The wait and worry over the return of deportees, and the tendering of Occupation honors to some, including a knighthood for Victor Carey, led to some hard feelings and bitterness in certain quarters. Although there were exceptions, the honors seemed to go to men in high places, and singling out some by necessity meant neglecting others.

As it became apparent that some Islanders would never return from deportation, it was also natural to question whether their leaders had done all they possibly could to protect the people. These immediate feelings slowly cooled over time into a shared belief that, given the circumstances, the States had acted with practicality and largely to good effect. Although Frank Falla believed that the resisters in Guernsey had never been properly acknowledged or compensated for their suffering under the Germans, and raised these issues in the late 1960s, he too defended many of the decisions made by the Island leaders under duress. So, over the decades, Islanders settled into a sense of their common experience and common efforts under Occupation, and they rebuilt the fortunes of Guernsey while relishing the stories of this strange and eventful period.[137]

As already discussed, various attacks on this common understanding have been made since the 1990s, challenges based on the official transcript of Occupation documents. In an odd way this battle, though in a new generation, points up the singularity of the Occupation years, and the disconnect experienced by Islanders in conveying their experience to outsiders. Those who went through the Occupation in Guernsey knew that their perspective was unique, and this became the basis of numerous jokes at the time. The isolation was certain, the Islanders kidded each other, to have an effect on their minds. Her son's doctor told Kitty that he was sure that he was no longer "*compos mentis.*" He believed that when evacuated friends and family returned, they would "take one look at us, shrug their shoulders and sigh: 'I suppose it must be the Occupation.'"[138]

Part of the Islanders' perspective could be summed up in the new traits that they expected to retain even once freedom and plenty returned. Many believed that they would never leave food on their plates again, or that they would "never throw things away"[139] after the Occupation was behind them. But these were little things. Dorothy Higgs was particularly eloquent on the larger issues that might divide those in Guernsey during these years from mainlanders and those who evacuated. She believed that when the war was at an end, there would be a "gap of ignorance that, perhaps, will never be bridged." Islanders had not experienced the time spent in air-raid shelters, the opportunity to engage in war work, the camaraderie of a whole nation united behind a single cause. Would they be able to bridge that sense of being remote from all these experiences? Or would they be "like foreigners, who know the language and grammar, but none of the idiom of these years"?[140] Then again, the ignorance would cut both ways, and how could they ever convey what it was like to live amidst their captors and to spend their time focused on the necessities of survival?

Dorothy had a dream around the time of the D-day invasion that showed the subconscious depth of her concerns. She dreamed that she was in an "English restaurant where everyone knew everyone else." She felt very out of things because she only knew a few people and had recently just returned from the "oubliette"—a small room or dungeon where a person is locked away, forgotten, and left to go mad. Then someone asked her what work she was engaged in and she was instantly embarrassed. How could she tell these people that she had only been "playing with goats and rabbits for four years"? So, with the cleverness that comes to us in dreams, Dorothy replied that she had been "investigating the life history of fleas and lice."[141]

As charmingly bizarre as Dorothy's dream was, it is a fair summary of Islander concerns as the war ended. Would they be treated as outsiders, as noncontributors to the war effort, despite the number of troops they had supplied and their role in helping to preserve their small corner of Britain? They had been locked away in their Island oubliette and perhaps forgotten; would they now be embraced and made to feel part of the British whole? Could anyone else relate to the experiences of their five years, to the makeshift recipes and amateur animal husbandry that spelled the difference between malnutrition and survival, to the small concerns and the acts of rhetorical resistance that were so important to Islander spirits?

The Islanders did find some tensions with returning family and friends. It can be imagined that young people returning to the Island after five years in the larger space of the mainland would find it cramped and narrow. Many of them left as children, but they now were coming back as teenagers, and settling into family life could not have been easy. Some would not stay, having in effect lost their home and family to the change in themselves while forced to be away for so long. And it seems that there were some sharp exchanges with returning friends to the effect that those who left had cut and run, and those who stayed had not helped to win the war.[142] Some of the less-measured mainland British attacks of the last few years, seeking to paint Channel Islanders with a broad brush as collaborators, come across as an echo of these earlier disputes.

I asked Alf Williams if, after the war, he felt closer to those who had shared his experience of Occupation. He thought only briefly and then said, "You mustn't ask me that because I'm afraid I can forget a lot quick and talk to anybody. I could forget that and carry on . . . half our youth we lost in the war." Alf's response brings up an interesting issue not always considered. We tend to think in terms of two different perspectives on the Occupation, of adults who evacuated versus adults who stayed, ignoring age as a primary variation. Just to open a new way to look at the blending of Islanders after the war, let us consider the experience of one of the many Le Page families in Guernsey. This was a family of five children, the youngest, Victor, being born on the day that the older children evacuated. This new brother explains quite well why the parents planned to stay for the near term. Although they fully expected to join their evacuated children later on, the Occupation started and the family was separated for the duration. The oldest son, Howard, who was fifteen at the time, evacuated with Elizabeth College, and the twelve-year-old sister, Marion, left with the Girls Intermediate. The third son, Bill, was nine years old and he also assembled to evacuate with the Hautes Capelles school. However, after waiting all day, Bill's school was rescheduled for the next day at 3 P.M., and the children were sent home for the night. It was just too much for Bill, and he "broke down" at home that night, his parents agreeing that he could stay with them in Guernsey.

Thus, Bill shared the Occupation with his parents, his brand new brother, and his little sister, Maud, three-and-a-half when the Germans came. When asked the same questions about what stood out for them, the three surviving children (Bill, Maud, and Marion) quite naturally have divergent answers. Bill, who was at a perfect age for forming memories, strongly remembers the five Germans billeted on the family, the time when an airplane flew low at night and the response was anti-aircraft fire ("the finest firework display ever seen"), and the train lines run across the Island—with attendant destruction of property—by the Germans in an Island that had never seen a train. And he remembers the hunger, influential enough that still today he feels that he must clean his plate and hates to see anything going to waste.

Maud, only eight-and-a-half when the Occupation ended, also remembers the billeted Germans, but she mainly recalls that the ordinary soldiers were kind to her, most likely because they missed their own families. She remembers that the golf links nearby was used by the Germans for storage, and that the children were allowed to wander around the area. But her memory of the railway line cutting through the Island is harrowing. On one particular day she saw men "dressed like tramps" working under the charge of a German. Now she knows that they were the Organization Todt, but what she remembers was watching the men and having one turn toward her. He had no nose, "just the holes in the face." It is little wonder that she was horrified, never went near the rail line again, and still retains the moment as a "flashbulb memory" of the Occupation.

Now think how radically different was Marion's experience as an evacuee. The connection to Guernsey was broken almost immediately when she only had time to receive one letter from her mother in the ten days after evacuation and before the Germans invaded and closed the communicative link. From then on, communication was a matter of 25-word messages every six months or so, with only an opportunity to find out that the family was well. Marion remembers that it was 1943 before she found out in one message that her new brother had been named Victor. It might be expected that she would see Howard, evacuated at the same time. But she only saw him once during the early months, and Howard would go on to join the military. She would not see him until after the war, when he was "de-mobbed" from the army and returned to Guernsey, together with his new wife. Marion had some stability, because although the evacuated Guernsey schoolchildren were billeted all around the town, the school was given their own three rooms in a primary school and stayed together with their teachers throughout their school years. As a group they participated in various war work projects, collecting money door-to-door for the Red Cross, weaving camouflage nets, and washing dishes at a local hospital.

During 1941, when Marion was staying at her first billet, a German plane came over and dropped two bombs on the village. Two rows of houses were destroyed on the main road, but had the bombs been released a second earlier, it would have been Marion's house that was hit. She would carry with her through life the distinct memory of the devastation that had come so close to her. Marion, too, had a difficult adjustment upon returning to Guernsey in 1945. She had finished school in 1944 and had been working at the Girl Guide Training House in the New Forest. Her life was now in England, and she anticipated returning there after a prolonged visit with family in Guernsey. But somehow, she settled in and stayed on in the Island despite her shyness, which made the adjustment back to Guernsey life that much more difficult.

In the Le Page children, we see the broad experience of the youth of Guernsey during the Occupation.[143] Their perceptions of the experience would vary according to age, and for many of the younger ones, the postwar period would meld seamlessly into what went before. However, the change was greatest for the older children who went away in 1940. Some, like Howard, who returned to live in Guernsey, came back as married veterans. Others, like Marion, felt like strangers—at least at first—disconnected from those they had left behind years ago. The Islanders did not just lose their young men that they gave to the war effort, many of whom would never come home. They lost the natural connection that they had with much of the young generation forced to spend their formative years away from Guernsey. The reverberations of the Occupation were not just psychological but also physical, and this impact was felt more in the children who remained in Guernsey throughout the war years. There have been some fascinating recent studies on the later health effects for those children who suffered through the extended period of food restriction in the Channel Islands. Studies conducted right after the war, and another study in 2002 showed that there were significant reductions in weight, height, and body mass index (BMI) short-term during the Occupation, and a significant long-term reduction in height. A more recent study revealed that average growth rates for Jersey schoolchildren, under the same food restrictions as Guernsey, were significantly lower than children in mainland Britain during the same period.[144]

There would be other ripple effects from the Occupation for those who were children and teenagers during that time. Menstruation for women coming of age during the Occupation in Guernsey was delayed by a full twelve months for girls born in 1930. Much like the studies on height, the impact of lower weight on the start of menstruation is not a surprise, and duplicates the modern understanding that eating disorders may have a similar effect, as may high levels of exercise. One recent study examined the breast-cancer rates for women who had experienced this delayed menarche due to Occupation conditions. Although the researchers were seeking some protective benefit, they found that the delay in menarche had the opposite effect and was associated with an increased risk of breast cancer.[145]

Perhaps, however, the restricted diet and lower weight would be protective for Islanders' hearts in later years? A recent study showed this not to be the case, and found that those who were children, adolescents, and young adults during the Occupation developed a significantly higher level of cardiovascular disease, and experienced more than twice the admissions to hospital for CVD than the cohort of Guernsey Islanders of the same ages who had evacuated to the mainland. The researchers concluded that this result was unlikely to be due to stress, because those who evacuated had the stress of adaptation to a new environment, and many experienced the additional trauma of air raids. The result appears to have mainly been influenced by food deprivation during the Occupation period.[146]

I mention these studies because they show that the Occupation was not simply a five-year experience, but one that had impact for years to come on those who lived through it. It is also clear that the Occupation deserves examination from a number of fields and is a resource not just for historians, archeologists, and rhetoricians but also for those who wish to study the effect of restricted diet on a community. But what of our diarists? What were their postwar experiences? Most of the diarists went on to lead full and peaceful lives in Guernsey, so much so that they leave the public record and much less is known of their subsequent lives.

The formidable Winifred Harvey "won" the Battle of Newlands, as her published diary was called, and returned to her home to live there until 1975, when age and infirmity forced her to leave.[147] She died the following year after a rich life of eighty-eight years. Kitty Bachmann's diary was published, with her evacuated daughter Diana de La Rue providing the charming illustrations of an Occupation that she only experienced through her family's stories. W. A.

Warry and his wife both survived the Occupation despite their separate health problems. There seemed to be little to write about after the war, and his diary lagged, with only occasional entries until 1952. He recorded that his wife Angeline had died suddenly on April 6, 1950, her seventy-fifth birthday, and was buried April 11 at the Candie Cemetery, followed a month later by her sister.[148] Bill carried on for another eleven years without his wife, dying in 1961 at the age of eighty-two.

Rev. Ord, that adept guide through the Occupation, stayed at Brock Road Church until 1948. His congregation wished for him to stay on longer, although he had far exceeded the number of years that the Methodist Church tended to leave a minister in one location. He left Guernsey to make way for a minister who had been through an illness and for whom the Island location was helpful to his convalescence.[149] His final ministry was in Farnham, Surrey, where he remained following his retirement until his death in 1978.[150] Our other prolific guide, Ken Lewis, ended the Occupation in the same romantic quandary that he had experienced throughout these years. On the same day in late April that he took Vera some lilies of the valley, he mentions that he dreamed the previous night that Brenda Parker had died and Mrs. Parker had been the one to break the news to him. Yet, three days later, he recorded that it was Brenda's twenty-first birthday, so she certainly was not dead to him.[151] I simply had to learn the outcome of this little love story and how life turned out for Ken, so I contacted his son, Nigel Lewis. Brenda actually married someone else and, as of 2004 when I heard from Nigel, was still living in Guernsey. Vera joined the WRENS after the war, an interesting proof that any casual contact she had with the young German soldiers was just youthful high spirits and not a negative reflection on her patriotism. The last that Nigel heard of her, she was living overseas.

But Ken did find love, and with someone who reflected his deeply held beliefs. His future wife, Jean, had evacuated to Rugby at the beginning of the Occupation, but when she returned, she attended the Methodist Church in St. Martin where Ken was a youth club leader. They had several children, and on Sundays after lunch, Ken used to read to the family from the diary, although Nigel said he "managed to gloss over the romantic bits." Ken died of a brain tumor in 1996, and it was then that his son decided that the diary should be in the Island Archives.[152] It is an incredible resource about life under Occupation.

But one of our diarists would not survive for the long-awaited reunion with evacuated family. The reader of Jack Sauvary's diary slowly watches Jack's health change over the years. He first mentions a problem in January 1943 as a weakness in his voice, despite his feeling well, no cough or cold or pain, but just "an awful effort" to speak. Jack was a little anxious about this and took some French medical concoction to get him through Mary's wedding. After all, he was giving her away and needed to come out strongly with the "I do." He does believe at this early point that he may need to give up smoking and see the doctor.[153] Thus begins the long road familiar to anyone dealing with serious illness, although in this case aggravated by the lack of means to properly diagnose or treat whatever he was experiencing.

It is interesting to gauge Jack's response to this initially mysterious affliction. On the one hand, when undergoing a serious of tests, he immediately equates it with his wife's fatal illness: "It seems to be the same game as with Mother, looking for something that shows no symptoms. I don't understand doctors."[154] On the other hand, Jack approached illness with his usual humor and hope. He tries various self-remedies, gargling with old port and glycerin, or sitting outside with his shirt open to sunburn his chest, figuring it to be as good as the radium treatments not available to him under Occupation conditions. When pulled into the Emergency

Hospital for tests and asked all the usual questions for admission, such as "where born?" Jack cheerfully added, "Where died? Emergency hospital." By Easter 1943, he was saddened that he could no longer sing with the choir on the great festival day, but hoped he would someday again: "We always live in hope, they say, if you die in the stairs, never despair."[155]

And so it went for the next two years, with tests alternating with the few attempted treatments that could be mustered in the Island. Jack's voice finally failed entirely, and his breathing made it difficult to climb hills. In January 1945, he was admitted to the Emergency Hospital so that he could be treated quickly if his breathing stopped. With the rest and care, not to mention the better food allowed at the hospital, Jack recovered some of his strength and breathing ability. But by 1945, it was clear to all that his only hope was that the Red Cross would arrange the evacuation of invalids so that he could get the deep x-ray/radium treatments that he needed. It is an interesting window into another time to find that Jack was being told that his problem was "purely functional," but at the hospital he found out, by the way his plates and dining utensils were marked, that he was being treated for a malignant growth.

By the end of February, despite the war going well, it seemed that the hospital ship would not come, and Jack's entries to his children take on a tone of farewell. He had asked Mrs. Rowe to look out after their "little things" and to keep them safe for his children's return. In March, Dr. Fox personally took Jack back to St. Sampson, a poignant trip that was quite obviously meant as a chance to say goodbye and settle his affairs. Jack was sad that all signs pointed to his not surviving to see his children again, but he treated it as "just misfortune to be stuck here like this" and unable to get lifesaving treatment. Jack tried later in March to stay at his home, but after three days it was obvious that he needed to be in the hospital. So, he said goodbye to old friends and the Front that looked out to sea, now so beautiful in the spring sunshine, and left his home for the last time.[156]

Holy Saturday was a difficult day for Jack physically, and for the first time, he wrote of himself in the past tense: "If only this war had finished in time, it might have made all the difference for me." And by the next day, Easter Sunday, he was poorly enough that he hoped it would be the last he would spend if he was going to feel this way. On Easter Monday, April 2, he managed to go with a blanket wrapped around himself to the women's ward for Communion, the last he expected to ever have on a festival week. But Jack never lost his interest in life or the affairs of the Island. Mr. De Garis, the man whose throat was slit in the milking incident, was in the bed next to him On Monday, three Germans were there typing out information on the attack, and Jack wrote, "Quite a lot of clicking for half an hour." And there the diary ended.

A letter appended in the published diary from a nurse at the hospital described how Jack's breathing grew worse and he was scheduled for a tracheotomy on April 5. He was doing well the night before and seemed happy, but grew worse the next morning and lapsed into unconsciousness.[157] So slightly over a month before the Occupation ended, kind and cheerful Jack, who wanted little more than a reunion with his children and grandchildren, died on April 5, 1945. He is buried in the St. Sampson's churchyard next to the wife he mourned so deeply. On the stone wall beside the grave are the memorial plaques to their children, Jack, Flo, and Kitty, a symbolic uniting of the family in death that could not occur in life.

Although this study of discourse, sense-making, and rhetorical resistance effectively ends with the close of Occupation, I want to mention two examples of public memory where there has been an effort made to convey the lived experience of those years. The first is a film

STATES OF GUERNSEY ISLAND ARCHIVES

K. M. "KITTY" BACHMANN

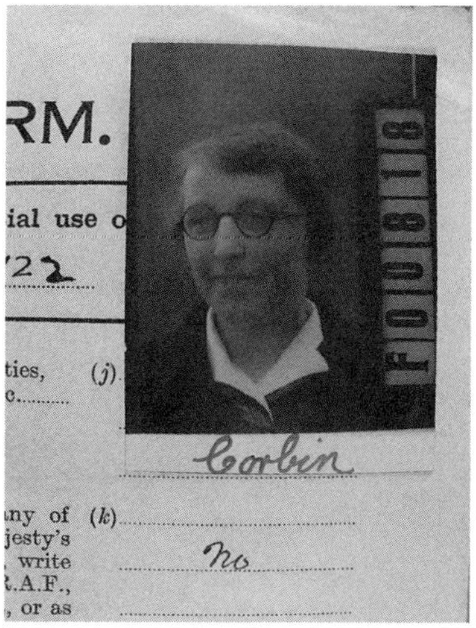

STATES OF GUERNSEY ISLAND ARCHIVES

GERTRUDE M. "GERTIE" CORBIN

STATES OF GUERNSEY ISLAND ARCHIVES

ELIZABETH DOIG

STATES OF GUERNSEY ISLAND ARCHIVES

REV. ROBERT DOUGLAS ORD

STATES OF GUERNSEY ISLAND ARCHIVES

WINIFRED HARVEY

STATES OF GUERNSEY ISLAND ARCHIVES

DOROTHY PICKARD HIGGS

Ken Lewis

States of Guernsey Island Archives

Arthur J. Mauger

States of Guernsey Island Archives

Ambrose Collas Robin

States of Guernsey Island Archives

J. C. "Jack" Sauvary

States of Guernsey Island Archives

William Arthur Warry

States of Guernsey Island Archives

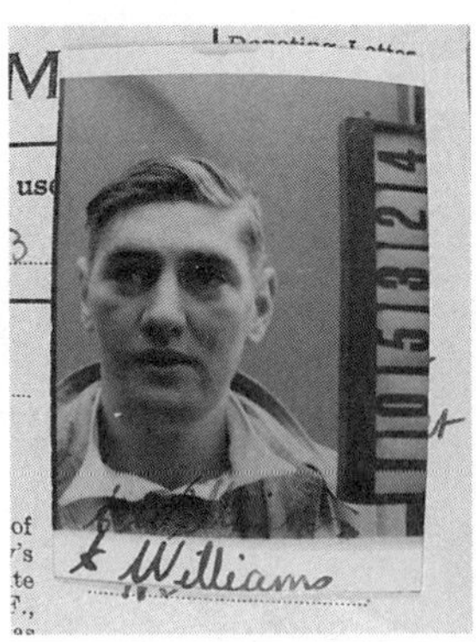

Alfred C. "Alf" Williams

States of Guernsey Island Archives

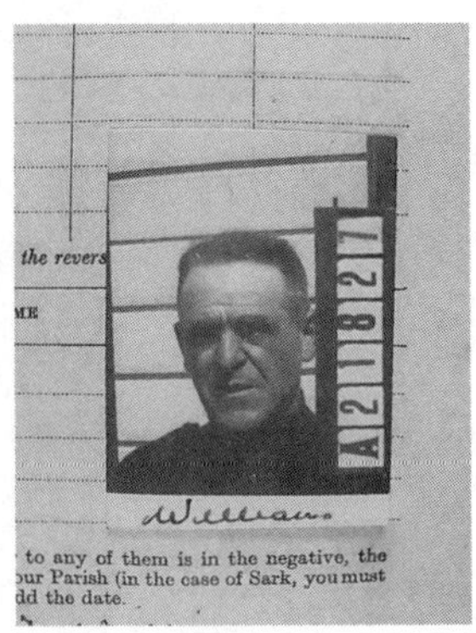

Herbert F. "Bert" Williams

States of Guernsey Island Archives

German Occupation Museum, Guernsey

A Taunting Poster from the Evacuation Period

German Occupation Museum, Guernsey

"Why Go Mad?" Poster from the Evacuation Period

German Occupation Museum, Guernsey

Marianne Grunfeld's Suitcase Left Behind at Duvaux Farm

German Occupation Museum, Guernsey

Suitcase Memorial by Jennifer Anne Snell

V-Sign Painted on the Front of a St. Peter Port House

Girls with V-Sign, Cartoon by Edmund Blampied

German Occupation Museum, Guernsey

A Guernsey Family Listens to Their Secret Wireless

German Occupation Museum, Guernsey

Statue of the Evacuated Child

made about the Channel Islands soon after Liberation, "starring" the Channel Islanders and some of the Germans, drafted as extras, who were still in the Islands doing cleanup. Directed by Gerald Bryant and produced by the British Ministry of Information, *Channel Islands 1940–1945* is, in effect, a public-relations film to let Britain know that the Channel Islands were working hard to be ready for business once again.[158] It was also a means to share some of the tales of being occupied by the Germans with the many people outside of the Islands interested in the experience. This 16-minute film takes its stylistic cues from the other British mobilization films and attempts to tap the same expectations for exciting viewing formed by the major cinema of the day. Therefore, the film of everyday life is punctuated by adventure sequences, and the narrator, while speaking from an Islander's standpoint, has that cynical, world-weary-yet-determined tone that became familiar in British Ministry of Information films of the war years.

The theme is established in the opening sequence: it is dark, and Islanders are seen lowering a small boat down a wall at the water's edge. Some men are keeping watch while others load cases into the boat and help to launch it out to sea. As the boat is rowed away from the Island, a group of men stand on the wall and wave as the narrator intones, "Good luck! When you get to England, tell them how we're getting on over here. Tell them we're having a tough time but the Germans can't get us down. And tell them more of us will be following you. And tell them in spite of everything we're managing to hear the BBC." It is this concept of carrying on under tough conditions and not allowing the enemy to prevail that carries through this little film.

It really is a fascinating view into the Occupation, as the Islanders had a final chance to wear their tattered everyday clothes as costumes for the film before they were discarded, burned, or folded away in attics as part of private memories. The film moves through scenes of want and make-do ("As for clothes, it was a case of mending and mending"), the disturbing sight of slave laborers ("We were sorry for those slave workers; we'd seen the way they were treated"), and the empty Market of the final year ("There was the black market if you could afford it, but for ordinary decent people it was always the same, 'No, I'm sorry. Nothing.'"). And there were the triumphs of the *Vega*'s arrival and the joy of Liberation ("We forgot we were hungry. We forgot everything except that we were free."). One response to Liberation that was discussed in this chapter is verified by a segment of the film. The film takes the standpoint that, as food poured in and the shops were newly filled with goods that had not been seen for years, it all seemed to be a dream to the Islanders: "We went about in a sort of daze. Hardly daring to touch anything for fear that we would wake up and find that it wasn't real."

Most interesting from the standpoint of this current study is the move made by the film to juxtapose the experience of the Islanders with that of their British mainland counterparts. It is an initial attempt to show mainlanders that although the Islanders had not slept in fallout shelters or suffered under bombardment as did British mainland civilians, they did experience the prolonged suffering of hunger and deprivation. A key moment to stake the ground of this position came during scenes of Liberation, when ragged and largely barefoot children were shown eating oranges while sitting on a seawall. The narrator explains, "Most of your children know what an orange looks like, but our younger ones had never seen one. They had to be shown how to peel one." This stance was strengthened when the film returned at Liberation to a couple, introduced earlier, who had struggled to feed their children during the Occupation: "Jack and Florey Steele, and that means all of us, had their first normal British meal: a cut off the joint and two veg. The sort of meal you've been having once a week ever since 1939." Perhaps the Islanders had not experienced the continuous threat of air raids, but, the narrator implies, although mainland Britons had been living under rationing, they had little idea of real hunger. It was an initial salvo in the brief post-Liberation war of comparative experience.

Despite the human interest of these more domestic scenes, the film justifies the Islanders' experience the most during the adventure sequences. First established is the response of Islanders during the arrival of the Germans, and the panoptical nature of Occupation as a whole. Early in the film, the narrator describes how "When the Germans arrived in 1940, our first reactions to them were probably the same as yours would have been." The script thus connects the patriotism and resistant nature of the Islanders to their British mainland counterparts. But here the visuals are particularly instructive. German tanks are shown rolling along the road by the water, and there is a cross-fade to an old man, the typical Islander attired in a working-class cap, looking down from a high window and spitting (the "first reaction" to the Germans demonstrated in a clear sign of contempt).

As a tank goes past a petrol station, an old woman with round glasses looks out her open window past her lace curtains and then withdraws, allowing the curtain to fall, obscuring her presence. Thus is shown not only the Islanders' antagonism to the occupying forces and their determination to stand apart from them in opposition but also the *sousveillance* that civilians would adopt as a primary tactic of resistance. The woman, who continues to monitor the troops while shielding herself from observation behind her lace curtains, provides a strong visual metaphor for this technique. The Islanders would constantly watch and "read" the Germans in their midst while drawing an impenetrable veil over their own activities.

But it would not be an adventure story without displays of overt resistance. The film shows two men in the dark of a small and secret room, listening to a hidden radio and writing by the light of a flickering candle. The narrator, having described German confiscation of goods, explains the scene: "But, worst of all, they stole the truth, and filled our newspapers with Goebbels and Haw Haw. The remedy was simple but dangerous. We ran our own with the help of the BBC." Then begins a section where the narrator describes GUNS and introduces Nick Robbins, a junior reporter, and his role in the underground news distribution. As the next series of visuals unfold, the narrator explains their importance in flat, unemotional tones: "The originator, Marchon of the *Guernsey Star*, was eventually caught and sent to Germany where he died, poor chap. Falla and Duquemin also went to prison."

A young man is shown typing a page headed Feb. 1943 and making the large V made out of small "v's" that was the hallmark of GUNS. Leaving his hidden room and heading down a dark staircase, he emerges into the daylight of the street past a sign in the window, "Advertise in The Star." Two German officers are shown at the top of a steep flight of Guernsey steps that the young man, attired in a trench coat straight out of any spy film, starts to run up. He stops and looks up as the Germans give each other the Nazi salute and go their separate ways. The young man turns, takes the typewritten sheets from their hiding place in his sock, and slides the papers through an opening under the door. Then comes a series of scenes to represent the flow of news. The young man knocking at a door and talking to an old woman, another young man selling papers and whispering to another man who stops to buy a paper, a woman milking a cow when a man comes up and whispers something to her. The narrator explains, "That's one of the ways news got around."

The final notable aspect of the film is the way that it handles collaborators and other traitors to the British cause. It does not take up the more delicate issue of so-called "horizontal collaboration"[159] and leaves the sexual dalliances of women with the German soldiers unmentioned. But the film is blunt about profiteers and informers:

> It was really a shame about our traitors, people who would spit on you for a handful of dirty marks. There wasn't many of them, but we shan't forget them. They used to write anonymous letters to the Gestapo telling them where they could find hidden radios. But the post office workers had a way of dealing with these letters. A great many of them never reached the Gestapo.

Postal workers are shown sorting mail. One middle-aged worker in the foreground, apparently Rev. Ord's friend, Henry Martin Lihou, playing himself,[160] pauses in his sorting to examine a letter. A close-up reveals that the letter has been very generally addressed to reach the commandant at the Grange Lodge, thus marking it as coming from an informant. The postal worker looks up to check if he is being monitored; then he quietly slips the letter in his pocket. The message of the sequence is clear: the Islanders did not accept the traitors in their midst and had their own means of dealing with them. It would not be dramatic, and perhaps not as satisfying to some, but under the right circumstances, it could be effective.

This is the message, too, in the little piece of retaliation hinted at in the close of the film. The Germans are shown as being set to the "thoroughly unpleasant job of removing the 200,000 mines they laid in four Islands. And that goes for the barbed wire, too. No one has suggested giving them gloves." The written description of this film in the Imperial War Museum where it is housed calls this specific reference "vindictive commentary," but it is much the favored style of humor of the time. It shows quite plainly where Islander sentiments reside, and makes the point that they had their own ways of balancing the books.

Before leaving the topic of public memory, a word should be given to the German Occupation Museum, founded and directed by Richard Heaume. Born during the final years of the war, Richard collected artifacts of the Occupation as a child and a young man, and it was to house his growing collection that he opened a museum in 1966. For many years he ran the museum rather like a hobby. However, his avocation became his vocation, and for many years he has directed the museum full time. I mention this evolution because the German Occupation Museum is an example of vernacular memorializing that over the years has gained official status. It is the Occupation as viewed by the average Guernseyman and woman who experienced it. Richard brings to the museum both the professional and careful quality of the historian and the warmth of familiarity with a given time and place. There is a charm to the mannequins used throughout to represent the Islanders, for they have that slightly stunned appearance of all figures frozen in place. Yet, dressed in the clothes of the day, especially in the Occupation Street addition to the main museum that shows a tableau of Guernsey life under Occupation, they are effective in "peopling" the displays and providing a glimpse into the war years of the Island.

The cabinets, corners, hallways, and even the canteen that plays music of the time and serves Guernsey *gâche* (a traditional type of raisin bread) are all stuffed with artifacts large and small, carefully labeled. The museum has become the Island's attic, and at first glance the jumble of items appear to be without an overall pattern, resembling our memories of historic events, particularly traumatic ones, when we relive them. Yet, this first impression is illusory, because the pattern to the layout of the museum is quite strong and reflects a distinct view of Occupation from the Islander's perspective. Unlike many modern museum displays that provide predigested sound bites of history, carefully wrapped in media to capture flagging attention spans, the German Occupation Museum expects from visitors an engagement with history in all of its complexity. It is a view shared by the Channel Islands Occupation Society that history is to be understood and faced for what it reveals, for good or ill. There is nothing of public relations or overt justification in the displays, for the museum takes a warts-and-all perspective on the events of the Occupation.

The main portion of the museum (taken separately from the Canteen, Occupation Street tableau, Fishermen's Memorial Room, and Liberation Room) unfolds much as the Occupation unfolded for the Guernsey civilians. On entering the museum, the visitor's eye is pulled down and to the right by the figure of a small child dressed for travel, his suitcase at his feet. It is in the interplay between the small figure and the first two rooms of the museum that we see an initial theme. The small figure represents the children evacuated before the onslaught of German power that drove the French and British forces from the shores of Dunkirk, and that swept up Guernsey in their wake. The first two rooms of the museum emphasize the power and military force of the German occupiers as they descended on demilitarized Guernsey. The cabinets from floor to ceiling are filled with weapons and uniforms—helmets, daggers, dress uniforms on mannequins, pistols, and all the other accoutrements of war. These are rooms much cherished by small boys who visit the museum.

But there is also a dual focus in these rooms, where the Island is viewed through the eyes of the young German soldiers coming to Guernsey. Paintings of their homeland, watercolors of the Island, folk art and carvings used to while away the time (including a never-completed dollhouse), letters home to sweethearts and families are displayed along with temporary grave markers of those Germans who never were to leave the Island. These rooms take much of the approach of Rev. Ord: acknowledging the humanity of the common soldier and differentiating him from the fearsome evil of the Nazi juggernaut that rolled across the Island.

The next two rooms thematically emphasize the panoptical Occupation and the rhetorical resistance. There are the "Don't Be Yellow" posters urging Islanders to stay, a bomb of the type deployed in the initial air raid that ended the opportunity to leave, and framed copies of newspapers now controlled by the Germans, opened to particularly important dates for Guernsey. It is in this room that a feeling is set up of unending surveillance and the monitoring of the population. In the following room comes the Islander response of resistance through the gathering and disseminating of information and the symbolic attempts to resist psychological control. In this room is the centerpiece of the museum: a tableau of a family in their kitchen, secretly listening to a wireless set. The father sits at the kitchen table with the wireless set on his lap; the mother stands watch at the window, a guard against surveillance by Germans or informers. And their little girl stands close by, her pets brought in for the night to spare them from the German stewpot. On the end of a cabinet is a wicked little visual joke: amid a series of references to food, such as recipes using carrageen moss for blancmange and ways of cooking with a sawdust burner, is a poster offering a £5 reward for the return of Mrs. De Guerin's white Scotch dog "Sarah."

Many aspects of Occupation life, from posters for amateur theatrics to homemade dolls, are displayed here. This room also contains a fascinating juxtaposition of collaborators and patriots. Anonymous letters sent by informers share the room with photos of fraternizing civilians with Organization Todt staff at a celebration of Hitler's birthday and Guernsey girls with soldiers at the La Valette Swimming Pools. Yet these are side by side with articles revealing the more overt campaigns of resistance. On display are the Victory brooches bearing the likeness of King George. There are the German warnings that were posted about marking walls with V's, and Edmund Blampied's cartoon of two girls who "committed the heinous crime of writing the letter "v" on a wall." And Red Cross messages are displayed here, with their coded language designed to thwart the German censor and send news off the Island.

The room that follows is a remembrance of Festung Guernsey (Fortress Guernsey) and the role the Island played in Hitler's plans for an Atlantic Fortress. The emphasis is upon the mines, the railway line, the gun emplacements, the heavy artillery, and the tunnels, all of which changed the face of the Island. It presents a tableau of a German POW clearing the mines from the beaches following Liberation. In tableau, too, is a memorial to the Organization Todt workers, one of whom is shown attired in ragged clothes and pushing a rail truck filled with soil from the construction of the many tunnels. The room that follows is also a tribute to those under imprisonment, although in a different sense. There is a display about the Guernsey Prison, so often filled to overflowing with Islanders. For the most part, however, the room concerns the deportees to the German camps at Laufen and Biberach, and displays homemade items from the camp. At the end of the room is a tableau of Ambrose Sherwill sitting in a mockup of the small British Camp Seniors' Room at Laufen.

The final room of the main portion of the museum is a small room located behind a prison door, a space given over to themes of martyrdom and memory. In this room are commemorated the resisters who died in Continental prisons (such as John Ingrouille), civilians who served prison terms for resistance (such as Winnie Green), and slave laborers who died throughout the Channel Islands. Hanging in a cabinet are the striped pyjama suits worn by German political prisoners who died at Sylt Prison Camp in Alderney. There is a special section set aside to commemorate the three Jewish women, Auguste Spitz, Therese Steiner, and Marianne Grunfeld, who were to be victims of the Holocaust. And beside a display about the fate of the Jews in Guernsey is a touching and disturbing item: Marianne Grunfeld's suitcase.

The focal point of the room is actually a sculpture of three suitcases by Jennifer Anne Snell, a locally born artist. Built out of concrete, they mirror the concrete fortifications that desecrated the Island's beauty. The suitcases are completed with original leather fittings and patches, bringing to mind all the piles of suitcases found when the Nazi death camps were liberated, and according to the artist, they are designed to reflect "travel, deportation, evacuation, and exile."[161] But this sculpture also functions to bring the museum full circle, back to the statue of the small boy with his cap, traveling jacket, and suitcase that greeted visitors at the entrance. It reflects, as does the museum as a whole, the journey through five years of Occupation taken by the Guernsey Islanders, and the memories shared only by those who traveled those years together.

We are rapidly losing the opportunity to directly tap the memories of discourse and rhetorical resistance as waged by the Channel Islanders. Many researchers eschew private memories because they consider them tainted by time and subject to the self-interest we all have in being the heroes of our own lives. These are legitimate concerns, but such problems with memory are generally part of the universal coping mechanism that all of us possess. The vagaries of memory, especially of traumatic events, usually provide a means for the mind to heal itself rather than an attempt to cover dark secrets. Except for private, contemporaneous accounts, it is unlikely that a true picture of the resistance of the powerless can ever emerge. In official accounts, written or overseen by those in power, we generally find in the descriptions of those under domination a similar dim and stolid compliance. What is not apparent in the official transcript is the extent to which this apparent compliance shelters acts of resistance. Performed compliance offers such a perfect mask that those reading official transcripts, even decades after events, are easily gulled into the same mistaken reading foisted on the dominant at the time.

Rarely is there available any type of private documentation revealing the unfiltered views and methods to thwart domination utilized by those under the control of others. Slaves in the South, forbidden legally to learn to read and write, expressed in the words of spirituals both their discontent and desire to escape.[162] But these views must be deciphered rather than read at face value. The discontent in many onerous political, business, or academic climates may leave no private paper trail at all behind them that can be read by subsequent generations. Those who wish to read only the officially sanctioned view of history found in public documents will find plenty to support a picture of happy slaves, contented women during times and places where they lacked legal rights, workers pleased with their lot, and widespread collaborators under conditions of military occupation. This, then, is the value of these private Guernsey diaries, written despite the difficulties and dangers involved, and offering an insight not just into means of resistance but also into the views of a general populace toward the actual profiteers, fraternizers, and collaborators in their midst.

The subtlety of rhetorical resistance, particularly under domination of arms, and its inability to effect an actual change in the power structure may foster little but contempt in some quarters. Repeatedly, the view is put forth that these acts of resistance were even welcomed by the Germans as a "safety valve" to dissuade wider revolt. Were these verbal and symbolic acts "a matter of hollow posing," a poor substitute for acts of overt aggression?[163] I agree here with James Scott that there is little sign from a social psychology perspective that the narratives, symbolic rituals, and small acts of defiance found in the hidden transcript of the powerless will lead to some kind of "harmless catharsis that helps preserve the status quo."[164] Instead, the "fires of resentment" are stoked by those resistant acts and narratives, just as grumbling and expressions of frustration in everyday life tend to feed rather than cool the flames of anger.[165]

And through these shared small acts and narratives, a connective web is formed of the like-minded, a community that may be called into action should the opportunity present itself. We should not expect to find acknowledgment of most forms of rhetorical resistance in either private or public writings by the Germans. As we have seen in this study, successful resistance is deftly hidden, and this understanding gives new who's-fooling-whom meaning to an unnamed German officer's view that the Guernsey Islanders were "obsequious peasants."[166] What is important in the case of Guernsey is that the Germans themselves treated the rhetorical resistance with some of the respect they would have accorded overt resistance, expending time, effort, and resources to come down hard on defiant Islanders. From the comically excessive response to the V-campaign to the arrests and subsequent deportation of Islanders for verbal defiance, acts of disrespect, and skirting the rules against wireless possession and news dissemination, the Germans verified the effectiveness of rhetorical resistance by their very response to it.

This examination of the Guernsey resistance has provided a tentative outline for a rhetorical resistance that is likely to arise in other conditions of extreme power differential. It remains to be seen if, under other situations of domination, there is a universal need for community support and clearly shared values as preliminaries for resistant acts. These elements, generally established through interpersonal communication, seem to be foundational before the symbolic elements of subversion are likely to develop to any great extent. In many cases, we could look for these elements as established in the home or within groups of friends. However, in some situations, these private nurseries of oppositional strength might be augmented by churches, with the clergy providing both practical support and the nurturing of a set of countervalues.[167] Thus, in studying instances where long-term opposition to domination remains primarily rhetorical, the first steps of analysis may be to identify the sources of support, to delineate the values shared by the community, and to detail how these vital preliminaries to resistance were communicated within those private and quasi-public spaces sheltered from panoptical surveillance. In onerous situations of domination, a new morality may also be forged: an "imperative to be honest and ethically responsible among those who counted as 'us,' contrasted with the distrust and duplicity in dealings with 'them' and with the official world generally."[168] Considering the multilayered complexities of community support, resistant acts, and ethical understandings, it is little wonder that the Guernsey Occupation has defied easy analysis.

When it comes to the structure of rhetorical resistance itself, as it emerges in other situations of long-term opposition to power, we might expect the specifics to vary from the three primary approaches noted in the Guernsey Occupation. The trio of rhetorical resistance elements identified here may serve, however, as touchstones for discovering other discursive and symbolic means of opposition. In other instances of a dominated population, do rumor and gossip serve the same functions of expression, information verification, and control that they did during the Occupation? Although it is unlikely outside of a political or wartime setting that propaganda would be a substantive factor, understanding the narratives—the jokes, stories, and folktales—of subjugated populations is a clear necessity to deciphering their hidden transcript. And finally, we should seek commonalities in the form that symbolic defiance takes across situations marked by a power differential. Each culture will have its resonant symbols and methods that are comfortable for average people to exploit, such as Joan of Arc and resistance poetry in World War II France,[169] and King Christian X and chain letters in Denmark during the same period.[170] And within countries and individual organizations, there are likely to be multiple subcultures, each with its own view of creative and effective means of symbolic subversion. Unique rhetorical resources may be tapped in each case to construct and deploy an effective counterbalance to oppression.

We are only at the beginning of understanding the nature and extent of Channel Island resistance, and more will be revealed as diaries and other contemporaneous documents make their way from attics and into the Island Archives. Physical artifacts, private writings, and personal memories all have something valuable to contribute when it comes to understanding this unique situation of a subjugated people and their quiet opposition to tyranny. As this study has revealed, one legacy of the Guernsey Occupation may be the lesson the wartime generation of Islanders has to teach us about the subtlety and persistence of rhetorical resistance.

Notes

INTRODUCTION

1. Diary of the Rev. R. Douglas Ord, vols. 1–7, 16 June 1940–12 May 1945, M0007066GY–M0007073GY, Priaulx Library, Guernsey [hereafter Ord], 176 (June 28, 1940).
2. Diary of Kenneth G. Lewis, Guernsey Island Archives, G06/10 W, 1-1-8-10, AS/LC 16-01, June 28, 1940.
3. Jack C. Sauvary, *Diary of the German Occupation of Guernsey, 1940–1945* (Upton-upon-Severn: Self Pub. Association, 1990), 25–26 (June 28, 1940).
4. Diary of Elizabeth Doig, 298904, Priaulx Library, Guernsey [herafter Doig], June 28, 1940.
5. Winifred Harvey, *The Battle of Newlands: The Wartime Diaries of Winifred Harvey*, ed. Rosemary Booth (Guernsey: Guernsey Press, 1995), 7–8 (June 27–28, 1940).
6. Harvey, *Battle of Newlands*, 7–8; *"Press" Diary of Island Life during the German Occupation* (Guernsey: Guernsey Press, n.d.), 4.
7. Harvey, *Battle of Newlands*, 7–8.
8. Diary of Arthur Mauger, AQ 374/13 to 25 (23 April 1939–7 August 1940), ledger book 21, Guernsey Island Archives [hereafter Mauger], June 28–29, 1940.
9. Frank Falla, *The Silent War* (London: Burbridge Ltd., 1994), 15. I am using the statistics for deaths and injuries provided by Falla and William M. Bell, *Guernsey Occupied but Never Conquered* (Exeter: Studio Publishing Services, 2002), 44. Some sources list 33 dead and a varying number of injured.
10. Sauvary, *Diary*, 25 (June 28, 1940).
11. See, for example, H. R. Kedward, *Occupied France: Collaboration and Resistance, 1940–1944* (Oxford: Basil Blackwell, 1985); H. R. Kedward, *Resistance in Vichy France: A Study of Ideas and Motivation in the Southern Zone, 1940–1942* (Oxford: Oxford University Press, 1978); Roderick Kedward and Roger Austin, eds., *Vichy France and the Resistance: Culture and Ideology* (London: Croom Helm, 1985); Christopher Lloyd, *Collaboration and Resistance in Occupied France: Representing Treason and Sacrifice* (New York: Palgrave Macmillan, 2003); Hanna Diamond and Simon Kitson, eds., *Vichy, Resistance, Liberation: New Perspectives on Wartime France* (Oxford: Berg, 2005).
12. François-Georges Dreyfus, ed., *Unrecognized Resistance: The Franco-American Experience in World War Two*, trans. Paul Seaton (New Brunswick, NJ: Transaction Publishers, 2004).
13. Lloyd, *Collaboration and Resistance*, 29.
14. Kedward, *Resistance in Vichy France*, 230.
15. Václav Havel provides the classic analogy when he writes that "'dissident movements' or even 'oppositions,' emerge, like the proverbial one tenth of the iceberg visible above the water"; Václav Havel, "The Power of the Powerless," trans. Paul Wilson, in *The Power of the Powerless: Citizens against the State in Central-Eastern Europe*, ed. John Keane (London: Hutchinson, 1988), 65.

16. Andrea Muhi Brighenti, "Resistance as Transformation," in *Roots, Rites and Sites of Resistance: The Banality of Good*, ed. Leonidas K. Cheliotis (New York: Palgrave Macmillan, 2010), 101–2.
17. Hazel R. Knowles Smith, *The Changing Face of the Channel Islands Occupation: Record, Memory, and Myth* (Houndmills, Basingstoke, Hampshire: Palgrave Macmillan, 2007), 187.
18. Louise Willmot, "The Channel Islands," in *Resistance in Western Europe*, ed. Bob Moore (London: Berg, 2000), 76.
19. Gillian Carr and Richard Heaume, "Silent Resistance in Guernsey: The V-Sign Badges of Alf Williams and Roy Machon," in *Channel Islands Occupation Review*, no. 32 (2004): 51.
20. Sandra Wentworth Bradley, quoted in Knowles Smith, *The Changing Face*, 187.
21. Willmot, "The Channel Islands," 75.
22. Douglas Ehninger, *Contemporary Rhetoric* (Chicago: Scott, Foresman, and Co., 1972), 3.
23. In her study of early modern women's spiritual narratives, Gae Lyn Henderson describes rhetorical resistance as "the attempt to revise truth in opposition to a reigning regime of power"; Gae Lyn Henderson, "The 'Parrhesiastic Game': Textual Self-Justification in Spiritual Narratives of Early Modern Women," *Rhetoric Society Quarterly* 37 (2007): 425.
24. Kerry Kathleen Riley, *Everyday Subversions: From Joking to Revolting in the German Democratic Republic* (East Lansing: Michigan State University Press, 2008), 22.
25. See, for example, such studies as Kerran L. Sanger, "Slave Resistance and Rhetorical Self-Definition: Spirituals as a Strategy," *Western Journal of Communication* 59 (Summer 1995): 177–92. A variety of excellent studies may be found in Gary Y. Okihiro, ed., *Resistance: Studies in African, Caribbean, and Afro-American History* (Amherst: University Press of Massachusetts, 1986).
26. Just as a very brief sampling, see Aileen S. Kraditor, ed., *Up from the Pedestal: Selected Writings in the History of American Feminism* (Chicago: Quadrangle Books, 1968); Nan Johnson, "Reigning in the Court of Silence: Women and Rhetorical Space in Postbellum America," *Philosophy & Rhetoric* 33 (2000): 221–42; Karlyn Kohrs Campbell, *Man Cannot Speak for Her: A Critical Study of Early Feminist Rhetoric*, vols. 1–2 (New York: Praeger, 1989); Lisa Gring-Pemble, "Writing Themselves into Consciousness: Creating a Rhetorical Bridge between the Public and Private Spheres," *Quarterly Journal of Speech* 84 (1998); Jacqueline Jones Royster, *Traces of a Stream: Literacy and Social Change among African American Women* (Pittsburgh, PA: University of Pittsburgh Press, 2000).
27. See Kent A. Ono and John M. Sloop, "The Critique of Vernacular Discourse," *Communication Monographs* 62 (1995): 19–46; Barbara Biesecker, "Michel Foucault and the Question of Rhetoric," *Philosophy & Rhetoric* 25 (1992): 351–64; Ronald F. Wendt, "Answers to the Gaze: A Genealogical Poaching of Resistances," *Quarterly Journal of Speech* 82 (1996): 251–73.
28. Nathaniel Hong, "Down With the Murderer Hitler!: Illegal Communication Strategies during the First Period of the German Occupation of Denmark," *Journalism Monographs* 146 (August 1994): 1–46.
29. Riley, *Everyday Subversions*, 22–27.
30. I have chosen to follow the lead of those in the Channel Islands who capitalize Occupation when referring specifically to the German Occupation of Guernsey and the other Channel Islands. I will also capitalize Island and Islanders when referring to Guernsey and the populace during this time.
31. Charles Cruikshank, *The German Occupation of the Channel Islands* (Guernsey: Guernsey Press, 1975).
32. Madeleine Bunting, *The Model Occupation: The Channel Islands under German Rule, 1940–1945* (London: Harper Collins, 1995).

33. Unfortunately, there are also incredible errors, some simple but some that are dead wrong and provide fuel for faulty conclusions. A critical analysis of *The Model Occupation* with a list of these errors was published by Linda Holt and Ward Rutherford, "'The Model Occupation'—Setting the Record Straight," *Channel Islands Occupation Review* 25 (1997): 49–72.
34. Bunting, *The Model Occupation*, 192–93. Even this chapter, filled with instances of resistance—some of which resulted in grueling prison terms, torture, and death—is entitled "Resistance? What Resistance?" This seeming desire for controversy has morphed into some unconscious comedy and journalistic shell games. In an article for *Travel Intelligence*, an online travel website, Vitali Vitaliev wrote a scathing article entitled "Island Legacy." Seeing in the Occupation museums, books about Occupation experiences, and work of the Channel Islands Occupation Society only a marketing strategy leading to "the trivialisation of human suffering" and "a certain glamourisation of the Nazis," Vitaliev paints a picture of Islander collaborators still "obsessed" with their "nice, civilised and invariably 'smartly dressed'" Nazi captors. And what does he put forth as proof of collaboration but a quote from the *Guernsey Evening Press* of November 15, 1944, lifted from an anti-Semitic diatribe against a "reptilian Hebrew," written by "a certain William Joyce, a local 'columnist'"; Vitali Vitaliev, "Island Legacy," *Travel Intelligence*, http://www.travelintelligence.com/travel-writing/island-legacy. Vitaliev's lack of awareness that William Joyce was the infamous "Lord Haw-Haw," the American-born but British-raised propaganda broadcaster transmitting from Germany and simply reprinted in the Nazi-controlled *Evening Press*, is simple ignorance. The fact that Vitaliev's article is reprinted on the guardian.co.uk website, renamed "Channel Islanders Showing Off Their Sites of Shame," and with the telltale, embarrassing section on Joyce deftly deleted, points to the *Guardian*'s desire for controversy; Vitali Vitaliev, "Channel Islanders Showing Off Their Sites of Shame," Sunday, January 3, 1999 (guardian.co.uk).
35. Bunting, *Model Occupation*, 321.
36. Bunting, *Model Occupation*, 322. She does not give the frightened historian's name, although it was presumably Peter Toombs.
37. Bunting, *Model Occupation*, 3.
38. Bunting, *Model Occupation*, 316. Bunting follows this stunning condemnation with the peculiar revelation that an Australian journalist, Roland le Folet Hoffman, committed suicide in Guernsey shortly after Liberation in disgust that there had been "signs of outright collaboration." She does not say what these signs were. This was truly a sensitive soul if, as an Australian, Hoffman killed himself because Channel Islanders let down mainland Britain.
39. Louise Willmot, "The Channel Islands," in *Resistance in Western Europe*, ed. Bob Moore (London: Berg, 2000), 83.
40. Willmot, "The Channel Islands," 84.
41. Mary Ann Shaffer and Annie Barrows, *The Guernsey Literary and Potato Peel Pie Society* (London: Bloomsbury, 2008).
42. See Knowles Smith, *The Changing Face*; Paul Sanders, *The British Channel Islands under German Occupation, 1940–1945* (Jersey: Jersey Heritage Trust/Société Jersiaise, 2005); Barry Turner, *Outpost of Occupation: How the Channel Islands Survived Nazi Rule, 1940–45* (London: Aurum Press, 2010); Gillian Carr, "The Archaeology of Occupation, 1940–2009: A Case Study from the Channel Islands," in *Antiquity* 84 (2010): 161–74. All of these are excellent resources. Paul Sanders focuses primarily on Jersey, but provides an analysis of the entire Occupation, utilizing many recently released documents. Dr. Knowles Smith is the one historian who pays attention to diary accounts in her broad examination of all of the Channel Islands. She provides a general refutation of scandal and discovers material that "overwhelmingly support[s] an honourable narrative

of occupation history, with a few blemishes" (254). Dr. Carr also brings new eyes to the analysis of Occupation artifacts from her perspective as an archaeologist, a very promising new line of research.

43. Partway through this project, I came upon a master's thesis in the archives by Alice Evans, "The Language of Occupation," written for the University of Warwick in 2002. Evans, too, sees the problem with public memory as it has recently been framed in a "binary opposition of accusation and defence." Evans uses the diary of her great-grandmother, Violet Carey, to examine "discourses of rumour, humour, and honour" that provided a means of self-understanding and coping during the Occupation; Alice Evans, "The Language of Occupation" (Master's thesis, University of Warwick, 2002), 8–12. Evans has since published her great-grandmother's diary, *Guernsey under Occupation: The Second World War Diaries of Violet Carey*, ed. Alice Evans (Gloucestershire: Phillimore and Co., 2009).
44. James C. Scott, *Domination and the Arts of Resistance: Hidden Transcripts* (New Haven: Yale University Press, 1990), xiii.
45. Scott, *Domination*, xiii.
46. Scott, *Domination*, xiii.
47. Scott, *Domination*, 19–20.
48. Scott, *Domination*, 27.
49. Scott, *Domination*, 137.
50. Scott, *Domination*, 18.
51. Scott, *Domination*, 2.
52. Jennifer Sinor, *The Extraordinary Work of Ordinary Writing: Annie Ray's Diary* (Iowa City: University of Iowa Press, 2002), 5.
53. Judy Nolte Temple, "Fragments as Diary: Theoretical Implications of the Dreams and Visions of 'Baby Doe' Tabor," in *Inscribing the Daily: Critical Essays on Women's Diaries*, ed. Suzanne L. Bunkers and Cynthia Huff (Amherst: University of Massachusetts Press, 1996), 78.
54. The complete diary is in the Priaulx Library in Guernsey. A rather poor photocopy of it is available in the archives of the Imperial War Museum, London.
55. Diary of Ambrose Collas Robin, 17 June 1940 to 18 May 1945, Priaulx Library, Guernsey, Control no. M0005622GY.
56. Diary of Herbert Williams, States of Guernsey Island Archives Service, AQ 380/03-2.
57. Diary of William Arthur Warry, University of Virginia, Special Collections, Microfilm 1688 MSS8138.
58. Who can resist the little doggerel from the time of these champions of women's education: "Miss Buss and Miss Beale, Cupid's darts do not feel, How different from us, Miss Beale and Miss Buss."
59. Dorothy Pickard Higgs, *Life in Guernsey under the Nazis, 1940–45* (Guernsey: Toucan Press, 2000).
60. K. M. Bachmann, *The Prey of an Eagle* (Guernsey: Guernsey Press, 1972).
61. Diary of Gertie Corbin, States of Guernsey Island Archives, Z009/19 AQ92/12.
62. Alex Aronson, *Studies in Twentieth-Century Diaries: The Concealed Self, Studies in Comparative Literature* (Lewiston, NY: Edwin Mellen Press, 1991), vol. 12: 1.
63. Aronson, *Studies in Twentieth Century Diaries*, vol. 2: vii, 110.
64. Bachmann, *Prey of an Eagle*, 120 (May 10, 1942).
65. Bachmann, *Prey of an Eagle*, 44 (November 7, 1940).
66. Bachmann, *Prey of an Eagle*, 37 (October 24, 1940).

67. Sauvary, *Diary*, 52 (January 28, 1941).
68. Sauvary, *Diary*, 54 (February 5, 1941).
69. Doig, February 22, 1944.
70. Bachmann, *Prey of an Eagle*, 185 (June 19, 1944).
71. Dorothy Sheridan, ed. *Wartime Women* (London: Heinemann, 1990), 2.
72. Higgs, *Life in Guernsey*, 18 (January 28, 1941).
73. Higgs, *Life in Guernsey*, 54 (February 15, 1945).
74. Harvey, *Battle of Newlands*, 1 (June 16–25, 1940).
75. Ord, 464 (March 14, 1943).
76. Bachmann, *Prey of an Eagle*, 120 (May 10, 1942).
77. Bachmann, *Prey of an Eagle*, 169 (January 27, 1944).
78. Higgs, *Life in Guernsey*, 41 (April 11, 1944).
79. Willmot, "The Channel Islands," 71.

CHAPTER ONE. THE PANOPTICAL OCCUPATION

1. Diary of the Rev. Douglas Ord, vol. 1–7, 16 June 1940–12 May 1945, M0007066GY–M0007073GY, Priaulx Library, Guernsey [hereafter Ord], June 16, 1940.
2. Dorothy Pickard Higgs, *Life in Guernsey under the Nazis, 1940–45* (Guernsey: Toucan Press, 2000), 9 (July 2, 1940).
3. Winifred Harvey, *The Battle of Newlands: The Wartime Diaries of Winifred Harvey*, ed. Rosemary Booth (Guernsey: Guernsey Press, 1995), 1 (June 18, 1940). The governor was Major-General A. P. D. Telfer-Smollett, who had only been in the post briefly (10 n. 7).
4. Roy McLoughlin, *Living with the Enemy: What Really Happened* (Jersey: Channel Island Publishing, 2003), 17.
5. McLoughlin, *Living with the Enemy*, 17.
6. Harvey, *Battle of Newlands*, 12 n. 24.
7. Harvey, *Battle of Newlands*, 6 (June 25, 1940).
8. K. M. Bachmann, *The Prey of an Eagle* (Guernsey: Guernsey Press, 1972), 26 (August 10, 1940).
9. Bachmann, *Prey of an Eagle*, 26–27 (August 10, 1940).
10. Bachmann, *Prey of an Eagle*, 25 (August 10, 1940).
11. Diary of Arthur Mauger, AQ374/13 to 25, ledger book 21, States of Guernsey Island Archive [hereafter Mauger], 22 June 1940.
12. Harvey, *Battle of Newlands*, 2 (June 17, 1940).
13. Harvey, *Battle of Newlands*, 2–3 (June 17, 1940).
14. Ord, 6 (June 20, 1940).
15. Harvey, *Battle of Newlands*, 5 (June 22, 1940).
16. Harvey, *Battle of Newlands*, 8 (June 27–28, 1940).
17. Harvey, *Battle of Newlands*, 3 (June 19, 1940).
18. Ord, 7 (June 16, 1940).
19. Ord, 5 (June 16, 1940).
20. Diary of Herbert Williams, States of Guernsey Island Archives Service, AQ 380/03 [hereafter Williams], June 22–30, 1940 (written in 1942).
21. The diarists do not mention some of the intriguing stories in popular culture describing people

leaving their homes to evacuate and then changing their minds. They returned home to find that thieves had stolen everything. Neighbors seem often to have been told to take food stuffs and whatever was small and of value to protect it from German hands. There is no indication that it was the neighbors who pillaged the houses of aborted evacuees, although they were certainly ineffective guards.

22. Harvey, *Battle of Newlands*, 15 (July 1, 1940).
23. Jack C. Sauvary, *Diary of the German Occupation of Guernsey, 1940–1945* (Upton-upon-Severn: Self Pub. Association, 1990), 115 (December 27, 1941).
24. Ord, 9 (June 22, 1940).
25. Mauger, June 19–20, 1940.
26. Ord, 8 (June 20, 1940).
27. Bachmann, *Prey of an Eagle*, 8 (July 18, 1940).
28. Sauvary, *Diary*, 25 (July 21, 1940, written later, presumably the 28th).
29. Sauvary, *Diary*, 37 (November 9, 1940).
30. Bachmann, *Prey of an Eagle*, 3–4 (July 13, 1940).
31. Harvey, *Battle of Newlands*, 3–4 (June 20–21, 1940). Actually, Winnie later reports that Bessie had asked R. O. Falla of the Controlling Committee personally to check on her mother.
32. Harvey, *Battle of Newlands*, 4 (June 21, 1940); Bachmann, *Prey of an Eagle*, 29 (August 10, 1940).
33. Harvey, *Battle of Newlands*, 5 (June 23, 1940).
34. Harvey, *Battle of Newlands*, 6 (June 35, 1940).
35. Ord, 6 (June 20, 1940).
36. Sauvary, *Diary*, 32 (September 29, 1940).
37. Bachmann, *Prey of an Eagle*, 28–29 (August 10, 1940).
38. Diary of Kenneth G. Lewis, vol. 1, Guernsey Island Archives, G06/10 W, 1–1-8–10, AS/LC 16–01 [hereafter Lewis], June 30, 1940.
39. Sauvary, *Diary*, 27 (June 30, 1940).
40. Harvey, *Battle of Newlands*, 11 n. 12, and 14 (June 20–July 1, 1940).
41. Harvey, *Battle of Newlands*, 3 (June 20, 1940).
42. Harvey, *Battle of Newlands*, 14 (July 1, 1940).
43. Higgs, *Life in Guernsey*, 9 (July 2, 1940).
44. Lewis, June 30, 1940.
45. Diary of Ambrose Collas Robin, 17 June 1940 to 18 May 1945, Priaulx Library, Guernsey, Control No. M0005622GY [hereafter Robin], July 1, 1940.
46. Lewis, July 1–14, 1940; Harvey, *Battle of Newlands*, 14 (July 1, 1940).
47. Lewis, July 1–14, 1940.
48. William M. Bell, *Guernsey Green: The Life and Times of Guernseyman Bill Green* (Guernsey: William M. Bell, 1992), 97–98.
49. Higgs, *Life in Guernsey*, 9 (July 2, 1940).
50. Sauvary, *Diary*, 27 (July 1, 1940).
51. Harvey, *Battle of Newlands*, 14 (July 1, 1940).
52. Stephen V. Ash, *When the Yankees Came: Conflict and Chaos in the Occupied South, 1861–1865* (Chapel Hill: University of North Carolina Press, 1995), 29.
53. The Channel Islands were part of the Duchy of Normandy for some two centuries or more, until King John lost mainland Normandy to the King of France in 1204. The Islands maintained their allegiance to the English Crown, becoming Crown dependencies with the right to their own laws, taxes, and governmental structure.
54. McLoughlin, *Living with the Enemy*, 66.

55. Bachmann, *Prey of an Eagle*, 31 (August 10, 1940).
56. McLoughlin, *Living with the Enemy*, 66–67.
57. Bill Green tells the story of being confronted by "two tall young blond Hitler youth types" who stopped him on the road in these early days. "Vitch vay London?" one asked, only to learn to his disappointment, "Over there, across the sea"; Bell, *Guernsey Green*, 99.
58. Hazel R. Knowles Smith, *The Changing Face of the Channel Islands Occupation: Record, Memory, and Myth* (Houndmills, Basingstoke, Hampshire: Palgrave Macmillan, 2007), 22.
59. Knowles Smith, *The Changing Face*, 21.
60. McLoughlin, *Living with the Enemy*, 25–26.
61. Bachmann, *Prey of an Eagle*, 6 (July 16, 1940).
62. Harvey, *Battle of Newlands*, 15 (July 1, 1940).
63. Bachmann, *Prey of an Eagle*, 25 (August 10, 1940).
64. Higgs, *Life in Guernsey*, 15 (October 1, 1940).
65. Michel Foucault, *Discipline and Punish*, trans. Alan Sheridan (New York: Vintage, 1995), 200.
66. Foucault, *Discipline and Punish*, 200.
67. Ken Tough, "The Identity Card System in Occupied Guernsey," in *Channel Islands Occupation Review*, no. 20 (1992): 32.
68. Paul Sanders, *The British Channel Islands under German Occupation, 1940–1945* (Jersey: Jersey Heritage Trust/Société Jersiaise, 2005).
69. William M. Bell, *I Beg to Report: Policing in Guernsey during the German Occupation* (Guernsey: Guernsey Press, 1995), 48.
70. Harvey, *Battle of Newlands*, 21 (August 18–25, 1940).
71. Lewis, December 2–3, 1940.
72. Harvey, *Battle of Newlands*, 36 (October 13, 1940); Diary of Elizabeth Doig 298904, Priaulx Library, Guernsey, October 14, 1940.
73. Harvey, *Battle of Newlands*, 43 (October 24–November 3, 1940).
74. Tough, "Identity Card," 33–35.
75. Sauvary, *Diary*, 35 (October 21, 1940).
76. Ken Tough, "Deportation from Guernsey 1942—Two Personal Accounts and a German Assessment," *Channel Islands Occupation Review*, no. 20 (1992): 72.
77. Ord, 103 (November 19, 1940).
78. Harvey, *Battle of Newlands*, 36 (October 11, 1940).
79. Anonymous diary, green cover, Priaulx Library, Guernsey, 7 (November 7, 1940).
80. Harvey, *Battle of Newlands*, 16 (July 1, 1940).
81. Ord, 36 (July 31, 1940).
82. Ord, 38 (August 1, 1940).
83. Ord, 37 (August 1, 1940).
84. Bell, *I Beg*, 61–62. Other sources, including later writing by Bell, portray Cheeseborough as a collaborator.
85. Harvey, *Battle of Newlands*, 16 (July 1, 1940).
86. Harvey, *Battle of Newlands*, 16 (July 1, 1940).
87. Mark Andrejevic, "The Discipline of Watching: Detection, Risk and Lateral Surveillance," *Critical Studies in Media Communication* 23, no. 5 (December 2006): 396–97.
88. Foucault, *Discipline and Punish*, 214.
89. John S. Bak, "Escaping the Jaundiced Eye: Foucauldian Panopticism in Charlotte Perkins Gilman's 'The Yellow Wallpaper,'" *Studies in Short Fiction* 31, no. 1 (Winter 1994): 39–46.
90. Foucault, *Discipline and Punish*, 201.

91. Lewis, November 12–13, 1940; Harvey, *Battle of Newlands*, 45 (November 14, 1940).
92. Lewis, October 21–22, 1940.
93. Robin, December 2, 1940.
94. Robin, December 24, 1940.
95. Ord, 124 (December 14, 1940).
96. Bachmann, *Prey of an Eagle*, 22 (August 3, 1940).
97. Williams, 19 (June 22–30, 1940).
98. Ord, 27 (July 10, 1940).
99. Ord, 98 (November 11, 1940).
100. Ord, 103 (November 19, 1940).
101. Harvey, *Battle of Newlands*, 43 (November 3–November 14, 1940).
102. Harvey, *Battle of Newlands*, 28 (September 3, 1940).
103. Ord, 51 (August 16, 1940).
104. Foucault, *Discipline and Punish*, 200.
105. Foucault, *Discipline and Punish*, 201.
106. Andrejevic, "Discipline of Watching," 396.
107. Foucault, *Discipline and Punish*, 205.
108. Steve Mann, "Sousveillance," http://wearcam.org/sousveillance.htm, 2002.
109. Robin, August 31, 1940.
110. Ord, 19 (July 1, 1940).
111. Ord, 19 (July 1, 1940).
112. Lewis, December 4–5, 1940.
113. Lewis, July 15–21, 1940.
114. Harvey, *Battle of Newlands*, 29 (September 8–12, 1940).
115. Ord, 51 (August 16, 1940).
116. Bachmann, *Prey of an Eagle*, 17 (August 10, 1940).
117. Ord, 23 (July 3, 1940).
118. Ord, 28 (July 11, 1940).
119. Harvey, *Battle of Newlands*, 50 (December 16, 1940).
120. Harvey, *Battle of Newlands*, 46 (November 16–December 2, 1940).
121. Ord, 250 (December 31, 1941).
122. Harvey, *Battle of Newlands*, 37 (October 20–27, 1940).
123. William M. Bell, *Guernsey Occupied but Never Conquered* (Exeter: Studio, 2002), 73–75.
124. Bell, *Guernsey Occupied*, 120–21.
125. Bell, *Guernsey Occupied*, 77–79.
126. Bell, *Guernsey Occupied*, 79.
127. Bell, *Guernsey Occupied*, 95.
128. Harvey, *Battle of Newlands*, 22 (August 30, 1940).
129. Bell, *Guernsey Occupied*, 121.
130. Bell, *Guernsey Occupied*, 123.
131. Bell, *Guernsey Occupied*, 125.
132. Harvey, *Battle of Newlands*, 36 (October 20–27).
133. Harvey, *Battle of Newlands*, 42 (October 24–November 3, 1940); Lewis, October 24, 1940.
134. Harvey, *Battle of Newlands*, 43 (November 3–November 14, 1940).
135. Bachmann, *Prey of an Eagle*, 44 (November 7, 1940).
136. Harvey, *Battle of Newlands*, 44 (November 3–November 14, 1940).

137. Harvey, *Battle of Newlands*, 56 (January 1, 1941).
138. Bell, *Guernsey Occupied*, 138.
139. Harvey, *Battle of Newlands*, 56 (January 1, 1941).
140. Harvey, *Battle of Newlands*, 44 (November 3–14, 1940).
141. Bachmann, *Prey of an Eagle*, 44 (November 7, 1940).
142. Bell, *Guernsey Occupied*, 165.
143. Lewis, June 19, 1942.
144. Lewis, April 15, 1942.
145. Diary of William Arthur Warry, University of Virginia, Special Collections, Microfilm 1688 MSS8138 [hereafter Warry], August 12, 1942.
146. Harvey, *Battle of Newlands*, 110 (October 29, 1942).
147. Diary of Herbert Williams, States of Guernsey Island Archives Service, AQ 380/03–2 [hereafter Williams], October 14, 1942.
148. Sauvary, *Diary*, 97 (August 25, 1941).
149. Ord, 442 (February 15, 1943).
150. Warry, June 6, 1943.
151. Ord, 337 (August 3, 1942).
152. Sauvary, *Diary*, 50 (January 21, 1941).
153. Sauvary, *Diary*, 103 (September 30, 1941).
154. Sauvary, *Diary*, 109 (November 22, 1941).
155. Sauvary, *Diary*, 134 (March 26, 1942).
156. Sauvary, *Diary*, 155–56 (July 12, 1942).
157. Ord, 273–74 (March 3, 1942).
158. Williams, 72 (October 14, 1942).
159. Higgs, *Life in Guernsey*, 27–28 (November 12, 1941).
160. Ord, 218 (October 9, 1941).
161. Ord, 217 (October 9, 1941).
162. Harvey, *Battle of Newlands*, 70 (March 20, 1941).
163. Harvey, *Battle of Newlands*, 98–101 (October 23–29, 1941).
164. Harvey, *Battle of Newlands*, 110 (October 29, 1941). Mrs. Clayton lived with Winnie off and on throughout the years.
165. Lewis, November 11, 1941.
166. Diary of Arthur Mauger, A2 374/23 25/8/1942–13/4/1944, ledger book 23, Guernsey Island Archives, January 19–27, 1943.
167. Sauvary, *Diary*, 171–72 (October 11–18, 1942).
168. Diary of Elizabeth Doig, 298904, Priaulx Library, Guernsey [hereafter Doig], February 24, 1942.
169. Doig, April 8, 1942.
170. Doig, October 8, 1942.
171. Doig, August 2, 1943.
172. Doig, September 19, 1943.
173. Ord, 305 (June 8, 1942).
174. Sauvary, *Diary*, 150 (June 8, 1942).
175. Sauvary, *Diary*, 152 (June 16, 1942).
176. Doig, June 8, 1942.
177. Doig, June 18, 1942.

178. Ord, 359 (September 15, 1942).
179. Warry, September 16, 1942.
180. Robin, September 20, 1942.
181. Ord, 359 (September 15, 1942).
182. Ord, 364 (September 18, 1942).
183. Harvey, *Battle of Newlands*, 148–49 (September 15–30, 1942).
184. Doig, September 27, 1942.
185. Harvey, *Battle of Newlands*, 152 (September 15–30, 1942).
186. Harvey, *Battle of Newlands*, 152 (September 15–30, 1942).
187. Warry, September 21, 1942.
188. Harvey, *Battle of Newlands*, 150 (September 15–30, 1942).
189. Sauvary, *Diary*, 168 (September 25, 1942).
190. Warry, September 21, 1942.
191. Warry, September 21, 1942. Unable to put out due to the weather, they were forced to sit up in their wet clothes with no water or lavatory in ships laden mainly with lice and fleas. In the morning they were given some coffee and bread (plus a hot meal at 10 A.M.), then told to go home and to report again on Wednesday. After "trailing down to the pier" on Wednesday, they were sent back home again. And thus the "cat and mouse game," as Winnie called it, went on until finally new ships of better quality came on Friday and put out for Germany with the deportees aboard. Unfortunately, this time lag gave the Germans more opportunity to review their exemption lists, and a number of people who thought they were safe found themselves suddenly on their way to Germany.
192. Harvey, *Battle of Newlands*, 171 (January 16–February 28, 1943).
193. Warry, February 12, 1943.
194. Harvey, *Battle of Newlands*, 171 (January 16–February 28, 1943).
195. Robin, February 17, 1943.
196. Warry, February 12, 1943.
197. Patrick R. Spence, David Westerman, Paul D. Skalski, Matthew Seeger, Robert R. Ulmer, Steve Venette, and Timothy L. Sellnow, "Proxemic Effects on Information Seeking after the September 11 Attacks," *Communication Research Reports* 22, no. 1 (February 2005): 40.
198. Spence et al., "Proxemic Effects," 40.
199. C. R. Berger and R. J. Calabrese, "Some Explorations in Initial Interaction and Beyond: Toward a Developmental Theory of Interpersonal Communication," *Human Communication Research* 1, no. 2 (1975): 99–112; C. R. Berger and J. J. Bradac, *Language and Social Knowledge: Uncertainty in Interpersonal Relations* (London: Edward Arnold Publishers, 1982); C. R. Berger, "Communicating under Uncertainty," in *Interpersonal Processes: New Directions in Communication Research*, eds. M. E. Roloff and G. R. Miller (Newbury Park, CA: Sage, 1987), 39–62.
200. See Berger and Bradac, *Language and Social Knowledge*.
201. See Berger, "Communicating," 1987.
202. D. E. Brashers, "Communication and Uncertainty Management," *Journal of Communication* 51 (2001): 478.
203. See Maria Miceli and Cristiano Castelfranchi, "Anxiety as an 'Epistemic' Emotion: An Uncertainty Theory of Anxiety," *Anxiety, Stress, and Coping* 18, no. 4 (December 2005): 294–95.
204. Harvey, *Battle of Newlands*, 78 (June 1–14, 1941).
205. Sauvary, *Diary*, 90 (July 31, 1941).
206. Sauvary, *Diary*, 88 (July 22, 1941).

207. Higgs, *Life in Guernsey*, 30–31 (August 5, 1942); Harvey, *Battle of Newlands*, 84 (July 29–August 5, 1941).
208. Bachmann, *Prey of an Eagle*, 31 (August 10, 1940).
209. Higgs, *Life in Guernsey*, 12 (August 3, 1940) and 15 (October 5, 1940).
210. Harvey, *Battle of Newlands*, 45 (November 15, 1940).
211. Williams, 88 (May 14, 1943).
212. Higgs, *Life in Guernsey*, 30 (August 5, 1942).
213. Bachmann, *Prey of an Eagle*, 136 (September 1, 1942).
214. Harvey, *Battle of Newlands*, 154 (September 15–30, 1942).
215. Higgs, *Life in Guernsey*, 45 (July 3, 1944).
216. Diary of Gertie Corbin, Z009/19 AQ92/12, States of Guernsey Island Archives, August 1943.
217. Ord, 54 (August 24, 1940).
218. Williams, 31 (May 11, 1942).
219. Higgs, *Life in Guernsey*, 34 (June 1, 1943).
220. Ord, 153 (April 11, 1941).
221. Harvey, *Battle of Newlands*, 125 (February 1–18, 1942).
222. Harvey, *Battle of Newlands*, 133 (no date).
223. Bachmann, *Prey of an Eagle*, 25 (August 13, 1942).
224. Harvey, *Battle of Newlands*, 87 (August 21, 1941).
225. Harvey, *Battle of Newlands*, 84 (July 28–August 5, 1941).
226. Ord, 444 (February 14, 1943).
227. Ord, 395 (October 13, 1942).
228. Ord, 189–90 (August 1, 1941).
229. Ord, 217 (October 9, 1941).
230. Ord, 960 (January 15, 1944).
231. Williams, 101 (July 31, 1943).
232. Robin, December 8, 1940.
233. Higgs, *Life in Guernsey*, 45 (July 2, 1944).
234. Robin, December 20, 1942.
235. Ord, 282 (March 28, 1942).
236. Bachmann, *Prey of an Eagle*, 9 (July 20, 1940).
237. Ord, 521 (June 6, 1943).
238. Harvey, *Battle of Newlands*, 174 (January 15–February 28, 1943).
239. Bachmann, *Prey of an Eagle*, 88 (November 14, 1941).
240. Warry, December 21, 1942.
241. Doig, Later addition to diary.
242. Ord, 348 (August 24, 1942).
243. Sauvary, *Diary*, 128 (February 4, 1942).
244. Lewis, April 19, 1943.
245. Warry, February 4, 1943.
246. Warry, September 21, 1943.
247. Robin, January 7, 1941.
248. Sauvary, *Diary*, 155 (July 9, 1942).
249. Bachmann, *Prey of an Eagle*, 8 (July 20, 1940).
250. Robin, May 20, 1941.
251. Harvey, *Battle of Newlands*, 63 (February 16–March 2, 1941).

252. Ord, 219 (October 10, 1941).
253. Hazel R. Knowles Smith, *The Changing Face of the Channel Islands Occupation: Record, Memory, and Myth* (Houndmills, Basingstoke, Hampshire: Palgrave Macmillan, 2007), 121.
254. Ord, 304 (June 4, 1942).
255. Tilman Allert, *The Hitler Salute: On the Meaning of a Gesture*, trans. Jefferson Chase (New York: Metropolitan Books, 2008).
256. Ord, 348–49 (August 24, 1942).
257. Ord, 202–4 (September 2, 1942).
258. Ord, 240 (November 20, 1941).
259. Ord, 218–31 (October 10–October 28, 1941).
260. Ord, 234 (November 1, 1941).
261. Ord, 247 (December 13, 1941).
262. Ord, 291 (April 25, 1942) and 334 (July 31, 1942).
263. Ord, 545 (July 7, 1943).
264. Robin, November 16, 1942.
265. James C. Scott, *Domination and the Arts of Resistance: Hidden Transcripts* (New Haven: Yale University Press, 1990), 118.
266. Susan Gal, "A Semiotics of the Public/Private Distinction," *Differences: A Journal of Feminist Cultural Studies* 13, no. 1 (2002): 85.
267. Scott, *Domination*, 151.

CHAPTER TWO. THE BEDROCK OF RESISTANCE

1. Jack C. Sauvary, *Diary of the German Occupation of Guernsey, 1940–1945* (Upton-upon-Severn: Self Pub. Association, 1990), 91 (August 4, 1941).
2. Sauvary, *Diary*, 98 (August 31, 1941).
3. James C. Scott, *Domination and the Arts of Resistance: Hidden Transcripts* (New Haven: Yale University Press, 1990), 117–18.
4. Scott, *Domination*, 118.
5. K. M. Bachmann, *The Prey of an Eagle* (Guernsey: Guernsey Press, 1972), 5 (July 16, 1940).
6. Bachmann, *Prey of an Eagle*, 110 (February 18, 1942).
7. Bachmann, *Prey of an Eagle*, 72–73 (June 4, 1941).
8. Bachmann, *Prey of an Eagle*, 42 (October 24, 1940).
9. Bachmann, *Prey of an Eagle*, 50 (January 2, 1941).
10. Dorothy Pickard Higgs, *Life in Guernsey under the Nazis, 1940–45* (Guernsey: Toucan Press, 2000), 11 (July 24, 1940).
11. Bachmann, *Prey of an Eagle*, 4 (July 13, 1940).
12. This terrible juxtaposition of grief and joy, Kitty called a true example of "the funeral baked meats coldly furnishing forth the marriage tables." But, she added, "We are indeed becoming almost accustomed to truth being stranger than fiction."
13. Bachmann, *Prey of an Eagle*, 17 (July 26, 1940).
14. Bachmann, *Prey of an Eagle*, 48 (January 2, 1941).
15. Sauvary, *Diary*, 117 (January 1, 1942).
16. It can only be hoped that most of these efforts were not on the order of one get-together

Mrs. Warry attended with a few friends. They had a lovely afternoon and enjoyed the cakes that one woman provided, any sweet or pastry being particularly welcome and more like the teas of old. When this woman returned home, her husband (a grower) asked her what had become of his bag of slug killer. They realized that she had mistaken the slug bait for flour and used it to concoct her cakes. Of course everyone had partaken of the cakes with enthusiasm and were beside themselves with worry over the possible consequences. Surprisingly, no one seemed to suffer any ill effects; Diary of William Arthur Warry, University of Virginia, Special Collections, Microfilm 1688 MSS8138 [hereafter Warry], June 6, 1943.

17. Diary of Kenneth G. Lewis, vol. 2, Guernsey Island Archives, G06/10 W, 1-1-8-10, AS/LC 16-01 [hereafter Lewis], April 7, 1943.
18. Lewis, December 29, 1942.
19. Bachmann, *Prey of an Eagle*, 43 (November 7, 1940) and 56 (January 19, 1941).
20. Diary of Herbert Williams, States of Guernsey Island Archives Service, AQ 380/03-2 [hereafter Williams], 64 (August 10, 1942).
21. Williams, September 28, 1943.
22. Sauvary, *Diary*, 61 (March 4, 1941), 69 (April 12, 1941), and 72 (April 23, 1941).
23. Sauvary, *Diary*, 184–85 (January 15, 1943), illustration 15.
24. E. B. Ebbeson, G. L. Kjos, V. J. Konecni, "Spatial Ecology: Its Effects on the Choice of Friends and Enemies," *Journal of Experimental Social Psychology* 12 (1976): 508–18.
25. Williams, 188 and 196 (January 2 and January 8, 1945).
26. Williams, 226 (March 2, 1945).
27. Lewis, October 17, 1942, and March 20, 1943.
28. All names for the family are pseudonyms.
29. Diary of Ambrose Collas Robin, 17 June 1940 to 18 May 1945, Priaulx Library, Guernsey, Control No. M0005622GY [hereafter Robin], July 30, 1942.
30. Lewis, July 30, 1944.
31. Lewis, April 6, 1945.
32. A pseudonym.
33. Island Police, Guernsey, Statement of Witness, September 1, 1940; Island Police, Report of Inspector Sculpher, September 3, 1940, Imperial War Museum archives.
34. Diary of the Rev. R. Douglas Ord, vols. 1–7, 16 June 1940–12 May 1945, M0007066GY-M0007073GY, Priaulx Library, Guernsey [hereafter Ord], 133 (February 28, 1941).
35. Winifred Harvey, *The Battle of Newlands: The Wartime Diaries of Winifred Harvey*, ed. Rosemary Booth (Guernsey: Guernsey Press, 1995), 63–64 (February 16–March 2, 1941). This is the same incident that resulted in a guard being placed on Mrs. Sherbrooke and Mrs. Kinnersley (see chapter 1). Upon investigation, the Germans found that the servant girls, rather than their mistresses, were sending signals to Allied parachutists.
36. Ord, 836 (July 26, 1944).
37. Ord, 180 (July 6, 1941).
38. Harvey, *Battle of Newlands*, 16–17 (August 1940).
39. Harvey, *Battle of Newlands*, 43 (October 24–November 3, 1940).
40. Sauvary, *Diary*, 77 (May 1941).
41. Sauvary, *Diary*, 173 (October 26, 1942).
42. Sauvary, *Diary*, 76 (May 17, 1941).
43. Sauvary, *Diary*, 43 (December 23, 1940).
44. Sauvary, *Diary*, 55 (February 9, 1941).

45. Sauvary, *Diary*, 141 (May 5, 1942).
46. Sauvary, *Diary*, 51 (January 25, 1941).
47. Sauvary, *Diary*, 114 (December 22–23, 1941).
48. Sauvary, *Diary*, 68 (April 4, 1941).
49. Sauvary, *Diary*, 85 (July 6, 1941).
50. Warry, May 12, 1943.
51. Robin, August 3, 1941.
52. Sauvary, *Diary*, 50 (January 21, 1941).
53. Paul Sanders, *The British Channel Islands under German Occupation, 1940–1945* (Jersey: Jersey Heritage Trust/Société Jersiaise, 2005), 152.
54. Sauvary, *Diary*, 131 (February 1942).
55. Diary of Elizabeth Doig, 298904, Priaulx Library, Guernsey [hereafter Doig], April 30, 1944.
56. Warry, March 31, 1943.
57. Sauvary, *Diary*, 198–99 (March 31–April 12, 1943).
58. Bachmann, *Prey of an Eagle*, 96 (December 2, 1941).
59. Bachmann, *Prey of an Eagle*, 131 (July 27, 1942).
60. Sauvary, *Diary*, 209 (June 9, 1943).
61. Williams, 107 (September 8, 1943).
62. Bachmann, *Prey of an Eagle*, 99 (December 19, 1941).
63. Warry, September 24, 1942.
64. Harvey, *Battle of Newlands*, 145 (August 19, 1942).
65. Sauvary, *Diary*, 97 (August 27, 1941).
66. When visiting Guernsey for research on this book, I stayed several times in a pleasant set of rental apartments in a quiet St. Peter Port neighborhood overlooking Castle Cornet. The house next door still had a perfect hole in a garden wall where the Germans had broken through for some never-completed project. Despite the many times the house had been renovated over the years, no one could part with this little piece of history in their back garden.
67. Williams, 116 (December 7, 1943).
68. Sauvary, *Diary*, 213 (November 7, 1943). Jack has this date as November 7, 1943, although all other accounts have it on December 7.
69. Sauvary, *Diary*, 213 (November 7, 1943).
70. When in September 1941 there were no dog biscuits left anywhere in the Island, she gave "some from her store" to her friends. It is noteworthy that she gives "some" of her biscuits away; perhaps she was just unable to part with the entire lot, the final acknowledgment that Rolfie was gone forever.
71. Harvey, *Battle of Newlands*, 60 (January 30, 1941).
72. Harvey, *Battle of Newlands*, 77 (May 23, 1941).
73. Lewis, December 2 and 3, 1940; Harvey, *Battle of Newlands*, 49 (December 3–17, 1940).
74. Sauvary, *Diary*, 40 (December 16, 1940).
75. Robin, January 7, 1941.
76. Robin, April 2, 1942. Robin goes on to write that this occurrence with Tim of normally curable illness followed by death "corresponds with the cases of several persons who have died during last autumn and winter," and it was this realization that "embitters the spirit."
77. Higgs, *Life in Guernsey*, 28 (December 14, 1941). Yet it would be Tinker who, being underfed and slowed by pregnancy in her hunting, could not drop her kittens and died on Good Friday the next year. "We miss her sadly," wrote Dorothy. Higgs, *Life in Guernsey*, 29 (April 8, 1942).

78. Bachmann, *Prey of an Eagle*, 71 (May 14, 1941).
79. Sauvary, *Diary*, 60 (February 27, 1941).
80. Sauvary, *Diary*, 193 (February 27, 1943).
81. Diary of Gertie Corbin, States of Guernsey Island Archives, Z009/19 AQ92/12 [hereafter Corbin], February 1941.
82. Hazel R. Knowles Smith, *The Changing Face of the Channel Islands Occupation: Record, Memory, and Myth* (Houndmills, Basingstoke, Hampshire: Palgrave Macmillan, 2007), 138–39. Paul Sanders provides the official death rate per 1,000 that was part of the official report on essential supplies (Jersey Archives Service L/D/25/M4/10); Sanders, 152.
83. Smith, *The Changing Face*, 139.
84. Ord, 265 (January 29, 1942) and 272 (February 28, 1942).
85. Harvey, *Battle of Newlands*, 135–36 (April 1942).
86. Sauvary, *Diary*, 142 (May 10, 1942).
87. Harvey, *Battle of Newlands*, 89 (August 25–September 12, 1941).
88. Doig, December 31, 1941.
89. Sauvary, *Diary*, 109 (November 18, 1941).
90. Bachmann, *Prey of an Eagle*, 151 (March 28, 1943).
91. Bachmann, *Prey of an Eagle*, 114 (March 19, 1942). His Occupation funeral was simple, like most, but on his coffin as it was lowered into the grave was a little posy of many different blooms. The card attached read, "To Dear Grandpa—The Oldest, from Peter-John—The Youngest." Great age sometimes was juxtaposed with great youth, as occasionally happens in the natural order of things. In the same week, Arthur Mauger wrote of the death of Mrs. George Sauvarin at the advanced age of 100 and 3 months and the death of Mrs. Wilson Le Pelley's newborn son, Geoffrey, at the age of 5 days (Diary of Arthur Mauger, A2 374/23 25/8/1942–13/4/1944, ledger book 23, States of Guernsey Island Archives [hereafter Mauger], June 14 and 19, 1943).
92. Warry, October 28, 1942.
93. Robin, June 30, 1943.
94. Sauvary, *Diary*, 242 (August 5, 1944).
95. Bachmann, *Prey of an Eagle*, 128 (May 25, 1942).
96. Corbin, November 1941; Bachmann, *Prey of an Eagle*, 86 (November 6, 1941).
97. Warry, December 31, 1942.
98. Robin, January 1941; Lewis, January 1, 1942.
99. Robin, April 15, 1941; Harvey, *Battle of Newlands*, 73 (April 23, 1941).
100. Corbin, February 1943.
101. Mauger, ledger book 23, February 8, 1943.
102. Sauvary, *Diary*, 208 (June 9, 1943); Harvey, *Battle of Newlands*, 185–89 (June 9, 1943).
103. Warry, December 10, 1942.
104. Warry, August 14, 1943.
105. Ord, 247 (December 10, 1941).
106. Sauvary, *Diary*, 212 (October 1943).
107. Ord, 614–15 (September 15, 1943).
108. Robin, February 24, 1941.
109. Ord, 242–43 (November 22, 1941); Robin, November 23, 1941; Sauvary, *Diary*, 110 (November 22, 1941).
110. Sauvary, *Diary*, 55 (February 8, 1941).
111. Sauvary, *Diary*, 67 (April 1, 1941).

112. Ord, 216 (October 10, 1941).
113. Sauvary, *Diary*, 139 (April 20, 1942).
114. Doig, April 17, 1942.
115. Warry, July 20, 1943.
116. Sauvary, *Diary*, 73 (April 30, 1941).
117. Sauvary, *Diary*, 100 (September 7, 1941).
118. Bachmann, *Prey of an Eagle*, 62 (March 29, 1941).
119. Harvey, *Battle of Newlands*, 193 (August 25, 1943).
120. Ord, 543 (July 5, 1943).
121. Ord, 216 (October 4, 1941).
122. Ord, 158 (April 29, 1941).
123. Higgs, *Life in Guernsey*, 24 (June 6, 1941).
124. Bachmann, *Prey of an Eagle*, 87 (November 6, 1941).
125. Warry, March 24, 1944.
126. Bachmann, *Prey of an Eagle*, 73 (June 4, 1941).
127. Ord, 216 (October 4, 1941).
128. Harvey, *Battle of Newlands*, 51 (December 17–26, 1940).
129. Higgs, *Life in Guernsey*, 33 (May 24, 1943).
130. Robin, September 12, 1941.
131. Lewis, February 9, 1942.
132. My mother was a teenager during the 1930s, growing up on a small Iowa farm. Her family did not have money, nor did they have clothes. In fact, she recalled vividly the year when she had to wear shoes they were given from a community collection, and she went to school in a pair of lace-up, pointed-toed boots from around 1910. It broke her stylish adolescent heart. Yet, she never recalled being hungry, simply because they were in a position to raise their own food. With the exception of the Dust Bowl states, it was an advantage to be in a rural location, for the worst food shortages were in urban areas.
133. Alfred Williams, personal interview, June 2004.
134. Harvey, *Battle of Newlands*, 215 (May 1–26, 1944).
135. Sauvary, *Diary*, 229 (June 7, 1944).
136. Higgs, *Life in Guernsey*, 30 (April 8, 1942).
137. Higgs, *Life in Guernsey*, 39 (March 7, 1944).
138. Higgs, *Life in Guernsey*, 39–40 (March 14–18, 1944).
139. Sauvary, *Diary*, 224 (March 26, 1944).
140. Higgs, *Life in Guernsey*, 48 (August 28, 1944).
141. Higgs, *Life in Guernsey*, 54 (February 15, 1945).
142. Bachmann, *Prey of an Eagle*, 148 (March 24, 1943).
143. Sauvary, *Diary*, 143 (May 17, 1942).
144. Sauvary, *Diary*, 177 (November 27, 1942).
145. Corbin, January 1942 and November 1942.
146. Harvey, *Battle of Newlands*, 111 (November 1942).
147. Bachmann, *Prey of an Eagle*, 109 (February 16, 1942).
148. Warry, September 17, 1942.
149. Harvey, *Battle of Newlands*, 169 (January 1943).
150. Bachmann, *Prey of an Eagle*, 109 (February 16, 1942).
151. Sauvary, *Diary*, 180 (December 28, 1942).

152. Sauvary, *Diary*, 29–30 (July 8, 1940).
153. John W. Jordan, "Sabotage or Performed Compliance: Rhetorics of Resistance in Temp Worker Discourse," *Quarterly Journal of Speech* 89, no. 1 (February 2003): 22.
154. K. M. Bachmann, *The Prey of an Eagle* (Guernsey: Guernsey Press, 1972), 3 (July 13, 1940).
155. Harvey, *The Battle of Newlands*, 104 (October 25, 1941).
156. Malcolm Smith, *Britain 1940: History, Myth, and Popular Memory* (London: Routledge, 2000), 2.
157. Smith, *Britain 1940*, 2.
158. Harvey, *Battle of Newlands*, 18 (August 11–17, 1940).
159. Harvey, *Battle of Newlands*, 29 (September 8, 1940).
160. Bachmann, *Prey of an Eagle*, 63 (March 31, 1941).
161. Sauvary, *Diary*, 46 (December 31, 1940).
162. Harvey, *Battle of Newlands*, 18 (August 11–17, 1940).
163. Harvey, *Battle of Newlands*, 18 (August 11–17, 1940).
164. Sauvary, *Diary*, 73 (April 30, 1941).
165. Sauvary, *Diary*, 75 (May 12–13, 1941).
166. Corbin, January 1943.
167. Corbin, March 1944.
168. Harvey, *Battle of Newlands*, 31 (September 15–22, 1940).
169. Higgs, *Life in Guernsey*, 9–10 (July 2, 1940).
170. Higgs, *Life in Guernsey*, 11 (July 24, 1940).
171. Higgs, *Life in Guernsey*, 14 (September 24, 1940).
172. Higgs, *Life in Guernsey*, 14 (August 18, 1940).
173. Higgs, *Life in Guernsey*, 17 (November 21, 1940).
174. Bachmann, *Prey of an Eagle*, 24–25 (August 10, 1940).
175. Bachmann, *Prey of an Eagle*, 24–25 (August 10, 1940).
176. Warry, May 31, 1944.
177. Lewis, December 17–18, 1940.
178. Sauvary, *Diary*, 41 (December 16, 1940); Harvey, *Battle of Newlands*, 49 (December 3–17, 1940).
179. Lewis, December 17–18, 1940.
180. Sauvary, *Diary*, 41 (December 16, 1940).
181. Higgs, *Life in Guernsey*, 18 (January 10, 1941).
182. Lewis, January 17, 1942. The newspaper article appended to Ken's diary says nothing of vaporized horses.
183. Bachmann, *Prey of an Eagle*, 107 (January 26, 1942); Sauvary, *Diary*, 122 (January 17, 1942); Harvey, *Battle of Newlands*, 122–23 (January 25, 1942).
184. Ord, 205–6 (September 8, 1941).
185. Harvey, *Battle of Newlands*, 122 (January 25, 1940).
186. Knowles Smith, *The Changing Face*, 190.
187. Ord, 272 (February 28, 1942).
188. Higgs, *Life in Guernsey*, 21 (March 13, 1941).
189. Higgs, *Life in Guernsey*, 19 (January 30, 1941).
190. Higgs, *Life in Guernsey*, 13 (August 11, 1940).
191. Higgs, *Life in Guernsey*, 32 (May 15, 1943).
192. Higgs, *Life in Guernsey*, 18–19 (January 28, 1941).
193. Harvey, *Battle of Newlands*, 83–84 (July 1941).

194. Bachmann, *Prey of an Eagle*, 41 (October 24, 1940) and 72–73 (June 4, 1941).
195. Ord, 385 (October 13, 1942).
196. Stephen Ash, *When the Yankees Came: Conflict and Chaos in the Occupied South, 1861–1865* (Chapel Hill: University of North Carolina Press, 1995), 39 and 45.
197. Doig, May 16, 1943.
198. Sauvary, *Diary*, 36 (October 21, 1940).
199. Higgs, *Life in Guernsey*, 24–25 (June 6, 1941).
200. Bachmann, *Prey of an Eagle*, 147 (March 25, 1943).
201. Higgs, *Life in Guernsey*, 32–33 (May 24, 1943).
202. Robin, February 23, 1944.
203. Ord, 532 (June 22, 1943).
204. Mauger, December 1940.
205. Warry, January 1943.
206. Robin, April 22, 1941.
207. Ord, 157 (April 24, 1941).
208. Lewis, May 13, 1942.
209. Lewis, March 31, 1945.
210. Sauvary, *Diary*, 90 (August 3, 1941).
211. Sauvary, *Diary*, 239 (July 21, 1944).
212. Robin, February 28, 1943.
213. Robin, February 13, 1944; Ord, 701–2 (February 13, 1944).
214. Lewis, April 21, 1944.
215. Sauvary, *Diary*, 94 (August 17, 1941).
216. Sauvary, *Diary*, 222 (January 30, 1944).
217. Sauvary, *Diary*, 246 (September 10–16, 1944).
218. Sauvary, *Diary*, 69 (April 11, 1941).
219. Harvey, *Battle of Newlands*, 45 (November 15, 1940).
220. Sauvary, *Diary*, 45 (December 25, 1940).
221. Robin, May 8, 1942; Harvey, *Battle of Newlands*, 48 (December 3–17, 1940).
222. Inke Arns and Sylvia Sasse, "Subversive Affirmation: On Mimesis as Strategy of Resistance," in *East Art Map: Contemporary Art and Eastern Europe*, ed. IRWIN (London/Ljubljana, 2005), 444.
223. Arns and Sasse, "Subversive Affirmation," 5.
224. Harvey, *Battle of Newlands*, 46 (November 16–December 2, 1940).
225. Bachmann, *Prey of an Eagle*, 11 (July 22, 1940).
226. Bachmann, *Prey of an Eagle*, 40 (October 24, 1940).
227. Sauvary, *Diary*, 109 (November 16, 1941) and 114 (December 24, 1941).
228. Robin, November 24, 1940.
229. Ord, 977 (January 15, 1945).
230. Ord, 101 (November 17, 1940).
231. Ord, 503 (May 15, 1943).
232. Bachmann, *Prey of an Eagle*, 35 (September 23, 1940).
233. Sauvary, *Diary*, 25 (June 1940).
234. Doig, April 4, 1943.
235. Higgs, *Life in Guernsey*, 16 (October 5, 1940).
236. Higgs, 29 (February 15, 1942).
237. Lewis, December 31, 1943.

238. Bachmann, *Prey of an Eagle*, 106 (January 26, 1942).
239. Bachmann, *Prey of an Eagle*, 106 (January 26, 1942).
240. Bachmann, *Prey of an Eagle*, 25 (August 10, 1940).
241. Bachmann, *Prey of an Eagle*, 14 (July 24, 1940).
242. Bachmann, *Prey of an Eagle*, 13 (July 24, 1940).
243. Sauvary, *Diary*, 31 (August 11, 1940).
244. Bachmann, *Prey of an Eagle*, 42 and 43 (November 6, 1940).
245. Bachmann, *Prey of an Eagle*, 54 (January 19, 1941).
246. Robin, October 10, 1941.
247. Robin, December 22, 1941.
248. Robin, August 9, 1941.
249. Robin, August 1, 1942.
250. Lewis, April 19–22, 1941.
251. Ord, 185 (July 19, 1941).
252. Higgs, *Life in Guernsey*, 23 (April 12, 1941).
253. Williams, 66 (September 13, 1942).
254. Higgs, *Life in Guernsey*, 25–26 (August 10, 1941).
255. Robin, December 22, 1941.
256. Harvey, *Battle of Newlands*, 77 (June 1–14, 1941).
257. Ord, 132 (January 25, 1941).
258. Bachmann, *Prey of an Eagle*, 56 (January 30, 1941).
259. Robin, March 11, 1942.
260. Bachmann, *Prey of an Eagle*, 131 (July 27, 1942).
261. Bachmann, *Prey of an Eagle*, 132–35 (August 15–September 1, 1942).
262. Bachmann, *Prey of an Eagle*, 33 (August 22, 1940) and 7 (July 18, 1940).
263. Bachmann, *Prey of an Eagle*, 56 (January 30, 1941).
264. Bachmann, *Prey of an Eagle*, 120 (May 10, 1942).
265. A pseudonym.
266. Lewis, November 19, 1940.
267. Lewis, April 29–May 1, 1941; June 18–20, 1941.
268. Lewis, May 26–30, 1942.
269. Lewis, July 2, 1943.
270. Lewis, August 6, 1942.
271. Lewis, December 19, 1942.
272. A pseudonym.
273. Lewis, September 15, 1943.
274. Michael Huspek, "Foucault on the 'Other Within,'" in *Transgressing Discourses: Communication and the Voice of the Other*, ed. Michael Huspek and Gary P. Radford (Albany: State University of New York Press, 1997), 99.
275. Huspek, "Foucault," 100–101.
276. Scott, *Domination*, 109.
277. Scott, *Domination*, 110.

CHAPTER THREE. REACHING FOR CONTROL

1. Diary of the Rev. R. Douglas Ord, vols. 1–7, 16 June 1940–12 May 1945, M0007066GY–M0007073GY, Priaulx Library, Guernsey [hereafter Ord], 152 (April 11, 1941).
2. James C. Scott, *Domination and the Arts of Resistance: Hidden Transcripts* (New Haven: Yale University Press, 1990), 184 and 165.
3. Scott, *Domination*, 149.
4. Scott, *Domination*, 155 and 137.
5. Scott, *Domination*, 184.
6. Scott, *Domination*, 196.
7. Scott, *Domination*, 184.
8. Gordon Allport and Joseph Postman, *The Psychology of Rumor* (New York: Russell and Russell, 1947); Warren Peterson and Noel Gist, "Rumor and Public Opinion," *American Journal of Sociology* 57, no. 2 (September 1951): 159–67; Ralph L. Rosnow, "Inside Rumor: A Personal Journey," *American Psychologist* 46, no. 5 (May 1991): 484–96; Ralph L. Rosnow, "Rumor and Gossip in Interpersonal Interaction and Beyond: A Social Exchange Perspective," in *Behaving Badly: Aversive Behaviors in Interpersonal Relationships*, ed. R. M. Kowalski (Washington, DC: American Psychological Association, 2001), 203–32.
9. Ord, iii–iv (1945).
10. Rosnow, "Inside Rumor," 485–87.
11. K. M. Bachmann, *The Prey of an Eagle* (Guernsey: Guernsey Press, 1972), 10 (July 20, 1940).
12. Diary of Ambrose Collas Robin, 17 June 1940 to 18 May 1945, Priaulx Library, Guernsey, Control No. M0005622GY [hereafter Robin], August 31, 1940.
13. Bachmann, *Prey of an Eagle*, 23 (August 3, 1940).
14. Ord, 831 (July 21, 1944).
15. Ord, 33 (July 23, 1940).
16. Ord, 63 (September 11, 1940).
17. Ord, 97 (November 10, 1940).
18. Ord, 106 (November 22, 1940).
19. Ord, 210 (September 24, 1941).
20. William M. Bell, *Guernsey Occupied but Never Conquered* (Exeter, UK: Studio Publishing Services, 2001), 165–66.
21. Diary of Kenneth G. Lewis, G06/10 W, 1–1-8–10, AS/LC 16–01, States of Guernsey Island Archives [hereafter Lewis], September 25–26, 1941.
22. Winifred Harvey, *The Battle of Newlands: The Wartime Diaries of Winifred Harvey*, ed. Rosemary Booth (Guernsey: Guernsey Press, 1995), 97 (September 20–27, 1941).
23. Ord, 210–14 (September 24–October 6, 1941).
24. Lewis, September 28–29, 1941.
25. Ord, 359 (September 15, 1942).
26. Bell, *Guernsey Occupied*, 223.
27. Jean-Noel Kapferer, "How Rumors Are Born," *Society* (July–August 1992): 53.
28. Kapferer, "How Rumors Are Born," 53.
29. Hans-Joachim Neubauer, *The Rumour: A Cultural History* (London: Free Association Books, 1999), 174.
30. Rosnow, "Inside Rumor," 485.

31. Ord, 210 (September 24, 1941).
32. R. L. Rosnow, J. H. Yost, and J. L. Esposito, "Belief in Rumor and Likelihood of Rumor Transmission," *Language and Communication* 6, no. 3 (1986): 189–94.
33. Scott, *Domination*, 147.
34. Ord, 180 (July 8, 1941).
35. Dorothy Pickard Higgs, *Life in Guernsey under the Nazis, 1940–45* (Guernsey: Toucan Press, 2000), 31 (September 8, 1942).
36. Jack C. Sauvary, *Diary of the German Occupation of Guernsey, 1940–1945* (Upton-upon-Severn: Self Pub. Association, 1990), 187 (January 28, 1943).
37. Robin, December 8, 1941.
38. Rosnow, "Inside Rumor," 485.
39. Harvey, *Battle of Newlands*, 95 (September 20–27, 1942).
40. Bernard Guerin and Yoshihiko Miyazaki, "Analyzing Rumors, Gossip, and Urban Legends through Their Conversational Properties", *Psychological Record* 56 (2006): 27.
41. Guerin and Miyazaki, "Analyzing Rumors," 30.
42. Scott, *Domination*, 145.
43. Harvey, *Battle of Newlands*, 29 (September 3, 1941).
44. Harvey, *Battle of Newlands*, 76 (May 11, 1942).
45. Bachmann, *Prey of an Eagle*, 97 (December 2, 1941).
46. Harvey, *Battle of Newlands*, 21 (August 27, 1940).
47. Michael Quinion, *World Wide Words*, http://www.worldwidewords.org/qa/qa-gra2.htm, page created October 20, 2001.
48. Diary of Mrs. Elizabeth Doig, Bib Id. 298904, Priaulx Library, Guernsey [hereafter Doig], September 11, 1943.
49. Harvey, *Battle of Newlands*, 178 (March 1–April 30, 1943).
50. Bachmann, *Prey of an Eagle*, 21–22 (August 3, 1940). The pseudonymous last name may have been provided by Kitty, or possibly by the editor of her published diary.
51. Bachmann, *Prey of an Eagle*, 22 (August 3, 1940).
52. Bachmann, *Prey of an Eagle*, 22 (August 3, 1940).
53. Hazel R. Knowles Smith, *The Changing Face of the Channel Islands Occupation: Record, Memory, and Myth* (Houndmills, Basingstoke, Hampshire: Palgrave Macmillan, 2007), 167. Knowles Smith does an excellent job of sorting through some of the indications that collaborators/fraternizers were a very small—though undoubtedly dangerous—part of the Channel Islands population. She relies on contemporary accounts from the general population, testimony of those who escaped the Islands during the Occupation, and some common-sense assessment of her own. In this last category, I would include her view that those so clearly worried about their many relatives and friends now sheltering in mainland Britain would be unlikely to do anything to aid an enemy bent on that nation's destruction; Knowles Smith, 163–80.
54. Bachmann, *Prey of an Eagle*, 22 (August 3, 1940).
55. Bachmann, *Prey of an Eagle*, 21 (August 3, 1940).
56. Madeleine Bunting, *The Model Occupation: The Channel Islands under German Rule* (London: Harper Collins, 1995), 5–6.
57. Bunting, *The Model Occupation*, 237. Bunting uses the letter to claim that the Home Office was "furious" that word of collaboration in the Channel Islands had leaked out.
58. Sauvary, *Diary*, 98 (August 31, 1941).
59. Sauvary, *Diary*, 256 (October 30, 1944).

60. Sarah R. Wert and Peter Salovey, "A Social Comparison Account of Gossip," *Review of General Psychology* 8, no. 2 (2004): 123.
61. Roy F. Baumeister, Liqing Zhang, and Kathleen D. Vohs, "Gossip as Cultural Learning," *Review of General Psychology* 8, no. 2 (2004): 112.
62. Baumeister et al., "Gossip as Cultural Learning," 116.
63. Wert and Salovey, "Social Comparison," 129.
64. Baumeister et al., "Gossip as Cultural Learning," 112.
65. Baumeister et al., "Gossip as Cultural Learning," 114.
66. Baumeister et al., "Gossip as Cultural Learning," 114.
67. Scott, *Domination*, 142.
68. Baumeister et al., "Gossip as Cultural Learning," 117.
69. Baumeister et al., "Gossip as Cultural Learning," 116–17; Wert and Salovey, "Social Comparison," 124.
70. Wert and Salovey, "Social Comparison," 124.
71. Baumeister et al., "Gossip as Cultural Learning," 115.
72. Scott, *Domination*, 131.
73. Scott, *Domination*, 129–31 and 142–43.
74. Higgs, *Life in Guernsey*, 32 (May 15, 1944).
75. Bachmann, *Prey of an Eagle*, 95 (November 26, 1941).
76. Bachmann, *Prey of an Eagle*, 95 (November 26, 1941).
77. Diary of William Arthur Warry, University of Virginia, Special Collections, Microfilm 1688 MSS8138 [hereafter Warry], June 29, 1942.
78. Ord, 231 (October 28, 1941).
79. Warry, November 6, 1943.
80. Doig, October 26, 1942.
81. Sauvary, *Diary*, 136 (April 4, 1942).
82. Sauvary, *Diary*, 165 (September 2, 1942).
83. Harvey, *Battle of Newlands*, 165 (December 1, 1942–January 16, 1943).
84. Robin, December 15, 1943.
85. Harvey, *Battle of Newlands*, 168 (December 1, 1942–January 16, 1943).
86. Robin, November 26, 1942.
87. Lewis, January 11, 1943.
88. Harvey, *Battle of Newlands*, 169 (December 1, 1942–January 16, 1943).
89. Lewis, January 11, 1943.
90. Harvey, *Battle of Newlands*, 169 (December 1, 1942–January 16, 1943).
91. Sauvary, *Diary*, 165 (September 2, 1942).
92. Bachmann, *Prey of an Eagle*, 100 (December 19, 1941).
93. Bachmann, *Prey of an Eagle*, 166 (January 4, 1944).
94. Sauvary, *Diary*, 215 (November 17, 1943).
95. Doig, November 28, 1943.
96. Doig, November 16, 1943.
97. Doig, September 11, 1943.
98. Doig, August 13, 1944.
99. Warry, June 18, 1943.
100. Warry, December 13, 1942.
101. Warry, December 25, 1942.

102. Ord, 517 (June 4, 1943).
103. Ord, 543 (July 5, 1943).
104. Lewis, March 29, 1943.
105. Wert and Salovey, "Social Comparison," 133.
106. Ord, 212 (September 28, 1941).
107. Scott, *Domination*, 128.
108. Wert and Salovey, "Social Comparison," 129.
109. Wert and Salovey, "Social Comparison," 125.
110. Wert and Salovey, "Social Comparison," 125–26.
111. Diary of Herbert Williams, States of Guernsey Island Archives Service, AQ 380/03–2 [hereafter Williams], 29–30 (May 11, 1942).
112. Williams, 48–49 (May 17, 1942).
113. Williams, 21 (1942–no further date).
114. Williams, 56 (June 12, 1942).
115. Wert and Salovey, "Social Comparison," 124.
116. Ord, 277 (March 7, 1942).
117. Ord, 278 (March 13, 1942).
118. Harvey, *Battle of Newlands*, 127 (March 1–31, 1942). Inspector Sculpher was deported to Germany with the other English-born.
119. Harvey, *Battle of Newlands*, 127 (March 1–31, 1942).
120. Knowles Smith, *The Changing Face*, 89.
121. Harvey, *Battle of Newlands*, 134 (no date).
122. Sauvary, *Diary*, 139 (no date).
123. Sauvary, *Diary*, 139 (no date).
124. Ord, 277 (March 7, 1942).
125. Harvey, *Battle of Newlands*, 127 (March 1–31, 1942).
126. Warry, June 1, 1943.
127. Scott, *Domination*, 118.
128. See Knowles Smith, *The Changing Face*, 88–90.
129. Knowles Smith, *The Changing Face*, 90.
130. Williams, 83 (April 24, 1943).
131. Wert and Salovey, "Social Comparison," 124.
132. Harvey, *Battle of Newlands*, 206 (January 1–February 29, 1944).
133. Robin, December 15–16, 1943.
134. Harvey, *Battle of Newlands*, 206 (January 1–February 29, 1944).
135. Williams, 120 (January 15, 1944).
136. Harvey, *Battle of Newlands*, 206 (January 1–February 29, 1944).
137. Robin, January 11, 1944.
138. Wert and Salovey, "Social Comparison," 124.
139. Harvey, *Battle of Newlands*, 117 (December 1941).
140. Stephen V. Ash, *When the Yankees Came: Conflict and Chaos in the Occupied South, 1861–1865* (Chapel Hill: University of North Carolina Press, 1995), 71.
141. Ord, 80 (October 11, 1940).
142. Williams, 64 (August 10, 1942).
143. Lewis, October 5, 1942.
144. Lewis, March 20, 1944.

145. Harvey, *Battle of Newlands*, 221 (June 7, 1944).
146. Bachmann, *Prey of an Eagle*, 168 (January 27, 1944).
147. Lewis, October 5, 1942.
148. Harvey, 207–10 (January 1–February 29, 1944).
149. Knowles Smith, *The Changing Face*, 177–78.
150. Ord, 593–94 (August 19, 1943).
151. Warry, July 19, 1943.
152. Williams, June 12, 1943.
153. Lewis, April 21, 1945.
154. Knowles Smith, *The Changing Face*, 178. In fact, Hazel Knowles Smith reports from records in the Jersey Archives that by the Germans' own estimate in May 1944, eighty babies had been born in all the Islands who were definitely from German fathers. Most likely this is an underestimation but shows the difficulty of assigning parentage.
155. Lewis, January 22, 1943.
156. *The Miniver Story* and Brief Encounter are emblematic of this theme that separation by war for many years was difficult for married couples, and perhaps perfect fidelity was an understandable casualty of the times. Of course, in many of these movies, the infidelity proves to only have been contemplated or simply an unfair rumor, and perhaps it is best not to believe gossip or rumors of infidelity.
157. Bachmann, *Prey of an Eagle*, 168 (January 27, 1944).
158. I was lucky enough to interview the late Alf Williams, a young man during the Occupation and a resister whose actions will figure into a later chapter. I suggested to him that I saw such love affairs as wholly natural, if unwise. Alf fixed me with a sharp look and said loudly, "Well that's because you've got some common sense!" (Private interview with Alf Williams, Summer 2004.)
159. Harvey, *Battle of Newlands*, 167 (December 1–January 16, 1943).
160. Williams, 122 (February 15, 1944).
161. Williams, 261 (April 25, 1944).
162. Ord, 869 (September 9, 1944).
163. Lewis, September 5, 1944.
164. Bachmann, *Prey of an Eagle*, 192 (September 8, 1944).
165. Harvey, *Battle of Newlands*, 241 (September 1–30, 1944).
166. Ord, 873 (September 20, 1944).
167. Harvey, *Battle of Newlands*, 64 (March 2–20, 1941).
168. Harvey, *Battle of Newlands*, 139 (June 1–30, 1942).
169. Bachmann, *Prey of an Eagle*, 184 (June 11, 1944). They actually had another odd encounter with "Wolfi," as they nicknamed him, based on the name he had them engrave once on a locket. One dark January night, P.J. was in howling pain from an earache when a knock came at the door. Kitty opened it only to have "Wolfi" breeze past her and go straight to the child, solemnly advising potato poultices, a folk remedy that his parents had successfully used when he suffered earaches as a child. For his part, P.J. "fairly boggled at the sight of the resplendent uniform" and for a moment forgot his pain. Seeing that he was not even offered a chair, "Wolfi" took his departure.
170. Bachmann, *Prey of an Eagle*, 157–59 (August 24, 1943).
171. Harvey, *Battle of Newlands*, 30–31 (September 15–22, 1940).
172. Jordan, "Sabotage or Performed Compliance," 30.
173. James C. Scott, *Domination and the Arts of Resistance: Hidden Transcripts* (New Haven: Yale University Press, 1990), 23–24.

174. Harvey, *Battle of Newlands*, 125 (February 7, 1942).
175. Harvey, *Battle of Newlands*, 178 (March 8, 1943).
176. Harvey, *Battle of Newlands*, 189 (June 22, 1943).
177. Harvey, *Battle of Newlands*, 205 (January 1–February 29, 1944).
178. Warry, March 20, 1943.
179. Williams, 79–80 (March 20, 1943).
180. Lewis, July 31, 1943.
181. Williams, 47–50 (May 18, 1942).
182. Williams, 244 (April 1–3, 1945).
183. See Bernard Weiner, *An Attributional Theory of Motivation and Emotion* (New York: Springer-Verlag, 1986).
184. Williams, 266 (May 2, 1945).
185. Williams, 261 (April 25, 1945).
186. Bunting, *The Model Occupation*, 5.

CHAPTER FOUR. UNDERSTANDING THE STORY

1. Diary of the Rev. R. Douglas Ord, 402, vols. 1–7, 16 June 1940–12 May 1945, M0007066GY–M0007073GY, Priaulx Library, Guernsey [hereafter Ord], November 21, 1942.
2. William L. Benoit, Andrew A. Klyukovaki, John P. McHale, and David Airne, "A Fantasy Theme Analysis of Political Cartoons on the Clinton-Lewinsky-Starr Affair, *Critical Studies in Media Communication* 18, no. 4 (December 2001): 379.
3. Victoria O'Donnell and Garth S. Jowett, "Propaganda as a Form of Communication," in *Propaganda: A Pluralistic Perspective*, ed. Ted J. Smith III (New York: Praeger, 1989), 54.
4. O'Donnell and Jowett, "Propaganda as a Form," 56.
5. Ted J. Smith, "Techniques of Deception," in *Propaganda: A Pluralistic Perspective* (New York: Praeger, 1989), 67.
6. Of course, when Hitler discussed this concept in chapter 10 of *Mein Kampf*, he accused the Jews of fostering the technique. Goebbels would later assign the consistent use of the Big Lie to Churchill, this false attribution serving as simply one further example of concealment and deception.
7. Ord, 98 (November 13, 1940).
8. Diary of Ambrose Collas Robin, 17 June 1940 to 18 Mary 1945, M0005622GY, Priaulx Library, Guernsey [hereafter Robin], 9 (February 9, 1941).
9. Robin, January 26, 1942.
10. Robin, January 19, 1944.
11. Robin, October 12, 1943.
12. Ord, 133 (February 28, 1941).
13. Ord, 165 (May 22, 1941).
14. Ord, 541 (July 4, 1943).
15. Ord, 536 (June 30, 1943).
16. Ord, 102 (November 19, 1940).
17. O'Donnell and Jowett, "Propaganda as a Form," 56.
18. Robin, October 19, 1940.

19. Ord, 207 (September 20, 1941).
20. Winifred Harvey, *The Battle of Newlands: The Wartime Diaries of Winifred Harvey*, ed. Rosemary Booth (Guernsey: Guernsey Press, 1995), 89–91 (September 1941).
21. Harvey, *Battle of Newlands*, 89–91 (September 1941).
22. Ord, 253 (January 1, 1942).
23. Diary of William Arthur Warry, University of Virginia, Special Collections, Microfilm 1688 MSS8138 [hereafter Warry], September 1942.
24. Robin, November 6, 1941. A similar type of ham-handed German propaganda tried to portray the British as disgruntled with the war effort. Ken Lewis went to Eileen's house to listen the "mystery voice" that kept interrupting the news on the BBC. The voice seemed to take the role of a discontented British citizen, although Ken believed that the voice "sounded foreign," popping in with "It's a lie," "Isn't it funny," "We want more milk for our children." When the announcer described an attack on a supply train, saying that the RAF pilot could see bullet holes from the strafing appear in the boiler, the voice interrupted with, "Why don't you say that they got splashed by the water from the engine?" Finally, the announcer acknowledged the voice as "the enemy trying to make himself heard," and the voice replied, "And it is heard." Ken believed that this gave the game away, acknowledging that it was a German rather than an estranged Briton delivering the critique; Diary of Kenneth G. Lewis, G06/10 W, 1-1-8–10, AS/LC 16–01, States of Guernsey Island Archives [hereafter Lewis], October 14, 1941.
25. Ord, 610 (September 10, 1943).
26. Ord, 275 (March 4, 1942).
27. Ord, 549 (July 7, 1943).
28. Harvey, *Battle of Newlands*, 31 (September 23, 1940).
29. Jack C. Sauvary, *Diary of the German Occupation of Guernsey, 1940–1945* (Upton-upon-Severn: Self Pub. Association, 1990), 32 (September 29, 1940).
30. Robin, October 10, 1940.
31. Harvey, *Battle of Newlands*, 29 (September 9–13, 1940).
32. Diary of Gertie Corbin, States of Guernsey Island Archives, Z009/19 AQ92/12 [hereafter Corbin], September 1941; Ord, 208 (September 20, 1941).
33. Robin, April 11, 1944.
34. Smith, "Techniques of Deception," 81.
35. Smith, "Techniques of Deception," 81.
36. Ernest G. Bormann, "The Symbolic Convergence Theory of Communication: Applications and Implications for Teachers and Consultants," *Journal of Applied Communication Research* 10, no. 1 (1982): 51.
37. J. F. Cragan and D. C. Shields, *Symbolic Theories in Applied Communication Research: Bormann, Burke, and Fisher* (Cresskill, NJ: Hampton, 1995), x.
38. Benoit et al., "A Fantasy Theme Analysis of Political Cartoons on the Clinton-Lewinsky-Starr Affair," 379.
39. Bormann, "Symbolic Convergence," 51.
40. Bormann, "Symbolic Convergence," 52.
41. Bormann, "Symbolic Convergence," 52.
42. Bormann, "Symbolic Convergence," 53–54.
43. Bormann, "Symbolic Convergence," 52.
44. Bormann, "Symbolic Convergence," 51–52.
45. Bormann, "Symbolic Convergence," 53.

46. Bormann, "Symbolic Convergence," 52.
47. Harvey, *Battle of Newlands*, 10–20 (August 11–17, 1940).
48. See Madeleine Bunting, *The Model Occupation: The Channel Islands under German Rule, 1940–1945* (London: Harper Collins, 1995), 83, for the original; and for the factual difficulties, see Linda Holt and Ward Rutherford, "'The Model Occupation'—Setting the Record Straight," *Channel Islands Occupation Review* 25 (1997): 49–72.
49. Ord, 239 (November 15, 1941).
50. K. M. Bachmann, *The Prey of an Eagle* (Guernsey: Guernsey Press, 1972), 92 (November 22, 1941).
51. Violet Carey Diary entry for October 24, 1942, in Alice Evans, "The Language of Occupation" (Master's thesis, University of Warwick, 2002), 99.
52. Robin, July 12, 1940.
53. Now, this tendency is not universal, for a reliance on self-deprecating humor is natural to some individuals. There was the tendency in both Kitty Bachmann's and Dorothy Higgs's epistolary accounts to tell funny stories about their own mistakes and foibles, possibly because these "letters" were addressed to family members. Jack Sauvary, however, was one diarist for whom gentle self-deprecation appeared regularly as part of his charm. During a time when he was feeling poorly, he mentioned that Mrs. Rowe had made him a "nice apple tart," Mr. Johns had provided him with "a little fat and liver," and even a plaice came his way, "all because I am sick." Jack follows this with, "I think I had better keep being sick!"—a little gold-bricking joke coming from someone who was anything but lazy and greedy; Sauvary, *Diary*, 111 (November 20, 1941).
54. Robin, October 10, 1940.
55. Ord, 78 (October 10, 1940).
56. James C. Scott, *Domination and the Arts of Resistance: Hidden Transcripts* (New Haven: Yale University Press, 1990), 41–42.
57. Harvey, *Battle of Newlands*, 48 (December 2, 1940). Dr. Richard Brosch served as the Kriegsverwaltungassessor (war administration assessor). His name as it appears in the original document (i.e., Brotsch) is used here in the transcribed conversation.
58. Sauvary, *Diary*, 121–22 (January 15, 1942).
59. Robin, October 5, 1940.
60. Bachmann, *Prey of an Eagle*, 137 (November 2, 1942).
61. Unlike the question-answer joke in the GDR revolution, there does not appear to have been one dominant type of joke structure in the Occupation; Kerry Kathleen Riley, *Everyday Subversion: From Joking to Revolting in the German Democratic Republic* (East Lansing: Michigan State University Press, 2008), 68–86.
62. Robin, March 30, 1943; Evans, Violet Carey Diary entry for April 7, 1943, 77–78.
63. Ord, 353 (September 7, 1942).
64. F. K. M. Hillenbrand, *Underground Humour in Nazi Germany, 1933–1945* (London: Routledge, 1995), xvi–xvii.
65. Lisa Tickner, *The Spectacle of Women: Imagery of the Suffrage Campaign, 1907–1914* (Chicago: University of Chicago Press, 1988), 163.
66. Ord, 522 (June 7, 1943).
67. Harvey, *Battle of Newlands*, 48 (December 2, 1940).
68. Ord, 178–79 (July 19, 1941).
69. Ord, 478 (April 4, 1943).
70. Sauvary, *Diary*, 118 (January 2, 1942).

71. Robin, 9–10 (March 12 and March 17, 1944).
72. Warry, June 8, 1942.
73. Robin, November 11, 1941.
74. Bachmann, *Prey of an Eagle*, 57 (February 7, 1941).
75. Bachmann, *Prey of an Eagle*, 90 (November 14, 1941).
76. Ord, 493 (May 2, 1943). The first thought is that Ambrose Robin might be this States official, but Robin describes himself as being at Brock Road Church that evening.
77. Ord, 493 (May 2, 1943).
78. Ord, 498 (May 7, 1943).
79. Robin, May 7, 1943.
80. Ord, 498 (May 7, 1943).
81. Hazel R. Knowles Smith, *The Changing Face of the Channel Islands Occupation: Record, Memory, and Myth* (Houndmills, Basingstoke, Hampshire: Palgrave Macmillan, 2007), 147.
82. Edwin Parks, "Occupied Guernsey 'let the minority go to the wall,'" *Guernsey Evening Press*, January 26, 1995.
83. Jurat John Leale, *Report of Five Years of German Occupation*, May 23, 1945, M0004390GY, Priaulx Library, Guernsey, section A.
84. John W. Jordan, "Sabotage or Performed Compliance: Rhetorics of Resistance in Temp Worker Discourse," *Quarterly Journal of Speech* 89, no. 1 (February 2003): 30.
85. Scott, *Domination*, 3.
86. Jordan, "Sabotage," 30.
87. Jordan, "Sabotage," 30 and 36.
88. Scott, *Domination*, 3.
89. Scott, *Domination*, 3.
90. Leale, *Report*, section C.
91. Lewis, October 9–12, 1940.
92. Lewis, November 23, 1942.
93. Leale, *Report*, section B.
94. Lewis, March 17, 1942.
95. Leale, *Report*, section D.
96. Knowles Smith, *The Changing Face*, 49–50.
97. Leale, *Report*, section B.
98. Knowles Smith, *The Changing Face*, 51.
99. It truly is an ancient trick, honed by rhetoricians of the Second Sophistic, the period of the Roman Empire when "speaking truth to power" was accomplished at the cost of one's life.
100. Ord, 39 (August 2, 1940).
101. Higgs, 12 (August 3, 1940).
102. Knowles Smith, *The Changing Face*, 33.
103. Scott, *Domination*, 110.
104. Leale, *Report*, section C.
105. Harvey, *Battle of Newlands*, 110 (October 29, 1941).
106. Williams, 20 (1942–no other date).
107. Leale, *Report*, section E.
108. Leale, *Report*, section D.
109. Leale, *Report*, section D.
110. Scott, *Domination*, 4.

111. Scott, *Domination*, 11.
112. Scott, *Domination*, 11.
113. Bunting, *Model Occupation*, 77–80.
114. Scott, *Domination*, 35.
115. Scott, *Domination*, 3 and 162.
116. Ord, 178 (July 6, 1941).
117. Ord, 180–81 (July 9, 1941).
118. Knowles Smith, *The Changing Face*, 31.
119. Ord, 180–81 (July 9, 1941).
120. Knowles Smith, *The Changing Face*, 32.
121. Ord, 180 (July 9, 1941).
122. Knowles Smith, *The Changing Face*, 32.
123. Lewis, May 8, 1943.
124. Harvey, *Battle of Newlands*, 211 (February 1944).
125. Knowles Smith, *The Changing Face*, 152.
126. Frederick Cohen, *The Jews in the Channel Islands during the German Occupation, 1940–1945*, 2nd ed. (Jersey: Jersey Heritage Trust, 2000), 15–16; Knowles Smith, *The Changing Face*, 155.
127. William M. Bell, *Guernsey Occupied but Never Conquered* (Exeter, UK: Studio Publishing Services, 2002), 16–17.
128. Knowles Smith, *The Changing Face*, 152–53.
129. Knowles Smith, *The Changing Face*, 153.
130. Cohen, *The Jews in the Channel Islands*, 19–21.
131. Bell, *Guernsey Occupied*, 130–31.
132. Bell, *Guernsey Occupied*, 127–28.
133. Bell, *Guernsey Occupied*, 127–28.
134. Ord, 88–89 (October 24, 1940).
135. Lewis, July 6, 1943.
136. Bachmann, *Prey of an Eagle*, 171 (April 14, 1944).
137. Cohen, *Jews in the Channel Islands*, 14.
138. Bell, *Guernsey Occupied*, 128.
139. Bell, *Guernsey Occupied*, 131. As required, Sculpher also reported on the one woman in Sark, Annie Wranowsky, who had a J on her passport. Wranowsky was questioned by the Dame of Sark and she denied any Jewish heritage, saying that the J (put on her passport when it was issued by the German Embassy in London in 1939) was a mistake.
140. It appears from Winifred Harvey's account that she was very aware of the slew of orders that came out at the same time. When the Italians, Austrians, and Germans had to report to the commandant, she recorded that they were asked "why they worked for the English, how they were treated and if they wanted to go home." Winnie added that she did not know how this affected the Hungarians, her concern for Rosa and Maria explaining her personal interest.
141. Harvey, *Battle of Newlands*, 37 (October 21–27, 1940).
142. Harvey, *Battle of Newlands*, 46 (November 16–December 2, 1940).
143. Robin, April 11, 1944.
144. Ord, 110 (November 28, 1940). It is not that the Guernsey Islanders were somehow free of all the easy stereotypes of the time. Ord went on to write, "A nation usually gets the kind of Jew it deserves. In Germany they have treated the Jew with medieval brutishness, but his skill in managing and acquiring money provokes others to jealousy"; Ord, 110 (November 28, 1940). This

opinion was based on Ord's understanding of centuries of restrictions imposed on the Jews in Germany and their resulting role in moneylending.

145. Cohen, *Jews in the Channel Islands*, 22.
146. Bell, *Guernsey Occupied*, 262.
147. Ord, 645 (November 4, 1943).
148. See Cohen, *Jews in the Channel Islands*, 31, for the way the Bailiff and Sculpher handled the businesses of evacuated Jews, avoiding the display of "Jewish Undertaking" signs.
149. Cohen, *Jews in the Channel Islands*, 39.
150. Cohen, *Jews in the Channel Islands*, 44.
151. Bell, *Guernsey Occupied*, 169–71.
152. Bell, *Guernsey Occupied*, 170.
153. Bell, *Guernsey Occupied*, 196–97. Rittmeister (Cavalry Captain) Furst von Oettingen was commonly known as "Prince." From March 1941, he was military commander of the Nebenstelle (the Island branch of the Feldkommandantur).
154. Bell, *Guernsey Occupied*, 180–81.
155. Cohen, *Jews in the Channel Islands*, 51.
156. Bell, *Guernsey Occupied*, 197–98.
157. Cohen, *Jews in the Channel Islands*, 51.
158. On a personal note, it is the basis of an ongoing joke by a colleague, who threatens to start a Christmas-tree farm on his mountain land simply for the pleasure of advertising "Greenberg's Christmas Trees."
159. Louise Willmot, "The Channel Islands," in *Resistance in Western Europe*, ed. Bob Moore (London: Berg, 2000), 69.
160. Bell, *Guernsey Occupied*, 198.
161. Ord, 289 (April 18, 1942).
162. Knowles Smith, *The Changing Face*, 156.
163. Ord, 458 (March 4, 1943).
164. Cohen, *Jews in the Channel Islands*, 52.
165. Knowles Smith, *The Changing Face*, 155.
166. Cohen, *Jews in the Channel Islands*, 53.
167. Cohen, *Jews in the Channel Islands*, 41–43.
168. Cohen, *Jews in the Channel Islands*, 62.
169. Cohen, *Jews in the Channel Islands*, 65.
170. Cohen, *Jews in the Channel Islands*, 50.
171. Ord, 458 (March 4, 1943).
172. Cohen, *Jews in the Channel Islands*, 54.
173. Leale, *Report*, section C.
174. Leale, *Report*, section B.
175. Madeleine Bunting, for example, includes the three women's deportation, along with a completely distorted version of the Nicolle and Symes affair, to charge the Committee with voluntarily handing over a chosen few in some form of devil's bargain with the Nazis. As she put it in an interview, "Morally if you sacrifice the few to save the many you should at least admit the fact"; Parks, "Occupied Guernsey 'let the minority go to the wall.'" But Bunting's opinion is sometimes based on factual inaccuracies. She states, for example, that the Guernsey police "arrested Therese and handed her over to the Germans"; Bunting, *Model Occupation*, 111. She further maintains that the letters first made publicly available in January 1993 were

proof "that island officials had tracked down Jews and handed them over to the Germans"; Bunting, *Model Occupation*, 317.

176. "Protocol of the Wannsee Conference, January 20, 1942," http://www.ghwk.de/engl/protengl.htm.
177. Indeed, Michaela Kipp has conducted some fascinating research arguing that even German soldiers involved in genocide in the occupied territories in Eastern Europe saw these acts as individual events based on narrow circumstances, rather than as part of an overarching plan; Michaela Kipp, "The Holocaust in the Letters of German Soldiers on the Eastern Front (1939–44)," *Journal of Genocide Research* 9, no. 4 (December 2007): 601–15.
178. Gary Saul Morson, *Narrative and Freedom: The Shadows of Time* (New Haven: Yale University Press, 1994), 234.
179. *Ship of Fools*, Columbia Pictures Corporation, 1965.
180. Leale, *Report*, section D.

CHAPTER FIVE. A SUBTLE RESISTANCE

1. Diary of the Rev. R. Douglas Ord, vols. 1–7, 16 June 1940–12 May 1945, M0007066GY–M0007073GY, Priaulx Library, Guernsey [hereafter Ord], 119 (December 14, 1940).
2. James C. Scott, *Domination and the Arts of Resistance: Hidden Transcripts* (New Haven: Yale University Press, 1990), 35.
3. James C. Scott, *Weapons of the Weak: Everyday Forms of Peasant Resistance* (New Haven: Yale University Press, 1985), 34.
4. Scott, *Domination*, 20.
5. Scott, *Domination*, 199.
6. Scott, *Weapons of the Weak*, 29–30.
7. K. M. Bachmann, *The Prey of an Eagle* (Guernsey: Guernsey Press, 1972), 39–40 (October 24, 1940).
8. Ord, 1:76 (September 29, 1940).
9. Diary of Ambrose Collas Robin, 17 June 1940 to 18 May 1945, Priaulx Library, Control No. M0005622GY [hereafter Robin], February 11, 1941, and March 1, 1941.
10. "A Dedication to François Marie Scornet, 1921–1941," http://www.francoisscornet.com/francoismain.php.
11. Hazel R. Knowles Smith, *The Changing Face of the Channel Islands Occupation: Record, Memory, and Myth* (Houndmills, Basingstoke, Hampshire: Palgrave Macmillan, 2007), 44.
12. Andrew R. Smith, "Violence and the Arts of Resistance: An Expedition in Critical Communicology," *Atlantic Journal of Communication* 16 (2008): 207.
13. Smith, "Violence," 199.
14. Smith, "Violence," 199.
15. Michel Foucault, *Fearless Speech*, ed. Joseph Pearson (Los Angeles: Semiotext(e), 2001), 11–19.
16. This was not a concern unique to the German Occupation. In the occupation of New Orleans, the patience with women's confrontational language and spitting reached an end when General Benjamin Butler issued an order declaring that any woman insulting or showing contempt for soldiers would be treated "as a woman of the town plying her avocation." This move earned the general the nickname of "Beast Butler" (and his picture a prominent location at the bottom of

many a Southern woman's chamber pot), but it cooled the verbal resistance if not the underlying discontent; Crystal N. Feimster, "General Benjamin Butler and the Threat of Sexual Violence during the American Civil War," *Daedalus* 138, no. 2 (Spring 2009): 126–34.

17. Jack C. Sauvary, *Diary of the German Occupation of Guernsey, 1940–1945* (Upton-upon-Severn: Self Pub. Association, 1990), 140 (May 3, 1942).
18. Diary of Gertie Corbin, States of Guernsey Island Archives, Z009/19 AQ92/12 [hereafter Corbin], September 1941.
19. Ord, 54 (August 24, 1940).
20. Winifred Harvey, *The Battle of Newlands: The Wartime Diaries of Winifred Harvey*, ed. Rosemary Booth (Guernsey: Guernsey Press, 1995), 22 (August 27, 1940).
21. Diary of Herbert Williams, States of Guernsey Island Archives Service, AQ 380/03–2 [hereafter Williams], 127 (May 20, 1944).
22. Harvey, *Battle of Newlands*, 134 (no date).
23. Harvey, *Battle of Newlands*, 144 (August 1942).
24. John W. Jordan, "Sabotage or Performed Compliance: Rhetoric of Resistance in Temp Worker Discourse," *Quarterly Journal of Speech* 89, no. 1 (February 2003): 35.
25. "John Ingrouille," display at the German Occupation Museum, Guernsey (viewed June 2003).
26. Smith, "Violence," 200.
27. Poppy M. Thompson, "Heil Churchill," article displayed at the German Occupation Museum, Guernsey (viewed June 2003).
28. Madeleine Bunting, *The Model Occupation: The Channel Islands under German Rule* (London: Harper Collins, 1995), 198.
29. Scott, *Domination*, 6.
30. Scott, *Domination*, 215–16.
31. Scott, *Domination*, 205.
32. Ord, 109 (November 23, 1940).
33. Saul Alinsky, *Rules for Radicals: A Practical Primer for Realistic Radicals* (New York: Vintage Books, 1971).
34. Quoted in William M. Bell, *Guernsey Occupied but Never Conquered* (Exeter, UK: Studio, 2002), 278.
35. Smith, "Violence," 207.
36. Ord, 568 (July 26, 1943).
37. Corbin, June 1941.
38. Diary of William Arthur Warry, University of Virginia, Special Collections, Microfilm 1688 MSS8138 [hereafter Warry], May 14, 1943.
39. See, for example, Bachmann, *Prey of an Eagle*, 163 (January 4, 1944); Harvey, *Battle of Newlands*, 159 (November 1–30, 1942) and 175 (March 8, 1943); Ord, 155 (April 15, 1941).
40. Ord, 155 (April 15, 1941).
41. Ord, 506 (May 13, 1943).
42. Robin, March 29, 1944.
43. Harvey, *Battle of Newlands*, 57 (January 1–15, 1941).
44. Williams, 188 (December 31, 1944).
45. Williams, 109–10 (September 30, 1943); Diary of Kenneth G. Lewis, G06/10 W, 1-1-8–10, AS/LC 16–01, States of Guernsey Island Archives [hereafter Lewis], October 1, 1943; Robin, October 3, 1943.
46. Scott, *Domination*, 18.

47. Bachmann, *Prey of an Eagle*, 170 (March 8, 1944).
48. Bachmann, *Prey of an Eagle*, 95–96 (November 27, 1941).
49. Bachmann, *Prey of an Eagle*, 154 (July 30, 1943).
50. Dorothy Pickard Higgs, *Life in Guernsey under the Nazis, 1940–45* (Guernsey: Toucan Press, 2000), 26 (October 2, 1941).
51. Ord, 309 (June 19, 1942).
52. Higgs, *Life in Guernsey*, 27 (November 12, 1941).
53. Sauvary, *Diary*, 154 (June 24, 1942).
54. Higgs, *Life in Guernsey*, 62 (postscript written in 1979).
55. Lewis, August 9, 1941.
56. Diary of Mrs. Elizabeth Doig, Bib Id. 298904, Priaulx Library, Guernsey [hereafter Doig], May 23, 1943. I am grateful to the librarians at the Priaulx Library for their aid in deciphering Elizabeth Doig's handwriting.
57. Lewis, May 28, 1943.
58. Lewis, July 8, 1943.
59. Lewis, February 19, 1944.
60. Lewis, July 5, 1943.
61. Ord, 537–40 (June 30, 1943) and 575–78 (July 31–August 2, 1943).
62. Ord, 320 (July 23, 1942).
63. Harvey, *Battle of Newlands*, 144 and 147n (August 1942).
64. Doig, August 31, 1942.
65. Ord, 357 (September 14, 1942).
66. Robin, August 16, 1942.
67. Ord, 270 (February 17, 1942).
68. Franklyn S. Haiman, "The Rhetoric of the Streets: Some Legal and Ethical Considerations," *Quarterly Journal of Speech* (April 1967): 99–114.
69. Michael L. Butterworth, "'Katie Was Not Only a Girl, She Was Terrible': Katie Hnidea, Body Rhetoric, and Football at the University of Colorado," *Communication Studies* 59, no. 3 (July–September 2008): 262. See also Kevin Michael Deluca, "Unruly Arguments: The Body Rhetoric of Earth First!, Act Up, and Queer Nation," *Argumentation and Advocacy* 36, no. 1 (Summer, 1999).
70. Scott, *Domination*, 32.
71. Scott, *Domination*, 37.
72. Warry, July 30, 1942.
73. Warry, April 20, 1944.
74. Scott, *Weapons of the Weak*, 273.
75. Jordan, "Sabotage or Performed Compliance," 27.
76. Jordan, "Sabotage or Performed Compliance," 29.
77. Jordan, "Sabotage or Performed Compliance," 29.
78. Robin, January 7, 1941.
79. Ord, 142 (March 19, 1941).
80. Lewis, March 19–22, 1941. The twelve hours of duty, performed by twenty men at a time and with the oversight of three policemen, went from 8:30 to 8:30, but actually meant two hours on duty and four hours off at a stretch. During the off hours they were allowed to sleep at San Elmo Hotel on the Forest Road, or at any nearby house.
81. Higgs, *Life in Guernsey*, 22 (March 17, 1941).

82. Harvey, *Battle of Newlands*, 65 (March 20, 1941).
83. Harvey, *Battle of Newlands*, 65 (March 20, 1941).
84. Doig, March 19, 1941.
85. Sauvary, *Diary*, 64 (March 21, 1941).
86. Ord, 142 (March 19, 1941), emphasis in original.
87. Higgs, *Life in Guernsey*, 48. Comically, she pondered whether she would be asked to sabotage the German batteries. This seemed a little beyond her small farmer capabilities, so she considered something more in line with her husbandry skills: "If I were told to steal all their rabbits I'd have a good try!"
88. Ord, 541 (July 1, 1943).
89. Robin, May 23, 1944.
90. Alfred Williams, private interview, June 2004. The tie between sabotage of the runway and any particular crash has not been authenticated and must be considered as a personal memory.
91. Knowles Smith, 202. Dr. Knowles Smith describes some of the truly harrowing treatment of several young Jersey Islanders who attempted these 1944–45 escape attempts, some of the fifty escapees from that Island between September 1944 and April 1945.
92. Louise Willmot, "The Channel Islands," in *Resistance in Western Europe*, ed. Bob Moore (London: Berg, 2000), 77.
93. Harvey, *Battle of Newlands*, 29 (September 9–13, 1940).
94. Harvey, *Battle of Newlands*, 29 (September 26–October 1, 1940).
95. Bachmann, *Prey of an Eagle*, 39 (October 24, 1940).
96. Harvey, *Battle of Newlands*, 33 (September 26–October 1, 1940).
97. Doig, September 28, 1940.
98. Sauvary, *Diary*, 34 (October 1940).
99. Williams, 57 (June 12, 1942).
100. Knowles Smith, *The Changing Face*, 204. Knowles Smith describes how the boys had been betrayed by a family member, and since they were arrested under Hitler's Night and Fog they were given no privileges. One of the arrested boys would die from tuberculosis and harsh treatment.
101. Lewis, June 29, 1942.
102. Williams, 61 (July 1942).
103. Corbin, June 1942.
104. Lewis, October 2, 1940.
105. Ord, 375 and 385 (October 3 and 13, 1940).
106. Harvey, *Battle of Newlands*, 192 (August 15, 1943).
107. Williams, 102 (August 15, 1943).
108. Bachmann, *Prey of an Eagle*, 159–60 (August 24, 1943).
109. Ord, 586 (August 15, 1943).
110. Lewis, November 8, 1943.
111. Madeleine Bunting, who devalues most resistant acts in the Occupation, has nothing but praise for those who escaped. Considering them to have "the most patriotic of motives," she apparently sees escapees as a cut above the average Islander, who experienced the retribution for escapes and was critical of the act; Bunting, *The Model Occupation*, 203.
112. Harvey, *Battle of Newlands*, 248 (November 5–12, 1944).
113. Bachmann, *Prey of an Eagle*, 200 (November 19, 1944).
114. Sauvary, *Diary*, 257–58 (November 4, 1944); Lewis, November 4, 1944; Williams, 170 (November 4, 1944); Harvey, *Battle of Newlands*, 248 and 258n (November 5–12, 1944).

115. Williams, 206 (January 25, 1945).
116. Ord, 567 (July 25, 1943).
117. Ord, 846 (August 9, 1944); Robin, August 2, 1944, and January 24, 1945; Williams, July 28, 1944, and January 25, 1945; William M. Bell, *I Beg to Report: Policing in Guernsey during the German Occupation* (Guernsey: Guernsey Press, 1995), 287.
118. Robin, December 1, 1940.
119. "HMS *Charybdis*," BBC Guernsey, http://www.bbc.co.uk/guernsey/content/articles/2004/10/06/hms_charybdis_feature.shtml.
120. Warry, November 13–14, 1943.
121. Diary of Arthur Mauger, A2374/23, 25/8/1942–13/4/1944, ledger book 23, Guernsey Island Archives [hereafter Mauger].
122. Warry, November 17, 1943.
123. Lewis, November 17, 1943.
124. Scott, *Domination*, 15.
125. "HMS *Charybdis*," BBC Guernsey, http://www.bbc.co.uk/guernsey/content/articles/2004/10/06/hms_charybdis_feature.shtml.
126. Smith, "Violence," 203.
127. Sauvary, *Diary*, 109 (November 18, 1941).
128. Lewis, June 19, 1942.
129. Sauvary, *Diary*, 69 (April 11, 1941).
130. Mary Ann Schaffer, *The Guernsey Literary and Potato Peel Pie Society* (London: Bloomsbury Publishing, 2008), 45.
131. Ord, 826 (July 13, 1944).
132. Harvey, *Battle of Newlands*, 64 (February 16–March 2, 1941).
133. Ord, 852 (August 14, 1944).
134. Doig, March 26, 1942.
135. Paul Sanders, *The British Channel Islands under German Occupation, 1940–1945* (Jersey: Jersey Heritage Trust/Société Jersiaise, 2005), 118–19; Bell, *Guernsey Occupied but Never Conquered*, 227–30; Richard Heaume, "Marie Ozanne," *Channel Islands Occupation Review* 23 (1995): 79–82.
136. Rosemary Booth, Introduction, in Harvey, *Battle of Newlands*, vii.
137. Harvey, *Battle of Newlands*, 49 (November 16–December 2, 1940).
138. Harvey, *Battle of Newlands*, 58 (January 15–28, 1940).
139. Harvey, *Battle of Newlands*, 120 and 129 (January 1942).
140. Harvey, *Battle of Newlands*, 154–55 (September 15–30, 1942).
141. Harvey, *Battle of Newlands*, 67 n. 12.
142. Smith, "Violence," 184.
143. Lewis, November 29, 1942.
144. Lewis, January 3, 1943.
145. Charles J. Rolo, *Radio Goes to War: The "Fourth Front"* (New York: G. P. Putnam's Sons, 1942), 11.
146. Rolo, *Radio Goes to War*, 12.
147. Rolo, *Radio Goes to War*, 141.
148. Robin, December 25, 1941.
149. Harvey, *Battle of Newlands*, 83 (July 1944).
150. Ord, 541 (July 1, 1943).
151. Rolo, *Radio Goes to War*, 173–74.

152. Rolo, *Radio Goes to War*, 176.
153. Rolo, *Radio Goes to War*, 177–78.
154. "International: Frivolous V," *Time* magazine, July 28, 1941, http://www.time.com/time/magazine/article/0,9171,795409–2,00.html.
155. Rolo, *Radio Goes to War*, 175.
156. Lewis, July 2–3, 1941.
157. Robin, July 9, 1941.
158. Robin, July 18, 1941.
159. Frank Falla, *The Silent War* (Guernsey: Burbridge Ltd., 1994), 57.
160. Ord, 184 (July 19, 1941).
161. Ord, 184 (July 19, 1941).
162. Ord, 185–86 (July 23, 1941).
163. Lewis, July 18, 1941.
164. Ord, 184–86 (July 19–July 23, 1941).
165. Ord, 185 (July 23, 1941).
166. Ord, 188 (July 30, 1941).
167. Lewis, July 31, 1941.
168. Harvey, *Battle of Newlands*, 83 (July 1941).
169. Lewis, August 13, 1941.
170. Lewis, August 1–3, 1941.
171. Archeologist Gillian Carr argues convincingly that the V-campaign went into a "more ephemeral phase." Based on artifacts, she traces its continuance in the camps to which Channel Islanders were deported in September 1942 and February 1943; Gillian Carr, "The Archaeology of Occupation and the V-sign Campaign in the Occupied British Channel Islands," *International Journal of Historical Archaeology*, published online at DOI 10.1007/sJ0761–010–0119–5 (June 24, 2010).
172. Alinsky, *Rules for Radicals*, 128.
173. Sauvary, *Diary*, 88 (July 23, 1941).
174. Harvey, *Battle of Newlands*, 83 (July 1941).
175. Gillian Carr and Richard Heaume, "Silent Resistance in Guernsey: The V-Sign Badges of Alf Williams and Roy Machon," *Channel Islands Occupation Review* 32 (2004): 52.
176. Private interviews with Alf Williams, Guernsey, 2003 and 2004.
177. Ord, 397 (November 16, 1942).
178. Alice Evans, ed., *Guernsey under Occupation: The Second World War Diaries of Violet Carey* (Chichester, UK: Phillimore, 2009), 107.
179. Ord, 537 (June 30, 1943). Gillian Carr has uncovered instances of Islanders also making badges and rings out of Island coins bearing the three lions *passant guardant* of the Guernsey Crest. Because the Germans stamped this crest on a number of items to prove their ownership of the Island, the wearing of the crest was an additional means for Islanders to reclaim their heritage; Carr, "A Campaign of Silent Resistance," *Research Horizons*, no. 5 (Spring 2008), 21, available at http://www.research-horizons.cam.ac.uk/images/fileupload/370.pdf.
180. Robin, July 2, 1943.
181. Lewis, July 1, 1943.
182. Alf Williams, personal interview, June 2003.
183. Alf Williams, personal interview, June 2003.
184. Warry, June 8, 1942.

185. Warry, June 15, 1942. Bert Williams was unique in having it affect his income as well. He was in the habit of copying down the words and melodies of the latest dance tunes, performing them with his band or selling them as sheet music to Guernsey musicians; Williams, 59 (June 28, 1942).
186. Ord, 121 (December 18, 1940).
187. Ord, 305 (June 8, 1942).
188. Ord, 586–87 (August 15, 1943).
189. Ord, 426 (January 18, 1943).
190. Ord, 422 (January 22, 1943).
191. Williams, 107 (September 8, 1943).
192. Lewis, September 8, 1943.
193. Robin, November 30, 1940.
194. Ord, 522 (June 10, 1943).
195. Ord, 798 (June 21, 1944).
196. Ord, 864 (August 29, 1944).
197. Lewis, July 30–August 18, 1944.
198. Corbin, August 1944.
199. Harvey, *Battle of Newlands*, 53 n. 14.
200. Higgs, *Life in Guernsey*, 41 (April 11, 1944) and 44 (June 22, 1944).
201. Bachmann, *Prey of an Eagle*, 197 (October 20, 1944).
202. Harvey, *Battle of Newlands*, 278–79 (April 26, 1945).
203. Ord, 500–501 (May 13, 1943).
204. Ord, 558 (July 16, 1943).
205. Ord, 353 (September 3, 1942); Robin, September 2, 1942.
206. Bachmann, *Prey of an Eagle*, 197 (October 20, 1944).
207. Ord, August 11, 1942.
208. Lewis, April 12, 1943.
209. Lewis, December 11, 1944.
210. Lewis, August 17, 1944.
211. Williams, 177 (December 3, 1944).
212. Warry, February 12, 1944.
213. Williams, 122 (February 15, 1944).
214. Lewis, January 11, 1943.
215. Bell, *Guernsey Occupied*, 277.
216. Ord, 396 (November 11, 1942).
217. Ord, 444 (February 15, 1943).
218. A pseudonym.
219. Lewis, June 29, 1944.
220. Ord, 419 (December 27, 1942).
221. Ord, 426 (January 18, 1943).
222. Ord, 981 (February 17, 1945).
223. Smith, "Violence," 202–3.
224. Ord, 395–96 (November 11, 1942).
225. Ord, 1009–10 (March 29, 1945).
226. Scott, *Domination*, 119 and 124.
227. Bachmann, *Prey of an Eagle*, 222–23 (March 26, 1945).

228. Sauvary, *Diary*, 265 (November 29, 1944).
229. Falla, *Silent War*, 98–100.
230. Bell, *Guernsey Occupied*, 274–75.
231. Falla, *Silent War*, 100–108.
232. Williams, 136–37 (June 25, 1944).
233. "Channel Island's World War II Forgotten Heroes Revealed," Channel 4 News, http://www.channel4.com/news/channel-islands-world-war-ii-forgotten-heroes-revealed, November 18, 2010; "WWII Prison Camp Archives Discovered in Guernsey," BBC News, http://www.bbc.co.uk/news/world-europe-guernsey-11779963; Stephen Bates, "Guernsey Files Reveal How Islanders Defied Nazi Occupation," http://www.guardian.co.uk/uk/2010/nov/18/guernsey-files-islanders-nazi-occupation.
234. Bell, *Guernsey Occupied*, 275–77.
235. Ord, 601 (August 31, 1943).
236. Scott, *Weapons of the Weak*, 301.
237. Scott, *Weapons of the Weak*, 29.
238. Yu Shi, "Chinese Immigrant Women Workers: Everyday Forms of Resistance and 'Coagulate Politics,'" *Communication and Critical/Cultural Studies* 5, no. 4 (December 2008): 377.

CONCLUSION

1. Diary of the Rev. R. Douglas Ord, vol. 6, 1 May 1944–25 October 1944, M0007071GY, Priaulx Library, Guernsey [hereafter Ord], 778–79 (June 6, 1944).
2. Jack C. Sauvary, *Diary of the German Occupation of Guernsey, 1940–1945*, ed. K. A. Sauvary (Upton-upon-Severn: Self Pub. Association, 1990), 228 (June 6, 1944).
3. K. M. Bachmann, *The Prey of an Eagle* (Guernsey: Guernsey Press, 1972), 180 (June 11, 1944).
4. Winifred Harvey, *The Battle of Newlands: The Wartime Diaries of Winifred Harvey*, ed. Rosemary Booth (Guernsey: Guernsey Press, 1995), 219 (June 5 and 6, 1944).
5. Diary of Herbert Williams, States of Guernsey Island Archives Service, AQ 380/03–2 [hereafter Williams], 130 (June 6, 1944); Harvey, *Battle of Newlands*, 219 (June 6, 1944).
6. Harvey, *Battle of Newlands*, 219 (June 5 and 6, 1944).
7. Sauvary, *Diary*, 232 (June 20, 1944).
8. Sauvary, *Diary*, 228 (June 6, 1944).
9. Ord, 780 (June 6, 1944).
10. Diary of William Arthur Warry, University of Virginia, Special Collections, Microfilm 1688 MSS8138 [hereafter Warry], June 7, 1944.
11. Ord, 796 (June 19, 1944); Harvey, *Battle of Newlands*, 223 (June 19, 1944); Warry, June 19, 1944; Sauvary, *Diary*, 231 (June 19, 1944); Bachmann, *Prey of an Eagle*, 185 (June 19, 1944).
12. Diary of Kenneth G. Lewis, Guernsey Island Archives, G06/10 W, 1–1-8–10, AS/LC 16–01 [hereafter Lewis], June 17, 1944.
13. Bachmann, *Prey of an Eagle*, 183 (June 11, 1944).
14. Diary of Mrs. Elizabeth Doig, Bib Id. 298904, Priaulx Library, Guernsey [hereafter Doig], July 23, 1944.
15. Doig, November 5, 1944.
16. Ord, 865–66 (August 31, 1944).

17. Diary of Ambrose Collas Robin, 17 June 1940 to 18 May 1945, Control No. M0005622GY, Priaulx Library, Guernsey [hereafter Robin], November 7, 1944.
18. Dorothy Pickard Higgs, *Life in Guernsey under the Nazis, 1940–45* (Guernsey: Toucan Press, 2000), 48 (August 28, 1944).
19. Higgs, *Life in Guernsey*, 44 (June 22, 1944).
20. Lewis, September 25, 1944.
21. Sauvary, *Diary*, 258–60 (November 9–11, 1944).
22. Harvey, *Battle of Newlands*, 250 (November 19–30, 1944).
23. Harvey, *Battle of Newlands*, 247 (October 21, 1944).
24. Harvey, *Battle of Newlands*, 252 (November 26–December 6, 1944); Corbin, November 1944; Sauvary, *Diary*, 262–64 (November 26–27, 1944).
25. Doig, November 5, 1944.
26. Harvey, *Battle of Newlands*, 247 (October 21, 1944).
27. Williams, 170 (November 4, 1944).
28. Williams, 171 (November 12, 1944).
29. Bachmann, *Prey of an Eagle*, 207 (December 14, 1944).
30. Higgs, *Life in Guernsey*, 52 (December 17, 1944).
31. Bachmann, *Prey of an Eagle*, 217 (January 18, 1945).
32. Ord, 946–47 (December 30–31, 1944).
33. Ord, 948 (December 31, 1944); Higgs, *Life in Guernsey*, 53 (December 31, 1944); Bachmann, *Prey of an Eagle*, 217 (January 18, 1945).
34. Higgs, *Life in Guernsey*, 54 (February 15, 1945).
35. Ord, 960 (January 15, 1945).
36. Harvey, *Battle of Newlands*, 263–64 (February 1–March 30, 1945).
37. Harvey, *Battle of Newlands*, 280 (May 4, 1945).
38. Warry, January 30, 1945.
39. Warry, January 11, 1945.
40. Hazel R. Knowles Smith, *The Changing Face of the Channel Islands Occupation: Record, Memory, and Myth* (Houndmills, Basingstoke, Hampshire: Palgrave Macmillan, 2007), 132–33.
41. Warry, January 7, 1945.
42. Bachmann, *Prey of an Eagle*, 207 (December 14, 1944).
43. Sauvary, *Diary*, 266 (December 2, 1944).
44. Williams, 193 (January 4, 1945).
45. Williams, 211 (February 4, 1945).
46. "Bean Jar or Bean Crock," The National Trust of Guernsey, http://www.nationaltrust-gsy.org.gg/content.aspx?p=102.
47. Winifred Harvey, *Battle of Newlands*, 253–66 (December 11, 1944–March 2, 1945).
48. Ord, 789 (June 11, 1944), 818 (July 7, 1944), and 867 (September 2, 1944).
49. Robin, September 1 and September 12, 1944.
50. Ord, 833 (July 24, 1944).
51. Robin, November 23, 1944.
52. Sauvary, *Diary*, 265 (November 29, 1944).
53. Warry, March 4, 1945.
54. Ord, 992 (February 28, 1945) and 996 (March 6, 1945).
55. Diary of Gertie Corbin, States of Guernsey Island Archives, Z009/19 AQ92/12 [hereafter Corbin], April 1945.

56. Harvey, *Battle of Newlands*, 260 (January 1–31, 1945).
57. Williams, 250–51 (April 8–9, 1945).
58. Sauvary, 265 (November 15, 1944); Williams, 195 (December 3, 1944).
59. Warry, November 30–December 1, 1944.
60. Warry, March 19, 1945.
61. Ord, 913 (November 18, 1944).
62. During a research trip to Guernsey a number of years ago, I was invited to go with Channel Islands Occupation Society members on a "ramble" with the visiting Jack Jabolinski, former driver to General Dini, the Luftwaffe commander of the Channel Islands. Jack, attired in his old uniform, visited the places he knew during the Occupation and told fascinating stories. At one point, he spoke casually of cats being stewed in a pot for a long period of time before they could be divested of fleas and mites enough to be edible.
63. Ord, 977 (February 11, 1945).
64. Williams, 193–98 (January 4–11, 1945).
65. Harvey, *Battle of Newlands*, 263 (January 1–January 31, 1945).
66. Harvey, *Battle of Newlands*, 262 (January 1–January 31, 1945).
67. Sauvary, *Diary*, 270–71 (December 20–22, 1944).
68. Bachmann, *Prey of an Eagle*, 210 (December 30, 1944).
69. Robin, November 2, 1944.
70. Williams, 251 (April 9, 1945).
71. Corbin, July 1944.
72. Ord, 1010 (March 30, 1945).
73. Harvey, *Battle of Newlands*, 265 (January 1–31, 1945).
74. Ord, 997 (March 8, 1945).
75. Ord, 1002 (March 11, 1945).
76. Warry, January 30, 1945.
77. Higgs, *Life in Guernsey*, 51 and 56 (December 6, 1944, and April 2, 1945).
78. Personal interview with Alfred Williams, June 2003, Guernsey.
79. Williams, 155 (September 30, 1944).
80. Lewis, September 20, 1944.
81. Williams, 155 (September 30, 1944).
82. Harvey, *Battle of Newlands*, 265 (March 2, 1945); William M. Bell, *I Beg to Report: Policing in Guernsey during the German Occupation* (Guernsey: Guernsey Press, 1995), 323–24.
83. Warry, April 2, 1945.
84. Ord, 1022 (April 13, 1945).
85. Lewis, April 12–13, 1945. The verdict of history seems to be that these were, indeed, the Georgian Russians. Both Richard Heaume and Alf Williams came to the conclusion that the use of a knife rather than a pistol and the brutality of the attack marked it as an assault by one or more of the Russian volunteer troops (Private interview with Richard Heaume and Alf Williams, 2003).
86. Jurat John Leale, *Report of Five Years of German Occupation, May 23, 1945*, M0004390GY, Priaulx Library, Guernsey.
87. Warry, March 4, 1945.
88. Robin, February 17, 1945.
89. Robin, May 5, 1945.
90. Robin, April 15, 1945.
91. Higgs, *Life in Guernsey*, 56–57; Bachmann, *Prey of an Eagle*, 218 (February 1, 1945).

92. Ord, 862 (August 25, 1944).
93. Harvey, *Battle of Newlands*, 260 (January 1–30, 1945).
94. Harvey, *Battle of Newlands*, 264 (March 2, 1945).
95. Bachmann, *Prey of an Eagle*, 195 (October 8, 1944).
96. Higgs, *Life in Guernsey*, 55 (March 11, 1945).
97. Bachmann, *Prey of an Eagle*, 225–26 (April 26, 1945).
98. Doig, April 22, 1945.
99. Ord, 1044 (May 8, 1945).
100. Ord, 1025 (April 16, 1945).
101. Ord, 1023 (April 14, 1945).
102. Robin, April 25, 1945.
103. Harvey, *Battle of Newlands*, 281 (May 6, 1945).
104. Harvey, *Battle of Newlands*, 281–82 (May 7, 1945).
105. Williams, 271 (May 7, 1945).
106. Harvey, *Battle of Newlands*, 280 (May 5, 1945).
107. Ord, 1041 (May 7, 1945).
108. Ord, 1042 (May 8, 1945).
109. Warry, May 8–9, 1945.
110. Harvey, *Battle of Newlands*, 282 (May 8, 1945).
111. Ord, 1043 (May 8, 1945).
112. Williams, 273 (May 8, 1945); Warry, May 9, 1945.
113. William M. Bell, *Guernsey Occupied but Never Conquered* (Exeter, UK: Studio Publishing Services, 2002), 363–68.
114. Harvey, *Battle of Newlands*, 283 (May 9, 1945).
115. Higgs, *Life in Guernsey*, 58 (May 6, 1945).
116. Ord, 985 (February 24, 1945).
117. Bachmann, *Prey of an Eagle*, 220 (February 5, 1945).
118. Williams, 234 (March 16, 1945).
119. Williams, 269 (May 5, 1945).
120. Williams, 261 (April 25, 1944).
121. Lewis, May 17, 1945.
122. Ord, 1043 (May 8, 1945).
123. Ord, 1043 (May 8, 1945).
124. Higgs, *Life in Guernsey*, 59 (May 10, 1945).
125. Williams, 277–93 (May 11–30, 1945).
126. Warry, May 13, 1945; Williams, 276 (May 10, 1945).
127. Warry, May 13, 1945; Williams 276 (May 10, 1945); Robin, May 18, 1945; Bachmann, *Prey of an Eagle*, 231 (Epilogue).
128. Warry, April 2, 1945.
129. Lewis, May 17, 1945.
130. Ord, 1049 (May 12, 1945).
131. Higgs, *Life in Guernsey*, 60 (May 10, 1945).
132. Williams, 277–78 (May 11–12, 1945).
133. Warry, May 9, 1945.
134. Williams, 278 (May 12, 1945) and 284 (May 19, 1945).
135. Williams, 292 (May 29, 1945).

136. See David Kynaston, *Austerity Britain* (New York: Walker and Company, 2008).
137. Knowles Smith, *The Changing Face*, 236–42.
138. Bachmann, *Prey of an Eagle*, 186–87 (June 29, 1944).
139. Sauvary, *Diary*, 255 (October 23, 1944).
140. Higgs, *Life in Guernsey*, 57 (April 18, 1945).
141. Higgs, *Life in Guernsey*, 41 (April 17, 1944).
142. Knowles Smith, *The Changing Face*, 238–39.
143. Questionnaires completed by Bill Le Page, Marion Legg (née Le Page), and Maud Smyth (née Le Page) in 2004.
144. George T. H. Ellison and Michelle Kelly, "Growth of Jersey Schoolchildren during the 1940–1945 German Occupation: Comparison with Schoolchildren on Mainland Britain," *Human Biology* 77, no. 6 (December 2005): 761–72.
145. I. S. Fentiman, D. S. Allen, and G. T. H. Ellison, "The Impact of the Occupation of Guernsey 1940–1945 on Breast Cancer Risk Factors and Incidence," *International Journal of Clinical Practice* 61, no. 6 (June 2007): 937–43.
146. Rosemary F. Head, Mark S. Gilthorpe, Allyson Byrom, and George T. H. Ellison, "Cardiovascular Disease in a Cohort Exposed to the 1940–45 Channel Islands Occupation," *BMC Public Health* 8 (2008), http://www.ncbi.nlm.nih.gov/pmc/articles/PMC2543024.
147. Harvey, *Battle of Newlands*, vi (Preface).
148. Warry, April 6, 1950.
149. Herbert Winterflood, "Testing Time in the Last Months of the War," *Guernsey Evening Press*, April 11, 1992.
150. Private e-mail communication with Michael Elstob, June 28, 2012.
151. Lewis, April 27 and 30, 1945.
152. Private e-mail communication with Nigel Lewis, November 18, 2004.
153. Sauvary, *Diary*, 184 (January 13, 1943).
154. Sauvary, *Diary*, 195 (March 15, 1943).
155. Sauvary, *Diary*, 238 (July 12–15, 1944), 200 (April 19, 1943), 201–2 (April 22, 1943).
156. Sauvary, *Diary*, 281–84 (February 23–March 18, 1945).
157. Sauvary, *Diary*, 285–87 (March 31–April 2, 1945); Addendum by Evelyn Monsell, June 21, 1945.
158. *The Channel Islands, 1940–1945*, film, Crown Film Unit, Ministry of Information, Great Britain, 1945, Imperial War Museum, UKY 727.
159. This is a term that crops up increasingly in such studies of occupation as Patrick Buisson's *1940–1945, The Erotic Years: Vichy or the Misfortunes of Virtue* (Paris: Albin Michel, 2008). Amusingly, it is also a current term in business collaboration and supply.
160. This assumption is based on comparing the facial features of the postal worker in the film to the photograph on Lihou's identity card.
161. Melissa Mason, "Sculptor's Suitcase Full of Memories," *Guernsey Evening Press*, April 7, 2001.
162. Kerran L. Sanger, "Slave Resistance and Rhetorical Self-Definition: Spirituals as a Strategy," *Western Journal of Communication* 59 (1995): 177–92.
163. James C. Scott, *Domination and the Arts of Resistance: Hidden Transcripts* (New Haven: Yale University Press, 1990), 185.
164. Scott, *Domination*, 187.
165. Scott, *Domination*, 186.
166. Louise Willmot, "The Channel Islands," in *Resistance in Western Europe*, ed. Bob Moore (London: Berg, 2000), 84.

167. This was the case in the early stages of the GDR revolution, where the Evangelical Lutheran Church played a vital role; Kerry Kathleen Riley, *Everyday Subversions: From Joking to Revolting in the German Democratic Republic* (East Lansing: Michigan State University Press, 2008), 24.
168. Susan Gal, "A Semiotics of the Public/Private Distinction," *Differences: A Journal of Feminist Cultural Studies* 13, no. 1 (2002): 87.
169. Gabriel Jacobs, "The Role of Joan of Arc on the Stage of Occupied Paris," in *Vichy France and the Resistance Culture and Ideology*, ed. Roderick Kedward and Roger Austin (London: Croom Helm, 1985), 106–22; Ian Higgins, "France, Soil and Language: Some Resistance Poems by Luc Berimont and Jean Marcenac," in *Vichy France and the Resistance Culture and Ideology*, ed. Roderick Kedward and Roger Austin (London: Croom Helm, 1985), 206–21.
170. Nathaniel Hong, "Down with the Murderer Hitler!: Illegal Communication Strategies during the First Period of the German Occupation of Denmark," *Journalism Monographs* 146 (1994): 1–46.

Bibliography

"A Dedication to François Marie Scornet, 1921–1941." http://www.francoisscornet.com/francoismain.php.

Alinsky, Saul. *Rules for Radicals: A Practical Primer for Realistic Radicals.* New York: Vintage Books, 1971.

Allert, Tilman. *The Hitler Salute: On the Meaning of a Gesture.* Translated by Jefferson Chase. New York: Metropolitan Books, 2008.

Allport, Gordon, and Joseph Postman. *The Psychology of Rumor.* New York: Russell and Russell, 1947.

Andrejevic, Mark. "The Discipline of Watching: Detection, Risk and Lateral Surveillance." *Critical Studies in Media Communication* 23 (December 2006): 391–407.

Arns, Inke, and Sylvia Sasse. "Subversive Affirmation: On Mimesis as Strategy of Resistance." In *East Art Map: Contemporary Art and Eastern Europe*, edited by IRWIN. London: Afterall, 2006.

Aronson, Alex. *Studies in Twentieth-Century Diaries: The Concealed Self, Studies in Comparative Literature.* Vol. 12. Lewiston, NY: Edwin Mellen Press, 1991.

Ash, Stephen V. *When the Yankees Came: Conflict and Chaos in the Occupied South, 1861–1865.* Chapel Hill: University of North Carolina Press, 1995.

Bachmann, K. M. *The Prey of an Eagle.* Guernsey: Guernsey Press, 1972.

Bak, John S. "Escaping the Jaundiced Eye: Foucauldian Panopticism in Charlotte Perkins Gilman's 'The Yellow Wallpaper.'" *Studies in Short Fiction* 31 (Winter 1994): 39–46.

Bates, Stephen. "Guernsey Files Reveal How Islanders Defied Nazi Occupation." http://www.guardian.co.uk/uk/2010/nov/18/guernsey-files-islanders-nazi-occupation.

Baumeister, Roy F., Liqing Zhang, and Kathleen D. Vohs. "Gossip as Cultural Learning." *Review of General Psychology* 8 (2004): 111–21.

"Bean Jar or Bean Crock." The National Trust of Guernsey. http://www.nationaltrust- gsy.org.gg/content.aspx?p=102.

Bell, William M. *Guernsey Green: The Life and Times of Guernseyman Bill Green.* Guernsey: William M. Bell, 1992.

———. *Guernsey Occupied but Never Conquered.* Exeter, UK: Studio Publishing Services, 2002.

———. *I Beg to Report: Policing in Guernsey during the German Occupation.* Guernsey: Guernsey Press, 1995.

Benoit, William L., Andrew A. Klyukovaki, John P. McHale, and David Airne. "A Fantasy Theme Analysis of Political Cartoons on the Clinton-Lewinsky-Starr Affair." *Critical Studies in Media Communication* 18 (December 2001): 377–94.

Berger, C. R. "Communicating under Uncertainty." In *Interpersonal Processes: New Directions in Communication Research*, edited by M. E. Roloff and G. R. Miller, 39–62. Newbury Park, CA: Sage, 1987.

Berger, C. R., and J. J. Bradac. *Language and Social Knowledge.* London: Edward Arnold Publishers, 1982.

Berger, C. R., and R. J. Calabrese. "Some Explorations in Initial Interaction and Beyond: Toward a Developmental Theory of Interpersonal Communication." *Human Communication Research* 1 (1975): 99–112.

Biesecker, Barbara. "Michel Foucault and the Question of Rhetoric." *Philosophy & Rhetoric* 25 (1992): 351–64.

Bormann, Ernest G. "The Symbolic Convergence Theory of Communication: Applications and Implications for Teachers and Consultants." *Journal of Applied Communication Research* 10 (1982): 50–61.

Brashers, D. E. "Communication and Uncertainty Management." *Journal of Communication* 51 (2001): 477–97.

Brighenti, Andrea Muhi. "Resistance as Transformation." In *Roots, Rites and Sites of Resistance: The Banality of Good*, edited by Leonidas K. Cheliotis, 95–107. New York: Palgrave Macmillan, 2010.

Brown, Roger, and James Kulik. "Flashbulb Memories." *Cognition* 5, no. 1 (1977): 73–99.

Bunting, Madeleine. *The Model Occupation: The Channel Islands under German Rule, 1940–1945*. London: Harper Collins, 1995.

Butterworth, Michael L. "'Katie Was Not Only a Girl, She Was Terrible': Katie Hnidea, Body Rhetoric, and Football at the University of Colorado." *Communication Studies* 59 (July–September 2008): 259–73.

Campbell, Karlyn Kohrs. *Man Cannot Speak for Her: A Critical Study of Early Feminist Rhetoric*. Vols. 1–2. New York: Praeger, 1989.

Carr, Gillian. "A Campaign of Silent Resistance." *Research Horizons*, no. 5 (Spring 2008): 21. http://www.research-horizons.cam.ac.uk/images/fileupload/370.pdf.

———. "The Archaeology of Occupation, 1940–2009: A Case Study from the Channel Islands." *Antiquity* 84 (2010): 161–74.

———. "The Archaeology of Occupation and the V-sign Campaign in the Occupied British Channel Islands." *International Journal of Historical Archaeology*, DOI 10.1007/sJ0761–010-0119–5, published online June 24, 2010.

———. "Occupation Heritage, Commemoration and Memory in Guernsey and Jersey," *History & Memory* 24, no. 1 (Spring/Summer 2012): 87–117.

Carr, Gillian, and Richard Heaume. "Silent Resistance in Guernsey: The V-Sign Badges of Alf Williams and Roy Machon." *Channel Islands Occupation Review* 32 (2004): 51–55.

"Channel Island's World War II Forgotten Heroes Revealed." Channel 4 News. http://www.channel4.com/news/channel-islands-world-war-ii-forgotten-heroes-revealed, November 18, 2010.

Cohen, Frederick. *The Jews in the Channel Islands during the German Occupation, 1940–1945*. 2nd ed. Jersey: Jersey Heritage Trust, 2000.

Corbin, Gertie. Diary of Gertie Corbin. Z009/19 AQ92/12, States of Guernsey Island Archives.

Cragan, John F., and Donald C. Shields. *Symbolic Theories in Applied Communication Research: Bormann, Burke, and Fisher*. Cresskill, NJ: Hampton, 1995.

Cruikshank, Charles. *The German Occupation of the Channel Islands*. Guernsey: Guernsey Press, 1975.

Deluca, Kevin Michael. "Unruly Arguments: The Body Rhetoric of Earth First!, Act Up, and Queer Nation." *Argumentation and Advocacy* 36 (Summer 1999): 9–21.

Diamond, Hanna, and Simon Kitson, eds. *Vichy, Resistance, Liberation: New Perspectives on Wartime France*. Oxford: Berg, 2005.

Doig, Elizabeth. Diary of Mrs. Elizabeth Doig. Bib Id. 298904, Priaulx Library, Guernsey, Channel Islands.

Dreyfus, François-Georges, ed. *Unrecognized Resistance: The Franco-American Experience in World War Two.* Translated by Paul Seaton. New Brunswick, NJ: Transaction Publishers, 2004.

Ebbeson, E. B., G. L. Kjos, V. J. Konecni. "Spatial Ecology: Its Effects on the Choice of Friends and Enemies." *Journal of Experimental Social Psychology* 12 (1976): 508–18.

Ehninger, Douglas. *Contemporary Rhetoric.* Chicago: Scott, Foresman and Co., 1972.

Evans, Alice. "The Language of Occupation." Master's thesis, University of Warwick, 2002.

Evans, Alice, ed. *Guernsey under Occupation: The Second World War Diaries of Violet Carey.* Gloucestershire, UK: Phillimore and Co., 2009.

Falla, Frank. *The Silent War.* London: Burbridge Ltd., 1994.

Feimster, Crystal N. "General Benjamin Butler and the Threat of Sexual Violence during the American Civil War." *Daedalus* 138 (Spring 2009): 126–34.

Foucault, Michel. *Discipline and Punish.* Translated by Alan Sheridan. New York: Vintage, 1995.

———. *Fearless Speech.* Edited by Joseph Pearson. Los Angeles: Semiotext(e), 2001.

Gal, Susan. "A Semiotics of the Public/Private Distinction." *Differences: A Journal of Feminist Cultural Studies* 13, no.1 (2002): 77–95.

Gring-Pemble, Lisa. "Writing Themselves into Consciousness: Creating a Rhetorical Bridge between the Public and Private Spheres." *Quarterly Journal of Speech* 84 (1998): 41–61.

Guerin, Bernard, and Yoshihiko Miyazaki. "Analyzing Rumors, Gossip, and Urban Legends through Their Conversational Properties." *Psychological Record* 56 (2006): 23–34.

Haiman, Franklyn S. "The Rhetoric of the Streets: Some Legal and Ethical Considerations." *Quarterly Journal of Speech* (April 1967): 99–114.

Harvey, Winifred. *The Battle of Newlands: The Wartime Diaries of Winifred Harvey.* Edited by Rosemary Booth. Guernsey: Guernsey Press, 1995.

Havel, Václav. "The Power of the Powerless." Translated by Paul Wilson. In *The Power of the Powerless: Citizens against the State in Central-Eastern Europe*, edited by John Keane. London: Hutchinson, 1988.

Heaume, Richard. "Marie Ozanne." *Channel Islands Occupation Review* 23 (1995): 79–82.

Henderson, Gae Lyn. "The 'Parrhesiastic Game': Textual Self-Justification in Spiritual Narratives of Early Modern Women." *Rhetoric Society Quarterly* 37 (2007): 423–51.

Higgs, Dorothy Pickard. *Life in Guernsey under the Nazis, 1940–45.* Guernsey: Toucan Press, 2000.

Hillenbrand, F. K. M. *Underground Humour in Nazi Germany, 1933–1945.* London: Routledge, 1995.

"HMS *Charybdis.*" BBC Guernsey. http://www.bbc.co.uk/guernsey/content/articles/2004/10/06/hms_charybdis_feature.shtml.

Holt, Linda, and Ward Rutherford. "'The Model Occupation'—Setting the Record Straight." *Channel Islands Occupation Review* 25 (1997): 49–72.

Hong, Nathaniel. "Down With the Murderer Hitler!: Illegal Communication Strategies during the First Period of the German Occupation of Denmark." *Journalism Monographs* 146 (August 1994): 1–46.

Huspek, Michael. "Foucault on the 'Other Within.'" In *Transgressing Discourses: Communication and the Voice of the Other*, edited by Michael Huspek and Gary P. Radford, 95–116. Albany: State University of New York Press, 1997.

"International: Frivolous V." *Time* magazine, July 28, 1941. http://www.time.com/time/magazine/article/0,9171,795409-2,00.html.

Island Police, Guernsey. Statement of Witness, September 1, 1940. Imperial War Museum Archives, London.

———. Report of Inspector Sculpher, September 3, 1940. Imperial War Museum Archives, London.

"John Ingrouille." Display at the German Occupation Museum, Guernsey (viewed June 2003).

Johnson, Nan. "Reigning in the Court of Silence: Women and Rhetorical Space in Postbellum America." *Philosophy & Rhetoric* 33 (2000): 221–42.

Jordan, John W. "Sabotage or Performed Compliance: Rhetorics of Resistance in Temp Worker Discourse." *Quarterly Journal of Speech* 89 (February 2003): 19–40.

Kapferer, Jean-Noel. "How Rumors Are Born." *Society* 29 (July–August 1992): 53–60.

Kedward, H. R. *Occupied France: Collaboration and Resistance, 1940–1944.* Oxford: Basil Blackwell, 1985.

———. *Resistance in Vichy France: A Study of Ideas and Motivation in the Southern Zone, 1940–1942.* Oxford: Oxford University Press, 1978.

Kedward, Roderick, and Roger Austin, eds. *Vichy France and the Resistance: Culture and Ideology.* London: Croom Helm, 1985.

Kipp, Michaela. "The Holocaust in the Letters of German Soldiers on the Eastern Front (1939–44)." *Journal of Genocide Research* 9 (December 2007): 601–15.

Knowles Smith, Hazel R. *The Changing Face of the Channel Islands Occupation: Record, Memory, and Myth.* Houndmills, Basingstoke, Hampshire: Palgrave Macmillan, 2007.

Kraditor, Aileen S., ed. *Up from the Pedestal: Selected Writings in the History of American Feminism.* Chicago: Quadrangle Books, 1968.

Kynaston, David. *Austerity Britain.* New York: Walker and Company, 2008.

Leale, Jurat John. *Report of Five Years of German Occupation.* May 23, 1945, M0004390GY, Priaulx Library, Guernsey.

Lewis, Kenneth. Diary of Kenneth G. Lewis. G06/10 W, 1-1-8-10, AS/LC 16-01, States of Guernsey Island Archives.

Lloyd, Christopher. *Collaboration and Resistance in Occupied France: Representing Treason and Sacrifice.* New York: Palgrave Macmillan, 2003.

Mauger, Arthur. Diary of Arthur Mauger. AQ 374/13 to 25, 23/4/1939–7/8/1940, ledger book 21, States of Guernsey Island Archives.

———. Diary of Arthur Mauger. A2 374/23, 25/8/1942–13/4/1944, ledger book 23, States of Guernsey Island Archives.

McLoughlin, Roy. *Living with the Enemy: What Really Happened.* Jersey: Channel Island Publishing, 2003.

Miceli, Maria, and Cristiano Castelfranchi. "Anxiety as an 'Epistemic' Emotion: An Uncertainty Theory of Anxiety." *Anxiety, Stress, and Coping* 18 (December 2005): 291–319.

Morson, Gary Saul. *Narrative and Freedom: The Shadows of Time.* New Haven: Yale University Press, 1994.

Neubauer, Hans-Joachim. *The Rumour: A Cultural History.* London: Free Association Books, 1999.

O'Donnell, Victoria, and Garth S. Jowett. "Propaganda as a Form of Communication." In *Propaganda: A Pluralistic Perspective*, edited by Ted J. Smith III, 49–64. New York: Praeger, 1989.

Okihiro, Gary Y., ed. *Resistance: Studies in African, Caribbean, and Afro-American History.* Amherst: University Press of Massachusetts, 1986.

Ono, Kent A., and John M. Sloop. "The Critique of Vernacular Discourse." *Communication Monographs* 62 (1995): 19–46.

Ord, Reverend R. Douglas. Diary of the Rev. R. Douglas Ord. Vols. 1–7, 16 June 1940–12 May 1945, M0007066GY-M0007073GY, Priaulx Library, Guernsey.

Parks, Edwin. "Occupied Guernsey 'Let the Minority Go to the Wall.'" *Guernsey Evening Press*, January 26, 1995.

Peterson, Warren, and Noel Gist. "Rumor and Public Opinion." *American Journal of Sociology* 57 (September 1951): 159–67.

"Press" Diary of Island Life during the German Occupation, 1940–45. Guernsey: Guernsey Press, n.d.

Quinion, Michael. *World Wide Words.* http://www.worldwidewords.org/qa/qa-gra2.htm (page created October 20, 2001).

Riley, Kerry Kathleen. *Everyday Subversions: From Joking to Revolting in the German Democratic Republic.* East Lansing: Michigan State University Press, 2008.

Robin, Ambrose Collas. Diary of Ambrose Collas Robin, 17 June 1940 to 18 May 1945, Control No. M0005622GY, Priaulx Library, Guernsey.

Rolo, Charles J. *Radio Goes to War: The "Fourth Front."* New York: G. P. Putnam's Sons, 1942.

Rosnow, Ralph L. "Inside Rumor: A Personal Journey." *American Psychologist* 46 (May 1991): 484–96.

Rosnow, Ralph L. "Rumor and Gossip in Interpersonal Interaction and Beyond: A Social Exchange Perspective." In *Behaving Badly: Aversive Behaviors in Interpersonal Relationships,* edited by R. M. Kowalski, 203–32. Washington, DC: American Psychological Association, 2001.

Rosnow, R. L., J. H. Yost, and J. L. Esposito. "Belief in Rumor and Likelihood of Rumor Transmission." *Language and Communication* 6, no. 3 (1986): 189–94.

Royster, Jacqueline Jones. *Traces of a Stream: Literacy and Social Change among African American Women.* Pittsburgh, PA: University of Pittsburgh Press, 2000.

Sanders, Paul. *The British Channel Islands under German Occupation, 1940–1945.* Jersey: Jersey Heritage Trust/Société Jersiaise, 2005.

———. "Managing Under Duress: Ethical Leadership, Social Capital and the Civilian Administration of the British Channel Islands During the Nazi Occupation, 1940–1945." *Journal of Business Ethics* 93 (2010): 113–129.

Sanger, Kerran L. "Slave Resistance and Rhetorical Self-Definition: Spirituals as a Strategy." *Western Journal of Communication* 59 (Summer 1995): 177–92.

Sauvary, Jack C. *Diary of the German Occupation of Guernsey, 1940–1945.* Upton-upon-Severn: Self Publishing Association, 1990.

Scott, James C. *Domination and the Arts of Resistance: Hidden Transcripts.* New Haven: Yale University Press, 1990.

Scott, James C. *Weapons of the Weak: Everyday Forms of Peasant Resistance.* New Haven: Yale University Press, 1985.

Shaffer, Mary Ann, and Annie Barrows. *The Guernsey Literary and Potato Peel Pie Society.* London: Bloomsbury, 2008.

Sheridan, Dorothy, ed. *Wartime Women: A Mass-Observation Anthology, 1937–45.* London: Phoenix Press, 1990.

Shi, Yu. "Chinese Immigrant Women Workers: Everyday Forms of Resistance and 'Coagulate Politics.'" *Communication and Critical/Cultural Studies* 5 (December 2008): 363–82.

Ship of Fools. Film. Columbia Pictures Corporation, 1965.

Sinor, Jennifer. *The Extraordinary Work of Ordinary Writing: Annie Ray's Diary.* Iowa City: University of Iowa Press, 2002.

Smith, Andrew R. "Violence and the Arts of Resistance: An Expedition in Critical Communicology." *Atlantic Journal of Communication* 16 (2008): 184–210.

Smith, Malcolm. *Britain 1940: History, Myth, and Popular Memory.* London: Routledge, 2000.

Smith, Ted J. "Techniques of Deception." In *Propaganda: A Pluralistic Perspective,* edited by Ted J. Smith III, 65–99. New York: Praeger, 1989.

Spence, Patrick R., David Westerman, Paul D. Skalski, Matthew Seeger, Robert R. Ulmer, Steve

Venette, and Timothy L. Sellnow. "Proxemic Effects on Information Seeking after the September 11 Attacks." *Communication Research Reports* 22 (February 2005): 39–46.

Temple, Judy Nolte. "Fragments as Diary: Theoretical Implications of the Dreams and Visions of 'Baby Doe' Tabor." In *Inscribing the Daily: Critical Essays on Women's Diaries*, edited by Suzanne L. Bunkers and Cynthia Huff, 72–85. Amherst: University of Massachusetts Press, 1996.

Thompson, Poppy M. "Heil Churchill." Article displayed at the German Occupation Museum, Guernsey (viewed June 2003).

Tickner, Lisa. *The Spectacle of Women: Imagery of the Suffrage Campaign, 1907–1914.* Chicago: University of Chicago Press, 1988.

Tough, Ken. "Deportation from Guernsey 1942—Two Personal Accounts and a German Assessment." *Channel Islands Occupation Review* 20 (1992): 72.

———. "The Identity Card System in Occupied Guernsey." *Channel Islands Occupation Review* 20 (1992): 32.

Turner, Barry. *Outpost of Occupation: How the Channel Islands Survived Nazi Rule, 1940–45.* London: Aurum Press, 2010.

Vitaliev, Vitali. "Island Legacy." *Travel Intelligence.* http://www.travelintelligence.com/travel-writing/island-legacy (last accessed June 12, 2012).

———. "Channel Islanders Showing Off Their Sites of Shame." *Guardian*, January 3, 1999.

"WWII Prison Camp Archives Discovered in Guernsey." BBC News. http://www.bbc.co.uk/news/world-europe-guernsey-11779963.

Warry, William Arthur. Diary of William Arthur Warry. University of Virginia, Special Collections, Microfilm 1688 MSS8138.

Weiner, Bernard. *An Attributional Theory of Motivation and Emotion.* New York: Springer-Verlag, 1986.

Wendt, Ronald F. "Answers to the Gaze: A Genealogical Poaching of Resistances." *Quarterly Journal of Speech* 82 (1996): 251–73.

Wert, Sarah R., and Peter Salovey. "A Social Comparison Account of Gossip." *Review of General Psychology* 8 (2004): 122–37.

Williams, Alfred. Personal interviews, 2003 and 2004.

Williams, Herbert. Diary of Herbert Williams. States of Guernsey Island Archives Service, AQ 380/03–2.

Willmot, Louise. "The Channel Islands." In *Resistance in Western Europe*, edited by Bob Moore, 65–92. London: Berg, 2000.

Index